VICTORIAN MAPS
OF ENGLAND

THE
ENGLISH COUNTIES
Delineated by
THOMAS MOULE.

VICTORIAN MAPS OF ENGLAND

◄◄◄◄◄◄ ● ►►►►►►

*The County and City Maps
of Thomas Moule*

EDITED AND INTRODUCED BY JOHN LEE

BATSFORD

First published in 2018 by
Batsford, an imprint of Pavilion Books Company Ltd

43 Great Ormond Street, London WC1N 3HZ

Devised, packaged and produced for Batsford by
The Pool of London Press, a division of Velodrome Media Limited.
www.pooloflondon.com   www.velodromemedia.com

A CIP catalogue record for this book is available from the British Library

ISBN 9781849944977

Reproduction by Mission, Hong Kong

Printed and bound by 1010 Printing International Ltd, China

20 19 18 17 16

10 9 8 7 6 5 4 3 2 1

This book can be ordered direct from the publisher at the website
www.pavilionbooks.com, or try your local bookshop.

CONTENTS

ENGLAND'S TOPOGRAPHER: THE WORLD OF THOMAS MOULE

BY JOHN LEE

The traditional printed map can only truly illustrate the past. Yet there is a considerable amount that can be learned about the distinct period when the map is produced and the way that its very production reflects developing trends, social movements and even significant historical shifts. The series of county and city maps produced by Thomas Moule in the 1830s are one of the finest examples of such a tension between the long draw of history and the impact of a feverish, impatient present. The 65 engraved maps were originally commissioned to accompany each of the county, and some of the city, descriptions in Moule's weighty 1837 two-volume publication *The English Counties Delineated*. However, given their refinement and quality, the maps enjoyed publication in a number of subsequent major volumes as feature illustrations, right up to the 1870s when some 30 of the maps were bound into Hume and Smollet's *The History of England* (George Virtue, London 1876–7). Their protracted life, and evident popularity, has meant that the maps have become celebrated as some of the finest cartographic productions of the Victorian age, although they were actually created in the reign of Victoria's predecessor William IV who adorns the original frontispiece. The new Queen came to throne in the June of 1837 just as the newly bound volumes of *The English Counties Delineated* made their first appearance in publisher George Virtue's Paternoster Row premises in London, delivered from the printer J.Unwin of St. Peter's Alley off nearby Cornhill.

Moule's work is celebrated as the very last decorative series of county maps to be published. In various forms, the maps have become highly collectable right up to the modern day, principally as single-sheet frameable pieces. This new volume, however, presents the collected series of Moule county and city maps alongside each of the author's original county text descriptions for the first time since original publication. It also includes

Thomas Moule's original Introduction to the book. Where space and interest has permitted, or in those cases where a city map was included in the bound pages of *The English Counties Delineated*, the city descriptions have also been worked in. The book seeks to explore Moule's work alongside the rapidly changing cartographic production methods of the time and the consequent explosion in mapmaking. It also aims to reassess, and to qualify, Moule's ongoing reputation as a proponent and revivalist of the Gothic style of decoration and explores how these maps reflect wider economic and social developments of what we now refer to as the Victorian age. These developments include the impact of the enclosure acts, the necessity for the 1832 Reform Act, the colossal revolutions in industry and communications, and the thundering impact of the first period of 'railway mania' (1836-1837) detailed in Moule's own Introduction. As the railway mania is taking place at the same time as Moule is having his various plates prepared for engraving, it would cause him to effect considerable updates to the map plates in the years that followed.

THOMAS MOULE

Thomas Moule (1784-1851) is remembered primarily now as a mapmaker in the broadest sense of the term. It is highly likely, however, that he would have preferred to be recognized, first and foremost, as a writer and antiquarian. He was born in the London parish of Marylebone on 14th January 1784 and is listed in the 1894 *Dictionary of National Biography* as commencing working life as a bookseller in Duke Street, Grosvenor Square in Mayfair between 1816 and 1823. He moved on to a role at the grand new buildings of the General Post Office, on St. Martin's Le Grand near to St Paul's Cathedral,

where his main duty was to decipher 'blind' letters, the addresses of which the general clerks could not make out. He continued this unique role throughout his working life whilst at the same time holding the office of chamber-keeper in the Lord Chamberlain's department, a position that gave him official residence in the Stable Yard at St. James's Palace.

These professional roles cannot have fully accounted for his time as, in addition to the monumental task of creating *The English Counties Delineated*, he made significant literary contributions throughout from the 1820s to the 1840s. The early part of his writing career was taken up compiling various bibliographies, including the *Bibliotheca Heraldica Magnæ Britanniæ. An Analytical Catalogue of Books in Genealogy, Heraldry, Nobility, Knighthood, and Ceremonies* (London, 1822) and a detailed work on classical architecture, *An Essay on the Roman Villas of the Augustan Age, their architectural disposition and enrichments, and on the Remains of Roman Domestic Edifices discovered in Great Britain* (London, 1833). Whilst working on *The English Counties Delineated* Moule was additionally engaged in writing the descriptions of the seven principal cathedrals in the first volume of *Winckle's Illustrations of the Cathedral Churches of England and Wales* (London, 1836) and further writing in *Antiquities in Westminster Abbey, ancient oil paintings and sepulchural brasses* (London,1825). Moule would also contribute the introductory text focusing on decoration and ornamental details to the major collection of line engravings by Henry Shaw FSA, entitled *Details of Elizabethan Architecture* (London, 1839). In this publication Moule displays a highly accomplished and elevated knowledge with descriptions of the architecture of Greece and Rome and the recent excavations at Herculaneum and Pompeii. His account of ornament and architectural details continues through the decoration of Pope Leo X's Vatican rooms by the painter Raphael, the Flemish exterior of Antwerp's town hall and concludes by tracing the development of ornament through the Elizabethan age up to the contributions of the British resident architect Inigo Jones.

Later in his career Moule saw the publication of his *The Heraldry of Fish: Notices of the principal families bearing Fish in the Arms* (London, 1842) with a most accomplished series of woodcuts from drawings made by his daughter. We are told, he had additionally completed the material for equivalent heraldic volumes on trees and birds. Moule also enjoyed an early partnership with the celebrated expedition artist and illustrator William Westall and contributed the descriptive text to the 59 views of historical buildings and locations in Westall's *Great Britain Illustrated* (London, 1830) as well as seven essays that appeared in the artist's *Illustrations of the Works of Walter Scott* (London, 1834). Whilst we have little historical record to draw from (apart from his own writings), it is possible to construct a picture of Thomas Moule as an emerging, accomplished historian and antiquary with some access to London's finest scholars, historians, architects and artists, frequenting institutions such as the Society of Antiquaries at Somerset House on the Strand, and the broader refined society, clubs and salons of Mayfair and St. James's. But little is truly known about the man himself and there are no contemporary records of what others thought of him. Moule was still in the service of the Lord Chamberlain when he died in his St. James's Palace residence early in 1851, leaving a widow and his daughter.

THE ENGLISH COUNTIES DELINEATED

The publication of *The English Counties Delineated* would be undertaken in two distinct stages. From May of 1830 separate 'part-works' of single counties would be released on the first day of each month. The page size was at the substantial quarto format (10 inches in height and 7.5 inches wide (254 x 190mm)). Enclosed in a distinctive yellow wrapper, each monthly release would include not only the county map, but also the standard signature of 16 pages containing the text description, including both those general county descriptions (as included as part of this volume) but additionally the highly detailed descriptions of every city, town, village and place of note. Statistical information was taken from the censuses of 1821 and 1831 while inspiration and research for these descriptions came from a broad range of provincial guides and a range of books on local antiquities. The back cover of the monthly issue would include an index, news of issues in progress, subscriber notices, advertisements and a steady run of favourable press clippings.

This serial style of publication was becoming popular in the 1830s with Charles Dickens adopting the model for his novels commencing with *The Pickwick Papers* in 1836. The model brought Moule's monthly releases within the reach of a broader range of non-book buying customers, and also provided a more positive cash-flow for those financing the publication. The not inconsiderable cost of producing the 10,000 printed copies of each issue was spread out over seven years with, it was hoped, forward issues being funded by steady sales. Each issue was sold at 1 shilling for the black and white version. The inclusion of a hand-coloured map would increase the price to 1s 6d (1 shilling 6 pence). All were made available singly and via subscription through the three London booksellers, George Virtue, Simpkin & Marshall and Jennings & Chapman under a joint imprint. The intention was that subscribers would collect each of the issues and, when complete, would have them bound up into a handsome single volume. Moule remarkably managed to maintain this rigorous monthly publishing cycle for five years. Although he did run into some inevitable problems caused, in the most part, by attempting to squeeze the text into the allocated number of pages. The London release was planned to fit into 32 pages

RIGHT: The title page of *Barclay's Universal English Dictionary* of the 1840s, published by George Virtue, showing a young Queen Victoria. These popular volumes would include a full set of Moule's county maps.

yet was eventually published at over 80 pages and some eighteen months late. Ironically, it was the only section that Moule did not write himself.

With completion of all the monthly serial issues, the creation in book form could commence. The resulting volume is fully titled *The English counties delineated; or a topographical description of England. Illustrated by a map of London, and a complete series of county maps. By Thomas Moule.* In his accompanying Preface Moule indicates that the publication was not without problems stating:

Since the commencement of its publication in May 1830, the proprietors of the work have been changed more than once; other untoward circumstances left the Editor, at one period, without even a hope of his labours being completed. He has to acknowledge the kind and liberal attention he received from the present proprietor, Mr G. Virtue, by whose spirited exertions alone the Editor was enabled to perform his duty, and to continue the account to the end. Mr Virtue's chief object has been to produce a work of obvious utility at a reasonable price, so as to place it within the reach of every class, not without incurring a very great expense, and a considerable risk.

Moule clearly felt he had found a kindred spirit in George Virtue. They had both started life as booksellers and demonstrably shared those early Victorian traits of self-belief, energy, confidence and a yearning for progress following the end of war with France. Virtue immediately recognized the value in what Moule had created for his general readership and indeed how he could onwardly benefit from both the text as well as the county and city maps.

Virtue, a successful and self-made publisher, achieved his early results by producing numbered, collectable versions of works by the established publishers of Paternoster Row. Soon he was publishing in his own right with premises on the Row's Ivy Lane from 1831 and selling works illustrated by Issac and George Cruikshank. He scored the equivalent of a bestseller with *A Guide to Family Devotion* by Dr. Alexander Fletcher (first published 1840) running to 30 editions. Virtue invested well, creating highly illustrated, popular publications combining engravings with descriptive text. In his *History of Booksellers: the old and the new* (London, 1873) Henry Curwen states 'Almost every engraver of any reputation in this country had been employed on one or other of Virtue's illustrated works' and credits Virtue as 'the first art publisher of his time'. Much of Virtue's success came from selling individual engravings (of which he is said to have created some 20,000 different ones) or in reusing printed engravings many times in the 100 or so illustrated books that he produced over his career. As mentioned earlier,

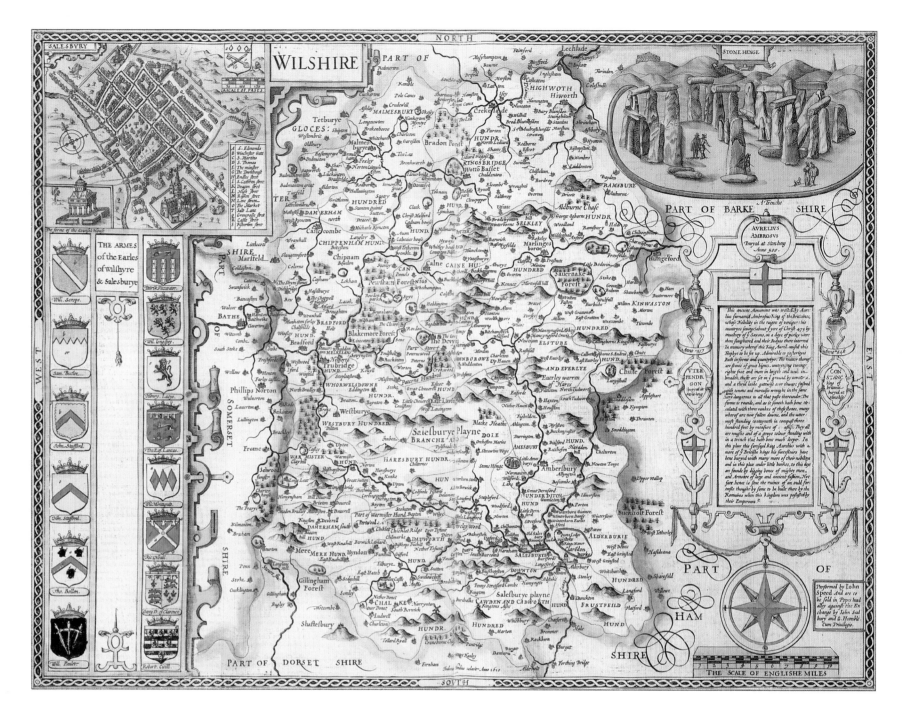

Moules county maps were reused by the Virtue company in the 1870s but he would also make significant use of them in the various successful editions of *A complete and universal English dictionary, by the Rev. James Barclay, illustrated by numerous engravings & maps. Revised by Henry W. Dewhurst, Esq.* that were to appear in updated forms in 1842, 1844, 1845, 1848 and 1852, and which would take Thomas Moule's map illustrations out to a much broader audience. Indeed it is these volumes that have provided the hand-coloured Moule's maps that make up this current publication.

Between them, Moule and Virtue had produced something approaching a Doomsday Book for the early Victorian age – a detailed account of every English city, town and village and their key features complete

ABOVE: John Speed's county map of Wiltshire published in his *Theatre of Greate Britaine* (1627). Through his use of a variety of decorative structural elements, extensive heraldry and vignette views of buildings and monuments, Speed was to have a significant influence on Moule's approach and cartography. *(Courtesy Batsford Archive/British Library)*

ABOVE RIGHT: A hand-coloured 1840s version of Thomas Moule's county map of the Isle of Thanet in Kent as originally engraved for inclusion in *The English Counties Delineated*. The cartographic historian Tony Campbell has suggested Moule's unconventional choice to depict Thanet as a stand-alone map was in response to requests from subscribers to the original part-work series. Note the subsequent addition of the London to Ramsgate railway line.

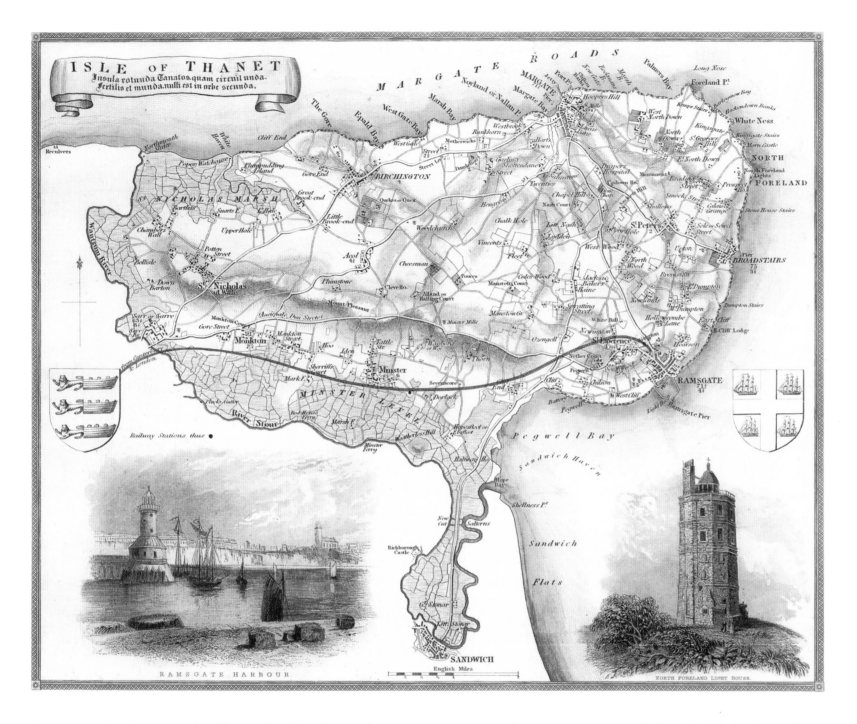

ISLE OF THANET

RAMSGATE HARBOUR.

NORTH FORELAND LIGHT HOUSE.

THE MAPS

The series of county maps that have become synonymous with his name were not drawn and engraved by Moule himself. Moule's creative skill lay in writing. For such a major personal undertaking he would certainly have fully specified what was required from each map, had a detailed input on each element and, given his clear expertise in ornament and decoration, it is inconceivable that his engravers would have been left to their own aesthetic whims to any great degree. Moule commissioned James Bingley, John Dower and William Schmollinger, three of London's leading artist-engravers. Yet he managed to carefully direct them to produce a successful series of maps that, while diverse in decorative styles, have an unmistakable consistency and uniformity.

The members of the assembled team were at the forefront of a technical revolution in the production of maps in which innovation and experimentation would spur advances throughout the course of the nineteenth century. The team benefitted equally from broader, uniquely national, developments that greatly enhanced the accuracy, usefulness and popularity of maps in Victorian Britain. The 1820s had seen the swift development of the steel engraving process replacing the more traditional use of copper plates, which had been pioneered in Italy and derived from the rudimentary woodcut. The new steel plates were more durable and, in a country becoming rapidly industrialized, were cheaper to produce. They could be used for the printing of many thousands of sheets while the softer copper plates displayed a significant reduction in crispness and fine line after some 500 impressions. The painstakingly slow process of plate-making was also significantly improved when engraving in steel which allowed engravers a greater ability to create delicate lighting effects and shading. At the same time the developing processes of the Industrial Revolution had directly contributed to great advances in the steam press, paper technology and the invention of a paper-making machine, all of which further improved the speed of production and output, and the quality and cost of printable sheets.

In their demand for apportioning strips of land, fields and in creating borders, the various British enclosure acts of the seventeenth and eighteenth centuries had to a small extent brought about the start of a process of accurately mapping the nation. The French Revolutionary and Napoleonic Wars, and the invasion threat that they posed, had further raised a new national consciousness. This prompted both the Society of Arts and the Royal Society into various initiatives, or calls to action, to bring British mapmaking more in line with its European neighbours. The country in which Sir Issac Newton had influenced major advances in mathematics,

with administrative details and records of the number of dwellings and inhabitants. The two original bound volumes of *The English Counties Delineated* run to a total of 978 double-column pages of text in the large quarto format and contain approximately 1.4 million words. There are a further 88 pages of index. Moule tells us that in the work's preparation his 'expensive diligence' had led him to personally visit every county in England apart from Devonshire and Cornwall. The span of material and straightforward data included is truly impressive. In the text, and in the broader publishing endeavour, Moule had one clear mission: to extol the 'ancientness' of England and celebrate those sites that embodied it. We have already noted his fervour for Britain's preserved monuments, and the

Romantic and antiquarian society in which he flourished. In his Preface to the book he sums up his principal intentions as follows:

Statistics are, however, made subordinate to a design of rendering the book instructive, by particularizing the most interesting and picturesque objects in the several counties, as well as scenes, situations, and prospects remarkable for extent or beauty … The admiration which the splendid remains of antiquity now very generally excite, rendered it desirable to notice all curious fragments of ancient architecture in the monastic buildings, churches and crosses of religious foundation; Anglo-Norman castles, the remains of feudal times; the castellated mansions of later date, and the Tudor houses of nobility and gentry.

trigonometry and astronomy had not been mapped in its entirety since the sixteenth century when methods were, at best, rudimentary. The developing communication network of turnpikes, canals, coach-houses and even newspapers was being built upon a loosely connected, unsophisticated and unregulated record. Up until the end of the eighteenth century mapmaking had been the preserve of a small number of individuals benefiting from the private patronage of the landowning aristocracy and local gentry who required a record of their own holdings and their setting.

Everything was to change in 1791 with the institution of the Ordnance Survey. Their mission was to chart and record the nation in unprecedented scale with both governmental authority and financial support. The process would start with the southern counties but would be painstakingly slow and be continually challenged by the pace of change brought about by industrial and urban development. However, by the 1820s the Survey had used the latest triangulation methods to produce a series of plain and unembellished maps of England to an unprecedented accuracy and to the separate scales of 25in=1 mile and 6in=1 mile. The Survey would institute a uniform and accepted system of signs and standards to depict topographical features and provide the associated administrative and statistical information.

The Survey would famously continue in its role but struggled in the first half of the century to survey Scotland and in particular the Highlands. This would go some way to explaining why Moule did not feature Scotland, and to a lesser degree Wales, in his own great cartographic work. Indeed the failure of the Ordnance Survey to accurately triangulate and record Scotland can be witnessed in Edward James Smith's illustration 'A Comparitive View of the Principal Hills of Great Britain' (*see page 27*) included by Moule in the first bound edition of his *English Counties Delineated*. Here the mountain Ben Macdui is incorrectly presented as the highest mountain in Britain dwarfing Ben Nevis by some 200 feet. Whilst Moule clearly states in Ben Nevis's favour in his own Introduction text, this points to a general lack of consistency, when it comes to the Highlands, in the first third of the century which would only be fully rectified in the 1880s.

The early publications of the Ordnance Survey would provide new, accurate cartographic data and large-scale maps for a host of commercial mapmakers in the early years of the nineteenth century. The cartographic historian David Smith writes, 'As the Ordnance tightened its grip on large-scale mapping, so private map-makers turned to the production of smaller-scale specialized maps which they could largely construct from Survey topographical data (following the official utilitarian style and standardization of content and appearance), but which would not compete with its sheets.'

Copyright had proved almost impossible to enforce and it was generally understood that, given the Survey's role as a funded national institution, the use of its published triangulation data, and indeed maps, was perfectly acceptable as long as such commercial maps were published at smaller scales. Firms such as the John Bartholomew & Sons, George Philip & Sons and latterly Edward Stanford Ltd would grow considerably on the back of this information, as would cartographers such Christopher and John Greenwood, William Henry Smith and, to a greater degree, John Cary whose output of functional county and canal maps over some 40 years was prolific, approaching some 600 pieces. Together they would lead a renaissance in British cartography, courtesy of the work of the Survey, in creating commercial maps with a level of accuracy never previously possible.

The influence of Cary and Smith's series of county maps is acknowledged by Thomas Moule in his Preface, as is that of the Rev. Thomas Cox's six-volume *Magna Britannia* (1720–31)(with small maps by Robert Morden), which certainly contributed to the structural model for *The English Counties Delineated*. However, the overriding influence on Moule's most celebrated book is the work of historian and cartographer John Speed (1552–1629). One has to see Moule's work as a continuation and development of Speed's. Both men considered themselves antiquarians and historians yet would become principally famous for the maps they had produced. Speed published his *Theatre of Great Britaine* and the accompanying *History* in 1627 and he was the first to show the whole of Britain, county by county, in map form. He was also the very first to incorporate a 'bird's eye' plan of the principal county town into each of his maps on the model of the German topographers and mapmakers Braun and Hogenberg. Some 50 of Speed's 73 town plans are the very first maps we have of these places.

It is very likely that Moule would have first come to Speed through his own deep interest in, and study of, heraldry. Speed's maps, like those from Moule that would follow him, carry an exhausting range of heraldic crests, shields and emblems relating to the families and institutions associated with the particular county or city depicted. All are arranged in intricate geometric and decorative structures often with architectural details and accompanying mythological, historical or genre figures. In a handful of his maps Speed also included actual famed buildings or sites such as royal palaces or monuments, including Stonehenge *(see page 8)*. Moule again would later develop each of these elements. However, Speed goes one step further in recreating historical events, such as battles, as part of his decorative scheme and, while Moule did not employ this device, there is no doubt that both men are consciously celebrating a distinct national pride. They celebrate England's (and in Speed's case Britain's) ancient and more recent history as well as its tangible form be it through monuments or indeed ruins. Speed started his career at the end of the Tudor dynasty and could be seen, through this first collection of county maps, to be recording the fabric and emerging identity of a nation, but also a countryside still scarred by the devastating impact of the Dissolution of the Monasteries in the previous century.

Moule had, of course, benefitted from the accuracy accorded by his access to the Ordnance Survey data and, unlike Speed, had the opportunity to include the principal roads and canals. He was also able to include significantly more accurate rendering of relief and hills, and the angle of their slope and gradient, through the newly developed technique of hachuring which had also been pioneered by the Ordnance Survey. Speed had simply adopted a series of molehills of varying heights and grouped them to suggest the location of the hills and undulating heights within any given county.

STYLE AND DECORATION

One of Moule's key achievements is his ability to marry the latest technical printing innovations with the emerging accurate data and rigour of the Ordnance Survey. However, what takes his work beyond that of his contemporaries, and ensures its continuing popularity, is the way that he developed John Speed's original aesthetic, and adapted it to the more refined and competitive marketplace of the early Victorian age. It is the conscious use of a range of decoration that takes Moule's maps beyond the plain, unapologetically utilitarian works of those larger concerns of the Greenwoods, Cary and Smith. Designed to appeal to a wide set of subscribers, the adoption by Moule of a fine artistic presentation and embellished treatment would give his series a unique appeal to collectors that would set it apart from its commercial competitors.

We have seen through his wider writings of the time that Moule was swiftly becoming a leading expert on historical decoration and ornament. He would no doubt have spent some of his limited spare time attending lectures, events and discussions with his fellow antiquarians, artists, writers, scholars and architects in the salons and societies of Mayfair, St James's and the Strand. Moule would use his unique knowledge of ornament to produce a beautiful series of maps complete with highly embellished borders, convincing cartouches, delicate embellishments and elaborate title arrangements.

Faced with such a large number of maps to produce, Moule chose to apply a real variety of historical artistic styles to the individual maps across the series, and would have been able to supply his fine engravers with no end of varied reference materials to work from, alongside their own pattern books. One only has to look at the wide variety of artistic styles exhibited across the displays of the Great Exhibition (1851) or glance at Owen Jones's book *The Grammar of Ornament* (1856) to see the styles available to the graphic artists of the time. In Moule's maps for counties such as Berkshire, Essex and Middlesex, Nottinghamshire, Surrey and Yorkshire (West Riding), strong classical elements are featured, from nymphs and river gods to Roman eagles, elegant drapery swags and laurel frames. In many cases the decorative scheme framing the maps is dictated directly by the buildings and monuments featured in the accompanying vignette views. The county map of Oxfordshire is perhaps the best example of this matching of architectural and decorative style. Here the neoclassical architecture of Blenheim Palace and Oxford's Radcliffe Camera are set off with a scheme featuring Doric and Corinthian columns and delicate motifs echoing the interior decoration of a Renaissance palazzo. The map decoration for Sussex even merges the Roman Baroque style with more delicate elements of foliage and lighter carved friezes of later French-style decoration. Throughout, those highly fashionable, neoclassical country houses of the aristocracy and gentry feature from Holkham Hall and Chatsworth to Harewood House and Woburn Abbey.

Whilst classical decoration and architecture play a significant role, Moule is more widely celebrated for his revival of Gothic decoration and architectural elements in his maps. His position as a writer on antiquities, and heraldry, will certainly have been a major influence here, but also the simple fact that the majority of Britain's native architecture, especially outside of the major urban centres, was predominantly Gothic in style. The Gothic churches and cathedrals are the main monuments featured in the county maps and, once again, Moule has selected and briefed a style of decoration and inclusion of Gothic elements to match. Ely Cathedral in Cambridgeshire is accompanied by a suitably articulated framework and cornice complete with niches, canopies, trefoil decoration, pendants, tracery and pointed arches. All this is set alongside Moule's heraldic crests and ecclesiastical figures. The pinnacles of Eaton Hall in Cheshire are mirrored by the floral stanchion decoration of the border above, and the heavy titling device of Gloucestershire reflects the Gothic 'pointed style' of Gloucester Cathedral and Tewkesbury Abbey. Niched medieval knights flank the map of the Isle of Man, while a rustic ploughman, reminiscent of many similar figures in Speed's maps, leads us into the richly articulated decorative border in the map of Bedfordshire.

Moule's deep interest in, and stylistic application of, Gothic architectural elements was part of a wider revival of the style which had been slowly underway since the middle of the eighteenth century and was closely allied to the Romantic movement. The revival would soon find its most celebrated flourish in the architectural work of Augustus Pugin. It is highly likely that Moule and Pugin would have known of each other through their direct connections to the Society of Antiquaries and their joint interests in heraldry and British architectural history. Both men clearly lamented the destruction wrought on medieval English architecture during the Dissolution of the Monasteries. Of the Gothic Moule wrote of his intention to direct 'the attention of the public to the finest specimens of architectural science', while Pugin was to go as far as calling for a return to the age of the High Church and Catholicism. There is nothing directly in Moule's writings to suggest he shared such a view, but he was a clear admirer of the Gothic age, its buildings and its direct link to the British landscape. In his Introduction (*see page 28*) he would recall the chasms of the banks of the River Wye, their 'roofs ornamented by nature's hand with stalactitical concretions of white and glistening spar, which seem like the fretted sculpture of Gothic architecture'.

The monastic remains provided Moule and his engravers with a consistent source of illustration for a high number of vignettes throughout the series of maps. These picturesque, pastoral views are inspired by a wider literary and pictorial trend within the Romantic movement, celebrating the beauty and power of nature. It is possible that his earlier writing work, describing the views of the artist William Westall and those inspired by Walter Scott, may have led Moule to introduce the vignette view alongside the more decorative elements of his maps. The cartographers Bowen and Kitchen had made similar use of vignette views between 1750–80, developing Speed's model, but did not enjoy the same technical advances, surveying accuracy and commercial opportunities that Moule did. Furthermore, the idea of the English pastoral view had taken on new significance and popularity in the first thirty years of the nineteenth century through the fêted paintings, and steel engravings, of Philip Wilson, John Constable and JMW Turner. The latter was to be constantly at work in the late 1820s and 1830s on a central series of watercolours, destined for the expanding steel engraving market, originally entitled 'Picturesque Views of England and Wales'. Moule seized on the vignette as a device to fill in the irregular spaces between the borders of the counties and the edges of his decorative frames, whilst also taking the opportunity to appeal further to public taste and increase the potential sales of his engraved maps.

***

Moule's descriptive writing in the town and county entries in *The English Counties Delineated* openly acknowledges the growing industrialization of the English cities, towns and the wider landscape. There is, however, little at all in his accompanying maps to suggest such an upheaval which saw the population of Britain double between 1801 and 1851. The depiction in Moule's maps of the simple, rustic life and medieval charm can be seen as a major reason for their continuing popularity and collectability. For many they would have represented an antidote to the relentless industrialization. Moule sought to celebrate the simple beauty and ancientness of England, whilst at the same time enjoying many of the developing benefits of the Industrial Revolution in the creation, production and sales of his books and associated maps. Indeed the Reform Act of 1832, and the changing political jurisdictions it brought about (resulting from population growth and urbanization), would force Moule to issue two separate double-size maps of England within ten months of each other in 1832. It is, however, the unrelenting growth of the railways in the 1830s and 1840s that would ultimately have the biggest effect on the British cities and countryside. In his Introduction Moule wrote:

Steam-engines and Rail-roads are not merely facilitating the conveyance of merchandize from one part of England to the other they are doing more—they are sealing the intercourse between mind and mind, and they are exciting demands for knowledge sending the desire for that knowledge into all the recesses of this empire, tending powerfully to the cultivation of the mental, as they are improving the physical, capabilities of the country.

Moule's own work for *The English Counties Delineated* was part of this revolution in communications, not only through its clear and accurate presentation of popular, decorative and attractive maps of the counties and cities, but also through Moule's incredibly detailed written descriptions of their every part. The irony will not have been lost on him when he learned that in including Moule's maps in editions of *Barclay's Complete and Universal English Dictionary* in the 1840s, Virtue had required that all of the principal railway lines of the 1830s, for the very first time in a county series, be engraved onto the original map plates. In some ways, through his work, Moule was laying the foundations for the great growth in leisure travel and associated guidebooks and maps – from the likes of Bradshaw's, Stanford's and W H Smith's – which developed in the second half of the nineteenth century. It would enable so many more to see the countryside and the monuments he so cherished.

INTRODUCTION TO
'THE ENGLISH COUNTIES DELINEATED'
1837

BY THOMAS MOULE

ENGLAND, the most considerable division of Great Britain, is bounded by Scotland on the north; by the German Ocean, or North Sea, on the east; by the English Channel, on the south, which divides it from France; and by Wales, the Atlantic Ocean, and the Irish Channel on the west. From north to south England is 450 miles in length, and is in some places 300 miles in breadth, from east to west, being about 1750 miles in circumference, containing a population which, in 1821, appears to have consisted of no less than 11,261,437 persons. The aspect of the country is various and delightful; in some parts verdant plains extend as far as the eye can reach, watered by copious streams. In others the pleasing vicissitudes of gently rising hills and bending vales, fertile in corn, waving with wood, and interspersed with meadows, offer the most delightful landscapes of rural opulence and beauty. Some tracts abound with prospects of the more romantic kind; lofty hills, craggy rocks, deep narrow dells, and tumbling torrents; nor are there wanting, as a contrast to so many agreeable scenes, the bleak barren moors and wide uncultivated heaths. These are constantly diminishing, in consequence of numerous enclosures and extension of cultivation. The native animals of England are the stag, of which a few are yet to be found in their natural state; the fallow deer, of which there are two kinds; the dog, of which there are various species and different breeds, adapted to the chace; the fox; the wild cat, which is still found in some woods; the martin, the badger, &c. The wild bulls of this island are known to exist at Chillingham castle, in

Northumberland, and the wild boar was formerly a native of this country, as also the wolf and the bear, but have gradually become extinct. The most remarkable of the birds, are the eagle, which is rarely met with; falcons of various species; the black cock, and the ptarmagan, found on the lofty hills of Cumberland.

The soil of England is various, consisting generally of clay, loam, sand, chalk, and gravel. Peat and mossy soils are common in the northern districts, and are also to be found, though more rarely, in the southern counties. No country in the world displays such a rich and uniform verdure for so large a portion of the year; while in more southern climates the bloom of nature withers under unintermitted and parching heats, or is obstructed in more northern latitudes by the influence of cold; nature is here refreshed in summer by frequent showers, and in the winter the cold is never so severe as to destroy vegetation. The indigenous fruits are few and of little value; but others have been introduced or brought to perfection by the skill and careful cultivation of the English gardeners. There is scarcely a farm of any extent in the south-western counties which has not an orchard attached to it of sufficient extent to supply the family with cider; but it is chiefly in the counties of Devon, Hereford, Worcester, Gloucester, Monmouth, and Somerset that cider and perry are made in large quantities for sale, and where the orchard forms a principal object of attention. Hops are cultivated to a considerable extent in the southern counties; timber grows abundantly in most parts of the country :—

Below me trees unnumbered rise, beautiful in various dyes:
The gloomy pine, the poplar blue, the yellow beech, the sable yew,
The slender fir that taper grows, the sturdy oak with broad spread boughs.

Here are some individual trees of extraordinary magnitude, particularly oak and elm trees; but generally the size of the trees in England bear no comparison with some described by travellers.

The mines and quarries of England afford a constant supply of valuable produce; coal is found in great abundance in the northern counties, and in Derbyshire, Staffordshire, and Shropshire; it is also found in Leicestershire, Warwickshire, and in some of the western counties; but those in the south are generally destitute of that article. Iron abounds in Shropshire, Gloucestershire, Derbyshire, and in the north of Lancashire; it is produced, although not in equal abundance, in other counties: the iron mines are of great antiquity, and are known to have been wrought before the Norman Conquest. Lead is produced in different parts, both in the south and north: these mines are very ancient, and are known to have been wrought in the time of the Romans. Tin is confined to Cornwall and the adjoining parts of Devonshire, and black lead to a small district in Cumberland. Mines of copper are wrought in Cornwall, Devonshire, Derbyshire, and partially in Yorkshire and Staffordshire. There are also mines of rock salt, pits of fullers' earth, potters' clay, &c.

The manufactures of England are of prodigious extent, not only is her own produce made into every variety of fabric and form for use or ornament, but the produce of other countries is imported in order to supply materials for the ingenuity of the numerous artisans; and such are the various devices, and complicated improvements, which science has invented for the abridgement of labour, such is the minuteness and skill with which the industry of the country is arranged and subdivided upon one vast and general plan, and so great is the capital employed that England is enabled, in all the countries to which her commodities are exported, to undersell the manufacturer in his own market. The superiority and cheapness of English manufactures has given them a preference in the markets of Europe and America. In addition to her commerce and manufactures England has extensive fisheries, both at home and abroad.

Literature, science, and all the liberal arts keep pace with the advancement of commerce in England; knowledge has become widely disseminated amongst all classes, and the various periodical publications which are circulated contribute to foster a general spirit of inquiry amongst the people, and to counteract that apathy to mental Pursuits, which is apt to grow up in a community purely commercial. In every town of note a newspaper is published, and there are besides other works, as magazines, reviews, and scientific journals, which serve to diffuse an ardour for liberal discussion.

COUNTIES

England is divided into forty counties, a division which appears to have been established in the Anglo-Saxon era, many of the counties being mentioned in history before the extinction of the Heptarchy, under the original name of shire, which, in its primitive signification, means a share, a division, and county is equivalent to earldom, a province or dominion of an earl. There are three counties-palatine, Lancashire, Cheshire, and Durham, with peculiar jurisdiction, and Cornwall, under the title of duchy, is settled by act of parliament on the king's eldest son. The shires of England were originally named from some remarkable particularity in the county or the capital town. Surrey, Sussex, and Middlesex from their relative situations, as well as Suffolk and Norfolk. Westmorland and Cumberland are sometimes called the middle shires. All are under the government of a shire reeve, or sheriff, a chief officer of the king.

THE RIDINGS

A Riding, or trithing, the original name, implies a third part; a mode of division in England now only peculiar to Yorkshire, but common to Lincolnshire, and some other counties in the Anglo-Saxon era.

LATHES

Lathe, the shire division peculiar to Kent, is stated in the laws of Edward the Confessor to have been the same with the Riding, but could not have comprised the third part of the shire, as in Kent, the only county in which it is named, no less than seven distinct Lathes occur. At present there are only five Lathes in Kent, each consisting of several hundreds. The Lathes were, probably, military divisions, connected with the establishment of the Cinque Ports, for defence of the coast against invasion. The court leet seems to have the same derivation; and Dymchurch Lathe, an annual court, is now held in Romney marsh, for the election of a bailiff, &c.

RAPES

The six intermediate divisions between the shire and the hundred in Sussex are called Rapes. These appear to have answered generally to the Lathes of Kent; but there is no mention of any court attached to the Rape. It was entrusted to the jurisdiction of an individual, and probably was a military district for the supply of a castle.

In Dorsetshire and Hampshire the hundreds are classed in divisions, simply so named.

HUNDREDS

The division of the southern parts of England into Hundreds is unquestionably of Anglo-Saxon origin, and was probably made in imitation of the Centena of Germany; but in what manner the name of hundred was applied is uncertain: indeed, there is scarcely any subject, connected with topography, that has caused so much controversy. Some authors have considered the hundred as relating to the number of heads of families, or the number of dwellings situated in the division; others to the number of hides of land therein contained. By analysing the Domesday Record, an able writer has proved that, as it regards the county of Bedford, the hundred anciently consisted of a hundred hides of land; the same is asserted by Mr. Baker to have been the case with the hundreds of Northamptonshire. Mr. Rickman, in the preliminary observations to the "Population Abstract," says that, "at least one hundred, which, in Saxon numeration, means one hundred and twenty, free men, householders answerable for each other, may be supposed originally to have been found in each hundred; and that the hundreds were regulated by the population, appears from the great number of hundreds in the counties first peopled by the Saxons. Kent and Sussex, when the Domesday Boke was compiled, each contained more than sixty hundreds, as at present. In Lancashire, a county of greater area than either, there are no more than six hundreds; in Cheshire, seven: and, upon the whole, so irregular is this distribution of territory, that, while several hundreds do not exceed a square mile in area, nor 1,000 persons in population, the hundreds of Lancashire average at 300 square miles in area; and the population contained in one of them, Salford hundred, is now above 320,000."

This irregularity seems to have been felt as an inconvenience as early as the reign of Henry VIII., when a remedy was attempted by ordaining divisions, which still exist in most of the English counties. These divisions appear to have been formed by a junction of small hundreds, as in Wiltshire, or a partition of large hundreds, as convenience required, in each particular case. But time, which had caused the irregularity of the ancient hundreds, gradually has the same effect in more modern arrangements. The divisions of Dorsetshire underwent a change in the year 1740.

One part of a hundred is sometimes found in the very middle of another, or several parts of a hundred scattered widely over a whole county. These ragged hundreds are supposed to have had heads of religious houses for their lords, or owners; whence it is presumed that the detached portions were acquisitions after the hundred came into their possession.

Several of the hundreds are strangely scattered; and instances are, probably, most frequent in Wilstshire; Winkley hundred, in Somersetshire; Faringdon hundred, in Berkshire; that of Barton Stacey, in Hampshire, and some others, are remarkable instances of this irregularity, still in existence. Parishes which extend into more hundreds than one, are numerous; as well as the number or places which lie at a distance from their own county or hundred.

The felling of a forest, the draining of a marsh, or the cultivation of a waste by the lord of the manor, would extend the limits of a hundred, in that direction; or whatever was gained or lost by purchase, by heirship, or by violence, must also have altered the boundary.

Hundreds were primarily denominated from places of rendezvous the situations of which have, in many instances, sunk into oblivion, with the disuse of the custom. The names of hundreds terminating in Low, received their names from some remarkable hill, as Totmon's low in Staffordshire; others from a tree as Crowthorn, and Grumbalds Ash, in Gloucestershire, the place where the hundred court was originally held. The jurisdiction of these hundred courts was afterwards transferred to the county courts, and remains so at present, excepting with regard to some; as the Chilterns, which have been by privilege annexed to the crown. These having still their own courts; a steward of these courts is appointed by the Chancellor of the Exchequer, with a salary of twenty shillings, and all fees belonging to the office, which, being an appointment of profit, the steward must vacate his seat in Parliament. The Chiltern is a name applied to the range of hills traversing Buckinghamshire, a little southward of its centre, and extending from Tring in Hertfordshire, to Henley in Oxfordshire.

WARDS

The four northern counties of Cumberland, Westmorland, Durham, and Northumberland are divided into Wards, so named from the warding or guarding necessary in that part of the country against the frequent excursions of the Scots.

At Alnwick, on the proclamation of the fairs, the adjacent townships send representatives to attend the bailiff, who keep ward all night in every quarter of the town, and are free of toll by this service. This is the most perfect remains of watch and ward now retained.

The Wards of the City of London are similarly named, from the guard or watch necessarily kept in them.

WAPENTAKES

The Wapentakes of Yorkshire and Lincolnshire are equivalent to the Hundreds, and the name literally signifies "To arms," from wappen, weapons, and tac, touch. The meeting was held sometimes at a distance from town, whence the division derived its name from some conspicuous natural object, as Barkston Ash, Skireake, or shire oak; the last is still remaining in the village of Hedingley, near Leeds, in Yorkshire.

SOKE, LIBERTY, &C.

Soke is a district wherein the power or liberty to administer justice, is exercised. It is used in Lincolnshire and Rutlandshire. Lythe is a liberty, or member, as Pickering Lythe in Yorkshire.

Districts of large extent are found under the name of Liberties, which affect the general course of law in the hundreds. In Dorsetshire, where this denomination chiefly prevails, the grants of some of these liberties are dated as late as the reign of Henry VIII. and even of Elizabeth.

PARISH

The Parish of the early Britons was synonymous with Diocese; the district submitted to the authority of a bishop, was originally called his parish. It is admitted by the most intelligent antiquaries that the distribution of the kingdom into parishes, in the present acceptation of the term, did not originate in any specific decree, but was the progressive work of ages, and was nearly completed by the end of the twelfth century. A comparatively few parishes was, it is true, formed in the Anglo-Saxon era; but being too extended in their boundaries for the accommodation of a dispersed population, were subsequently divided in the Anglo-Norman period.

Selden, speaking of Domesday Boke, in his history of tythes, says that, "In certain counties, as Somerset, Devon, Cornwall, and some few others, a parish church is rarely noticed; but, in others, churches very often occur." In the time of King James, according to Camden, there were 9284 parishes; and, in 1821, there were 10,693 parishes in England.

In modern times the boundary of every parish has been settled with precision; an exactness produced by the laws for the relief of the poor, by which a motive for ascertaining the boundary of a parish continually subsists. When this began to take place, the parishes of the northern counties were found to be much too large, thirty or forty square miles being there no unusual area of a parish; and in general the parishes in the north average at seven or eight times the area of those in the southern counties. According to the last Report of the Poor Law Commissioners in 1837, 7942 parishes were formed into 363 Unions for the administration of relief.

Soon after the restoration of King Charles II., a law was passed permitting townships and villages, although not entire parishes, to maintain their own poor; and under this law the townships northward of the rivers Humber and Dee have become as distinctly limited, as if they were separate parishes; but the townships still seem liable to separation and partition.

Mr. Davidson, clerk of the peace for the county of Northumberland, arranged the townships of that county under their several parishes, in the year 1777; and W. W. Carus Wilson, Esq., an active magistrate in Westmorland, did the same for that county, in the year 1802.

The place which gives the name to the whole parish, is the designation under which the several townships will be found arranged, although it frequently happens that the place is less important than its subordinate township; but this arrangement could not be avoided without departing from the customary manner of denomination.

EXTRA PAROCHIAL PLACES

Besides the Parishes, and their tythings or townships, there are many places in England, not contained within the limits of any parish, and thence called extra-parochial. These places are found usually to have been the site of religious houses, or of ancient castles, the owners of which did not permit any interference with their authority, within their own limits; and in early times the existence of such exemptions from the general government of the kingdom, is not surprising. In the language of the ancient law of England such places were not geldable, nor shire ground; and as the sheriff was then the receiver-general in his county, extra-parochial places were neither taxable, nor within the ordinary pale or civil jurisdiction; and the inhabitants are still virtually exempt from many civil duties and offices, served not without inconvenience by others, for the benefit of the community at large. The number of such places is not inconsiderable, although, difficult to be discovered; more than two hundred are probably enumerated in this work; and the subject is worthy of attention, as the acquisition or new land, by reclaiming forests, drainage of fens, or embankment from the sea, furnishes occasion for endeavouring to establish extra-parochial immunities.

POPULATION

From the summary of population returns, reduced into order by John Rickman, Esq., and printed by command of Parliament, a valuable document to the topographical historian, it appears that the population of England was, in 1700, .. 5,475,000 persons.

in 1801, .. 8,331,434

in 1811, .. 9,538,827

in 1821, .. 11,261,437

in 1831, .. 13,089,338

and that the increase in the last thirty years has been 4,757,904.

The amount of population throughout this work has uniformly been taken from the census of 1821; the following census of 1831 having been made while this work was in progress, it would, consequently, have been improper partially to have adopted that as a guide.

It is to be observed that the returns are always given in parochial districts, which are very seldom coincident with the boundaries of the towns, whence a difficulty arises in correctly estimating the population of large towns.

REFORM IN THE REPRESENTATION OF THE PEOPLE IN 1832

As the act of parliament was passed and carried into execution during the progress of this work, it is necessary to state the most important of the changes that were made, with a view to a more comprehensive parliamentary representation.

The Boroughs Disfranchised were,

In KENT—Queenborough, New Romney. In SURREY—Gatton, Bletchingley, and Haslemere. In SUSSEX— Bramber, East Grinstead, Winchilsea, Seaford, and Steyning.

In BUCKINGHAMSHIRE—Wendover and Amersham. In NORFOLK— Castle Rising. In SUFFOLK—Dunwich, Orford, and Aldeburgh.

In CORNWALL—St. Michaels, Bossiney, St. Mawes, East and West Looe, St. Germains, Newport, Camelford, Tregony, Saltash, Callington, Fowey, and Lostwithiel. In DEVONSHIRE—Beeralston, Plympton, and Okehampton. In DORSETSHIRE—Corfe Castle. In HAMPSHIRE—Stockbridge, Whitchurch, Yarmouth, and Newtown Isle of Wight. In SOMERSETSHIRE—Ilchester, Milborne Port, and Minehead. In WILTSHIRE—Old Sarum, Ludgershall, Hindon, Great Bedwin, Heytesbury, Wootten Basset, and Downton.

In HEREFORDSHIRE—Weobly. In SHROPSHIRE—Bishops Castle.

In NORTHAMPTONSHIRE—Higham Ferrers and Brackley.

In LANCASHIRE—Newton. In WESTMORLAND—Appleby. In YORKSHIRE—Aldborough, Boroughbridge, and Hedon.

Boroughs in which the Number of Representatives is reduced from Two to One each, are

In KENT—Hythe. In SURREY—Ryegate. In SUSSEX—Midhurst, Horsham, Arundel, and Rye.

In SUFFOLK—Eye.

In CORNWALL—Liskard, Launceston, St. Ives, and Helston. In DEVONSHIRE—Ashburton and Dartmouth. In DORSETSHIRE— Wareham, Lyme, and Shaftesbury. In HAMPSHIRE—Petersfield and Christchurch. In WILTSHIRE—Westbury, Wilton, Malmesbury, and Calne.

In BERKSHIRE—Wallingford. In OXFORDSHIRE—Woodstock. In WORCESTERSHIRE—Droitwich.

In LINCOLNSHIRE—Grimsby.

In LANCASHIRE——Clitheroe. In NORTHUMBERLAND—Morpeth. In YORKSHIRE—Northallerton and Thirsk.

New Boroughs to return Two Members to Parliament, are

In KENT—Greenwich. In MIDDLESEX—The Tower Hamlets, Finsbury, and Marylebone. In SURREY—Lambeth. In SUSSEX—Brighton.

In DEVONSHIRE—Devonport.

In GLOUCESTERSHIRE—Stroud. In STAFFORDSHIRE— Wolverhampton, and Stoke-upon-Trent.

In WARWICKSHIRE—Birmingham.

In CHESHIRE—Macclesfield, and Stockport. In DURHAM—Sunderland. In LANCASHIRE—Manchester, Bolton, Blackburn, and Oldham. In YORKSHIRE—Leeds, Sheffield, Bradford and Halifax.

New Boroughs which return One Member each to Parliament, are

In KENT—Chatham.

In SOMERSETSHIRE—Frome.

In GLOUCESTERSHIRE—Cheltenham. In STAFFORDSHIRE—Walsall. In WORCESTERSHIRE—Dudley, and Kidderminster.

In CUMBERLAND—Whitehaven. In DURHAM—Gateshead, and South Shields. In LANCASHIRE—Ashton-under-Lyne, Bury, Rochdale, Salford, and Warrington. In NORTHUMBERLAND—Tynemouth. In WESTMORLAND—Kendal. In YORKSHIRE—Huddersfield, Wakfield, and Whitby.

The Boroughs which were specially regulated by Clauses of the Reform Act, 1832, are the following :—

New Shoreham in Sussex, now includes the whole of the Rape of Bramben with the exception of some parts, which are included in the Borough of Horsham.

Aylesbury, in Buckinghamshire, includes the Hundred of Aylesbury.

Penryn, in Cornwall, includes the town of Falmouth.

Melcombe Regis, in Dorsetshire, returns two Members only, instead of four.

Cricklade, in Wiltshire, includes the Hundreds of Highworth, Cricklade, Staple, Kingsbridge, and Malmesbury, excepting that part of the last Hundred included within the Borough of Malmesbury.

East Retford, in Nottinghamshire, includes the Hundred of Bassetlaw, and all places within the boundary or limit of that Hundred.

The following alterations were made by the Reform Act of 1832, in the several Counties of England :—

Essex, Kent, Surrey, and Sussex were divided, and two Members are returned for each division. Hertfordshire now returns three Members to Parliament.

Norfolk and Suffolk are divided, and return four Members each. Buckinghamshire and Cambridgeshire return three Members each. Cornwall, Devonshire, Hampshire, Somersetshire, and Wiltshire return four Members each; and Dorsetshire returns three Members. The Isle of Wight returns one Member.

Gloucestershire, Shropshire, Staffordshire, and Worcestershire return four Members each. Berkshire, Herefordshire, and Oxfordshire now return three Members each.

Derbyshire, Leicestershire Lincolnshire, Northamptonshire, Nottinghamshire, and Warwickshire return four Members for each.

Cheshire, Cumberland, Durham, Lancashire, and Northumberland have been divided, and two Members are returned for each division, in each county. Yorkshire returns two for each Riding.

The Counties of England now return 144 Members; the cities return 50, the Universities 4, and the boroughs 273, making a total number of 471 Members of Parliament for England: the number of the Commons, including Scotland, Ireland, and Wales, is 658 Members.

CHURCHES

The nature and value of the benefice is described in every parish. Rectories are the most numerous class of benefices, and are usually the richest. A rectory is the entire parish church, with all its rights, glebe, tithe, and other profits; a living, whereof the predial tithe is not impropriated. When the living is in the hands of a layman, it is an impropriation. An appropriation is when the living is in the hands of a bishop, college, or religious house, a serving of a benefice to the perpetual use of some foundation which has obtained the king's licence to appoint a vicar to officiate for them.

At the dissolution of monasteries, most of these appropriations devolved to the crown, and were conveyed to laymen; whence they are called impropriations, as being improperly in the hands of laymen.

A great portion of benefices is in the patronage of the crown, of the bishops, of ecclesiastical dignitaries and corporations, and of opulent individuals.

The first forms, rules, rites, and ministers of the Christian Church, received Greek denominations; its whole vocabulary was derived from the Greek language. The bishops bore Greek names; and the whole church might be called more Greek than Roman; although the church flourished, and first received a decided form and hierarchy, at Rome. The first fruits and tenths was a fund collected from the church before the Reformation; these were paid to the Pope, and made applicable to carrying on the secular government of Rome. Henry VIII. contrived to apply these tenths and first fruits to state purposes in this country. Previously the value of rectories were ascertained by the taxation of 1254, 38th Henry III., made by Walter, Bishop of Norwich, called the Norwich taxation; and by that of Pope Nicholas IV. in 1291, the 20th Edward I.

In 1535, 26th Henry VIII., a return was made, which gave a survey of all the ecclesiastical lands and revenues of the country in that period. This valuation, known by the name of Liber Regis, or the King's Book, is kept up to the present time, in the Remembrancer's Office. The valuation in the King's Book, in many cases, determines whether a living be tenable with a fellowship or a college, or not. In taking a second living compatible with a former, regard must be had to this valuation in the King's Book; and it is according to the same valuation, that the presentation must have a stamp of a greater or lesser value.

Besides the chapels belonging to the larger parishes, there are free chapels, independent of the rector, and some parochial chapelries, differing only in name from parishes; but they are not numerous.

MONASTERIES

A considerable portion of the landed property in the kingdom having been in the possession of the monastical, clerical, and military orders, an account is given in this work of all the abbeys, priories, and houses of friars, formerly in England. So extensive were the temporal possessions of the religious institutions, that there were few parishes which were not, in part, claimed by the regular orders, or in which the religious had not an interest. Of the number of religious houses existing in 1535, 186 belonged to the Benedictine order, 173 to the Austin canons, and 103 to the Cistercians; the rest, in smaller proportions, amongst the numerous orders. The valuation, at the time of the dissolution, is chiefly taken from that of Speed, in his "Historie of Britain," being the gross incomes of the religious foundations, of which Dugdale gives only the clear revenues; but other valuations, from competent authorities, are occasionally inserted. The names of the persons to whom the estates were granted after the dissolution, are given in most instances, and those of the present proprietors, whenever they could be obtained. A description of the most beautiful, but delapidated remains of the conventual buildings, which yet adorn the country, is introduced as a means of directing the attention of the public to the finest specimens of architectural science.

ORTHOGRAPHY

The spelling of the names of various places, has been found to differ very much; and, as a proof of the unsettled state of orthography, seventeen methods of spelling Wainfleet in Lincolnshire, the birth-place of the founder of Magdalen College, Oxford, is mentioned by Dr. Chandler, in his life of that prelate.

The original names of places have been very often confounded and neglected; and in the changes made by time and caprice, the topographer has to contend with innumerable corruptions. There is no greater difficulty in topographical and genealogical researches, than in ascertaining precisely the spelling of a proper name. Burghley is adopted, in the history of Hatfield house, in Mr. Robinson's "Vitruvius Britannicus," as most agreeable to contemporary authority and as approaching nearest to its evident derivation from Burgh and Ley, simply meaning the town field; although Burleigh, it must be confessed, is frequently used in works of acknowledged authority, and is not more improper than the titles of Earl of Stradbroke, derived from Stradbrook, a village on his lordship's estate in Suffolk, or that of Viscount Goderich, which is taken from Goodrich castle in Herefordshire.

ROADS

The principal Roads in the kingdom are those by which the mail-coaches travel, branching from the metropolis to the most distant points in every required direction; amongst many improvements of the Roads suggested by Mr. Telford, it may be mentioned that all high hedges and trees are now cut down, and the sloping banks near the roads removed, that they may be kept open to the sun and air.

The improvements in the inland department of the General Post-office, which have been made since this book was commenced in 1830, are numerous and extensive. The following post towns have been established within that period, in addition to those which formerly existed.

Bognor, Robertsbridge, and St. Leonards, in Sussex; March, in Cambridgeshire, and Long Stratton, in Norfolk.

In the Western Counties—Callington, Redruth, Ilfracombe, Ivybridge, Torquay, Torrington, Stony Cross, Ilchester, South Petherton, Wincanton, Hindon, Swindon, Wily, and Woodyates.

In the Oxford circuit—Chalford, Coleford, Newnham, Bilston, Cheadle, Eccleshall, Droitwich, and Malvern.

In the Midland Counties—Belper, Matlock, Ashby de la Zouch, Barton on Humber, Spittal, Dunchurch, Leamington, Solihull, Southam, and Welford.

In the Northern Counties—Altringham, Chester le Street, Rushyford, Garstang, Felton, Catterick, Dewsbury, Driffield, Goole, Huddersfield, Market Weighton, Pocklington, and Selby; besides Bridgend, Builth, Chirk, Corwen, Crickhowell, Llanelly, Llangatock, Narbeth, Pwllheli, Rhayader, and St. Clears, in Wales.

A list of the principal Roads is necessary, to show how the several Counties are connected, and the facilities of travelling.

1. The Dover road, the most frequented in England, being the

readiest passage to France and the Downs, is through Dartford, Rochester, Sittingbourne, and Canterbury, to Dover.

2. The Brighton road is through Croydon, Reigate, Crawley, and Cuckfield, to Brighton.

3. The Hastings and St. Leonard's road is by Seven Oaks, Tunbridge Wells, Robertsbridge, Battle, and Hastings, to St. Leonards.

4. The Portsmouth road is through Kingston, Guildford, and Petersfield, to Portsmouth.

5. The Southampton and Poole road is through Staines, Farnham, Alton, Winchester, Southampton, and Ringwood, to Poole.

6. The Falmouth and Penzance road leads through Bagshot, Harford Bridge, Overton, Andover, Salisbury, Blandford, Dorchester, Bridport, Axminster, Honiton, Exeter, Oakhampton, Launceston, Bodmin, Truro, and Falmouth, to Penzance.

7. The Exeter road, *via* Yeovil, is through Staines, Andover, Salisbury, Shaftesbury, Yeovil, Crewkerne, Chard, and Honiton, to Exeter.

8. The Exeter, Devonport, and Falmouth road is through Bagshot, Whitchurch, Andover, Amesbury, Ilchester, Ilminster, Honiton, Exeter, Ashburton, Plymouth, Devonport, Liskeard, Lostwithiel, St. Austel, and Truro, to Falmouth.

9. The Bath, Exeter, and Devonport road passes through Hounslow, Maidenhead, Newbury, Marlborough, Devizes, Bath, Wells, Bridgewater, Taunton, Collumpton, Exeter, Chudleigh, Newton Abbot, and Totness, to Devonport.

10. The Bristol and Pembroke road is through Hounslow, Maidenhead, Newbury Calne, Bath, and Bristol, to Cardiff, Swansea, Carmarthen, and Pembroke.

11. The Stroud road is through Maidenhead, Henley, Abingdon, Faringdon, Fairford, Cirencester, and Stroud.

12. The Gloucester and Monmouth road passes through Hounslow, Maidenhead, Oxford, Witney, Northleach, Cheltenham, Gloucester, Ross, Monmouth, and Abergavenny, to Carmarthen.

13. The Worcester and Ludlow road passes through High Wycombe, Oxford, Moreton in Marsh, Worcester, and Tenbury, to Ludlow.

14. The Birmingham, Shrewsbury, and Holyhead road, is through Stony Stratford, Towcester, Daventry, Dunchurch, Coventry, Birmingham, Wolverhampton, Shiffnall, Shrewsbury, and Oswestry, to Holyhead.

15. The Banbury, Birmingham, and Stourport road, is through Aylesbury, Bicester, Banbury, Southam, Warwick, Birmingham, and Kidderminster, to Stourport.

16. The Chester road is through Dunstable, Woburn, Northampton, Lutterworth, Hinkley, Atherston, Tamworth, Lichfield, Stafford, Nantwich, and Tarporley, to Chester.

17. The Liverpool road is through St. Albans, Stony Stratford, Towcester, Daventry, Dunchurch, Coventry, Coleshill, Lichfield, Stone, Newcastle, Knutsford, and Warrington, to Liverpool.

18. The Manchester and Carlisle road passes through Redburn, Dunstable, Woburn, Northampton, Market Harborough, Leicester, Loughborough, Derby, Asbourne, Macclesfield, Manchester, Preston, Lancaster, Burton, Kendal, and Penrith, to Carlisle.

19. The Halifax road passes through Woburn, Newport Paynell, Market Harborough, Leicester, Loughborough, Nottingham, Chesterfield, Sheffield, and Huddersfield, to Halifax.

20. The Leeds road passes through Barnet, Welwyn, Hitchin, Bedford, Higham Ferrers, Kettering, Uppingham, Oakham, Melton, Nottingham, Mansfield, Chesterfield, Sheffield, Barnsley, and Wakefield, to Leeds.

21. The Wetherby and Carlisle road is through Barnet, Welwyn, Baldock, Stilton, Stamford, Grantham, Newark, Ollerton, Worksop, Doncaster, Pontefract, Wetherby, Boroughbridge, Gretabridge, Brough, Appleby, and Penrith, to Carlisle.

22. The Lincoln and Hull road passes through Waltham Cross, Baldock, Peterborough, Bourne, Folkingham, Sleaford, Lincoln, and Brigg, to Hull, on the opposite side of the Humber.

23. The Boston and Louth road is through Waltham Cross, Ware, Arrington, Caxton, Huntingdon, Peterborough, Spalding, Boston, and Spilsby, to Louth.

24. The York and Edinburgh road is through Waltham Cross, Ware, Arrington, Huntingdon, Stilton, Stamford, Grantham, Newark, Barnby Moor, Doncaster, Ferrybridge, Tadcaster, York, Easingwold, Thirsk, Northallerton, Darlington, Durham, Newcastle, Morpeth, Alnwick, Belford, Berwick, and Dunbar, to Edinburgh.

25. The Cambridge, Lynn, and Wells road, is through Ware, Royston, Cambridge, Ely, Downham, Lynn, Snettisham, and Burnham, to Wells.

26. The Newmarket and Norwich road is through Bishops Stortford, Littlebury, Newmarket, Bury St. Edmunds, Thetford, and Attleborough, to Norwich.

27. The Ipswich and Norwich road is through Ingatestone, Witham, Colchester, Ipswich, Stoke, and Long Stratton, to Norwich; the Yarmouth road is the same as that of Norwich to Ipswich, when it passes thence through Wickham Market, and Yoxford, to Yarmouth.

RAIL-ROADS

Rail-roads, presenting an increased celerity of movement, were introduced into this country in the beginning of the seventeenth century, and were employed in some of the collieries at Newcastle-on-Tyne. A description of them, as constructed in the year 1676, may be found in "The Life of the Lord Keeper North." These Rail-roads were of wood, and for a long time made but little progress in improvement. Cast-iron Railroads are stated to have been used at the colliery belonging to the Duke of Norfolk, near Sheffield, in the year 1776.

A Steam Carriage was invented and brought into use by Trevithick, upon the Rail-road of Merthyr Tydvil, in South Wales, in the year 1804; but the locomotive engine was not brought to perfection till 1830, upon the Liverpool and Manchester Rail-road; (*see page 80*).

The Rail-roads of England which have been executed, and are now in operation, about thirty in number, are here placed in the order in which they were completed.

1. The Surrey Railway, from the Thames at Wandsworth to Croydon, nine miles in length, was opened about the year 1802, for the conveyance of lime, chalk, and agricultural products, to London, and for the return of coals and manure for the use of the country through which it passes; horses are the motive power employed; and it was never intended for the conveyance of passengers.

2. The Croydon, Merstham, and Godstone Rail-road, formed in 1803, is a continuation of the Surrey Rail-way.

3. The Forest of Dean Rail-road, opened in 1809, for the conveyance of timber, coals, iron, ore, and other minerals, found in the forest, for shipment at Bullo Pill, on the river Severn, near Newnham, whence it proceeds to the summit of a hill in Dean Forest; it is in length about seven miles and a half.

4. The Severn and Wye Rail-road, opened in 1809, affords an easy communication between the rivers Severn and Wye, and the collieries and quarries in Dean Forest. It commences at Lydbrook, on the Wye, and

terminates at the lower verge below Newerne, in the parish of Lydney. It is connected with the Severn at Nass point, by a canal, one mile in length. The extent of Rail-road, including nine branches laid from the main line, to coal and other mines, is about twenty-six miles.

5. The Monmouth Rail-road, opened in 1810, runs from Howler Slade, in Dean Forest, to the town of Monmouth; and has several branch Rail-roads communicating with various quarries and collieries near to the main line.

6. The Hay Rail-road commences at Parton Cross, in the parish of Eardisley, in Herefordshire; and, after passing through a mountainous district, by a circuitous course of twenty-four miles, ends at the wharf of the Brecon and Abergavenny canal. This road is of great advantage to the owners of the property through which it runs, by affording facilities for the transit of mineral and other products.

7. The Kington Rail-road is a continuation of the Hay Rail-road from Parton Cross to Kington, and thence to the lime works, near Burlinjob, in Radnorshire: its length is about fourteen miles.

8. The Lanviangel Rail-road commences at Lanviangel Crucorney, in Monmouthshire, and ends on the bank of the Brecon and Abergavenny canal, two miles N.W. from the latter town, a distance of about six miles and a half.

9. The Grosmont Tramroad, or Rail-way, is a continuation of the Lanviangel Rail-road, and ends at the Langua bridge, on the Monnow, between Abergavenny and Hereford, a distance of nearly seven miles, in the course of which a difference in the level of 166 feet is accomplished.

10. The Mamhilad Rail-road commences at Usk bridge, and ends at Mambilad, three miles north from Pontypool, a distance of five miles.

11. The Gloucester and Cheltenham Rail-road commences at the Knap toll-gate, Cheltenham, and ends at the basin of the Gloucester and Berkeley canal, in the City of Gloucester, a distance of about nine miles. It is the means of suplying the town of Cheltenham with coal at a cheap rate.

12. The Mansfield and Pinxton Rail-road commences at Bullshead lane, Mansfield, and ends at Pinxton basin, near Alfreton, Derbyshire, where it communicates with a branch of the Cromford canal, passing above eight miles through a country abounding with minerals. A branch of this Rail-road begins about a mile a half from Pinxton basin, and passes eastward towards the Codnor Park works. The main line is proposed to be united to the Midland Counties Rail-road.

13. The Plymouth and Dartmoor Rail-road commences at Prince Town, on Dartmoor, and ends at the Sound at Sutton Pool, Plymouth, including

a branch from the lime works at Catsdown; its length, through a very circuitous route, is about thirty miles, passing one of the most interesting specimens of woodland scenery in the county, before it reaches Roborough Down.

14. The Stratford and Moreton Rail-road for supplying Moreton in the Marsh, Stow is the Wold, and other places through which it passes, with coal, and for conveying back to Stratford-on-Avon, stone, and agricultural produce; the length is sixteen miles, with a branch to Shipston-on-Stour, extending two miles and a half.

15. The Stockton and Darlington Rail-road, the earliest considerable project of the kind, was the first upon which locomotive steam engines were used. The extension to the Tees mouth, crosses the river by a suspension bridge, and proceeds by Stainsby, Stainton, Acklam, Newport, Middlesborough, Leventhorp, and Ormsby, to the river Tees.

16. The Clarence Rail-road beings at Samphire Beacon, on the banks of the Tees, in Durham, and joins the Stockton and Darlington Rail-road at Sim Pasture. By means of this Rail-road several valuable coal-fields and lime-stone quarries have been move effectually and cheaply connected with the port of Stockton. The main line is only fifteen miles and a half long; but there are six branches, extending, collectively, more than thirty miles. The city of Durham branch quits the main line at Stillington, in Redmarshall parish, for Durham. The Stockton branch from the old Durham and Yarm road, to Stockon-on-Tees. The Deanery branch from Sim Pasture to Bishops Auckland. The Sherburn brance from Ferry hill to the lime and coal-works at Sherburn. The Byers Green branch from Ferry hill to Byers Green; and the Chilton branch from the Durham branch to Chilton in the parish of Merrington.

17. The Redruth and Chasewater Rail-road for conveying the rich mineral produce of the district to a place of shipment, begins in the eastern side of Redruth, in Cornwall, whence it proceeds round Carnmarth hill to Twelve Heads, and then to Point Quay, a shipping port on the river Fal, at the head of Carreg road, in the parish of Feock. The length of the main line is more than nine miles; but there are, besides, four branches, amounting together more than five miles.

18. The Rumney Rail-road takes its name from the river Rumney, along the bank of which it runs from Abertyswg, in Bedwelty parish, Monmouthshire, to Pye Corner, in Bassaleg parish, when it joins the Sirhowey Rail-road, about two miles and a half W. from Newport. Its length is nearly twenty-two miles; and it is used for the conveyance of the abundant mineral products of the district through which it passes.

19. The Cromford and High Peak Rail-road from the Cromford canal in Derbyshire, to the Peak Forest canal, at Whaley Bridge, opened in 1829, is thirty-four miles in length, passing over high land. An ascent of 990 feet above the level of the Cromford canal is accomplished by means of several inclined planes, up which wagons are drawn by stationary steam engines: the summit level is maintained for twelve miles and a half; and the Rail-road, in its course, passes through a hill by a tunnel, nearly three furlongs is length; fifty-two bridges and archways have also been built upon it. This Rail-road opens a convenient communication for trade between the counties of Derby, Nottingham, and Leicester, the town of Manchester, and the port of Liverpool.

20. The Portland Rail-road is a line of little more than miles in length, from the Priory lands in Portland Island, to the stone piers, Portland Castle, Dorsetshire.

21. The Heck and Wentbridge Rail-road to convey stone procured at Wentbridge and Smeaton, in Yorkshire, for shipment; is rather circuitous in its course of about seven miles and a half to the Knottingley and Goole canal, part of the Aire and Calder navigation.

22. The Liverpool and Manchester Rail-road, the most important hither completed, has been fully described at *page* 80., in regard to its course, length, and manner of construction.

23. The Bolton and Leigh Rail-road, one of the branches of Liverpool and Manchester line, begins at the canal, near Bolton-le-Moors, and proceeds through various collieries to a branch of the Leeds and Liverpool canal, communicating with the Duke of Bridgewater's canal at Leigh, with a short extension to connect the towns of Bolton and Leigh. The length of the Rail-road is little more than nine miles, and the trade is carried on by means of locomotive steam engines.

24. The Warrington and Newton Rail-road, another branch of the Liverpool and Manchester line, enables the town of Warrington to partake of the advantages resulting from easy communication with the great commercial towns and with the coal-fields in its neighbourhood.

25. The Canterbury and Whitstable Rail-road was opened in May, 1830, to give facilities to the trade between London and Canterbury. It begins at the river Stour, Canterbury, and proceeds by St. Dunstans and Hackington through Clowes Wood, part of the Forest of Blean, to Whitstable bay. Its length is six miles and a quarter, formed into a series of inclined planes, a great part of which are of too great an inclination to allow of locomotive power; and stationary steam engines are here provided. On part of the line, which is nearly level, locomotive engines are used; at the

distance of a mile and a quarter from Canterbury, is a tunnel about half a mile long. The highest point of the line about midway, is 220 feet above the level of the sea at Whitstable.

26. The Bristol and Gloucestershire Rail-road is part of an extensive plan to establish a Rail-road between Bristol and Birmingham; a length of nine miles is only constructed from Cuckold's Pill, near the floating dock, Bristol, in a north-easterly direction through various collieries to Coal-pit Heath, near Westerleigh, in Gloucestershire.

27. The Leeds and Selby Rail-road, opened in 1834. It is intended to continue this line to Hull, establishing a communication between the manufactories of Yorkshire and the Baltic.

28. The Leicester and Swannington Rail-road for the supply of coal and lime-stone to Leicester, begins at the Leicestershire and Northamptonshire Union canal, in Leicester, and proceeds N.W. through a tunnel a mile and a quarter long, to the northern side of Swannington, in the parish of Whitwick, nearly sixteen miles in total length. It is to be continued to the Ashby de la Zouch Rail-road, with a branch to Cole Orton.

29. The London and Greenwich Rail-road is the first executed Rail-road having its commencement in the metropolis. The opening was celebrated on 14th December, 1836, by the Lord Mayor, Sheriffs, Aldermen, and gentlemen connected with science. Five trains of carriages started conveying 1,500 persons, and performing the journey of three miles to Deptford, in less than eight minutes. It was projected by Colonel Landmann; the surveyors and architects were Messrs. Smith and Newman; and the contractor Mr. Mackintosh: the success of the whole is considered to be due to the exertions of George Walker, esq., the managing director. The royal assent to the act for its formation, was given in 1833.

The viaduct is composed of about 1000 arches, eighteen feet in span, and twenty-two feet high; a form of construction rendered necessary by the number of streets over which the line is carried. The Deptford Pier Rail-road is carried from the main line, at the High-street, Deptford, to the river side; and a pier is now constructing to facilitate the embarkation and landing of passengers by steam vessels. This Rail-road will probably become the channel by which other lines of road, as the Croydon and South Eastern may enter the City of London.

30. The Whitby and Pickering Rail-road, seventeen miles in extent, by which the hilly and inconvenient road between those towns is in a great degree superseded, was opened in May, 1836. It is not intended for steam carriages; but the travelling is effected partly by horses, and partly by inclined planes.

The tour, by the Rail-road, is through Eskdale, the picturesque vale of Goathfand, Newton Dale, &c.; and illustrations of the scenery on this line have been published, from drawings by G. Dodgson.

31. The Newcastle and Carlisle Rail-road, of which seventeen miles were opened to the public in 1834, and forty-nine in 1836. Before it enters the valley of the Tyne, it encounters some difficult country; and the river scenery of the Tyne, viewed from the Rail-road, is exceedingly beautiful. Coal, stone, and agricultural produce, are the chief articles conveyed. This communication between the eastern and western coasts of England, is expected to be very beneficial; to Carlisle, in particular.

The following Rail-roads are now in active progress; involving, in their construction, a sum of money indicating a degree of private wealth and enterprise, such as no time or country but England has ever exhibited, and suggesting an idea of the aggregate riches of the country, which it is startling to contemplate.

The London and Southampton Rail-road by Vauxhall, Wimbledon, north of Guildford, to Basingstoke, Winchester, and Southampton, nearly seventy-five miles.

The great Western Rail-road connecting Bath and Bristol with London, and terminating on the Birmingham line, about four miles from the station in London, includes a long tunnel, on an inclined plane, at Box, near Chippenham, in Wiltshire.

The London and Birmingham Rail-road, an important undertaking, is very shortly to be opened.

The principal entrance of the London station, erected from designs by *P. Hardwick*, is on the northern side of Euston Square; the line of road passes by the valley of Brent to Watford, Berkhampstead, Fenny Stratford, near Northampton, Daventry, Rugby, and Coventry, to the station at Birmingham, the entrance to which is now erecting, from designs by *Hardwick*. There are several tunnels required to carry the line through the different ridges that cross its course; one of these at Watford exceeds a mile in length. By this means, good levels have been secured; and the distance of 111½ miles will be performed in five hours and a half.

The Grand Junction Rail-road continues the London and Birmingham line northward, by Wolverhampton, Penkridge, Stafford, on the western side of Newcastle, and the Potteries, through Cheshire to Warrington and Newton, where it joins the Liverpool and Manchester Rail-road at a point equidistant from each of these towns. This district traversed requires no tunnels; but, across the valley of the Weever, in Cheshire, is a viaduct of twenty arches, of sixty feet span, and more than sixty feet above the level of the valley.

The North Union Rail-road is another branch, formerly known as the Wigan Rail-road, which completes a distance of twenty-one miles from Newton to Preston, including a viaduct across the valley of the Ribble at Penwortham.

The Preston and Wyre Rail-road will continue the line to the harbour of Wyre on the southern side of Lancaster bay, a length of nearly 300 miles from Southampton to Preston. Here a town, to be named Fleetwood, is proposed to be built; and docks constructed for the accommodation of shipping. Its proximity to the lakes, by means of steam boats plying across the bay of Morecambe, will make it the nearest route to that beautiful district, by many miles.

The Midland Counties Rail-road is to proceed from the London Rail-road at Rugby, passing by Lutterworth, Leicester, and Loughborough, to Pinxton, near Alfreton, in Derbyshire, where it is to join the Mansfield Rail-road, crossed by branches near its northern extremity, to Nottingham and Derby.

The North Midland Rail-road is a continuation to be carried from the end of the Derby branch, by Chesterfield and Rotherham to Leeds, opening a new way to London, from the manufacturing district of Yorkshire.

A Northern and Eastern Rail-road is to connect London and York with a branch from Cambridge to Norwich and Yarmouth. The line is by Bishops Stortford, Cambridge, Huntingdon, Peterborough, Lincoln, and Gainsborough. At York it is to be connected with a proposed Rail-road to Newcastle-on-Tyne.

A Great North of England Rail-road is proposed to connect London with York, and to continue the line to Glasgow and Edinburgh.

An Eastern Counties Rail-road from London to Yarmouth, is intended to be carried through Brentwood, Chelmsford, Colchester, Ipswich, and Norwich, to Yarmouth.

A London and Brighton Rail-road it proposed by different routes, and by different engineers, Stephenson's and Rennie's.

A Birmingham and Gloucester Rail-road is intended to pass near Bromsgrove, Droitwich, Tewksbury, and Worcester, to Cheltenham. A grand connexion Rail-road is also proposed from Gloucester to Worcester, Stourbridge, and Wolverhampton, to Birmingham, giving an advantage to the Stourbridge and Kidderminster manufactories.

A Bristol and Exeter Rail-road is contemplated to pass by way of Clevedon and Weston, Bridgewater, and Taunton, a distance or about seventy-two miles.

A Manchester and Chester Junction Rail-road is proposed, and also a Manchester and Leeds Rail-road; the district over which the last must travel is exceedingly difficult.

A Birmingham and Derby Junction Rail-road, and a North Midland Rail-road from Derby to Leeds, are projected.

The London Grand Junction Rail-road will join the London and Birmingham line near the Regent's Canal, St. Pancras, and proceed thence to Skinner-street, in London; another called the Birmingham, Bristol, and Thames Rail-road, will proceed from the London and Birmingham line at Harlesdon Green to the basin of the Kensington canal.

Steam-engines and Rail-roads are not merely facilitating the conveyance of merchandize from one part of England to the other they are doing more—they are sealing the intercourse between mind and mind, and they are exciting demands for knowledge; sending the desire for that knowledge into all the recesses of this empire, tending powerfully to the cultivation of the mental, as they are improving the physical, capabilities of the country.

RIVERS AND INLAND NAVIGATION

England has numerous Rivers, which are not only of essential importance in facilitating the communication with the interior, and thus giving vigour to commerce and industry, but add greatly to the beauty and picturesque scenery of the country. The most considerable of these Rivers on the eastern coast are the Thames, the Blackwater, the Stour, the Orwell, the Deben, the Alde, the Blyth, the Yare, the Glaven, the Ouse, the Nen, the Witham, the Humber, the Eske, the Tees, the Wear, the Tyne, and the Tweed.

The Eastern Coast is less remarkable for the characteristic beauty of its Rivers, than the Western: on which coast are the Solway Frith, the Eden, the Poebeck, the Lune, the Ribble, the Mersey, the Dee, the Wye, the Severn, the Avon, the Parret, the Taw, the Torridge, the Camel, the Heyl, the Fal, the Fowey, the Looe, the Tamar, the Plym, the Dart, the Exe, the Lyme, the Wey, the Medina, the Anton, the Arun, the Adur, the Ouse, the Rother, the Swale, and the Medway.

The Western Ports of England, so called at the Custom House, are Rochester, Feversham, Ramsgate, Deal, Dover, Rye, Newhaven, Shoreham, Arundel, Chichester, Portsmouth, Southampton, Cowes, Poole, Weymouth, Lyme, Exeter, Dartmouth, Plymouth, Looe, Fowey, Falmouth, Gweek, Truro, Penzance, Scilly, St. Ives, Padstow, Bideford, Barnstaple, Ilfracombe,

Minehead, Bridgewater, Bristol, and Gloucester.

The Northern Ports of England are Leigh, Maldon, Colchester, Harwich, Ipswich, Woodbridge, Aldborough, Southwold, Yarmouth, Clay, Wells, Lynn, Wisbech, Boston, Grimsby, Hull, Bridlington, Scarborough, Whitby, Stockton, Sunderland, Newcastle, Berwick, Carlisle, Whitehaven, Lancaster, Preston, Liverpool, Chester, Douglas, Isle of Man, and Chepstow.

The Inland Navigation of England is chiefly indebted to the magnificent undertakings of the Duke of Bridgewater, a nobleman who spent his time and fortune in pursuits that well entitle him to be called the benefactor of his country. The first canal projected by Brindley, and constructed at the expence of his grace, from his estate at Worsley to the town of Manchester, was completed in 1760; since which time the greatest part of the canals in England have been formed, and brought nearer to perfection, than in any other part of the world. The introduction of Rail-roads have now given a check to the progress of Inland Navigation.

In 1795, the canals in one county, Staffordshire, exceeded 200 miles in length: the improvement and extent of the Potteries, was mainly facilitated by the convenience of water carriage; and, at the same time, the land near the canals rapidly advanced in value, by a communication being opened, and by the introduction of manure.

The Adur River, in Sussex, was improved in 1807, from Bainbridge to Shoreham Harbour.

The Aire and Calder Navigation, Yorkshire, has been improved by a canal from the Aire at Haddesley, to the Ouse at Selby, made in 1774; and by a canal from Knottingley to Goole, opened in 1826.

The Alford Canal, Lincolnshire, constructed in 1828, extends from Alford to the sea, near Anderby, five miles eastward, where is a harbour and pier.

The Ancholm River Navigation, Lincolnshire, from Brigg to the Humber, was made under the direction of *Rennie*, in 1825.

The Andover Canal, Hampshire, constructed in 1789, from Andover, crosses the River Anton, passes Stockbridge and Romsey to Redbridge, near Millbrook, on the Southampton water, at the point where the tide meets the River Test.

The Arun River, Sussex, was improved in 1785, from Houghton bridge to New bridge, near Pulborough, whence a Canal is cut parallel with the river to Pallenham Wharf, where the river becomes navigable; and another Canal is cut from Greatham bridge to New bridge, shortening the distance arising from the winding of the river. The length to the Port of Arundel is twenty-six miles; and in 1793 piers and improvements were

made in the harbour of Little Hampton, by cutting a new channel through the sea beach: here the trade is increasing.

The Ashby de la Zouch Canal, Leicestershire, to the Coventry Canal, near Nuneaton, is continued to the Lime works at Ticknall, in Derbyshire, and by another line to those at Cloud hill, in Leicestershire, opened in 1805.

The Ashton-under-Lyne Canal, Lancashire, forms part of a line of Inland Navigation between the Irish Sea and the German Ocean, passing through Ashton to Manchester, Rochdale, and Lancaster.

The Avon River, Wiltshire, was made navigable from Salisbury to Christchurch, in Hampshire, in 1666, but the works were destroyed by a flood; and it is only navigable at spring tides about two miles from the sea.

The Avon River, Warwickshire, was made navigable in 1793, from Stratford-on-Avon to Evesham, Pershore, and Tewksbury, where it falls into the Severn.

The Avon and Frome Rivers of Gloucestershire were improved in the reigns of William III., George II., and George III., under the direction of the Corporation of Bristol, whose jurisdiction extends to Hanham Mills. The Port of Bristol was improved in 1803; and the Bristol Dock Company constructed a dam across the Avon at Redcliff, in 1806.

The Avon River, Somersetshire, on Lower Avon, is navigable from Bath, and was improved in 1807.

The Axe River, Somersetshire, from Lower Weare to the entrance into the Bristol Channel, nine miles, was greatly improved in 1803.

The Barnsley Canal, Yorkshire, was opened in 1799; it is connected with a Rail-road to Silkston, near Wakefield.

The Basingstoke Canal, Hampshire, made in 1793, passes Odiham by Grewell hill tunnel, half a mile long, to Aldershot and the River Wey, about three miles above its junction with the Thames.

The Baybridge Canal, Sussex, opened in 1827, exteeds from Baybridge to Binesbridge, near West Grinstead, where the navigation of the River Adur commences.

Beverley Beck, Yorkshire, from Beverley to Hull, is maintained and improved by the Corporation of Beverley, under an Act of Parliament in 1744.

The Birmingham Canal Navigation, Warwickshire, consists of a Canal from Birmingham to Bilston and Antherley, near Wolverhampton, communicating with another Canal between the Severn and Trent, with cuts to several coal mines; a Canal from Riders Green in Staffordshire, to Broadwater engine, and another from Birmingham, which joins the Coventry Canal at Fazeley, near Tamworth. These Companies were united in 1784, and they have since joined the last Canal to the Trent and Mersey Navigation, and have opened a communication between that and the Worcester Canal.

The Birmingham and Liverpool Junction Canal, made in 1828, extends from Tettenhall, near Wolverhampton, where it joins the Worcestershire and Staffordshire Canal, to Norbury and Drayton, across the River Tern to Audlem and Nantwich in Cheshire, and joins the Ellesmere and Chester Canal, near Dorfold Hall, a distance of thirty-nine miles.

The Bourn Eau Navigation, Lincolnshire, was improved in 1781, from Bourn to the River Glen, at Tongue end, opening a communication with the Port of Boston.

The Bradford Canal, Yorkshire, completed in 1744, extends from the Leeds and Liverpool Canal at Shipley, to Bradford.

The Abergavenny Canal, Monmouthshire, completed in 1805, extends from Brecon to Abergavenny, and to the Monmouthshire Canal, near Pontypool, crossing the River Avon, and passing through a short tunnel; it also communicates with several iron works, collieries, and lime-stone quarries, by Rail-roads.

The Duke of Bridgewater's Canal in Lancashire, from Worsley Mill to Manchester, was opened in 1760. In 1776, this Canal was united with the Trent and Mersey Canal, at Preston Brook; and in 1795, a Canal to Pennington, near Leigh, has since connected it extent with the Leeds and Liverpool Navigation, by which means a vast extent of commercial intercourse is facilitated by this Canal.

The Bridgewater and Taunton Canal, Somersetshire, was completed in 1825, between those towns.

Bude Harbour and Canal, Cornwall; this harbour was improved in 1819, and a Canal cut to Thornbury, in Devonshire, a branch of which extends towards Launceston.

The Bure River Navigation, Norfolk, from Colteshall to Aylsham bridge, was improved in 1773.

The Bure, Yare, and Wavency Rivers, Norfolk, running into Yarmouth Haven, were improved in 1772.

The Caistor Canal, Lincolnshire, was formed in 1793, from Moorton, near Caistor, to the river Ancholme at South Helsey.

The Calder and Hebble Navigation was formed by Smeaton, from the Aire and Calder Navigation to the Rochdale Canal, with a cut at Salterhebble to Bailey Hall, near Halifax; made in 1825.

The Cam, or Granta River, Cambridgeshire, was made navigable in 1813, from Clayhithe Ferry to Queen's Mill, about seven miles.

The Camel River, Cornwall, has a tide-way navigation from Guinea Port, near Wade Bridge, to the see at Padstow.

The Canterbury Navigation: the River Stour, from Canterbury to Sandwich, was improved in 1825, and a jetty, 1000 feet in length, is proposed.

The Carlisle Canal, Cumberland, from the eastern side of Carlisle to Fishers Cross, Bowness, on the Solway Frith, was commenced in 1819, and has superseded the circuitous navigation or the Eden river.

The Chelmer and Blackwater Navigation, Essex, from Chelmsford to the tide-way at Colliers Reach, on the Blackwater, includes a canal uniting the rivers and a canal from Heybridge, near Maldon, to the basin at Colliers Reach, opened in 1796.

The Chesterfield Canal, Derbyshire, was made in 1776, from Chesterfield through a coal district, and entering Yorkshire at Shire Oaks, passes near Worksop and East Retford to the Trent at Stockwith.

The Colne River, Essex, was made navigable from the Hithe at Colchester, to Wivenhoe on the coast, in 1781.

The Coombe Hill Canal, Gloucestershire, made in 1792, extends from Coombe Hill to Fletcher's Leap, Deerhurst, on the Severn, near Tewksbury.

The Coventry Canal, Warwickshire, opened in 1790, extends from Coventry to Fazeley, where it joins the Birmingham and Fazeley Canal, and then is continued to Fradley Heath, near Alrewas, in Staffordshire, where it joins the Trent and Mersey Canal.

The Cromford Canal, Derbyshire, constructed in 1790, crosses the rivers Derwent and Amber to Butterley Park, and Codnor Park iron-works, and joins the Erewash Canal, near Langley Bridge, Heanor.

The Crouch River, Essex, is a tide-way navigation for sixteen miles.

The Darent River, Kent, is navigable, as a tide-way, four miles above its junction with the Thames.

The Dart River, Devonshire, has a tide-way navigation for twelve miles above the mouth.

The Dearne and Dove Canal, Yorkshire, was completed in 1800, from Barnsley to the river Don, at Swinton.

The Deben River in Suffolk, it navigable as high as Woodbridge; and there is a dock at Ramsholt, six miles below Woodbridge.

The Dee River, Cheshire, is navigable from Chester to the sea.

The Derby Canal, formed in 1793, extends from the Erewash Canal at Little Eaton, through Derby, to the Trent and Mersey Canal, which joins the river Trent at Swarkston.

The Derwent River, Derbyshire, was made navigable from Derby to the Trent, in 1720; but, on the opening of the Derby Canal, the navigation on this river was discontinued.

The Derwent River, Yorkshire: the navigation of this river, from Malton to the Ouse, at Barmby on the Marsh, was extended to Yedingham Bridge, in 1805; it is the property of Earl Fitzwilliam.

The Dorset and Somerset Canal, from the river Stour to the Kennet and Avon Canal, near Bradford, was commenced in 1803; but is not completed.

The Driffield Navigation, Yorkshire, was improved in 1817; it extends from the town of Driffield to the river Hull, near the mouth of the Aike Beck.

The Droitwich Canal, Worcestershire, from Droitwich to the river Severn, was formed by Brindley, in 1768.

The Dudley Canal Worcestershire, was executed in 1796, and extends from the Worcester and Birmingham Canal, near Selly Oak, entering the Lapal Tunnel near Stonehouse, and passing another tunnel beyond Halesowen, joins the Birmingham Canal near Tipton Green.

The Don River Navigation, Yorkshire, from Tinsley to the river Ouse, several miles below Doncaster, with cuts to avoid the windings of the river, was completed in 1826.

The Ellesmere and Chester Canal, projected in 1772, and improved in 1830, extends from Ellesmere on the Mersey to the Dee at Chester, whence it joins a branch of the Trent and Mersey Canal at Middlewich, and proceeds to Hurleston, where a cut unites it with the Birmingham and Liverpool Canal: it afterwards enters Shropshire, near Whitchurch, and joins the Montgomeryshire Canal. At the eastern extremity of the Vale of Llangollen the Ellesmere Canal passes over the river Dee by the Aqueduct of Pontcysylte, which was opened in 1805.

The Erewash Canal, Derbyshire, was made in 1777, from the Cromford Canal to the river Trent, near Sawley; in its course it unites with a branch of the Derby Canal, and joins the Nutbrook Canal, near Sandyacre.

The Exeter Canal, Devonshire, is constructed parallel with the river Exe; and the navigation was improved in 1829.

The Foss Navigation, Yorkshire, from Stillington to the Ouse, near York, was made in 1801.

The Foss Dyke Navigation in Lincolnshire, it an ancient canal, extending from the Witham, near Lincoln, to the river Trent at Torksey.

The Gipping River, Suffolk, from Stowmarket to Ipswich, was made navigable in 1793.

The Glastonbury Navigation, Somersetshire, from Glastonbury to the river Brue at High Bridge, and thence to the sea, was improved in 1827.

The Gloucester and Berkeley Canal, Gloucestershire, opened in 1827, is a ship canal, for the purpose of avoiding the tedious passage of the Severn; it commences on the southern side of Gloucester, and joins the estuary of the Severn at Sharpness point, near Berkeley.

The Grand Junction Canal, commenced in 1793, is more than ninety miles in extent from Braunston in Northamptonshire, near Daventry, where it joins the Oxford Canal. After passing Craunston tunnel it proceeds to Norton; at Wedon, the canal is carried across a valley to Stowe Hill, by a raised embankment of earth, about half a mile long and thirty feet high, being nearly parallel with the bells in Wedon church steeple. A cut from Northampton joins the canal, which then passes Blisworth tunnel, and is joined by a cut from Fenny Stratford, which crosses the river Ouse at Woolverton. The line rises to the Wendover branch, and continues to ascend to the summit level at Tring, descending again by Hemel Hempstead and Rickmansworth to Harefield, Uxbridge, and Norwood; it intersects the Brent River, and joins the Thames at Brentford. From Norwood it forms a junction with the Paddington Canal, by which, and by the Regent's Canal, another communication is formed with the Thames and the metropolis.

The Grand Surrey Canal commences near Addington-square, Camberwell-road, crosses the Kent-road to Peckham, towards the Docks at Rotherhithe. It was formed in 1811.

The Grand Union Canal, Leicestershire, was made in 1810 from the Union Canal at Grimley, in Leicestershire, to the Grand Junction Canal, near Long Buckley, in Northamptonshire, with a cut from Market Harborough. It is forty-five miles in length.

The Grand Western Canal, Devonshire, formed in 1812, extends from Topsham to Exeter, Tiverton, and Wellington to Taunton, where it joins the river Tone.

The Grantham Canal, Lincolnshire, was made in 1793, from Grantham to the river Trent, near Nottingham, with a cut to Bingham, near Newark.

The Gresley Canal, Staffordshire, from the colliery at Apedale to Newcastle-under-Lyne, was made by Sir Nigel Gresley, in 1775.

The Hereford and Gloucester Canal, commenced in 1792, is only completed from Gloucester to Ledbury, including a tunnel at Oxenhall, near Newent, more than a mile in length.

The Hertford Union Canal, to connect the River Lea Navigation with the Regent's Canal at Old Ford, near Bethnal Green, was commenced in 1824.

The Horncastle Navigation, Lincolnshire, opened in 1802, is an improvement of the river Bain, from Horncastle to Tattershall, and

of the Tattershall Canal to the river Witham; it also includes the navigation of the Witham to the Foss Dyke Canal at Lincoln.

The Huddersfield Canal, made in 1806, forms part of one of the lines of Inland Navigation between the Irish Sea and the German Ocean. From Huddersfield it communicates with Sir John Ramsden's canal to join a canal from Manchester, and thrice crosses the river Colne by aqueducts ascending to a summit level near Marsden, 656 feet above the surface of the sea, being higher than any other canal in England. It also passes under Pule Hill and Brunn Top, and crosses the river Tame repeatedly.

The Isle of Dogs Canal, Middlesex, formed in 1807, now belongs to the West India Dock Company.

The Itchin Navigation, Hampshire, was improved in 1820; it extends from the City of Winchester to the tide-way in Southampton water, a distance of fourteen miles.

The Ivel River, Bedfordshire, is navigable from Shefford to its junction with the Ouse at Tempsford, six miles below Biggleswade. The works have not long been completed.

The Ilchester and Langport Canal, Somersetshire, was formed in 1795, and connects Ilchester with the river Parret at Langport.

The Kennet and Avon Canal, Wiltshire, was opened in 1810. It extends from the river Kennet at Newbury to Hungerford, Bedwin, and Crofton; to Devizes, Semington, and Bradford, to the river Avon at Bath. In 1813, the proprietors purchased the Kennet River Navigation from Newbury to the Thames at Reading. The Kennet and Avon Canal Also communicates with the Wiltshire and Berkshire Canal at Semington, near Steeple Ashton; with the Frome Canal at Widbrooke, Bath, and with the Somerset Coal Canal, near Bradford. It is carried over several rivers by aqueducts, one of which, over the Avon at Limpley Stoke, is of excellent architecture.

The Kensington Canal, Middlesex, was formed in 1826, from the western extremity of Kensington to Counters Creek, on the Thames.

The Lancaster Canal, completed in 1819, extends sixty miles from Kendal to Hincaster Green Tunnel, across Stainton Ceck, by Milnthorp and Burton, Westmorland, to Lancaster. It then crosses the Lune by an aqueduct of five arches, and passes Garstang to Preston; a Rail-road crosses the Ribble, and the canal is thence continued through a tunnel to Bark Hill, near Wigan. It also joins the Leeds and Liverpool Canal.

The Lark River, Suffolk, was improved in 1817; it is navigable from Mildenhall to its junction with the Ouse, above Littleport.

The Lea River Navigation, Hertfordshire, commences at Hertford, and, passing Ware, joins the Stort River Navigation, near Hoddesdon; thence it

extends to Waltham Abbey, Wanstead, and Bromley, to Bow Creek, on the Thames, near Bromley: it communicates with the Regent's Canal, and with the Limehouse Canal, which joins the Thames, above the Isle of Dogs. It was completed in 1824.

The Leeds and Liverpool Canal, Yorkshire, was completed in 1816, and is in entire length more than 127 miles. It has opened a communication between Liverpool and Hull, furnishing a means of transit for the produce of nature and art through districts noted for manufactures. A branch from Wigan to Leigh, opened in 1821, communicates with Manchester.

The Leicester Navigation, completed in 1797, extends from the Loughborough Canal to the Soar, at Quorndon, which river, and the Wreke, are made navigable to Leicester.

The Leicestershire and Northamptonshire Union Canal, completed in 1805, forms a communication between Leicester and the river Nen, near Northampton, by its junction with the Grand Junction Canal at Foxton, near Market Harborough, to which town is a cut. At Soddington, about six miles northward, the canal passes through a tunnel half a mile in length.

Tke Leominster Canal, Herefordshire, completed in 1826, commences at Kington, and passing Leominster and Tenbury, joins the river Severn at Stourport. It is forty-six miles in extent; and crosses the river Lugg at Kingsland, also passing through two tunnels; one at Pensax, in Worcestershire, is nearly two miles and a quarter in length.

The Liskeard and Looe Canal, Cornwall, formed in 1825, extends from Moorswater, near Liskeard, to Talland Pill, West Looe.

The London and Cambridge Junction Canal, formed in 1814, extends from the river Cam, near Clayhouse Sluice, in Cambridgeshire, to the Stort Navigation, near Bishops Stortford.

The Louth Canal, Lincolnshire, improved in 1828, extends from Louth, by the river Ludd, to Alvingham, and thence to Tetney Haven, on the sea coast, near the mouth of the Humber.

The Lune River, Lancashire, was improved in 1807; the estuary forms the harbour of Lancaster.

The Macclesfield Canal, Cheshire, formed in 1826, extends from the Peak Forest Canal, near Marple, to the Trent and Mersey Canal, at Talk on the Hill, in Staffordshire; twenty-nine and a half miles.

The Manchester, Bolton, and Bury Canal, Lancashire, completed in 1805, crosses the rivers Roch and Irwell in its course.

The Market Weighten Canal, Yorkshire, made in 1772, extends from that town to the Humber.

The Medway River, Kent, between Maidstone and Halling, was widened and improved in 1824.

The Mersey and Irwell Navigation, Lancashire, was improved in 1794, forming a communication between Manchester and Liverpool.

The Monmouthshire Canal, completed in 1802, extends from Pont Newynydd to the river Usk and Newport, near Pontypool; it is connected with the Abergavenny and Brecon Canal, and by cuts and rail-roads with various collieries and iron-works.

The Nen River, Northamptonshire, from Northampton to Peterborough, was improved in 1794; and the navigation of the river at Bedford Level, through part of Cambridgeshire, was also previously improved.

The Nen and Wisbech River Navigation, was improved in 1829, at the outfall of the river Nen, draining the lands and altering the line of the navigation.

The Newcastle-under-Lyne Canal, constructed in 1795, extends from Newcastle to the Trent and Mersey Navigation, at Stoke-upon-Trent. The Newcastle-under-Lyne Junction Canal, forming a communication between the Gresley Canal and the preceding was made in 1798.

The Newport Pagnel Canal, made in 1814, extends to the Grand Junction Canal at Great Linford, on the Ouse, three miles distant.

The North Level Navigation, Cambridgeshire, commences at the Nen outfall, and extends to Clows Cross, with a cut thence to the Old Eau at Blackhorse Sluice, near Crowland; it was completed in 1830.

The North Walsham and Dilham Canal, Norfolk, was made in 1812, from the river Bure at Dilham, to North Walsham and Antingham on the Ant.

The North Wiltshire Canal, formed in 1813, extends from the Wiltshire and Berkshire Canal, near Swindon, to the Thames and Severn Canal, near Latton, passing the town of Cricklade in its course.

The Norwich and Lowestoft Navigation is a ship canal, executed in 1827, from Norwich to Cuckenham and Raveningham Mill, where a canal joins the river Yare to the river Waveney, whence at Oulton Dyke is a cut to Oulton Broad, forming a connexion with Lake Lothing; at the eastern end of which is a cut to the sea, with a tide lock for the admission of vessels.

The Nottingham Canal, from the Cromford Canal to the river Trent, near Nottingham, was made in 1793.

The Nut Brook, or Shipley Canal, Derbyshire, constructed in 1793, extends from the collieries at Shipley and West Halton, to the Erewash Canal, near Stanton, by Dale.

The Oakham Canal, Rutlandshire, completed in 1800, extends from Oakham to the Melton Mowbray Navigation, near that town.

The Ouse River, Sussex, was improved to 1814, from Cuckfield to Lewes and Newhaven, where it falls into the sea.

The Ouse River, Yorkshire, was improved in 1770, from Linton, as well as the Swale, and other contributary rivers; a great trade is carried on between the city of York and the junction of the Ouse with the Humber, as it unites with several canals and rivers from the manufacturing districts of Lancashire.

The Little Ouse, or Brandon and Waveney River, Norfolk, was improved in 1810, in its course from Thetford to Santon Downham, and Brandon.

The Ouse and Larke Navigation was in 1827 consolidated with the Little Ouse, with the New Bedford River, and with the Eau Brink cut to Lynn.

The Great Ouse River, Bedfordshire, was improved in 1663, by making the Old Bedford River, and by completing the New Bedford River.

The Oxford Canal, completed in 1829, extends from the Coventry Canal at Longford, to Marston Wharf and Banbury, to the Thames at Oxford. It is carried over a valley at Brinklow, and over the Swift and Avon Rivers at Casford and Clifton. The canal also passes through a tunnel near Fenny Compton, upwards of three quarters of a mile in length, and through another under the street and churchyard of Newbold, in Warwickshire.

The Peak Forest Canal, opened in 1800, extends from Limestone Rock in the Peak forest, by Chapel Milton, Bugsworth, Whaley Bridge, and Marple, to Ashton-under-Lyne, where it joins the Manchester and Oldham Canal.

The Pocklington Canal, Yorkshire, from Street Bridge, near Pocklington, to the river Derwent, at East Cottingwith, was made in 1815.

The Portsmouth and Arundel Canal, Hampshire, constructed in 1828, opens a navigable communication between the southern coast and various other parts of England, and affords the means of transmitting military stores to Portsmouth, without the risk of capture in time of war. The length of the line, from the river Arun to Chichester, is about twelve miles; thence to the canal at Cosham, is fifteen miles; and the canal to Portchester Lake, is one mile and a quarter.

Sir John Ramsden's Canal, constructed in 1774, extends from the river Calder, near Cooper's bridge, to the head of the Huddersfield Canal, Yorkshire.

The Regent's Canal, Middlesex, formed in 1821, derives importance from the facility it affords to the commercial intercourse between different parts of London and the surrounding country. It commences at the Paddington branch of the Grand Junction Canal, passes through a tunnel under Maida Hill, towards the Regent's Park. Camden Town, Pancras, and Pentonville, under Islington, and the New River, with a branch to Finsbury. It then crosses the Kingsland, Hackney, Mile-end, and Commercial roads, to the Thames at Limehouse.

The Ribble River, Lancashire, was improved in 1806, from Penwortham Bridge, near Preston, to the sea.

The Rochdale Canal, Lancashire, executed in 1807, extends from the Calder Navigation, at Sowerby Bridge, to Hebden Bridge, Todmorden and Warland, then to Littleborough and Rochdale; but is continued through Manchester to the Duke of Bridgewaters' Canal at Castlefield, and joins the Manchester and Oldham Canal at Piccadilly Wharf. It is also to be connected with the river Irwell, agreeably to an Act of Parliament in 1836.

The Rother River, Sussex, was made navigable in 1791, from Midhurst to the river Arun, near Stopham Bridge. It belongs to the Earl of Egremont.

The Royal Military Canal, Kent, was constructed for military purposes, in pursuance of a plan for the defence of the coast against invasion; but in 1807 was applied to the service of commerce. It extends from the tide-way at Shorncliff to Hythe, Rye, and Winchilsea to Cliff end.

The Saint Column Canal, Cornwall, was constructed in 1773, by John Edyvean, Esq., of St. Austel, to the sea at Towan Bay.

The Salisbury and Southampton Canal was commenced in 1800; but only part of the line between Southampton and Redbridge, where it joins the Andover Canal, has been completed.

The Sankey Canal, Lancashire, constructed in 1756, to form a communication between St. Helens and the Mersey, was the first of the kind in England. The canal, about a mile from Newton, is now crossed by a viaduct of the Liverpool and Manchester Rail-road, the height of which is seventy feet from the surface of the canal. In 1830 this navigation was extended to Widness Wharf, West Bank, where it communicates with the Mersey.

The Severn River Navigation, Shropshire, was improved in 1811.

The Severn and Wye Canal and Rail-road, formed in 1822, crosses the Forest of Dean nearly from north to south; the extent of which is about twelve miles.

The Sheffield Canal, made in 1815, connects the town of Sheffield with the river Don.

The Shrewsbury Canal was constructed in 793, from Shrewsbury to the Shropshire Canal at Rockwardine Wood. It passes through a tunnel near

Ateham, and crosses the river Tern by an aqueduct of cast iron.

The Shropshire Canal, formed in 1788, extends from the Donnington Wood Canal, Lilleshall, to the Severn at Coalport, below Coalbrook Dale. In its course are three inclined planes, worked by steam engines; the first at Donnington Wood, a second at Stirchley, near Shiffnall, and a third at Hay, near the Severn.

The Sleaford Navigation, Lincolnshire, formed in 1794 extends from Sleaford Castle Causeway, through the town along the course of the mill-stream and Kyme Eau, to near Chapel Hill, on the river Witham, about thirteen miles and a half.

The Soar River Navigation, or Loughborough Canal, Leicestershire, constucted in 1776. It extends from the Rushes at Loughborough, to Bishop's Meadow, Garendon, on the river Soar, which falls into the Trent.

The Somersetshire Coal Canal, formed in 1802, is a communication between the coal mines at Radstock, and the Kennet and Avon Canal at Limpley Stoke, between Bradford and Bath.

The Staffordshire and Worcestershire Canal, completed in 1790, extends from Stourport on the Severn, to Hay Wood in Staffordshire, where it unites with the Trent and Mersey Navigation, passing Kidderminster and Penkridge.

The Stainforth and Keadby Canal, Lincolnshire, formed in 1809, passes the towns of Thorne and Crowle in its course from the river Don to the Trent, at Keadly, in the parish of Althorp.

The Stort River, Hertfordshire, was made navigable in 1766, from Bishops Stortford to the river Lea.

The Stourbridge Canal, Worcestershire, formed in 1782, extends from that town to Waresley Brook, where it crosses the river Stour and joins the Staffordshire and Worcestershire Canal.

The Stratford-on-Avon Canal, Warwickshire, completed in 1821, connects the town of Stratford with the Worrester and Birmingham Canal at King's Norton.

The Stroud Navigation, Gloucestershire, made in 1776, extends from Wallbridge, near Stroud, to the river Severn at Framilode.

The Tavistock Canal, Devonshire, was constructed in 1803, from the river Tavy at Tavistock, to the tide-way of the river Tamar at Morwelham Quay. At Morwelham Down it passes a tunnel cut through solid rock, a mile and a half in length, and crosses the Lumbourn, near Crebor, by an aqueduct fifty feet above the surface of the river beneath. A collateral cut from the aqueduct to Millhill bridge, is also completed.

The Tees Navigation, Yorkshire, was improved in 1828, when a canal was made from Portrack into the Tees, near Newport, in the chapelry of Acklam, Yorkshire.

The Thames River, formerly navigable to Cricklade in Wiltshire, by the completion of the Thames and Severn Canal, was made navigable to Lechlade, distant from London by water, 146½ miles, with a fall of 258 feet.

The Thames and Medway Canal, formed in 1824, obviates the necessity of a circuitous passage of vessels round the Nore, from Gravesend to Strood.

The Thames aad Severn Canal, thirty miles in length, completed in 1813, extends from the Stroud Canal to the Thames at Lechlade, passing through a tunnel at Saperton, near Cirencester, more than two miles in length.

The Tone and Parrett Navigation, Somersetshire, was made in 1707, from the Grand Western Canal at Taunton, to the tide-way in Bridgewater Bay.

The Torridge Canal, Devonshire, was formed in 1823, by Lord Rolle.

The Trent river Navigation was improved in 1794, from Burton on Trent to the Humber, a distance of 117 miles, with a fall of 118 feet.

The Trent and Mersey Canal, in length ninety-three miles, was completed in 1827, from Wilden Ferry, where the Derwent joins the Trent, to Runcorn Gap, on the Mersey.

The Warwick and Birmingham Canal, executed in 1796, extends from the Digbeth, branch of the Birmingham Canal at Birmingham, to Saltisford, Warwick.

The Warwick and Napton Canal, Warwickshire, completed in 1809, extends from the Warwick and Birmingham Canal at Budbrook, to the Oxford Canal at Napton on the Hill.

The Wear River, Durham, was improved in 1830, from Durham to its estuary at Sunderland.

The Weaver River Navigation, Cheshire, was improved in 1829, from Frodsham to Winsford Bridge, and a communication opened between this river and the Mersey.

The Welland River, Lincolnshire, was improved in 1794, from Stamford to Market Deeping, Crowland, and Spalding, to its estuary in the Wash.

The Wey River, Surrey, was made navigable from Godalming to its junction with the Thames, near Weybridge, in 1760.

The Wey and Arun Junction Canal, formed in 1813, extends from the river Wey at Shalford, near Guildford, to the Arun Navigation at Newbridge.

The Wiltshire and Berkshire Canal, completed in 1821, extends from Abingdon to Swindon, and joins the Kennet and Avon Canal at Semington; it is fifty-two miles in length.

The Wisbech Canal, constructed in 1794, extends from the New river at Wisbech, to the old river at Outwell, six miles.

The Witharn River, Lincolnshire, was improved in 1829, from Lincoln to Boston, five miles below which town it terminates in the Wash.

The Worcester and Birmingham Canal, completed in 1815, is twenty-nine miles in length from Birmingham to its junction with the Severn at Diglis, below Worcester.

The Wreke and Eye Rivers, Leicestershire, were improved in 1800, under the name of the Leicester and Melton Mowbray Navigation.

The Wye and Lugg Rivers, Herefordshire, were improved in 1809, from Hay to the Severn.

The Wyrley and Essington Canal, Staffordshire, made in 1794, extends from Wyrley Bank to the Birmingham Canal, near Wolverhampton, and joins the Coventry Canal, near Huddlesford.

THE HILLS OF ENGLAND

The Plate (see page 27) representing a comparative view of the principal Hills of Great Britain, engraved from a drawing by Mr. Edward James Smith, for this work, shows their perpendicular heights above the level of the sea at low water, according to Colonel Mudge's survey, and other competent authorities. This mode of reference was considered better than any lengthened dissertation, and leaves little to be said on the subject.

Throughout the whole length of England, from the county of Cornwall to Cumberland, are ranges of Hills which may be considered as forming one connected chain along the western side of the country. It begins at Carnbre Hill, in Cornwall, and the following ranges occur in immediate succession— Hengston Hill, Rippon Tor, and the numerous Tors on Dartmoor Forest; the Haldon Hills, known to mariners as the High Blue Lands of Devonshire; Bredon Hill, the Quantock Hills, Pildon Hill, the Mendip Hills of Somersetshire, an extensive range, but of no extraordinary elevation; the Clay Hills, and the Cotswold Hills of Gloucestershire. These are succeeded by the Malvern Hills of Worcestershire, the Wrekin of Shropshire, Weaver Hill of Staffordshire, Axe Edge, and the Peak Forest of Derbyshire, of considerable height; Blackstone edge, Pendle Hill, Pennygent, Ingleborough, and Whernside, in Yorkshire, and the Fells of Cumberland, where the highest mountains in England are to be found; these are Helvellyn, Skiddaw, and Saddleback—and the chain is continued by the range of the Cheviot Hills and the Pentland Hills of Scotland. The steepest face of this ridge is on the western side, particularly towards Wales; and there the largest river, the Severn, has its source, receiving its principal tributaries from the eastern side.

Two lower ranges of Hills also extend across the country, one of which reaches from Dorsetshire into Kent, along the coast of the English Channel, but has no river of any magnitude; while the other stretches in an irregular waving line from the Isle of Portland to the Wolds of Lincolnshire and Yorkshire.

The line which is formed by this last range of Hills, passes on the western side of Wiltshire and Oxfordshire, and through the high lands of Northamptonshire, Leicestershire, and Nottinghamshire nearly to Scarborough. The eastern side of this range gives rise to the river Thames, and to the Humber, with its confederate streams.

Professor Brande, one of the most pleasing authors on the subject, says it would be difficult to select a better spot for the study of geology, than Great Britain. Every variety of rock is presented under its various aspects; and though, in foreign climes, nature may have more liberally dispersed the sublime, she has no where more instructively or delicately diversified the earth's surface, than in the small space allotted to the British Isles.

The crust of the earth, it is well known, presents three distinct series of substances. The first, coeval with the world, it primitive, or primary rocks, generally found in huge masses or blocks, not regularly stratified, and affecting, in their fractures and fissures, a vertical arrangement. Sometimes they are of a perfectly homogeneous texture, commonly hard and durable, and sometimes composed of two or three ingredients blended together; they are generally crystalline in their texture, and usually constitute the loftiest mountains.

The transition rocks, the second series, are of more recent formation, and seem to have resulted from some great catastrophe, probably the deluge, tearing up and modifying the former order of things; they are less lofty than the former, and in many instances present a slaty texture; they seem to have been deposited in strata or layers, which are seldom either vertical or horizontal, but variously inclined to the horizon.

The secondary rocks, or third class, owe their formation to partial or local revolutions, as indicated by their structure and situation; and are nearly if not quite horizontal in their position. In their texture they are soft, and consequently easy of decay; they appear rather as mechanical deposits, than as chemical compounds, which have resulted from fusion, crystallization, or solution. These different series are tolerably regularly arranged in regard to each other. The primary rocks form the bases upon which the others rest; the transition are immediately recumbent upon these; and are again succeeded

by the varieties of secondary rocks, and by their detritus constituting alluvial matter and soils.

A section of the south of England, from the coast of Cornwall in the west, to London in the east, furnishes a good exhibition of the phœnomena of stratification alluded to. It begins at the Land's End with primitive rocks, massive and amorphous. Upon this rest several species of transition rocks, especially slates of different kinds, having various inclinations; and these are succeeded by secondary strata, deviating more and more from the vertical, and acquiring the horizontal position; and ultimately is attained the alluvial matter upon which the metropolis stands. It is principally clay; and has once, perhaps, formed the mud at the bottom of a salt-water lake.

Proceeding from London northwards, towards the Scotch border, the order of stratification is reversed; and traversing a highly interesting series of secondary rocks, some of the primitive series is arrived at in Cumberland. The whole arrangement is such as to include the highest and oldest rocks upon the western side of England, forming an uninterrupted chain, extending from the Land's End in Cornwall to Cumberland, and thence to the northern extremity of Scotland. So that the length of Great Britain, and its general shape, appear in a considerable degree dependant upon this chain of mountainous land, and upon two lower ridges, which extend in one direction from Devonshire, through Dorsetshire, Hampshire, and Sussex, into Kent; and in another, nearly from the same point, to the east of Yorkshire. The western ridge is broken in upon in several places by plains and rivers, giving rise to many chasms in the great chain.

Of the primitive rocks, one of the most abundant in nature, and the most useful in its application, is granite; so called from its appearing to be made up of a number of distinct grains, or particles. It constitutes the basis upon which all other rocks appear to lie; and its essential component parts are quartz, feldspar, and mica. Quartz is the substance commonly called rock crystal; it is sometimes met with in mountain masses, which usually present a conical appearance. The quartz is milk white, and of a more or less granular texture. Feldspar, the next constituent, is a compound body, and an important component of several other rocks. The decomposing feldspar of Cornwall, is abundantly employed in the English porcelain manufactories; and as it contains no iron, it retains its perfect whiteness. Mica, the third and last, is a well marked compound mineral; the extreme tenuity of the plates into which it may be divided, and their elasticity, renders it very useful for the enclosure of objects to be submitted to microscopic inspection.

In some specimens of granite these components may be distinctly

traced and separated from each other; but sometimes the particles are so small as to produce a compound, which, to the unaided eye, will seem almost homogeneous. There is, therefore, fine and coarse-grained granite; the former abundant in Scotland, the latter in Devonshire and Cornwall. The Cornish granite is remarkable for the well-defined and large crystals of feldspar it contains, and which may be seen in many parts of London, where this rock has been used for paving, and where the crystals of white feldspar have become evident in the mass, from the constant attrition to which it has been subjected. It is of this stone that Waterloo Bridge is mainly constructed. The colour of granite is principally dependant upon that of the feldspar it contains, though a dark mica will often give it a gloomy hue : it is commonly grey or reddish.

There are two rocks very closely allied to granite, and usually associated with it; slaty granite or gneiss, composed of precisely the same materials as granite, but slaty in its fracture, owing to the comparatively large quantity of mica it contains; and mica slate, a compound of mica and quartz, of a slaty texture, and also deriving its leading characteristic from the large quantity of mica it contains.

The aspect of a granite district in nature is subject to variation; it, however, exhibits traits sufficiently peculiar, which are readily recognised by the traveller in his approach to it. In Cornwall, and in some parts of Ireland, especially in the county of Donegal, the granitic rocks are marked by the bold and abrupt precipices which they present to the attacks of the ocean; and by the barren and dreary aspect of the inland plains, that seem like fields in which blocks of the stone have been torn from their beds, and indiscriminately scattered over the moss grown surface. The elevation of these districts is not considerable: the granite is coarse grained, and splits into immense blocks, separated from each other by natural seams, and appearing like the ruins of edifices constructed by a giant race. In other cases granite forms irregular and broken peaks of prodigious elevation, and does not split into the blocks and masses just alluded to. This is the case in the Alps and Pyrenees, in the highest Scotch mountains, in the Hartz, and in the Tyrol.

Some kinds of granite are prone to decomposition, crumbling down into a fine clay; but, in general, granite is the most durable of nature's productions, and long resists the destroying hand of time; as a building material, therefore, it is almost unrivalled; among the examples are London Bridge, and the Duke of York's Column.

In Wales there is very little granite; in the north of Scotland it is abundant; and in England it occurs in Cornwall, Devon. Westmorland and Cumberland. It is also met with in smaller quantities in Worcestershire, at the Malvern hills; and in Leicestershire in Charnwood forest.

To the class of massive unstratified rocks belongs Porphyry, a substance which is ranked among the primitive formations. Its essential constituent is feldspar; and genuine porphyry may be defined as massive feldspar, containing embedded crystals of the same substance. Any rock including distinct crystals of feldspar is called porphyritic; as porphyritic granite, &c. The colour of porphyry, which is usually reddish, brown, and green, is principally derived from the base, or paste, including the crystals. The common aspect of porphyry is that of blocks and masses, not very unlike some of the varieties of granite; but its fragments are generally smaller, and are in a more decaying condition. Porphyry is an extremely durable material for architectural purposes; and as such was highly esteemed among the nations of antiquity. It is met with in many parts of Britain; and in the north the porphyry districts are of singular grandeur, as at the base of Ben Cruachan, on the banks of the Awe; and amidst the precipices of Ben Nevis, the highest of the British mountains.

The British porphyries are many of them of great beauty, and might well be substituted in all ornamental purposes for the more rare and expensive foreign varieties.

The aspect of syenitic rocks is allied to that of granite and porphyry; the terra syenitic is derived from Syene, in Upper Egypt, where this rock is plentiful, and was used for architectural purposes by the Egyptian and Roman sculptors. These rocks may be observed rising from the slaty district of St. David's in Pembrokeshire; and in Cumberland, near Wastdale and Buttermere. A beautiful syenite occurs in Leicestershire at Markfield Knoll, a hill in Charnwood forest.

Another substance belonging to the same class of rocks, is Serpentine; its appearance is singularly picturesque and beautiful; and it forms a delightful contrast to the sublimity of granitic districts. Serpentine has its name from the variety of tints which it exhibits, such as bright red, green, brown, yellow, and their various shades; and it often is prettily traversed by veins of a soft substance, to which the term steatite, or soapstone, has been given.

Some of the varieties of serpentine admit of a tolerable polish, and such are very desirable for many ornamental purposes. Serpentine is seen in Cornwall in characteristic beauty, forming part of the Lizard promontory on the Southern coast of the county. It appears in variously-shaped and coloured blocks and masses; it forms natural arches, columns, and caves; and the district is of very singular interest, from many concomitant circumstances, especially from the blocks of porphyry, upon which the serpentine is

incumbent, and the veins of granite associating with those of steatite which pervade it.

Steatite is a substance of different tints of grey and green; and, from its very singular unctuous feel, has been called soap stone. It is somewhat abundant in the serpentine of Cornwall, one of the masses of which is called the Soapy rock; it is here carefully collected for the porcelain works of Worcester and Swansea, in which it forms a very important ingredient.

Marble is the last of the rocks belonging to this class. It is also very abundant in the secondary rocks, but its characters are there different. Serpentine and marble are sometimes blended together, and they then form a valuable compound for ornamental purposes, which has been called Verd Antique.

This is a highly important series of rocks; as a class they present analogies which distinguish them from their superincumbent neighbours, and give them the stamp of a peculiar and distinct formation, either formed before organic beings, or under circumstances which have destroyed such remains. In these rocks is seldom observed any regular stratification; they are mostly constituted of amorphous, irregular, and various masses, and present no appearances of having been deposited from water. They are crystalline aggregates; and they are deeeper in their situation than other rocks, which always appear incumbent upon them, and often elevated, or heaved, as it were, by their operation. They often break through the beds or layers that cover them, and rise to a very great elevation.

The highest mountains in Britain are composed of granite and its associates; but these are mere trifling protuberances upon the earth's face, when compared with the exceeding heights of the Alpine chain, or the yet more elevated mountains of South America, and of Asia, which consist of the same materials.

The reason why these excessive elevations present nothing but primitive rocks, and especially granite, excepting, indeed, where they are volcanic, may not at first appear quite obvious, for in the low lands the primitive are generally covered by secondary strata, which were also once, probably, incumbent upon their loftiest summits. It is likely that the destructive agencies of the elements have been so powerfully exerted in these elevated and unprotected regions, that the secondary rocks have yielded to their unceasing attacks, and have been earned towards the valleys by the rills and torrents, while granite and its durable accompaniments, have more obstinately opposed the inroads of such resistless assailants.

At the same time, however, it will seem probable that the granitic mountains have themselves suffered tremendous degradation, and that,

at a former period, their summits were beyond their present elevation. All this will appear more clear when the general characters of mountain chains, and the phenomena of their decay, are taken into account. But several circumstances present themselves, which announce the influence of destructive agents upon these apparently invulnerable materials. Prodigious masses of granite are often found among the secondary strata that form the valleys under primary mountain chains; they are insulated and unconnected with any general mass of the same material; and the more distant they are from the granite range, the more they are rounded and smoothened upon the surface.

In Cornwall, granite is sometimes of very rapid decomposition and the streams which traverse these districts deposit a finely-divided earthy matter, resulting principally from the feldspar, and much used in the Potteries. Carglaise tin mine is situated in a decomposing granite of this kind, and presents a spectacle highly worthy the attention of the curious. The mine is a vast chasm in the granite rocks, and exposed to the day. The tin ore and short rock traverse it in abundant veins; and the surrounding peaks strongly remind the beholder of a miniature representation or model of the Alps.

Of the transition or stratified rocks, one leading and general circumstance may be observed in regard to them, which is, that they never attain the great elevation of the primary bodies. The next peculiarity of the secondary rocks that presents itself, is their containing fragments, pebbles, and organic remains; in the oldest of these rocks, fragments are often found, and rounded pebbles, whence is learnt their origin from former rocks. Upon these, beds occur which contain remains of shells, corals, and fish, all of marine origin, and oftentimes the races ore extinct. Approaching the newer rocks, relics of quadrupeds, now no longer known, are observed; and following the deposition of strata, remains of lizards, crocodiles, elephants, deer, and some other animals, are found; and occasionally are discovered districts containing land and sea-shells in alternating layers.

The secondary rocks are the chief repositories of metallic substances, and by their decomposition and decay they furnish the principal materials of the soil in which the vegetable has its habitation, and consequently upon which the existence of animals ultimately depends.

Of the secondary rocks, clay slate may be first noticed; it is extremely abundant, and generally immediately incumbent upon the primary series. The varieties of slate are applied to various useful purposes; that which is easily separable into thin plates, compact, sonorous, and not injured by the application of a moderate heat, is employed for roofing houses.

A Comparative View of some of the PRINCIPAL HILLS in GREAT BRITAIN

"Hills peep o'er Hills and Alps o'er Alps arise"

London is chiefly supplied from Bangor, in Carnarvonshire, and from the neighbourhood of Kendal, in Westmorland.

Slate often contains fragments of other rocks, embedded masses, and nodules of various kinds, frequently pebbles, and occasionally a few impressions of shells; it also often derives a green colour from the presence of a mineral called chlorite, consisting of oxide of iron, united to siliceous and aluminous earths. The slates containing embedded matters, are called grauwacke-slates; or, when of a less slaty fracture, simply grauwacke, a substance which is abundant in this country.

The slate district of England is of considerable extent, and neither wants sublimity nor grandeur; it follows the great primary chain, before alluded to, as running north and south upon the west side of England: in Cornwall the slate is seen immediately incumbent upon granite; and the slaty districts form very beautiful scenery upon many parts of the coast. The term killas has been applied to it by the miners.

Nothing can exceed the scenery about Looe, Fowey, and the country between it and Falmouth; and upon the north coast Tintagell is yet more remarkable.

There is some grauwacke in many parts of Cornwall; the best marked specimens are from Mawnan, near Falmouth, where it alternates with clay slate.

Advancing northwards, the mountain chain is broken by the lowlands of Lancashire; but, in Westmorland and Cumberland, slate again presents itself, plentifully accompanied by grauwacke, which contributes to the enchanting scenery of the lakes. As black peaks and precipices strewed with slippery and cutting fragments, mark the mountains of common slate, so have the grauwacke rocks peculiarities by which they are recognised, and which are no where more evident than in the rounded summits that embosom Derwentwater. In their forms, tints, and outlines, there is something indescribably delightful; and they present the rare union of the sublime and beautiful.

The varieties of mountain limestone are the substances that next occur; they are frequently seen immediately incumbent upon clay slate, and are further distinguished from primitive limestone, or statuary marble, by having a less decidedly crystalline texture. Where this rock lies directly upon slate, it contains few organic remains; but where red sandstone is interspersed between it and the slate rocks, or in proportion as it is distant from the primary and slate rocks, the reliefs of organization become more frequent. It then abounds in remains of corals and zoophytes, which now are not known to exist. It often is traversed by veins of calcareous spar, and presents

a great variety of colours. It is abundant in Devonshire, Derbyshire, and Yorkshire. At Plymouth, this rock is seen immediately incumbent upon slate, in a quarry between Devonport and the town; its colours are red and grey, streaked with white crystalline veins. It is also seen to great perfection in the Breakwater quarries at Oreston.

Slate districts often present very curious inflexious and incurvations of their strata. The slate at Plymouth, and the grauwacke of Clovelly, in the north of Devon, and the killas upon the coast of Cornwall, near Charlestown, are in many places very singularly contorted; and sometimes small undulations present themselves in the laminæ, exactly resembling those left by the ebbing tide upon a gently reclining sand bank. These appearances may, perhaps, be referred to the action of water upon the materials, before they were consolidated.

The aspect of a country of mountain limestone is peculiar, and generally extremely picturesque. The hills, which, in this country at least, are not very lofty, abound in precipices, caverns, and chasms; and, when upon the coast, form small promontories, and jut out in low, but grotesque pillars. The even surfaces are covered with a stinted turf; but the rifts and cracks contain often a soft, rich soil, in which stately timber trees flourish. The chasms of limestone rocks are often filled with a fine clay, which has, perhaps, sometimes been derived from the decomposition of shaly strata, or sometimes deposited from other causes, in the fissures; and the singularities of aspect, and much of the beauty of this rock, is referable to these peculiarities. Thus, upon the banks of the Wye, large and luxuriant trees grace the abrupt precipices, and jut forth from what appears a solid rock. Their roots are firmly attached in some crevice, filled with a favourable soil. Sometimes rivers force their way through the chasms; at other times they are empty, and the roofs ornamented by nature's hand with stalactitical concretions of white and glistening spar, which seem like the fretted sculpture of Gothic architecture.

The views of Dovedale, of Matlock and its vicinity, and the caves of Castleton, are admirably illustrative of the scenery of mountain limestone.

The banks of the Avon, in the vicinity of Chepstow, are of mountain limestone. The rock is there impregnated with bitumen, and hence exhales a peculiar and fetid odour when submitted to the blows of the axe or hammer. This is by no means uncommonly the case where the limestone rock, as in the present instance, is in the vicinity of coal.

Mountain limestone is an excellent material for building; and many of its varieties are sufficiently indurated to receive a good polish, and are thus employed for ornamental purposes, being cut into vases, chimney pieces,

and the like. Where they abound in corals, and other organic remains, these frequently add to their beauty.

The colours of transition limestone are various; but its essential constituent part is always carbonate of lime. The black variety known under the name of Lucullite (so called, because admired by Lucius Lucullus,) or black marble, is often tastefully manufactured and ornamented by etching upon its surface; it is found in Derbyshire, and appears to derive its colour from carbonaceous matter.

The next rock that occurs in point of succession is red sandstone: it often rests upon slate; and then, from its position, has acquired the term of old red sandstone. But a similar substance, or nearly so, also is found lying upon mountain limestone, in which case it has been called red marl, or new red sandstone. Entering upon this substance, we come upon distinctly stratified ground; it is very abundant in England, especially in Lancashire, Cheshire, Staffordshire, Shropshire, and Worcestershire; and independent of its embowelled treasures, for it is connected with coal and rock salt, its surface is generally favourable to vegetation, and its soil sufficiently luxuriant.

Red sandstone rocks are seen in some parts of Britain, in great beauty and perfection, especially where they occur on the coast, or are intersected by rivers. At Ilfracombe the old red sandstone of the Somersetshire coast is seen lying upon slate; and the junction is interesting to the geologist, the sandstone becoming somewhat slaty, and the slate having a tendency to a granular fracture.

The slates, grauwackes, and limestones, are in this country the principal seats of the metallic ores; and they form scenery, which, gradually decreasing in grandeur and sublimity, increases in softness, variety, and luxuriance. Gypsum, or sulphate of lime, known also under the name of plaster stone, selenite, and alabaster, occurs in abundance in many parts of the red strata. Near Tutbury in Staffordshire, and near Nottingham, it is found in blocks and veins; and lately a variety, new in England, has been found, called anhydrite. These minerals constitute valuable materials for the ornamental manufactures of Derbyshire.

In Cheshire, the red sandstone contains immense beds of common salt, most abundant in the valley of the Weaver, and near Middlewich, Northwich and Nantwich; it is accompanied by gypsum. The first stratum was discovered upwards of 160 years ago in searching for coal.

Coal is the most important product of these middle strata. What is called a coal field or district, or sometimes a coal basin, may be regarded as a concavity, varying greatly in extent, from a few to many miles, and containing numerous strata or seams of coal, of very various thickness, alternating with sandstone, clays, and soft slate, or shale, containing impressions of vegetables, and sometimes the remains of fresh water shell-fish. The parallelism of these strata is generally well preserved. The whole arrangement is seldom any where quite horizontal, and never vertical, but almost always more or less inclined. Beneath each stratum of coal, there is often one of soft clay, or clunch, which rarely contains the organic remains of the overlying shale; and although the alternating strata of coal be very numerous, it is seldom that more than three or four will afford profitable occupation to the miner. The upper seam is commonly broken and impure; and few beds, less than two or three feet in thickness, are followed down to any considerable depth. The depth of the mines will, of course, greatly vary, according to the inclination of the strata, the time they have been worked, and other circumstances. The deepest mines are in the counties of Durham and Northumberland; and the thickest beds are found in Staffordshire; the most productive vary from six to nine feet.

Leaving the districts of red sandstone and red marl, a change is observable in the general aspect of the country. There are no steep or abrupt precipices; the hills assume a more picturesque and luxuriant character, and the rugged features of primary country are here softened down into gentle slopes and verdant plains. The rocks which now occur are chiefly varieties of limestone and sandstone, particularly prolific in organic remains; among them are discerned a number of species, of which no living semblance is now in existence.

Corals, zoophytes, ammonites, belemnites, nautili, and a variety of other fossil remains, are found in the argillaceous limestones, which succeed in position to the red sandstone, and are often called white and blue lias limestone. The coast of Dorsetshire, between Weymouth and Lyme, presents a very interesting section of these strata; and their continuation through the country is well entitled to the notice of the geologist.

These strata are succeeded by a species of stone, called Bath stone, from its abundant occurrence in the vicinity of that city; and freestone, or oolite, of which Portland stone is a notorious variety. There then commonly occur various sandstones, with veins of chert, and oxide of iron; and, lastly, chalk, and superincumbent alluvial matter.

In England, chalk is a very abundant formation; and the round backed hills covered with verdure, which mark the eastern counties, are very characteristic of it. Salisbury plain and Marlborough Downs form a centre, whence the chalk emanates, in a north-eastern direction, through the Chiltern hills of Buckinghamshire, and the Counties of Bedford and Cambridge, and terminates on the Norfolk coast. In an easterly direction,

it traverses Hampshire, Surrey, and Kent, and terminates at Dover; and another arm, passing through Sussex, forms the South Downs, and the lofty promontory of Beachey Head.

Parallel ridges of sandstone generally accompany the chalk; and in Wiltshire, Berkshire, and some other counties, large blocks of granular siliceous sandstone lie scattered upon its surface; of these the celebrated remains, Stonehenge, appear to have been constructed, with the exception of one of the blocks, which is of greenstone. The lower beds of chalk are generally argillaceous, or marly, and contain no flints, and few organic remains. The upper beds abound in fossil relics, of the kinds before alluded to, and in flints, sometimes regularly arranged in distinct nodules, at other times remarkably intersecting the chalk in thin seams. The formation of flints has been much speculated upon; but no plausible theory has yet been adduced in regard to it.

In the south of England the chalk is covered with gravel and clay, the history of which is extremely curious, on account of the fossils they contain, and the evidence they afford, of repeated inundations of salt and fresh water upon the same spot. There are two celebrated concavities filled with such materials, which have been called the London and the Isle of Wight basins. The former is bounded by the chalk hills proceeding from Wiltshire to the south of the Kentish coast, in one direction, and to the northern point of the Norfolk coast, in another; and it is open to the ocean upon the Essex, Suffolk, and Norfolk coasts, which show sections of its contents.

The numerous wells which have been dug in the neighbourhood of London, and the canals, tunnels, and other excavations, and public works that have been carried on, have lately developed many curious facts respecting the contents of this basin.

Greenstone, basalt, amygdaloid, and toadstone, are a singular and important series of rocks, which occur indiscriminately in primary and secondary countries; and are not less varied in their characters and aspects, than in their situation.

It is the remark of an able writer in the "Mining Journal," that the neglect of one of the most interesting, and apparently most obvious branches of scientific research, geology, was the result of many causes, one or two of which only will be here alluded to. The spirit of ancient philosophy disdained the slow and laborious process of patiently investigating natural phenomena; and it was not till the lofty, but severe genius of Bacon, had firmly established the inductive system of philosophy, that a science like geology could be cultivated with success.

It was necessary, also, that the kindred sciences of chemistry and mineralogy should have made considerable progress, before any successful enquiry could be instituted into the nature of the earth, and the position and relations of its constituent masses. Another obstacle to the cultivation of geology at an earlier period arose from the obscurity in which the phenomena it investigates are veiled by nature. The internal parts of the earth are, with few exceptions, excluded from view; those portions exposed to examination are few and far between; often, indeed, obscure and deceptive; and thus it happens that numerous and accurate observations, and extensive powers of generalization, were required, before geology could be placed on a firm foundation, and attract that attention which it deserved.

To have accomplished this important task fell to the lot of Werner, of Freyberg, who is deservedly looked up to as the father of geological science. Many important facts had previously been observed, and many remarkable anticipations had been indulged in by different gifted individuals; but it was reserved for Werner to combine these scattered fragments; to add to them his own close observation and precise mineralogical knowledge, and, finally, to combine these materials into a beautiful and harmonious, though, as it has since been proved, faulty theory; a circumstance so far unavoidable in an infant science, that it detracts but little from his great and original merits. The profession of Werner, as a miner, gave him numerous and valuable facilities for personal observation of geological phenomena; the principal errors into which he fell, were those of supposing that the limited portion of Germany, with which he was acquainted, might be considered as representing the structure of the whole globe; and, as the operation of existing geological causes was then very imperfectly understood, he was led to admit of explanations, founded on imaginary phenomena and gratuitous assumptions.

Dr. Hutton, of Edinburgh, and his able illustrator, Professor Playfair, were well acquainted with the phenomena of the older one pyrogenous rocks, and established on their observations a bold, and in many respects a just theory, but almost entirely opposed to that of Werner; and in the discussion and support of these opposite views, too much of the attention of the earlier geologists was unfortunately, directed.

Hasty theories, founded on imperfect knowledge, warmly espoused, and keenly contested, were little calculated to advance an infant science; and in the early part of the present century a clear perception of this truth appears to have prevailed among many of the principal cultivators of geology in this country. It was seen by them that a vast collection of facts, apart from theoretical considerations, was at that period the great object to be attained; that a concentration of all their powers to effect this great and laborious task was requisite; that frequent meetings and communications between geologists could alone remove the narrow and limited views then entertained; and that, finally, a convenient and accessible depository for their labours was essential. These were the considerations which chiefly influenced the founders of the Geological Society, which originated in 1807, and for some time consisted of little more than the private meetings of some of the chief cultivators of geological science in this country.

The volumes of transactions which have been published bear witness to the zeal and energy of the fellows of this society; and the names of Greenough, one of its earliest supporters, of Lyell, Buckland, Sedgwick, Murchison, De la Beche, and others, are sufficient to prove the very high degree of talent enrolled among its members.

During a recent examination of Devonshire, Professor Sedgwick and R. J. Murchison discovered a raised beach in Barnstaple and Bideford Bay, which forms at intervals a series of low cliffs from the mouth of the Taw to the bold headland of Baggy Point, a distance of three miles. The greatest thickness of the beach is forty-five feet, and its base is about three feet above the highest tidal level. The top presents eight or ten feet of angular fragments of the adjacent rocks, imbedded in clay. Beneath this superficial covering are twenty-five feet of finely laminated sand, passing downwards into masses of hard calcareous grit; and the base of the beach consists of indurated conglomerate or shingle, which fills up the inequalities in the surface of the ancient rocks constituting that part of Devonshire. The thickness of these lower beds is about eleven feet. The sands are generally arranged in horizontal layers, but they sometimes present an appearance of false bedding, common in tertiary and secondary formations. Fragments of shells of existing species occur in the sand as well as in the calcareous grit and conglomerate.

Though the base of the beach, as already stated, is generally not more than three feet above high water mark, yet at Baggy Point it rises rapidly to the north to an altitude of seventy feet, and the shingle in parts is nineteen feet thick; thus presenting the greatest quantity of coarse materials at the point where it attains the greatest elevation.

The beaches in Cornwall, with respect to the character they present, maybe divided into three classes;—1. High shingle beaches, or accumulations formed at high water level on rocky shores;—2. Mid water beaches, composed of pebbles and fragments of shells, more or less confusedly disposed;—and 3. Low water beaches, made up of beds of small gravel alternating with sand and layers of shells, and formed below the line constantly covered by the sea.

Of the first of these classes, the raised beds of coarse shingle, and rounded blocks near the Land's End are prominent examples; of the second, the elevated shingle beach at Plymouth; and of the third, the ancient beaches north of St. Just's Bay, and south of New Quay. There are no vestiges of similar phenomena on coasts formed of precipitous cliffs, or on the opposite low shores of Pembrokeshire. With respect to the latter, the mounds of blown sand, by which they are bordered, have for ages ceased to increase; and it is therefore inferred that the sandy beaches, which since supplied the loose materials, are now permanently submerged beneath the sea.

This introduction to the description of the English Counties may be concluded with the following observations;—England has four points of strength; two are physical, her coal and her iron; and two of them are moral, the freedom of the press, and the trial by jury; and these sources of strength are mutually conservative of each other, for should any attempt be made to destroy the two last, the two first are admirably adapted to defend them.

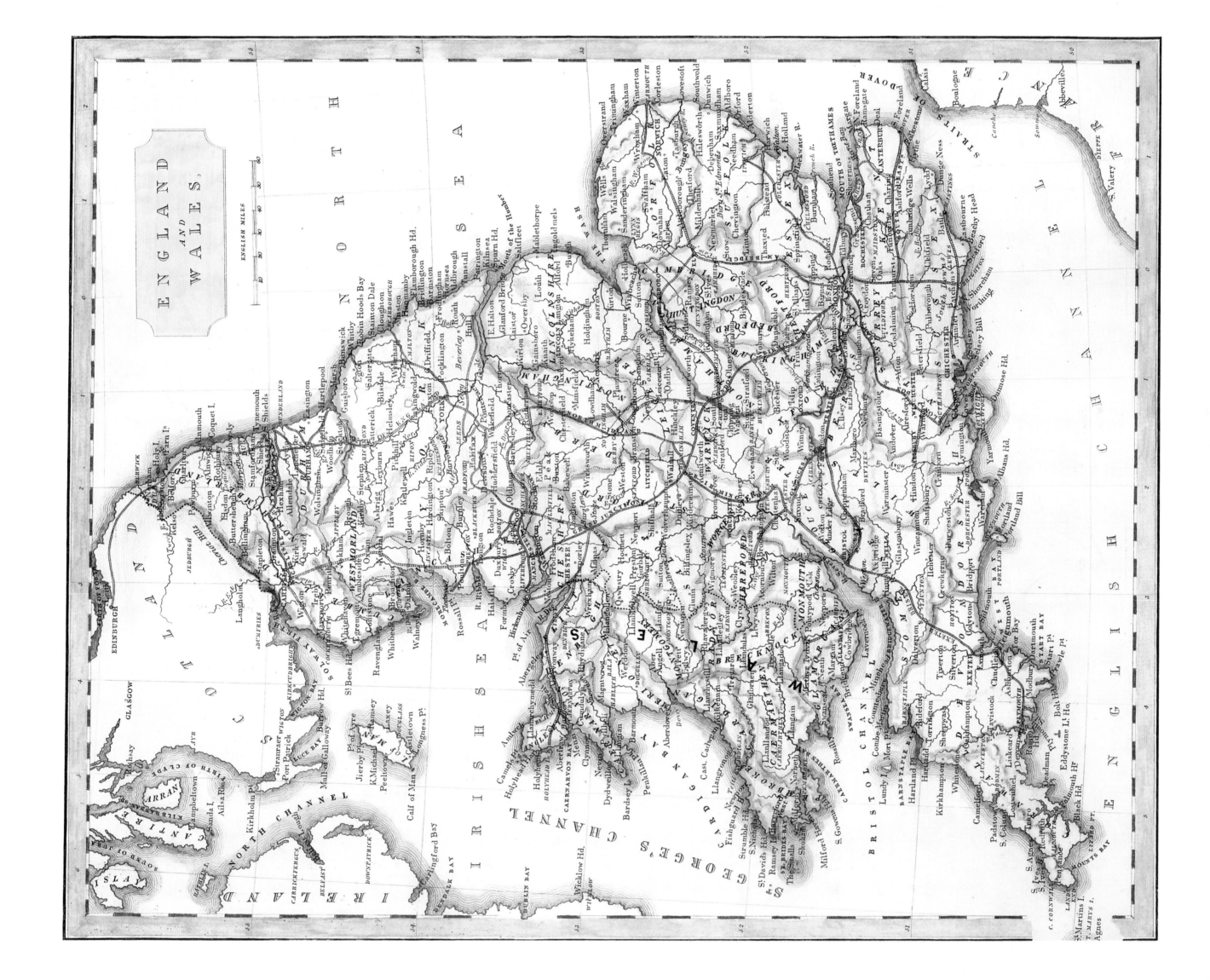

ENGLAND AND WALES.

ENGLISH MILES

BEDFORDSHIRE

THIS county, one of the smallest in England, is bounded on the north by Northamptonshire and Huntingdonshire; on the east by Cambridgeshire; on the south by Hertfordshire; and on the west by Buckinghamshire. It is about thirty-four miles in length, twenty in breadth, and about a hundred and forty-five miles in circuit. The British inhabitants of this county were called the Cassii, or Catteuchlani, by the Romans, under whom it formed part of Britannia Prima, and was included in the district of Flavia Cæsariensis. It is crossed by the Ikeneld-street, and the Watling-street, both of which are supposed to have been originally British roads: a third ancient road is the Roman military way which came from Hertfordshire to the station near Sandy, and thence passed to the Hermen-street, at Godmanchester, or Durolipons. The Roman stations in Bedfordshire are Durocobrivæ, Dunstable, and Salenæ, Sandy; but the Roman antiquities which have been discovered are not numerous. Totternhoe Castle, and Maiden Bower, are remarkable British earth-works. During the Anglo-Saxon Heptarchy this county became part of the kingdom of Mercia, and was afterwards comprised within Denelege, or the Danish jurisdiction. The castles of the early lords of Bedfordshire were at Bedford, Odell, or *Wahul*, Bletshoe Cainhoe, Eaton Socon, Risinghoe and Segenhoe. Eaton Bray, Luton Hoo, Willington, Cockayne Hatley, and Houghton Conquest, were noble mansions of early date. There were formerly abbeys at Warden and Woburn, and priories at Bissemede, Caldwell, Chicksand, Dunstaple, Elstow, Harold, Market-street, and Newnham. There were ancient hospitals at Bedford, Dunstable, Farleigh, Hockliffe, and Toddington; and a preceptory of knights hospitallers at Melchbourn. This county is in the diocese of Lincoln, and province of Canterbury. Bedford is the county-town; besides which there are nine market-towns, 121 parishes, 15,412 houses, and 83,716 inhabitants. It sends four members to Parliament; two for the borough of Bedford, and two for the county, who at present are the Marquess of Tavistock, and Sir Peter Payne, Bart. The surface of this county is broken into small hills and valleys: towards the south, a range of chalk eminences rises to a considerable height, sometimes projecting into the lower grounds in a bold and abrupt manner. Some very rich meadow-lands, terminated on the north by sandy hills, extend in a line from the middle of the county to its south-eastern extremity: the western side is flat and well cultivated, producing great quantities of beans. The vale of Bedford is an extensive corn district, its natural fertility being much increased by the overflowing of the Ouse. The north-eastern part of the county is noted for its abundant produce of barley. Fine woods are interspersed throughout the whole of the county, the timber of which is occasionally felled, and sent to the sea coast by the Ouse. The rivers of Bedfordshire are the Ouse, Ivel, Lea and Ouzel. The Ouse enters this county in its course from Buckinghamshire at Turvey, whence it passes between Carlton and Harold, and near Sharnbrook, in a very winding direction, to the town of Bedford, where it becomes navigable. Thence it flows to Barford and Tempsford, where it unites with the Ivel, and pursues its direction to Huntingdonshire, quitting the county below Eaton Socon, near St. Neots. The Ivel rises near Baldock, in Hertfordshire, and enters Bedfordshire near Stotfold. At Arlsey it is augmented by the Hiz, from Hitchin, and at Langford by another stream from Shefford. At Biggleswade the Ivel becomes navigable, and passes Girtford near Sandy, and Blunham, to Tempsford, where it falls into the Ouse. The river Lea, whose course is principally through Hertfordshire, rises near Houghton Regis, in this county, and runs through the whole extent of Luton parish. The river Ouzel rises near Whipsnade, and leaving Eaton Bray on the east, separates this county from Buckinghamshire, in its course to Leighton Busard. No navigable canal passes through Bedfordshire, but the Grand Junction canal comes up to Leighton Busard. The principal manufacture of this county is thread-lace, which is made in every part of the county, excepting in a few villages, where it has been superseded by the straw manufacture, which prevails in the neighbourhood of Dunstaple and borders of Hertfordshire. Lord Grantham is the Lord Lieutenant of the county.

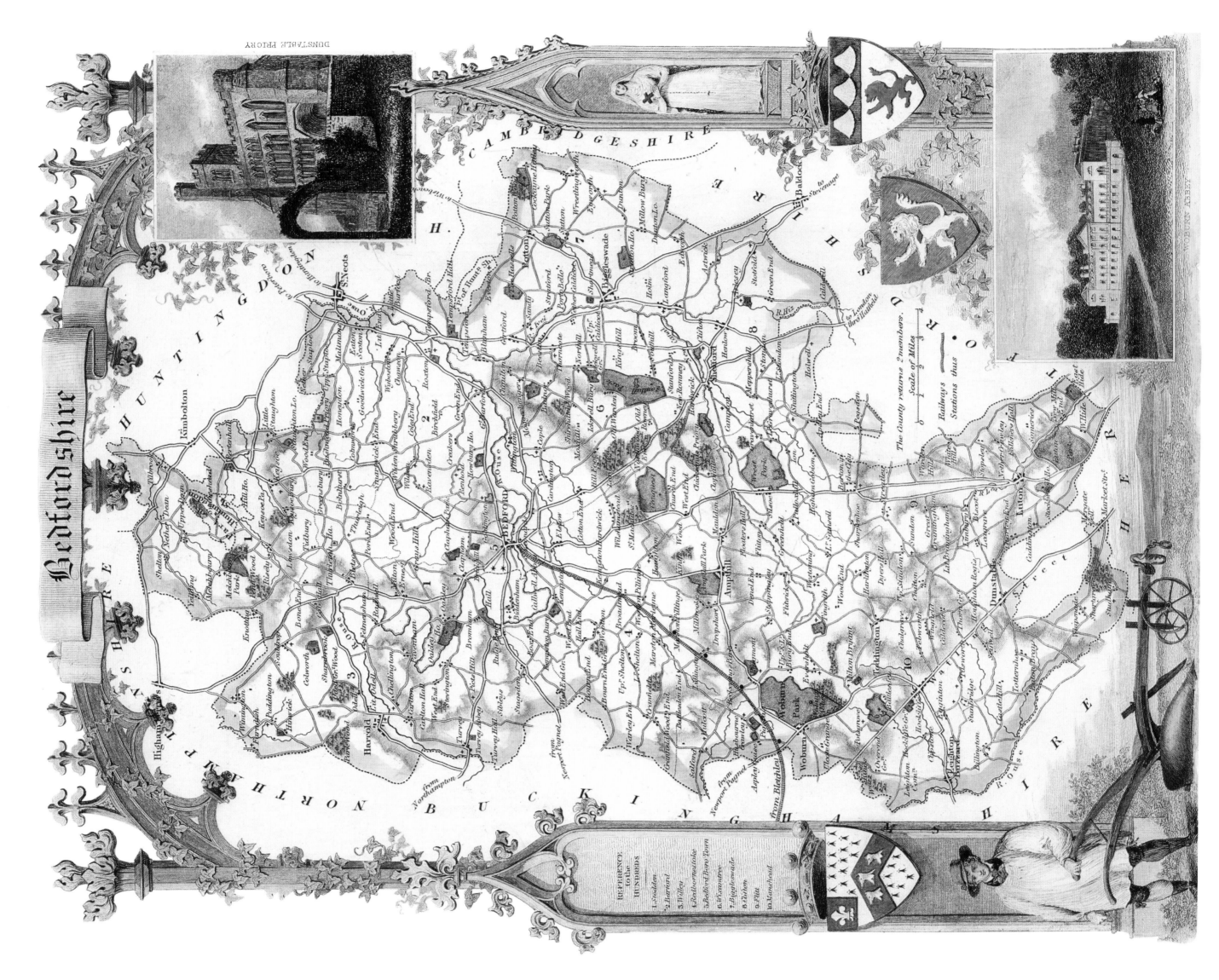

DUNSTABLE PRIORY

Bedfordshire

CAMBRIDGESHIRE

HUNTINGDON

NORTHAMPTONSHIRE

BUCKINGHAMSHIRE

HERTFORDSHIRE

BEDFORD

Kimbolton

St. Neots

Harrold

Woburn

Luton

Dunstable

Leighton Buzzard

Biggleswade

The County returns 2 members.

Scale of Miles

Railways, Stations thus

REFERENCE to the HUNDREDS.
1. Seddon
2. Barford
3. Willey
4. Redbornstoke
5. Bedford Three Town
6. Wixamtree
7. Biggleswade
8. Clifton
9. Flitt
10. Manshead

BERKSHIRE

This county is bounded on the north by Oxfordshire and Buckinghamshire, from which it is separated by the Thames; on the east by Surrey; on the south by Hampshire, and on the west by Wiltshire; its north-west corner just meets a small point in Gloucestershire. It was inhabited by the Attrebatii, Bibroces and Segontiaci, before the island was divided into Roman provinces, when it was included in Britannia Prima, and during the Saxon Heptarchy, in the kingdom of Wessex. In 889, when Alfred a native of Wantage, divided the kingdom into counties, it received the name of Berocscire. The shape of the county is irregular, being about 42 miles long, 28 broad and about 130 in circumference, comprising 148 parishes, 4 borough towns, and 8 other market towns; containing at the last census 24,705 houses, and 131,977 inhabitants, of whom 8873 families are returned as being employed in trade and manufactures. A part of this county lies in Oxfordshire, and a part of Wiltshire is in this county. It is in the province of Canterbury, and the diocese of Salisbury. It sends nine members to Parliament; being two for the county, two for Windsor, two for Reading, two for Wallingford, and one for Abingdon. The principal river is the Thames; it has also the Kennet, the Loddon, the Ocke, the Isis, the Auborne, the Cole, the Emme, and the Lambourn. The western and middle parts of the county are fertile; the eastern is chiefly occupied by Windsor Forest and its appendages. A range of chalk hills crosses from Oxfordshire, and bounds the noted vale of White Horse. The air is esteemed healthy even in the vales. It is well stored with timber, particularly oak and beech. Its principal manufactories are woollen, paper, sacking, and sail cloth. Besides its navigable rivers, it has the Kennet and Avon Canal from Reading to Hungerford, and the Wiltshire and Berkshire Canal from Abingdon, through Wantage, to Trowbridge in Wiltshire. The Roman Watling-street, from Dunstable, enters Berkshire at Streatley, and crosses the county to Marlborough. Another Roman road, from Hampshire, enters this county, and passing to Reading and Newbury, there divides and branches off to Marlborough and Cirencester. Near Wantage there is a Roman camp of a quadrangular form; at Lawrence Waltham is Castle Acre, a Roman fort, and near Denchworth, is Cherbury Castle, supposed to have been a fortress of Canute. Uffington Castle near Farringdon is said to be Danish; and near it is Pendragon Hill, supposed to be the burying place of Uter Pendragon, a British prince. Berkshire was constituted an Earldom by James I., who created Francis Lord Norris, Earl of Berkshire, Jan. 28 1620; the title became extinct at his death but was revived by Charles I., who created Thomas Lord Howard of Charlton, Earl of Berkshire Feb 5 1626, whose descendant is Thomas Howard, now Earl of Suffolk and Berkshire. This county was the residence of our ancient Kings at Wantage, Wallingford Castle, Letcombe Regis, and Reading Palace, as well as Windsor, which has long been famous for its magnificent Castle, originally founded by William the Conqueror. Besides Cumberland Lodge, Cranbourn Lodge, and other residences belonging to the Crown, the very ancient mansion at Wytham, the seat of the Lord Lieutenant, and above one hundred and fifty seats of noblemen and gentlemen, are in this county.

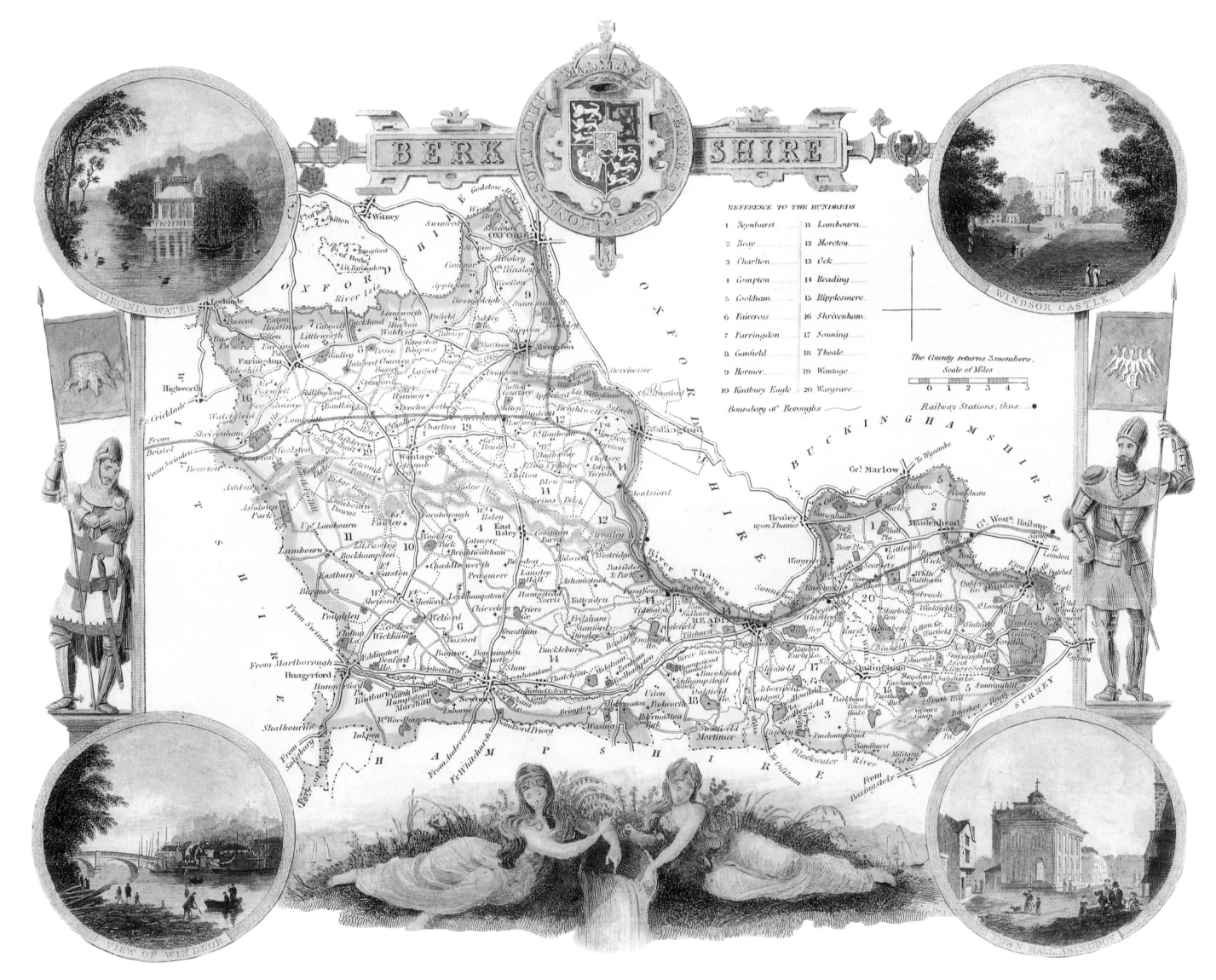

BERKSHIRE

REFERENCE TO THE HUNDREDS

1	Reynhurst	11 Lambourn
2	Bray	12 Moreton
3	Charlton	13 Ock
4	Compton	14 Reading
5	Cookham	15 Ripplesmere
6	Faircross	16 Shrivenham
7	Farringdon	17 Sonning
8	Ganfield	18 Theale
9	Hormer	19 Wantage
10	Kintbury Eagle	20 Wargrave

Boundary of Boroughs ....

Railway Stations, thus ....•

The County returns 3 members.

Scale of Miles

0 1 2 3 4 5

VIRGINIA WATER

WINDSOR CASTLE

VIEW OF WINDSOR

TOWN HALL ABINGDON

BUCKINGHAMSHIRE

THIS county is bounded on the north by Northamptonshire; on the north-east by Bedfordshire and Hertfordshire; on the east by Middlesex; on the south and south-west by Berkshire and the river Thames; and on the west by Oxfordshire. Its greatest length is about forty-five miles, its breadth eighteen miles, and it is about one hundred and thirty-eight miles in circumference. The British inhabitants were the Cassii and Dobuni; and under the Romans the county formed a part of Britannia Superior, and was subsequently included in the Roman district of Flavia Cæsariensis. The only station ascertained is Magiovintum, Fenny Stratford. The Watling-street entered the county near Brickhill, and proceeded perfectly straight through Fenny Stratford to Stoney Stratford, where it crossed the Ouse into Northamptonshire. All traces of the Roman causeway are obliterated by the present turnpike road; but no doubt is entertained of its line, whatever difference of opinion there may be in determining the site of the stations upon it. The Ikenild-street entered the eastern side of the county near Edlesborough, and preserving its course on the edge of the Downs left Tring on its left, and crossing the road from Aylesbury to London left Halton on the right, and proceeded to Wendover, Ascot and Calverton, and entered Oxfordshire near Chinnor. A mosaic pavement and Roman coins have been discovered at High Wycombe, an amphora was found on Wavendon heath, and a small glass vessel, and some spear heads have been dug up near Dinton. During the Anglo-Saxon Heptarchy this county was under the government of the Kings of Mercia, and was afterwards comprised in Denelege, or the Danish district. On the summit of the hill at West Wycombe are the remains of a circular encampment. At Danesfield, on the banks of the Thames, is an entrenchment nearly circular, with a double vallum, known by the name of Danes Ditch. There are also encampments near High Wycombe, Cholebury, Hedgerley Dean, Medmenham; and at Ellesborough are earthworks on the side of the Chiltern Hills, near which is a high circular mount called Kimble Castle. A considerable mound of earth, under the name of Grimsdyke, runs nearly east and west through part of this county. At Brill was a palace, which is said to have belonged to the Mercian Kings, and was the occasional residence of our monarchs of the Norman line so late as the reign of Henry III. Cheynies, or Isenhampsted, was a royal palace in the reign of Edward I.; and at Princes Risborough is an entrenchment supposed to be the site of the Black Prince's palace. The seats of the early Lords of Buckinghamshire were at Bolebec and Winslow, but there are no remains of the buildings of any ancient castles in this county; some earthworks point out the site of those which formerly existed at Lavendon and Whitchurch, and that at Castlethorpe or Hanslape

Castle, the seat of the Manduits. There are no earthworks remaining to mark the site of Newport Pagnell Castle, unless that near the river called Hill Close be assigned to it. The gatehouse of a castellated mansion at Barstall still remains. Lipscombe-house and Thornton-house have both been modernized; but Gayhurst, built in the reign of Elizabeth, has undergone little alteration. There were formerly abbeys at Bittlesden, Lavendon, Medmenham, Missenden and Nutley; and priories at Ankerwyke, Bradwell, Burnham, Chetwood, Little Marlow, St. Margaret's, Newington Longueville, Ravenstone, Snelleshall, Tickford and Wing. The college of the Bonhommes at Ashridge after its dissolution was for some time a royal palace, and was occasionally inhabited by Queen Elizabeth; and the royal college of Eton is still flourishing. Buckinghamshire is in the province of Canterbury and diocese of Lincoln, excepting six parishes in the diocese of Canterbury, and four in that of London. Aylesbury and Buckingham are assize-towns, besides which there are twelve market-towns. The county contains 201 parishes, 24,876 houses, and 134,086 inhabitants. It sends fourteen members to Parliament, two for Amersham, two for Aylesbury, two for Buckingham, two for Great Marlow, two for High Wycombe, two for Wendover, and two for the county, who at present are the Marquess of Chandos and John Smith, Esq.

The face of the county is much varied; the southern parts are occupied by the Chiltern Hills, which are chiefly composed of chalk, as their name is supposed to imply; and although very inferior to the northern districts in respect to richness of soil, have been rendered extremely productive by the mode of cultivation adopted. In that part of the county which borders on Bedfordshire, about Broughton and the Brickhills, the soil is a deep sand. The fertility of the Vale of Aylesbury is quite proverbial, as well as the saying, in reference to the produce of corn and cattle, "Buckinghamshire Bread and Beef." Camden speaks of the numerous flocks of sheep in the Vale of Aylesbury loaded with wool, and Fuller says the biggest bodied sheep in England were bred in this Vale: but at present sheep-farming is on the decline, although great numbers of oxen are fed in the Vale of Aylesbury for the London markets. The dairies in the Vale furnish large quantities of butter by contract to the London dealers; and in the neighbourhood of Aylesbury ducks are reared early in the spring and sent to the metropolis. The southern division of the county produces large quantities of fine beech; nearly a sixth part of the land in this part is supposed to be covered with that wood. Camden, indeed, derives the name of the county from Bucken, beech-trees, in the Anglo-Saxon language: but whatever be its etymology, it is evident that the county was named from the town of Buckingham; and although

beech-woods abound in some parts, these are remote from the county town, where the soil in the neighbourhood is not favourable to their growth. The rivers of this county are the Ouse, Colne, Thame, Ouzel, Wick, Loddon, and the Thames, which last is the boundary and chief ornament of the southern part; it divides Buckinghamshire from Berkshire, and passes Medmenham, Marlow, Hedsor, Taplow, Boveney, Eton and Datchet. The Colne separates this county from Middlesex, and passes near Denham and Iver to Colnbrook, whence it proceeds to Horton and Wyrardesbury, and falls into the Thames between Ankerwyke and Staines. The Thame rises near the borders of the county in Hertfordshire, and flowing through the Vale of Aylesbury, and receiving the waters of several small streams, enters Oxfordshire near the town of Thame, where it unites with the Isis. The course of the Ouse through Buckinghamshire, or as a boundary to it, is very circuitous. It first becomes a boundary to this county near Turveston, separating if from Northamptonshire, and having passed Westbury divides Buckinghamshire and Oxfordshire, and enters this county at Water Stratford; whence it passes to Buckingham and Thornton, and becomes a boundary between Buckinghamshire and Northamptonshire, and beyond Stoney Stratford enters the county a second time, and passes near Wolverton, Haversham, Stanton Barry, Linford and Lathbury, to Newport Pagnell; thence between Gayhurst and Tyringham to Olney, Clifton Reynes and Newton Blossomville, and passing between Brayfield and Turvey forms for a short distance a boundary between Bedfordshire and this county, which it quits near Snelson in the parish of Lavendon. The Ouzel is a boundary between Bedfordshire and Buckinghamshire, from Eaton Bray to Linchlade, whence it flows near Stoke Hammond and Water Eaton to Fenny Stratford, Simpson Walton, Woolston and Willien to Newport Pagnell, where it falls into the Ouse. The river Wick rises at West Wycombe, thence passing High Wycombe it flows by Woburn and falls into the Thames near Hedsor. The Grand Junction canal enters Buckinghamshire near Wolverton, passes Linford by Woolston, Woughton, and Simpson to Fenny Stratford; thence it follows the course of the Ouse to Grove, and near Marsworth quits the county.

The principal site of the lace manufacture in this county is Hanslope and its immediate vicinity; but it prevails for fifteen or twenty miles round in every direction; it is carried on to a great extent in and about Olney, where veils and lace of the finer sort are made. The manufacture of paper is carried on in the neighbourhood of Wycombe, and there are several mills on the Wick employed for that purpose. Stowe-House is the seat of His Grace the Duke of Buckingham and Chandos, K.G., Lord Lieutenant of the County.

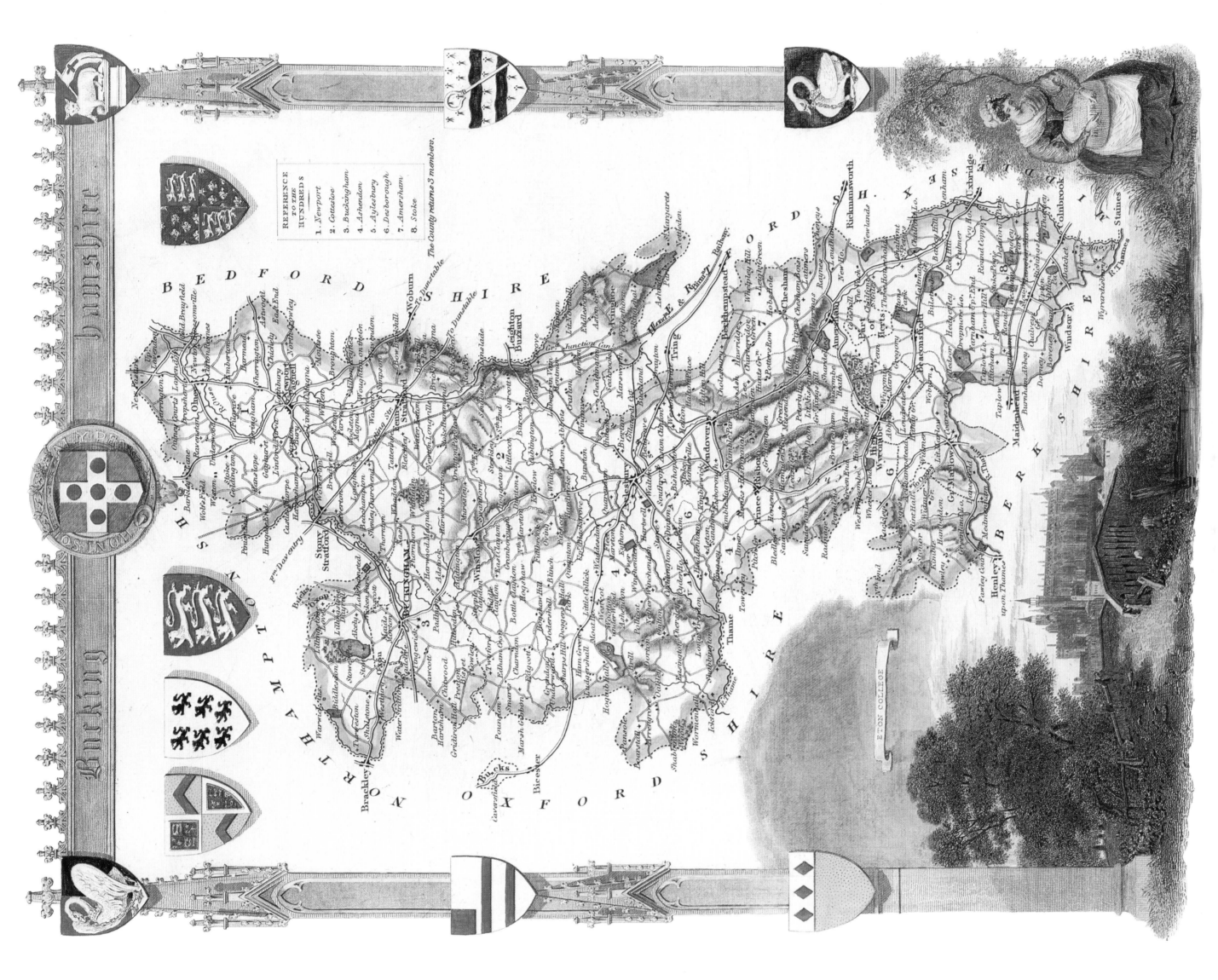

Buckinghamshire

REFERENCE
TO THE
HUNDREDS

1. Newport
2. Cottesloe
3. Buckingham
4. Ashendon
5. Aylesbury
6. Desborough
7. Amersham
8. Stoke

The County returns 3 members.

ETON COLLEGE

CAMBRIDGESHIRE

THIS county is bounded on the north by Lincolnshire and Northamptonshire; on the east by the counties of Norfolk and Suffolk; South by Essex and Hertfordshire; and on the west by Huntingdonshire and Bedfordshire. Its greatest length is about 45 miles, and the breadth about 30 miles, and in circumference it is about 130 miles. The British inhabitants the Iceni and Cenomanni. In the first division of Britain, under the Romans, Cambridgeshire formed a part of Britannia Superior, and under the last division was included in the district of Flavia Cæariensis. The whole county is traversed by ancient roads, in a great variety of directions, two of which are, with reason, supposed to be British; others are evidently Roman. The Ikenild-street enters the county near Newmarket, goes through Ickleton, over Fulmere field, to Royston, where it crosses the Ermin-street, and keeps on the side of the chalky hills to Baldock and Dunstaple. The British Ermin-street entering Cambridgeshire at Royston, kept to the left of the present turnpike-road to Caxton and Godmanchester. A great Roman road, which connected the colonies of Colchester and Chester, enters this county from Withers-field, in Suffolk, and bearing nearly from east to west, passes through Horseheath Park, leaving Balsham on the right, crosses the Ikenild-street, and proceeds very straight over the open country to Gogmagog Hills, through Fen Stanton to Godmanchester, in its way to Leicester. Another Roman road led through Cambridgeshire, from the north-eastern coast of Norfolk, to St. David's; this road passed through Littleport to Ely, Stretham, and near Landbeach and Impington to Cambridge and Barton, bearing towards the Roman station at Sandy. Although Cambridgeshire was surrounded by Roman towns of considerable importance, one station only appears to have been within the county, and that was Cambridge itself, generally supposed to have been the Camboritum of Antoninus's Itinerary. Few Roman antiquities have been discovered in the county, except on the site of the station at Camboritum or Cambridge, where coins and earthenware of various kinds, particularly of the red Samian ware, and Roman utensils, have been frequently found. After the expulsion of the Romans, this county became part of the kingdom of the East Angles, and was subsequently comprised within Denelege or Danish jurisdiction. On the highest part of Gogmagog Hills is Vandlebury, a large circular encampment; and at Kingsbedges, in the parish of Chesterton, are the remains of Arbury, a large circular camp; and some of the earth-works on the site of the castles at Camps and Bourn are supposed to be the remains of British camps. The most remarkable earth-works in the county are the Devil's Ditch and Fleamdyke. The castles of its ancient lords were at Cambridge, Wisbeach, Bourne, and Camps. Barham Hall, Childerley, Downham Palace, Madineley, Kittling, and Sawston Hall, are ancient houses. There were formerly abbeys at Denny and Thorney; priories at Anglesey, Barham, Barnwell, Ely, Fordbam, Linton, Marmond, Spinney, and Swavesey; and nunneries at Chateris, Ikelington, Swaffham, and Waterbeach, besides the Benedictine nunnery of St. Radegund at Cambridge; and it is certain that no county in England produces a richer display of ancient church architecture. Cambridgeshire is in the province of Canterbury, and diocese of Ely, excepting a few parishes in Norwich and Rochester. Cambridge is the county-town, and Ely is a city. There are in the county 7 market-towns, 165 parishes, 20,869 houses, and 121,909 inhabitants: it sends six members to Parliament, two for the University, two for the town of Cambridge, and two for the county, which last are Lord F. G. Osborne, and Henry John Adeane, Esq.

The face of the country exhibits considerable variety; the northern part, including the Isle of Ely, is for the most part fen land, comprising nearly half of the Bedford Level, intersected with canals and ditches, and abounding with windmills for conveying the water from the land into channels provided for carrying it off to the sea. The most considerable rising ground in this part of the county is that on which the city of Ely stands. The south-western part of the county is varied by gently rising hills, with downs, open corn-fields, and a considerable portion of wood, from Wood Ditton to Castle Camps; but in other parts the county is very bare of timber. Gogmagog Hills, south-eastward of Cambridge, are the highest in the county, and command a very extensive view. The land is chiefly arable, producing an abundant supply of corn, of which a considerable quantity is sent to the London markets. The cultivation of hemp and flax is practised near Wisbeach, and the neighbourhood of Ely is particularly famed for the production of garden vegetables. A district of the county formerly called "The Dairies," comprehended the parishes of Shengay, Wendy, Whaddon, &c.; but the dairy farms in this district are now not so considerable as those in the parishes of Chatteris, Mepal, Sutton, Swavesey, Over, Willingham, Cottenham, Rampton, Landbeach, Waterbeach, Stretham, Ely, Littleport, Soham, and Fordham. In Cottenham and Willingham the cheese is made which goes by the name of Cottenham cheese. Soham is also famed for its cheese. The rivers of Cambridgeshire are the Ouse, the Cam, the Glen, the Nen, the Lark, and the Rhee. The Ouse, now called the Old Ouse, enters the county near Earith-bridge, in the parish of Haddenham; and forming the boundary between the Isle of Ely and the rest of the county, passes Stretham to Upware, where it receives the Cam, and a few miles below Ely receives the Lark, and becomes the boundary between Cambridgeshire and Suffolk. The Cam is formed by the Rhee, which enters this county at a point where Bedfordshire and Hertfordshire meet it, and flows to Granchester, where it meets another stream rising at Henham in Essex. At Granchester, the Cam or Granta acquires its name, and passes through Cambridge to Upware, where it joins the Ouse. The river Nen, in its old course, enters this county at Benwick, and runs through March and Upwell to Outwell, where it enters Norfolk, and finally discharges itself into the Ouse at Salter's Lode. The Nen, in its present course, divides Huntingdonshire from the Isle of Ely, till it enters the isle, and passes Whittlesea and Wisbeach to Cross Keys Wash. There is a navigable canal from Peterborough, by Whittlesea, to the Old Nen, a little below Benwick. A navigable canal, called The Forty Foot Drain, enters the Isle of Ely near Ramsey Mere, and passes between Chatteris and Doddington to Welches Dam, where it enters the Old Bedford river, and leaves the county westward of Welney. Most of the canals which intersect the Isle of Ely in various directions were made for the purpose of drainage, but the greater part of them are applicable also to the purposes of navigation. The Hundred Foot river is the main channel for vessels passing from the upper to the lower parts of the Ouse. The Old Bedford river is scarcely ever employed for the purposes of navigation, excepting the lower part near Denver Sluice. There is a short canal from the Ouse, commencing near Barway, to Soham; another to Reach, and a third to Burwell. The rivers abound with fish; pike and eels are plentiful, and esteemed very fine: in addition to the more common fish, smelts are caught in considerable quantity in the New Bedford river. A paper manufactory is carried on Sawston, and a manufactory of earthenware and white bricks has been long established at Ely, made from the gault found in that neighbourhood. There are also several mills in the county for preparing oil from cole and rape seed. Wimpole, near Arrington, is the seat of the Earl of Hardwicke, Lord Lieutenant of the County.

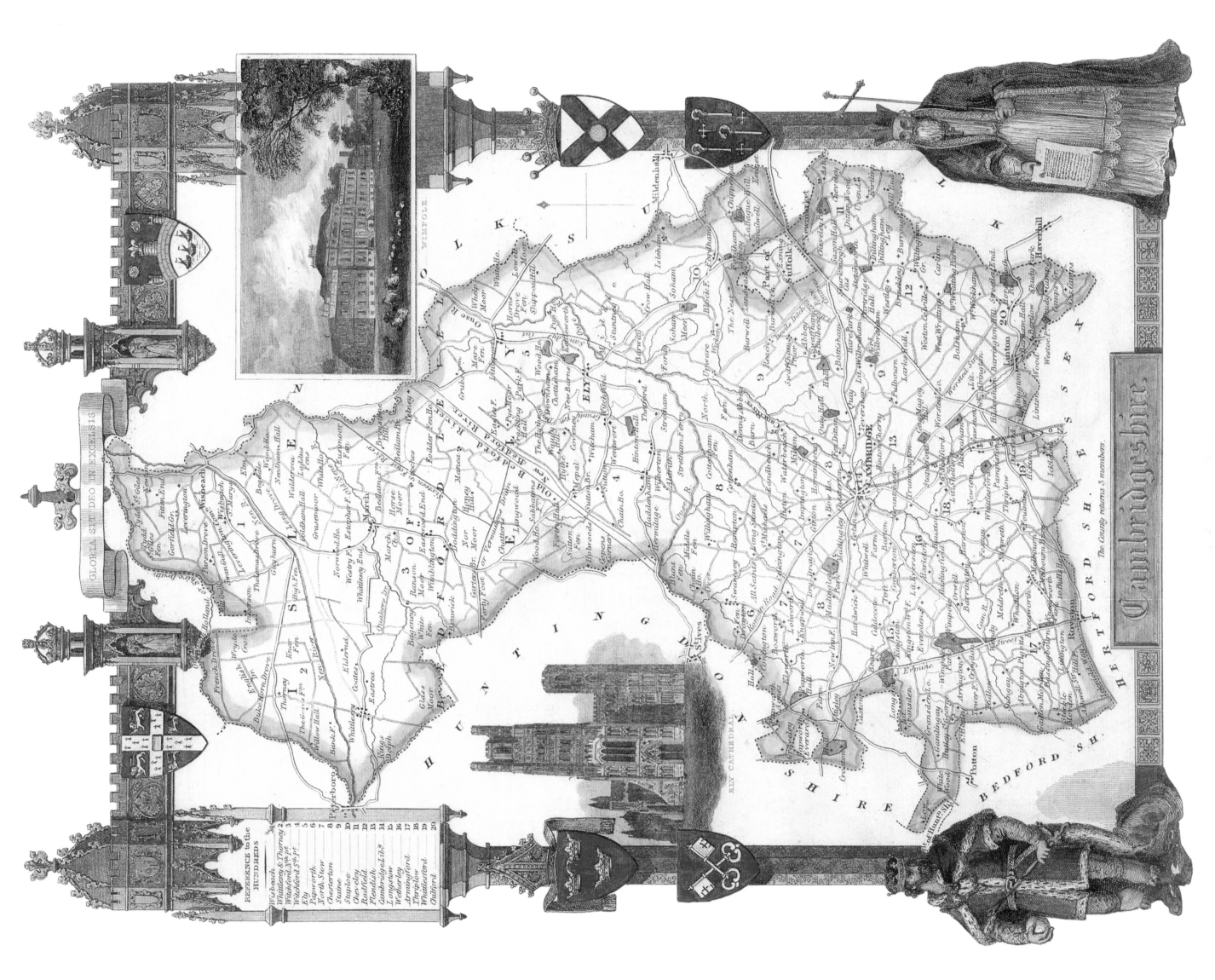

Cambridgeshire.

The County returns 3 members.

GLORIA SIT DEO IN EXCELSIS.

WIMPOLE

ELY CATHEDRAL

REFERENCE to the HUNDREDS

Wisbeach 1
Whittlesey & Thorney 2
Witchford No: pt. 3
Witchford S:th pt. 4
Ely 5
Papworth 6
North Stow 7
Chesterton 8
Staine 9
Staploe 10
Cheveley 11
Radfield 12
Flendish 13
Cambridge Lib.ty 14
Longstow 15
Wetherley 16
Armingford 17
Thriplow 18
Whittlesford 19
Chilford 20

NORFOLK

SUFFOLK

ESSEX

HERTFORDSH.

BEDFORD SH.

HUNTINGDON SHIRE

TOWN AND UNIVERSITY OF CAMBRIDGE

CAMBRIDGE is locally situated in the Hundred of Flendish, fifty miles north from London by way of Royston, and fifty-one miles by way of Ware. It is distant eighty-six miles north east from Oxford. The Town derives its name from the river Cam, or Grant, and is said to have extended from Grantchester, a castle two miles south westward of the town, to Chesterton on the north east, its total length having been three miles on the western banks of the Cam. It is at present above a mile in length, and more than half a mile in breadth, and about three miles in circumference, containing 2,594 houses, and 14,142 inhabitants. The situation of Cambridge is a perfect level, the Town being encompassed by the Colleges of the University, with their beautiful groves and gardens on both sides of the river, over which are several bridges, both public and private, but the streets, notwithstanding the recent improvements, are in general narrow and winding. Entering the Town by Trumpington-street, Downing College, with its graceful porticos, is on the right, and near the beginning of the street, is the Pitt Press and Addenbroke's Hospital, Peter House, Pembroke and Katherine Halls succeed, and nearly opposite the last is Benet College, lately rebuilt; in the centre of the Town is a group of magnificent buildings, comprising Great St. Mary's, or the University Church, the Senate House, the Public Library, and the superb Chapel of King's College, on the banks of the Cam. On the right of Bridge-street is Jesus College-lane and the road to Newmarket; the rural appearance of Jesus College, makes this entrance of the town frequently preferred for picturesque beauty. St. Andrew's-street, on the road from the Gogmagog hills and Colchester, contains Emmanuel and Christ's Colleges, and passing Trinity Church, leads to Bridge-street and Sidney College. Beyond the Bridge, over the Cam, is Magdalen College, and the remains of the ancient

Castle, on the road to Huntingdon; to the right of which are the roads to Chesterton and the City of Ely.

In the centre of the Town, behind Great St. Mary's Church, is Market Hill, where the markets under the jurisdiction of the University, are held. The chief Market for corn, &c. is on Saturday, but there is a Market every day in the week, excepting Sunday, and Monday for poultry and butter: the latter is made up in pounds, consisting of slender rolls a yard long, for the convenience of division into sizes for the use of the colleges; a grant quantity of butter in firkins, chiefly from Norfolk and the Isle of Ely, is also sent hence to London. Although very little fruit is grown in the town, no place is more plentifully supplied with it. The Petty Cury and Market-street, intersecting each side of the Market-place, lead into Bridge-street, and in an oblique

direction from Market Hill is Pease Hill, the Fish Market, &c., the last abundantly supplied with freshwater fish, from the Isle of Ely. Benet-street, denominated from the Church and College, leads into Trumpington-street.

The Corporation of the Borough of Cambridge, consists of a mayor, a high steward, a recorder, twelve aldermen, twenty-four common-councilmen, four bailiffs, a town clerk, and other officers. The Mayor upon entering into office, takes an oath to maintain the privileges, liberties and customs of the University, and on the day of his election, has the privilege of bestowing the freedom of the town on any one person he may think proper. The Town Hall, built in 1782, contains a room about 70 feet by 28 feet in dimension, in which concerts are occasionally performed. The arms of the Town are: *Gules, on a fess arched three towers or, all masoned sable : in chief a fleur de lis between two roses of the second, and in base a river proper, thereon three vessels of one mast each sable. Crest on a mount vert, a quadrangular castle with four towers domed, in front two ports, all or, masoned sable; supporters, two sea horses proper, finned and maned or.* The Borough of Cambridge returns two members to Parliament, a privilege granted by King Edward I.; the present members are the Right Hon. Thomas Spring Rice, one of the secretaries to the Treasury, and George Pryme, Esq. The Assizes are always held here.

The Town of Cambridge is divided into four Wards, viz. Bridge Ward, which extends from Jesus-lane to castle-end. High Ward, which extends from the entrance of the Town from Trumpington to St. John's College-lane. Preacher's Ward, which extends from the southern part of St. Andrew's-street to Jesus-lane. Market Ward, which contains the Market-place, and the streets, rows, and lanes adjoining. In the Town are fourteen Parishes, and the Churches of St. Mary and St. Sepulchre are interesting objects of observation.

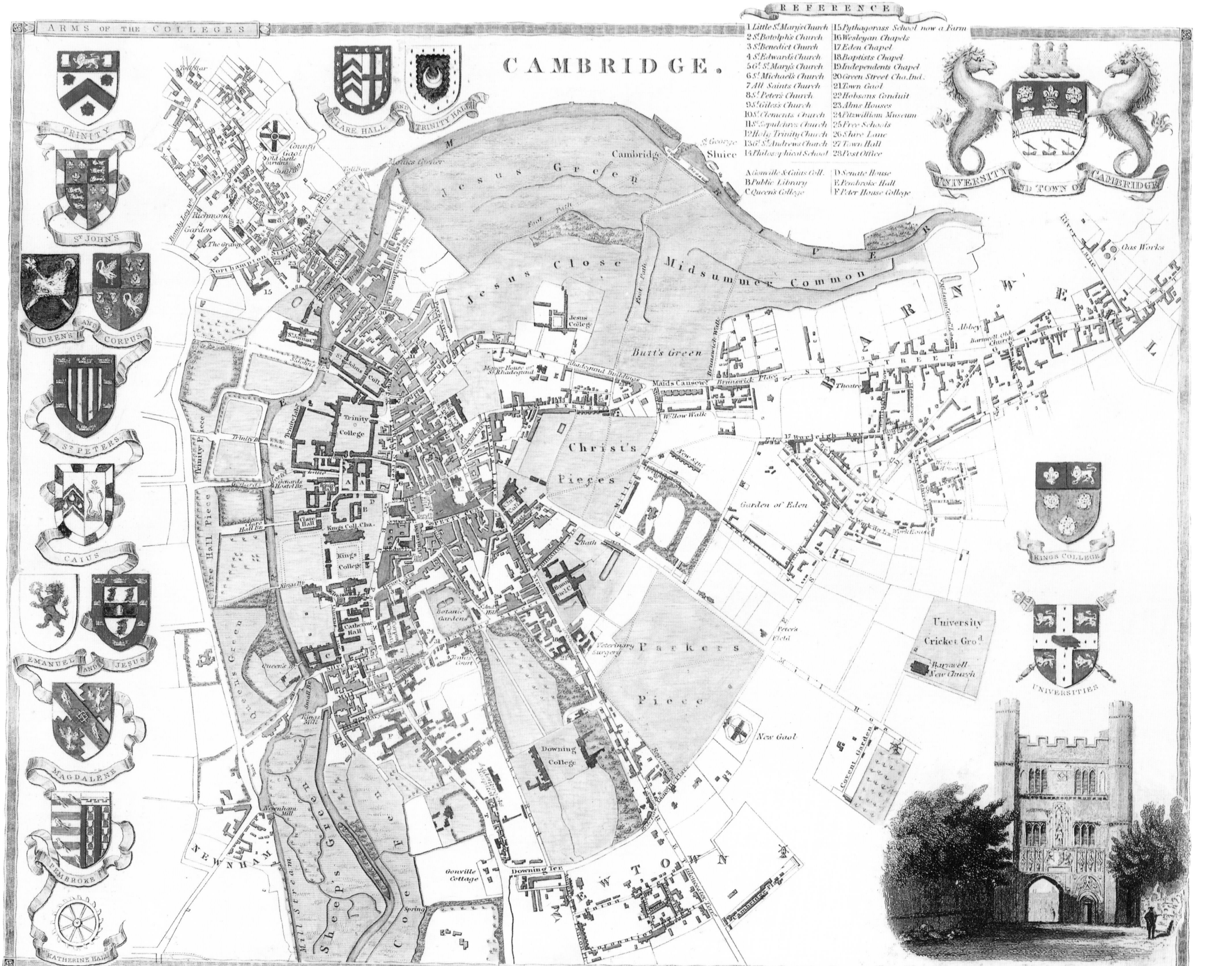
CAMBRIDGE.
ARMS OF THE COLLEGES
TRINITY
St JOHN'S
QUEENS AND CORPUS
St PETERS
CAIUS
EMANUEL AND JESUS
MAGDALENE
PEMBROKE
KATHERINE HALL
CLARE HALL AND TRINITY HALL
UNIVERSITY AND TOWN OF CAMBRIDGE
KINGS COLLEGE
UNIVERSITIES
TRINITY COLLEGE
REFERENCE
1 Little St. Mary's Church
2 St. Botolph's Church
3 St. Benedict Church
4 St. Edward's Church
5 Gt. St. Mary's Church
6 St. Michael's Church
7 All Saints Church
8 St. Peter's Church
9 St. Giles's Church
10 St. Clements Church
11 St. Sepulchre's Church
12 Holy Trinity Church
13 Gt. St. Andrews Church
14 Philosophical School
15 Pythagorass School now a Farm
16 Wesleyan Chapels
17 Eden Chapel
18 Baptists Chapel
19 Independents Chapel
20 Green Street Cha. Ind.
21 Town Gaol
22 Hobsons Conduit
23 Alms Houses
24 Fitzwilliam Museum
25 Free Schools
26 Shire Lane
27 Town Hall
28 Post Office
A Gonville & Caius Coll.
B Public Library
C Queen's College
D Senate House
E Pembroke Hall
F Peter House College
Jesus Green
Jesus Close
Midsummer Common
Jesus College
Butt's Green
Christ's Pieces
Trinity College
Kings College
Clare Hall
Catherine Hall
Botanic Gardens
Parkers Piece
University Cricket Grod
Barnwell New Church
New Gaol
Downing College
Garden of Eden
Covent Garden
Gonville Cottage
Downing Ter.
NEWTON
NEWNHAM
Sheep's Green
Coe Fen
Mill Stream
Queens Green
Clare Hall Piece
Trinity Piece
Newnham Mill
Kings Mill
Richmond Garden
The Grange
Northampton Street
Cambridge
St. George Sluice
RIVER CAM
BARNWELL
Gas Works
Theatre
Maids Causeway
Brunswick Place
Burleigh Row
Abbey
Barnwell Old Church
Veterinary Surgery
Peter's Field
Mill Road

CHESHIRE

This county is bounded on the north by Lancashire and Yorkshire; on the east by Derbyshire and Staffordshire; on the south by a detached portion of Flintshire aud Shropshire and on the west by Flintshire and Denbighshire: at the northwestern extremity between the estuaries of the Dee and Mersey, it is bounded by the Irish Sea. The greatest length of this county is fifty-eight miles, the breadth thirty miles, and the circumference one hundred and twelve miles. It takes its name from the ancient city of Chester, and in the earlier periods of history, formed part of the territories of a British tribe called the Cornavii. Under the Romans, the county was included in Britannia Superior, and it became part of the province of Flavia Cæsariensis: the Roman stations were Deva, Chester; and Condate, Kinderton. Upon the division of England into three great districts by Alfred, Cheshire was included in Mercenleage, or the Mercian jurisdiction. In the reign of William the Conqueror, Cheshire obtained the privileges of a county palatine. The Earl of Chester had his barons, one of whom was hereditary constable, and another hereditary steward; assembled parliaments, established his courts of law, and exercised almost every act of regal authority, until the death of John Le Scot Earl of Chester, in 1237, when King Henry III. granted the earldom of Chester to his son Prince Edward. King Richard II. erected it into a principality, but under his successor Cheshire again became a county palatine, and the Kings' eldest sons were from time to time created Earls of Chester; but its privileges were much abridged in the reign of Henry VIII.

The authority of the judges and officers of the great session of the county palatine extends over the counties of Chester and Flint, and one seal is used for both counties. The King's writ does not run in the county palatine, but all writs issuing from the superior courts are directed to the chamberlain, who issues his mandate to the sheriff. The present chamberlain is the Earl of Stamford; the vice-chamberlain Hugh Leycester, Esq., who generally presides in the Exchequer court twice in the year. The assizes for the county are held at Chester, the Epiphany and Easter quarter sessions at Chester, and the Midsummer and Michaelmas sessions at Knutsford. The ancient castles in this county were at Chester, Pulford, Dunham, Frodsham, Halton, Beeston, Shotwick, and Holt. There were formerly abbeys at Chester, Combermere, Stanlaw, and Vale Royal; the priories were those of Birkenhead, Mobberley, Warburton, and Norton. The knights hospitallers had a preceptory at Barrow.

This county contains one city and twelve market-towns; eighty-six parishes, nine of which are in the city of Chester; 47,094 inhabited houses, and 270,098 inhabitants. Most of the Cheshire parishes are of great extent and comprise numerous townships. The county is in the province of York

and diocese of Chester. It returns four members to Parliament, two for the city of Chester and two for the county: the present members for the county are Earl Grosvenor and George Wilbraham, Esq.

The greater part of Cheshire exhibits a uniform flat surface, and has few woods of any extent; the principal hills are those on the borders of Derbyshire, a range of hills in the hundred of Broxton, Bucklow hills, Frodsham hills and Alderley edge, a singular insulated hill in the hundred of Macclesfield; the view from this hill and those from Halton and Beeston castles, from Mowcop and Shutlingslow hills, from Carden cliff and Overton Scar, and from the western edge of De la Mere forest, are amongst the most remarkable for richness and extent of any in the county. Although Cheshire has now but few woods, it had in former times some very extensive forests; De la Mere and Macclesfield forests were large tracts of waste land. The forest of Wirrall, disforested in 1376, is now in cultivation. The quantity of timber growing in the county, in hedgerows and coppices, exceeds the general average of the kingdom; it is principally oak: there are also extensive plantations of Scotch firs and larches in De la Mere forest. The rivers of Cheshire are the Dee, the Mersey, the Weever, the Dane, the Bollin, the Peover, the Wheelock, and the Tame; the other smaller rivers are the Gowy, the Besley, Ashbrook, the Biddle, the Croco, the Birkin, the Mar, Grimsditch, the Walwarn, the Lea and Flookersbrook. The Dee rises in Merionethshire and enters the county near Aldford; thence it passes by Eaton and Eccleston to Chester. From Chester bridge the river Dee navigation to the sea was cut in 1754; near Flint Castle it becomes an estuary of three miles wide. The Mersey is formed by the junction of the rivers Etheron and Goyt, and passes from Stockport to Liverpool; at Runcorn Gap it communicates with the Trent and Mersey canal and the Duke of Bridgewater's canal and below extends itself into a grand estuary, three miles in width, receiving in its course the navigable river Weever. Opposite to Liverpool, its width is only one mile, where it forms a fine channel, very commodious for shipping, and about five miles distant falls into the Irish Sea. The Weever rises on Bulkeley heath, passes Risley, by Cholmondeley Castle, to Wrenbury, by Audlem and Nantwich to Winsford, thence by Vale Royal and Eaton to Hartfordbridge and Northwich, where it is joined by the Dane, and soon afterwards by the Peover: the river then passes Frodsham and Rocksavage to Weston, where it joins the Mersey. The river Dane rises in Macclesfield forest, near the Three Shire Mere, and enters the county about three miles from Congleton, whence it passes by Davenport to Cranage bridge and Byley bridge, near Davenham or *Daneham*, to Northwich, where it falls into the Weever. The Bollin rises in Macclesfield forest from several heads, the two

principal of which issue from the foot of Shutlingslow hill; it passes Sutton, Macclesfield, Bollington, Prestbury, and Newton, Wilmslow, Pownall, Ringey, Ashley, Dunham, Bollington, and Warburton, to Rixton, where it falls into the Mersey. There are several lakes, called meres or pools, in Cheshire: Ridley pool, formerly one of the largest, has been drained and converted into tillage: here are Comber Mere, Bar Mere, a mere in Rosthern parish, Comberbach Mere, Oakhanger Mere, Pick Mere, Rosthern Mere, Tatton Mere, Chapel Mere, and Moss Mere, all abounding with the more common sort of fish. Few counties derive so many advantages from the internal intercourse which has been produced by artificial navigation as Cheshire. The canals, which intersect various parts of the county, are the Duke of Bridgewater's, the Trent and Mersey, the Ellismere, the Chester and Nantwich, and the Peak forest canals. The staple commodities of this county are cheese and salt; the former has long been celebrated, and one of its principal articles of exportation, as is supposed, from a very early period. The richest and best cheese is said to be produced from land of an inferior nature; but the greatest quantity from the richest land. Amongst the districts most celebrated for making the prime cheese, may be reckoned the neighbourhood of Nantwich for a circuit of five miles; the parish of Over; the greatest part of the banks of the Weever, and several farms near Congleton and Middlewich. The Cheshire brine-pits, where the salt is made, are at Nantwich, Lawton, Wheelock, and Roughwood; in the townships of Anderton, Bechton, Leftwich, Middlewich, and in the neighbourhood of Northwich and Winsford. Rock or fossil salt forms an important staple commodity of the county: it is found abundantly in the townships of Witton, Winsham, and Marston near Northwich. The fossil salt is of two kinds, the one white and transparent, the other of a reddish brown; the former has been found by analysis to be an almost pure muriate of soda; the latter to contain a certain portion of earth, whence its colour is derived. Potatoes are cultivated in Cheshire to a great extent, for exportation, in the neighbourhood of Altrincham and Frodsham, and in the hundred of Wirrall. The cotton manufacture is carried on in several parts of the county, particularly at Stockport and its vicinity: muslin and calico are made at Macclesfield; and there are silk mills at Macclesfield Congleton and Stockport. The manufacture of hats at Stockport, of shoes at Sandbach and Nantwich, and of gloves at Chester and Nantwich, is extensive. Tanning is carried on throughout the whole county, but more particularly in the middle and northern parts. According to Fuller, the author of the "English Worthies," the Cheshire gentry are remarkable for their numbers, their antiquity, their loyalty, and their hospitality. Dunham Massey, near Knutsford, is the seat of the Earl of Stamford and Warrington, Lord Lieutenant of the County.

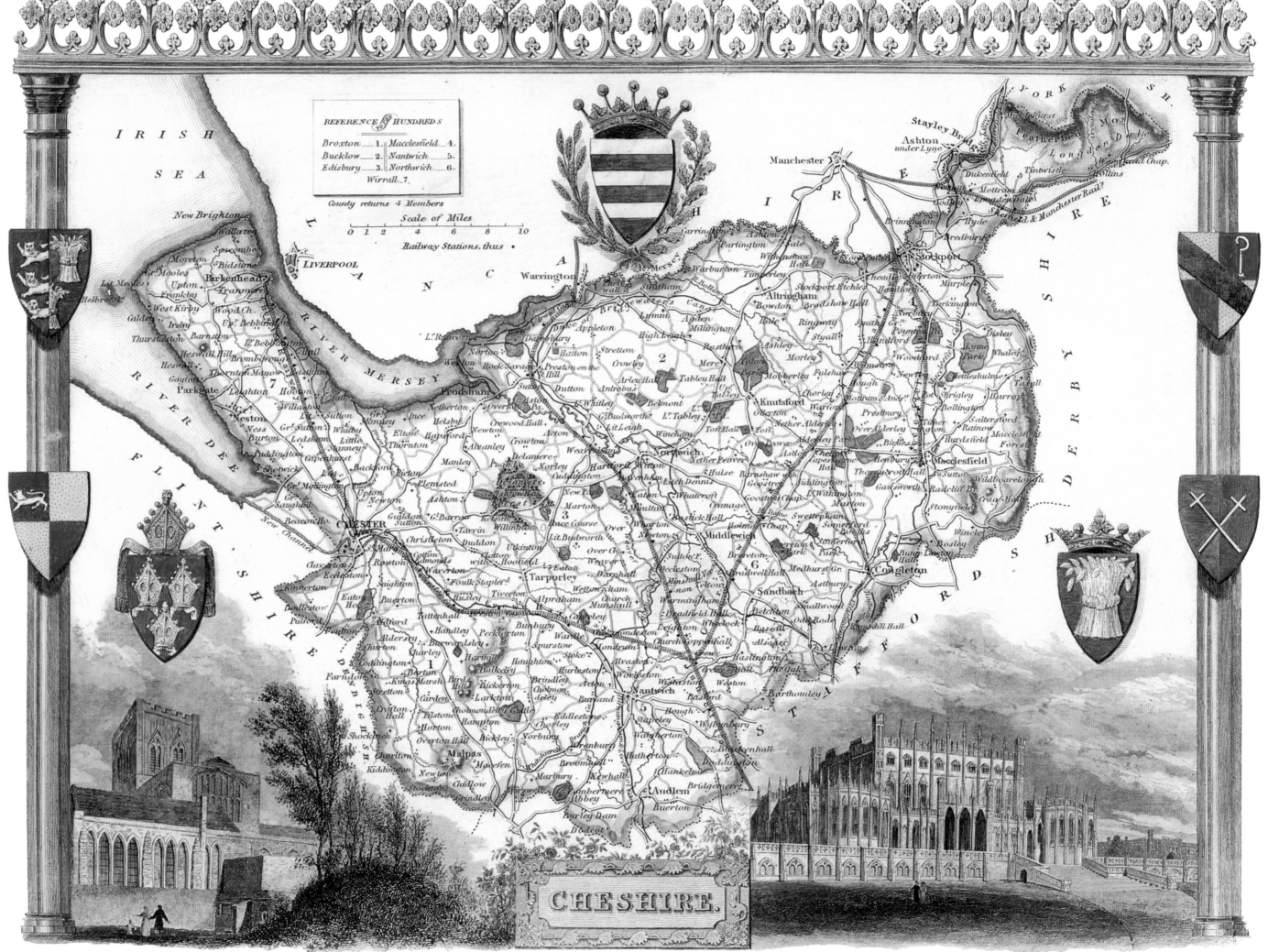

CHESHIRE.

CHESTER CATHEDRAL

EATON HALL

CORNWALL

THIS County forms the western extremity of the kingdom; the extreme point called "The Land's End," is three hundred and ninety-one feet above the level of the sea. The Lizard Point, its south-western extremity, is the spot whence all ships leaving the Channel date their departure from England; and for romantic scenery is rarely to be surpassed in the kingdom. Cornwall is bounded on the north by the Bristol Channel, on the east by Devonshire, and on the south by the English Channel. Its extent from the Land's End to the Devonshire border, is about 79 miles, its greatest breadth, from north to south, about 43 miles, and its reputed circumference is about 250 miles.

The British inhabitants were called Cornubii, or the men of the promontory. Before the coming of the Romans, the Danmonii had usurped the dominion; under the Romans, this district was included in their first division of the island, and formed part of Britannia Prima. Cornwall abounds with memorials of its early inhabitants, consisting of large unwrought stones, placed erect, either singly or in circles, or with others laid across, and tumuli of stones or earth. Two of the most remarkable upright stones are at Bolliet, in the parish of St. Burien. On the downs, between Wadebridge and St. Columb, is a line of stones, generally called the Nine Maids. Circles of erect stones are very frequent in this country, where they are known by the name of Dawnsmen, or the Stone-Dance. The monument called the Hurlers, originally consisted of three circles; and a singular monument at Bodinar, called the Crellas, is a double circle. It is most probable, that these circles of upright stones were applied to purposes of religion, although the opinion of those who consider them as peculiarly referable to Druidical rites, does not appear to be supported by the few notices which are to be met with on that subject, in the writings of the ancients. All the authors who were contemporary with the Druids, uniformly assert that their religious rites were confined to groves of oak, whilst these stone monuments chiefly abound in the most desert parts, where, in all probability neither oaks, nor any other trees, ever grew; and similar ones are found in almost every part of the world, although the Druids are supposed to have been chiefly confined to Britain and Gaul.

There are also in Cornwall several circular enclosures with walls of stone or earth, on the inside of which are rows of seats, having been originally intended for the exhibition of sports of various kinds, they are known by the name of Rounds, or "Plân an guare," the place of sport. Two of the most remarkable of these works are the Rounds of St. Piran and St. Just.

Barrows and cairns, tumuli of earth and stone, are found in several parts of Cornwall, most of which may be considered as the sepulchral monuments of the Britons, although, no doubt, some of them, especially those which have been found to contain neatly executed urns, may be referred to the Romans or Romanized Britons.

Another kind of stone monument found in this county, is the Cromlech, which there is every reason to suppose sepulchral, consisting of a large flat stone, in an horizontal position, supported by several others fixed upright in the ground. It is commonly known by the name of the Quoit, or the Giant's Quoit. Lanyon Quoit is raised so high that a man on horseback may sit under it.

Cornwall has produced few Roman antiquities, excepting coins, which have been discovered in great abundance in the western part of the county. Our knowledge of the Roman Stations in Cornwall, is as defective as that of the Roman Roads, of which fragments are met with in all parts of the county; but it is difficult to point out the situation of Roman settlements, and more so to determine their names.

During the Anglo Saxon Heptarchy, Cornwall was comprehended in the kingdom of Wessex. The castles of its ancient lords were at Tintagel, Launceston, Boscastle, St. Mawes, Pendennis, St. Michael's Mount, Trematon, Restormel, Tregony, St. Leven, Truro, Pengersick, Bossiney, Cambre, Chûn, Fowey, Kernejack, Kimick, Pellin, Pentilly, and Boscajal. There were priories at Bodmin, St. Benets near Lanhivet, St. Germains, Launceston, St. Michael's Mount, and Tywardreth; and collegiate churches at St. Buriens, Constantine, and Glaseney.

Cornwall contains 30 market towns, 203 parishes, 43,873 houses, 257,447 inhabitants. It returns fourteen members to parliament; two for Bodmin, one for Helleston, one for Launceston, one for Liskeard, two for Falmouth and Penryn, one for St. Ives, two for Truro, and four for the county; who at present arc Sir William Molesworth, Bart., of Pencarrow, near Bodmin, William Lewis Salusbury Trelawney, Esq. of Harewood near Tavistock, members for the eastern division : and Edward William Wynne Pendarves, Esq. of Pendarves near Falmouth, and Sir Charles Lemon, Bart., of Carclew near Penryn, members for the western division.

The high grounds of Cornwall, through which chiefly the great roads pass, present a dreary prospect, but there is a great deal of beautiful scenery near the southern coast, particularly at east and west Looe, Fowey, and Polperro, and on the banks of the Lynher, near Trematon Castle and Nottar Bridge. The Bay of Falmouth, and Mount's Bay, are exceeded in beauty by none in the kingdom. Many of the valleys are well wooded, particularly in the south eastern part of the county, and the neighbourhood of Lostwithiel and Bodmin. Cornwall has also its share of the beautiful scenery on the banks of the Tamar. Some of the most remarkable and interesting scenery in the county, is that which occurs along a line of bold and abrupt coast, bounded by the Atlantic Ocean and the British Channel, where amidst a great variety of striking objects may be enumerated the magnificent groups of granite rocks at the Land's End, Cape Cornwall, and Castle Treryn, the rocks at Tintagel, and the stupendous rock near Basset's Cove, with a lofty perforation, called Tabbin's Hole. The principal rivers of this county, are the Tamar, the Lynher, the Tidi, the Seaton, the Looe, the Fowey, the Fal, the Hel, the Heyl, and the Alan or Camel. The inland navigation is assisted by the St. Columb, Polbrook, and Tamar Canals. The produce of Cornwall is tin, copper, lead, most of the semi metals, China stone and clay, slate, Cornish diamonds or transparent quartz, pilchards and other fish. Mount Edgecumbe, in Devonshire, is the seat of Earl Mount Edgecombe, the Lord Lieutenant of Cornwall.

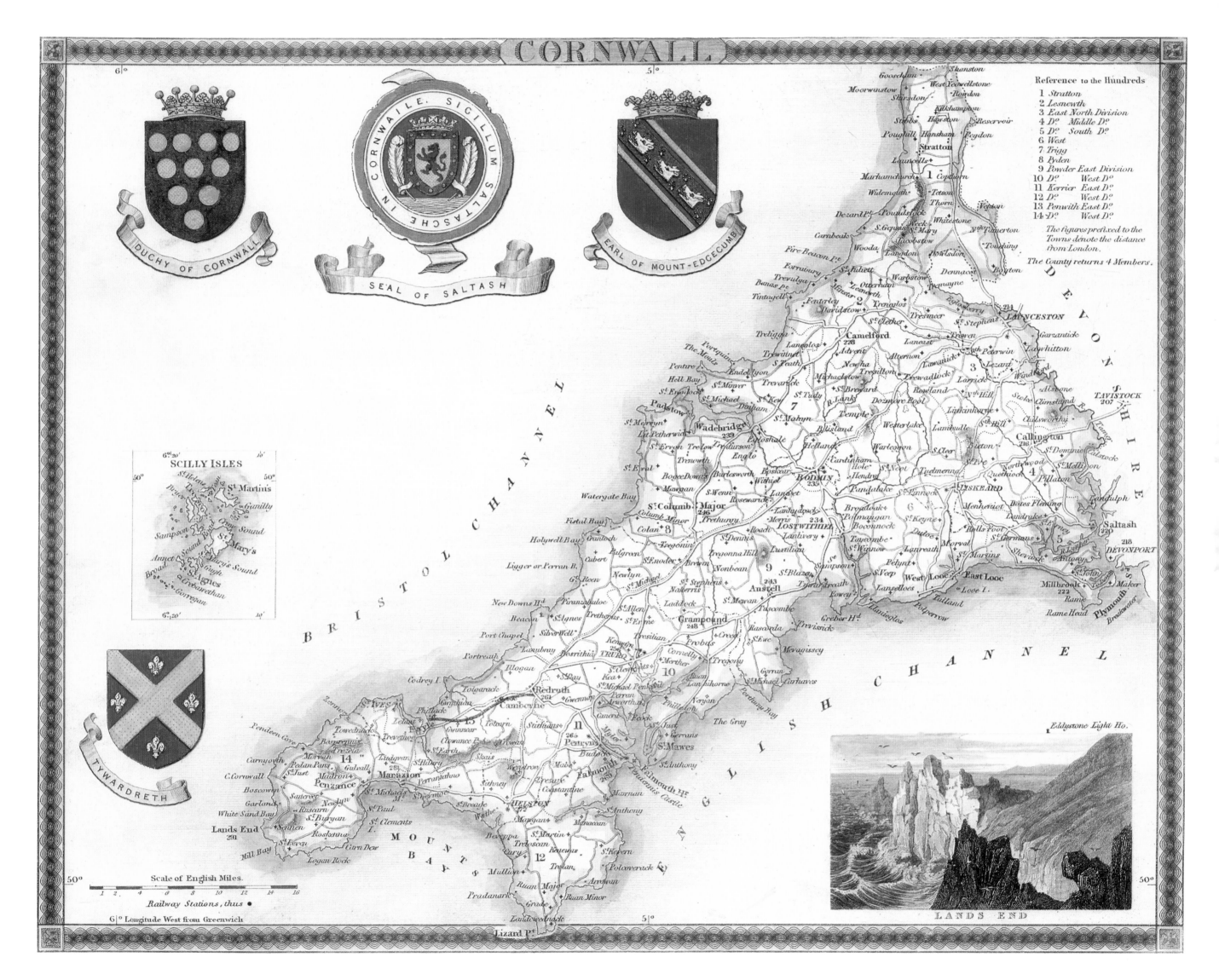

CORNWALL

Reference to the Hundreds

1 Stratton
2 Lesnewth
3 East North Division
4 Dᵒ. Middle Dᵒ
5 Dᵒ. South Dᵒ
6 West
7 Trigg
8 Pyden
9 Powder East Division
10 Dᵒ. West Dᵒ
11 Kerrier East Dᵒ
12 Dᵒ. West Dᵒ
13 Penwith East Dᵒ
14 Dᵒ. West Dᵒ

The figures prefixed to the Towns denote the distance from London.

The County returns 4 Members.

DEVONSHIRE

BRISTOL CHANNEL

ENGLISH CHANNEL

SCILLY ISLES

St Martin's
St Mary's
St Agnes

Launceston
Stratton
Camelford
Wadebridge
Padstow
St Columb Major
Bodmin
Lostwithiel
Liskeard
Callington
Saltash
Devonport
Plymouth
East Looe
West Looe
Truro
Redruth
Camborne
St Ives
Penzance
Marazion
Helston
Falmouth
Penryn
St Mawes
Grampound
Lands End
Lizard Pt

MOUNT'S BAY

Eddystone Light Ho.

LANDS END

Scale of English Miles.
2 4 6 8 10 12 14 16

Railway Stations, thus ●

6° Longitude West from Greenwich

5°

CUMBERLAND

This county is bounded on the north by Scotland; on the east by Northumberland and Durham; on the south by Westmorland and Lancashire; and on the west by the Irish Sea. Its greatest length from north east to south west is about seventy-two miles and its breadth about thirty-eight miles; the circumference is two hundred and twenty-four miles. Cumberland formed part of the territory of the Brigantes, and its inhabitants from an early period were called Cumbri. Under the Romans this county was part of Britannia Inferior, and afterwards was comprised within a district named Valentia. During the Anglo-Saxon Heptarchy the county formed part of the kingdom of Northumberland. Cumberland was sometimes under the dominion of the kings of Scotland and sometimes under the kings of England, till the year 1237, when it was finally annexed to the Crown of England by King Henry the Third, but for more than three centuries afterwards was seldom long exempt from invasion, or the depredations of raids and forays. It was not until the union of the kingdoms, on the accession of James the First to the English throne, that the residents of both borders were relieved from the misery of hostile inroads. British antiquities are numerous in this county, but the most considerable are Long Meg and her Daughters near Little Salkeld; a circle of stones eastward from Keswick; the Gray Yawd on King Harry Fell; Sunken Kirk at Swinside; and another circle of stones near it. This county became of importance to the Romans in a military view, which appears from the lines drawn across it by them at different periods, to enable them to resist the incursions of their northern enemies; but the British inhabitants, who formed the mass of its population, preserved their own manners long after the departure of the Roman army, and the remains both of British and Roman antiquity are to be met with in every part of it. In tracing the Roman wall, there are found at unequal distances, but in the most advantageous military position, several large fortresses, surrounded by deep ditches, defended by walls of earth or stones: these *castella* are invariably of a square or oblong form; the Romans always preferring a regular figure where the ground and other circumstances would permit its use. Several hypotheses have been formed regarding this celebrated wall, but the most general opinion seems to be, that some of the Roman generals, perhaps Agricola, about A.D.79, might draw a line of forts from Solway Frith to the mouth of the Tyne; that A.D.121, the Emperor Hadrian connected these forts by a *vallum* of turf with a ditch on its northern side that A.D.210 Severus constructed a wall of hewn stone northward of Hadrian's line, protected by three hundred turrets, by eighty-one towers at intervals of a mile, and by eighteen stations at the average distance of four miles, the whole forming a regular and compact defence from the eastern to the western sea. Finally, about A.D.448, when the Romans were on the point of leaving the island, Gallio of Ravenna, their general, assisted the British inhabitants in giving the wall of Severus a complete repair. This extraordinary work is yet seen in many parts of the county, running over the mountains and wastes at an elevation even now of five or six feet, and nearly nine feet thick attended by a fosse fifteen feet deep: its length from Newcastle to the station at Bowness is about seventy four miles. The stations on the wall are Amboglana, Burdoswald; Petriana Cambeck fort; Aballaba, Watch Cross; Congavata, Stanwix; Axelodunum, Burgh on the Sands; Gabrocentum, Drumburgh; and Tunnocelum, near Bowness. Other Roman stations, are Derventio, Papcastle; Virosidum, Ellenborough; Olenacura, Old Carlisle; Voreda, Old Penrith; Arbeia, Moresby or Irby; Bremetenracum, Whitbarrow or Brampton; Apiatorium, Bewcastle; Castra exploratorum, Netherby on the Esk; and Luguballium, Carlisle. No county in England, excepting Northumberland, has produced so great a number of Roman altars and inscribed stones as this, in consequence of the numerous military stations it contained. In Horsley's Roman Antiquities of Britain, the engravings of altars and sculptured stones amount to seventy-five, and the place where each was found is expressed. Lysons's *Magna Britannia* contains one hundred and forty-one and facsimiles are given of the most remarkable. The collection of antiquities, relative to Cumberland, at Netherby contains a great variety of sculptured stones, coins, iron and brass weapons, pottery, and other remains. The castles of its early lords were at Carlisle, Corby, Castle Carrock, Naworth, Rose Castle, Penrith, Egremont, Cockermouth, Kirk Oswald, Greystoke, Dacre, Armathwaite, Linstoke, Millom, Scaleby, Bew Castle, Dunwalloght, Hay, High, Head Castle, Wulstey, Askerton and Highgate. The ancient mansions retaining in part their original form are Muncaster, Irton Hall, Netherby, Netherhall, Dalston, Henthwaite, Lamplugh, Drumburgh, Harbybrow, and Hardrigg Hall. There were formerly abbeys at Calder and Holme Cultram, and priories at Armathwaite, St. Bees, Lanercost, Seton, and Wetheral. This county besides the city of Carlisle, contains 19 market-towns, 104 parishes, 27,246 houses, and 156,124 inhabitants, and according to the Reform Bill of 1832, returns nine members to Parliament,—two for the city of Carlisle, two for Cockermouth, one for Whitehaven, and four for the county: the Right Hon Sir James Robert George Graham, Bart. of Netherby, and William Blamire, Esq. of Thackwood, are members for the eastern division; Viscount Lowther of Whitehaven Castle, and Edward Stanley, Esq. of Ponsonby Hall, are members for the western. The surface of the county is much diversified; the northern and western parts are generally level, excepting in the course of several rivers, the banks of which are in several places well wooded and very beautiful. The eastern and southern parts of the county are chiefly occupied by mountains, many of which are of considerable height: between these and the level parts are lower ranges of smooth hills, distinguished by the appellation of Fells. A mountainous district forms the eastern boundary, but the summits of the hills are very little broken. The numerous mountains in the south-western part of the county present a great variety of grand and picturesque forms, and are accompanied by lakes of considerable extent. The valleys are highly cultivated, and in many parts well wooded, forming altogether some of the most remarkable and beautiful scenery in the kingdom. The principal mountains are Black Comb, Skiddaw, Saddleback, Bow Fell, Grasmere Fell, Helvellyn Hardknot, Wrynose, High Pike, Pillar, Sca Fell, and the Screes; several of these are very precipitous and rugged. The principal rivers of this county are the Eden and the Derwent; other rivers of note are the Bleng, the Calder, the Caldew, or *Caldbeck*, the Cocker, the Croglin, the Dudden, the Eamont, the Ellen or *Elne*, the Enn, the Esk, the Esk of Allerdale, the Gelt, the Greeta, the Irt, the Irthing, the Kershope, the Kingwater, the Leven or *Line*, the Liddell, the Lowther, the Mite, the Nent, the Petterell, the Sark, the Tees, the Tyne, the Wampool, the Wiza, and the Waver. The principal lakes of the county are Derwent Water, Bassenthwaite, Buttermere, Crumock, Lowerwater, Ennerdale, Wast Water, Thirlmere, and Devock Lake. The chief of the smaller lakes, or Tarns as they are here called, are Burn Moor Tarn, at the head of the Mite; Two Tarns, near Sellafield and Bray; the Stank, near Abbey Holm; Martin Tarn; Over Water; a lake near Anthorn; a lake near Rowcliffe; Wadling Tarn; Talkin Tarn; and Tindale Tarn, near the borders of Northumberland. This county affords a considerable variety of mineral productions, including numerous specimens of copper and lead ores. At the head of Borrowdale is the celebrated mine of wadd or black lead; and the mountainous part produces a great variety of plants, which are of rare occurrence in other parts of the kingdom. The only mineral water is the medicinal spring at Gilsland, celebrated for the cure of cutaneous disorders. The north-western part of the county is the principal corn district; in the north-eastern the turnip and barley system is very prevalent. The north-east, south-east, and southern parts of the county are chiefly appropriated to grazing. Amongst its productions for the use of the table, are cranberries, which grow in great profusion on the moors and are sold at Longtown and other markets, and also sent in barrels to London. The principal manufacturing district is Carlisle, where the cotton manufactory is carried on to a great extent. The Earl of Lonsdale, K.G., is Lord Lieutenant of the County; but his principal seat Lowther Castle is in Westmorland.

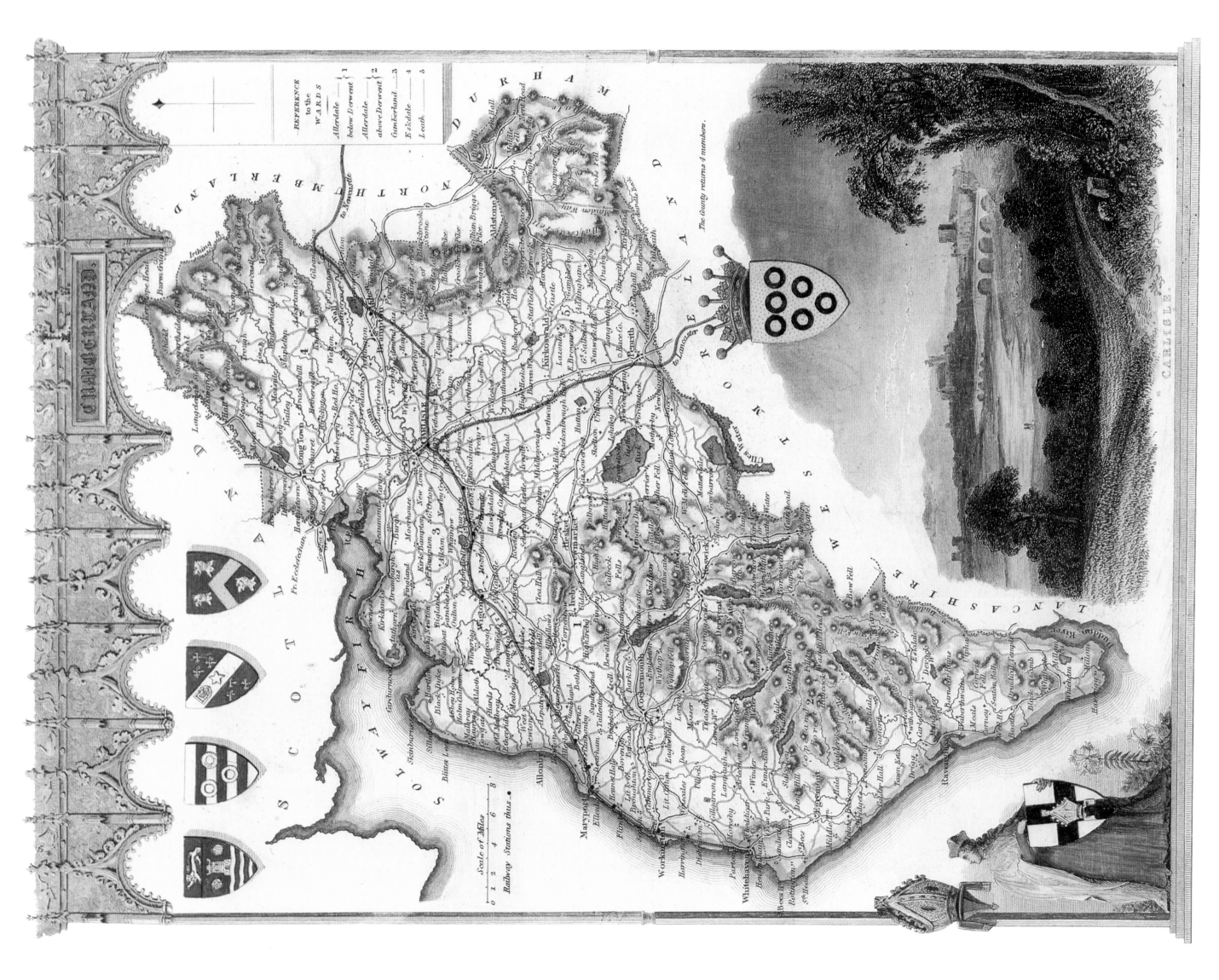

CUMBERLAND

REFERENCE to the WARDS

Allerdale below Derwent ——— 1
Allerdale above Derwent ——— 2
Cumberland ——— 3
Eskdale ——— 4
Leath ——— 5

NORTHUMBERLAND

DURHAM

SCOTLAND

SOLWAY FIRTH

WESTMORELAND

LANCASHIRE

The County returns 4 members.

Scale of Miles

Railway Stations thus ●

CARLISLE.

DERBYSHIRE

This county, situated nearly in the middle of the island, at an equal distance from the east and west seas, is bordered on the north by Yorkshire and part of Cheshire; on the east by Nottinghamshire; on the south by Leicestershire; on the west by Staffordshire and Cheshire. In extent it is about fifty-five miles long, thirty-three miles broad, and two hundred and four miles in circumference. It was included in the Roman province Flavia Cæsariensis, inhabited by Coritani. The Roman stations were Derventio, Little Chester; Ad Trivonam; Berry Farm; Aquæ, Buxton; and Lutudarum, Chesterfield. There are circles of stones at Arbor Low, and Nine Ladies; an earthwork at Staden Low, Cair's work on Hathersage moor. During the Saxon Heptarchy this county formed a part of the kingdom of Mercia. There were formerly abbeys at Beauchief and Dale, and castles at Bolsover, Castleton or Peake, Codnor and Mackworth. Derbyshire contains one county town, eleven market-towns, 116 parishes, 40,054 inhabited houses, and 213,333 inhabitants. It is in the province of Canterbury, and in the diocese of Lichfield and Coventry. This county returns four members to Parliament,—two for Derby; and two for the shire, the present members being Lord G.A.H. Cavendish, and F. Mundy, Esq., of Markeaton Hall. The general appearance of the county is extremely dissimilar, its southern and northern parts exhibiting a striking contrast; the former is not particularly remarkable for hills or valleys, but the latter is eminently distinguished by a long and continued succession of both. From this irregularity of surface, the upper and middle parts of the county are generally denominated the High and Low Peake; the southern part has not received any particular appellation. The mountainous tract of country commencing in the Low Peake, extends northward in one great chain varying in breadth, and at length forms the very elevated tract called the High Peake,—a region of bleak, barren heights, and extended moors, interspersed with deep valleys, through which small streams take their course. The scenery is here in many parts romantic and sublime; but beauty is only resident in the valleys, the high ground being dreary and sterile, serving by way of contrast to heighten the charms of the dales and valleys by which it is intersected. The most considerable eminences in this part of the county are Axe Edge and Kinder Scout; the first is situated near Buxton, and the last rises in the centre of the north-western angle of the county. The Low Peake abounds with eminences of various heights and extent on the eastern side of the county; there is

MATLOCK IN 1790.

also a high ridge of considerable length and extent, beginning on the south of Hardwick, and continuing in another direction to the extremity of the county, where it enters Yorkshire. The seven wonders of the Peake, as they are here denominated, are St. Anne's Well, Poole's Hole, the Ebbing and Flowing Well, Elden Hole, Mam Tor or the shivering mountain, the Peake Cavern, and Chatsworth. The southern part of Derbyshire is in general pleasant and well cultivated; while the mountainous part is distinguished from the rest by the greater quantity of rain which falls in it. The large tract on the eastern side of the county, extending from Stanton, Dale, and Morley to the borders of Yorkshire, abounds with coal, and is covered with a clay of various colours, black, gray, brown and yellow but principally the last; and is in some places mixed with a large proportion of sand. In the valleys near the banks of the larger rivers, the soil is very different from that of the adjacent parts, and has evidently been altered by depositions from inundations. Peat bogs exist in the northern parts of the county, even on the highest mountains; and in some of them, trees have been found nearly perfect. There are many mineral and medicinal waters, and chalybeate springs are numerous. The mineral productions are lead, iron, calamine, and coal; iron-stone, grit-stone, lime-stone, fluor-spar, and gypsum. The rivers are the Amber, Ashop, Barbrook, Burbadge, Crawley, Derwent, Dove, Ecclesburn, Erwash, Ethrow, Goyt, Gunno, Headford, Henmore, Ibber, Idle, Lathkill or Larkill, Martin-brook, Mease, Mersey, Morledge, Noa, Rother,

Schoo, Trent, and the Wye. The Trent enters this county from Staffordshire at a little distance south of Catton, and for several miles forms the south-western boundary of the county; but taking a more easterly direction near Newton Solney, it flows by Twyford and Swarkestone to the confines of Leicestershire; and after continuing its course between the counties for some miles finally quits Derbyshire near Sawlcy. The Derwent rises in the mountainous district of the High Peake, and is soon increased by various small torrents, which flow from the moorlands that inclose its spring. One of these issues directly from the cavern of Castleton, where it bursts into light under a natural arch, after its subterraneous passage, fertilizing the valley of Hope in its way. Another rivulet forms in its descent of Middleton Dale, where piles of rocks rise in successive clusters, so as to imitate the artificial formation of pillars. Soon after it emerges from its native wilds, the Derwent forms the principal ornament of Chatsworth, and has its current afterwards enlarged by the waters of the Wye. Both rivers thus united traverse the delightful vale of Darley, environed by fertility, and encompassed by lofty rocks, which inclose in their romantic scenery the baths of Matlock; whence flowing through several deep valleys, it at length enters the cultivated dale extending to Derby, where suddenly turning to the east it passes to the wide plain enlivened by the Trent, into which it flows on the Leicestershire border near Wiln. The Dove springs from the base of Axe Edge, near the town of Buxton, and proceeding in a south-easterly direction divides this county from Staffordshire; near Ashborne, the Dove receives the Manifold and in the vale of Uttoxeter adorns the grounds of Doveridge; then flowing beneath the walls of Tutbury Castle it falls into the Trent below Burton. This river, in the earlier part of its course, forms the beautifully romantic dell of Dove Dale, winding between almost perpendicular hills, fringed with wood and abounding in bold projecting rocks, which often turn the torrent from its course. The canals are the Ashby-de-la-Zouch, Chesterfield, Cromford, Derby, Erwash, Nutbrook, Peake Forest, and the Trent and Mersey. The manufactures which are carried on in Derbyshire are various and extensive. With Nottinghamshire and Leicestershire it partakes of the manufacture of stockings and lace; with Yorkshire in that of iron and of woollen cloth; and with Lancashire in the manufacture of cotton; and to these may be added silk, and the ornaments of Derbyshire spar. Chatsworth and Hardwick Hall are the seats of the Duke of Devonshire, K.G., Lord Lieutenant of the County.

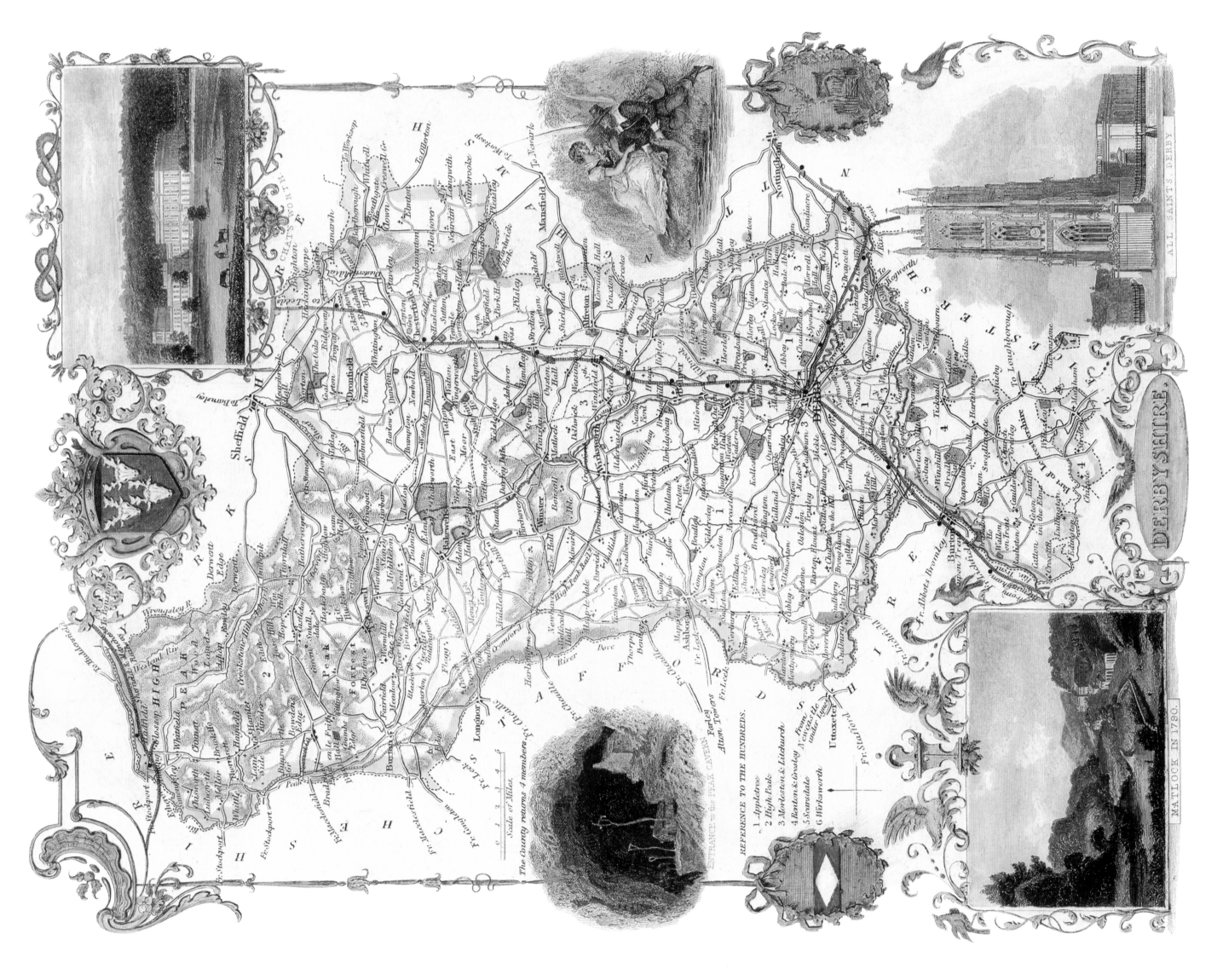

ALL SAINTS DERBY.

DERBYSHIRE.

MATLOCK IN 1780.

ENTRANCE to the PEAK CAVERN.

REFERENCE TO THE HUNDREDS.

1 Appletree
2 High Peak
3 Morleston & Litchurch
4 Renton & Gresley
5 Scarsdale
6 Wirksworth

The county returns 4 members &c.

Scale of Miles.
0 1 2 3 4

DEVONSHIRE

THIS county is bounded on the north by the Bristol Channel, on the east by Somersetshire and a small part of Dorsetshire; on the south it is bounded by the English Channel, and on the west by Cornwall, from which it is almost entirely separated by the River Tamar. Its length from east to west is about sixty-nine miles, its breadth from north to south about sixty four miles, and in circumference it is nearly three-hundred miles. The British inhabitants of this County were the Danmonii; there are several Celtic remains on Dartmoor and in other parts of the county; a few bridges, near the sources of the rivers on the Moor, are supposed to be British: at Drews Teignton is a Cromlech Kistvaen, and circles of Stones, and a Monumental Stone at Yealmton, of great antiquity. By the Romans this County was included in the province named Britannia Prima, and there were Roman Stations at Isca Danmoniorium, Exeter, at Moridunum, Seaton or Honiton, and at Tamare or Tamerton. During the Anglo-Saxon Heptarchy, the county was comprehended in the Kingdom of Wessex, and continued to be so until the incorporation of the whole into one Monarchy, by Egbert. The Castles of its ancient Lords were Rougemont Castle, in Exeter, Oakhampton, Barnstaple, Powderham, Exeter, Dartmouth, Plymton, Plymouth, Totnes, Berry Pomeroy, Kingswear, Tiverton, Compton, Godsborough, Henney, Lydford, Torrington, and the Castle in St. Nicholas Isle. There were Abbeys in this County at Buckland, Buckfastleigh, Dunkeswell, Ford, Frithelstoke, Hartland, Newenham, Tavistock, and Torr; Priories at Barnstaple, Modbury, Plymton, and Totnes : and Nunneries at Legh near Tiverton, and Polleshoo.

Devonshire contains one City, 37 Market Towns, 471 Parishes, 71,489 Houses, and 439,040 Inhabitants. It returns twenty-two Members to Parliament; one for Ashburton, two for Barnstaple, one for Dartmouth, two for Devonport, two for Honiton, two for Plymouth, two for Tavistock, two for Tiverton, two for Totnes, two for the City of Exeter, and four for the County, who at present are the Honorable Hugh Fortescue, Viscount Ebrington, and the Honorable Newton Fellowes, Members for the Northern Division, and the Right Honorable Lord John Russell, and John Crocker Bulteel, Esq. Members for the Southern Division.

A remarkable feature in the surface of this county is an almost constant succession of hills and valleys. The hills generally of a similar height, often steep and precipitous, on the eastern side especially, with their tops rounded and sloping, are cultivated to their very summits, or skirted with woods and coppices. The intervening vallies are generally in a high state of cultivation, and freely diversified by enclosures, meadows, orchards, woods, and water. In other parts of the county, extensive moors and barren wastes, form a striking contrast with scenes of rich fertility and most luxuriant vegetation. The whole is intersected by numerous rivers sometimes falling over precipices, dashing over rocky bottoms, and through deep ravines, or winding quietly through open plains, and expanding into noble estuaries.

Devonshire abounds with picturesque and romantic scenery, as well as with extensive views, and has been denominated, with reference to the mildness of its climate, the Italy of the West. On the eastern extremity of the County, are the Blackdown hills, a continuation of the ridge, which runs through a great part of the kingdom. White Down, between Collumpton and Tiverton, Broad Down and East Down are barren tracts, but between Honiton and Exeter, is one of the richest vales in the kingdom with a constant succession of the finest views. Towards Haldon, a contrast is afforded by the gradual rising of the hills, into commons bordering upon Dartmoor, on which High Tor forms a conspicuous object in the distance. The valley of the Exe, differs widely in appearance, from this mountainous district, but in some parts, has an irregular surface, with considerable elevations, particularly between Tiverton and Exeter, and between the last place and Collumpton. The central and northern parts of the County, preserve the vale character, and the southern is a fine, richly wooded, well cultivated country, generally level, with the exception of the South Hams; this district is popularly termed the Garden of Devonshire, from its fertility. Dartmoor, so named from the Dart, to which it gives rise, as it does to most of the rivers of Devonshire, is the highest ground in the County, and constitutes the south-western part, on the north of the South Hams. The hills between Tiverton and South Molton are dreary, and have no attractions, excepting by contrast with the finer portions of the County, and of a similar character, is the Down between Challacombe and the Bristol Channel. Exmoor in its general features, resembles Dartmoor, and is usually described as belonging to Devonshire, but the whole of the forest itself is in Somersetshire. The valley of the Culme, is more level than any other part of the County and the lowest spot, (according to some writers in the whole island,) is said to be between Chudleigh and Ashburton, near the Coal works of South Bovey.

From the perpetual recurrence of hills in this county, and their steepness, together with the depth and narrowness of the roads, between high fences, all prospect of the country is shut out, excepting on the open tops of the hills, and where there are no enclosures The most remarkable distant views are from Haldon, overlooking the vale of Exe, those of Black Down over the vale of Culme, from Pinhoe, and other heights in that vicinity, overlooking the City of Exeter. From Little Haldon is a view of the Channel, the Exe, and the Teign; on Holcombe Down is a prospect towards the West of Teignmouth with the river; Shaldon Hill and the Ness; the coast from Babbicomhe Bay to Tor Point; the Oar Stone and Lead Stone; over the hills of Torbay, and beyond are the Dartmouth and Brixham Hills. Towards the east is Dawlish, with a most extensive line o' coast.

DEVONSHIRE

REFERENCE to the HUNDREDS

1 Braunton
2 Sherwill
3 South Molton
4 Fremington
5 Shebbear
6 Hartland
7 Black Torrington
8 Winkley with
9 North Tawton
10 Crediton
11 West Budleigh
12 Witheridge
13 Bampton
14 Tiverton
15 Halberton
16 Hemyock

17 Axminster
18 Colyton
19 Ottery St. Mary
20 East Budleigh
21 Cliston
22 Hayridge
23 Lifton
24 Tavistock
25 Roborough
26 Plympton
27 Ermington
28 Stanborough
29 Coleridge
30 Haytor
31 Teignbridge
32 Exminster

33 Wonford

County returns 4 Members

Scale of Miles

0 1 2 4 6 8 10 12 14 16 18 20

Railway Stations, thus •

GUILDHALL, EXETER.

SCVTVM SALVS

FORTE   DVCVM

EXONIENSIS EPISCOPI

PLYMOUTH AND DEVONPORT

PLYMOUTH, at the mouth of the Plym, near its junction with the Ocean, 43 miles S.W. from Exeter and 216 from London, contains 2384 houses and 21,591 inhabitants, including the parishes of St. Andrew and Charles the Martyr; but under the general denomination of Plymouth may be comprised the Borough, Stonehouse, Devonport, Stoke, and Morice town, with the adjoining villages of Oreston, Turnchapel, Catdown and Torpoint, which form together a town inferior to few in the kingdom, for extent and population. Plymouth is situated on a fine bay, opening directly into the English Channel, and maintains by its port a constant communication with the whole world.

The older parts of the town, Briton Side and Treville Street, are narrow, but in Custom House Lane the access to the quay has been much improved from Woolster Street, Brunswick Terrace, Gascoign Place, Tavistock Street, Park Street, Portland Square, Frankfort Street, George Street, St. Andrew's Terrace, and Princes Square are amongst the modern improvements. The Plymouth Leat, a stream conducted from Dartmoor by Sir Francis Drake, supplies the town with water, and in its progress works the mills at Roborough, Widey, and Mill bay. The corporation consists of a mayor, elected by the freeman annually on St. Lambert's Day, 17th September, and as chief magistrate of the Borough, is assisted in his duties by the justice, (the mayor of the preceding year,) a recorder, and two senior aldermen, there is also a chamberlain, three serjeants at mace, and two town corporals; the general quarter sessions are held in the Guildhall, situated at the junction of Whimple Street, Market Street and Broad Street. In the hall is a portrait of King George IV th. when Prince Regent, by *Hoppner*. The arms of the town are: *Argent, a saltier vert, between four castles sable;* the arms surmounted by a coronet of fleur de lis, and having two lions rampant guardant for supporters, and motto Turris fortissima, est Nomen Jehovah. The Exchange was erected in 1813, on the side of the Mitre Chapel in Woolster Street, and is conveniently situated near the Custom House and Quays. A colonnade surrounds an open area, whence a staircase of granite leads to the great room, the chamber of commerce, &c. The port of Plymouth comprehends many harbours, but Sutton Pool and Catwater alone are connected with the town. Sutton Pool is divided at its entrance from Catwater, by two piers projecting from the Barbican and Teats Hill, which were constructed in the years 1791 and 1799. The harbour, with several quays and warehouses, is the property of the Duke of Cornwall, but the dues are leased to the Sutton Pool Company. The Barbican quay and others belong to the Corporation of Plymouth, and some are private property. The Custom-House, erected in 1820, fronts the parade, or Coal Quay; it was built from designs by *D. Laing*. Catwater is situated at the mouth of the Plym, and forms an excellent road for the large class of merchant ships, being defended from the south-westerly gales by Mount Batten. Its security has been greatly increased since the construction of the Breakwater. The property of this harbour is claimed by the Corporation of Plymouth, and the jurisdiction of their coroner is bounded by an imaginary line drawn from the Bear's Head at Catdown to the Fishes' Nose at the Victualling Office point. The corporation of Saltash is entitled to certain dues, and the lord of the manor of Plymton claims the right of fishing in the northern parts of the harbour. A market place, erected in 1804, occupies not less than three acres in extent, into which open three gates, from East Street, Cornwall Street, and Drake Street; the cattle market is on the eastern side, within the walls are the butchery, fish market, butter market, green market, and corn market: the days on which the market is held, are Monday, Thursday, and Saturday in every week. A spring fair in April has been revived, but the fair called the Great Market, in November, is most resorted to, it originally continued only three days, but the time has been extended to a week. The principal manufactories in the town are of soap, sailcloth, twine, and thread, there is also a manufactory of earthenware at Coxside, and a considerable iron foundry in George's Lane.

On the Hoe, or *Haw*, a hill which extends from Catwater to Mill bay, is a public promenade, commanding a prospect of an extensive range of marine and land scenery, looking sea ward the whole Sound and the distant channel open to the view; midway the dark line of the Breakwater presents itself, stretching across the sound between the Mew Stone and Penlee Point. Nearer on the eastern side are the mouth of the Catwater and Mount Batten; on the west, St. Nicholas's Island and the entrance to Hamoaze, having on the one side Staddon Heights, rugged and barren, and on the other Mount Edgecumbe, crowned with groves. The land view presents the town of Plymouth with the groves of Tothill, the river Lary, Saltram woods, Newenham Park, Hemerdon, and the Tors of Dartmoor in the distance. From the West Hoe is a view of Mill Bay and the Marine Barracks, the Naval and Military Hospitals, Stoke, the town of Devonport, Hamoaze, and the Cornish hills bound the prospect. The Citadel, from its elevated situation at the eastern extremity of the Hoe, is a protection to both the town and harbour. On the lower part and on the parapets above, several pieces of cannon are mounted, which are fired on all occasions of public rejoicing. The entrance to the citadel from the town is through two gates, with drawbridges, &c., that which opens immediately upon the citadel is enriched with the royal arms and other sculptured devices. The citadel was built in the reign of Charles II., and has been kept in repair as a military station; the ramparts, nearly three quarters of a mile in circuit, command in every direction, extensive and beautiful views. The Victualling Office is situated below the eastern rampart of the citadel, and extends from the pier at Sutton Pool to the mouth of the Catwater Harbour. The entrance from the town is on Lambhay Hill, and near this point are the agents' offices, &c.; on the western side are capacious granaries and cellars, store-houses and biscuit lofts. There are two bake-houses, where biscuit for the navy is baked. A succession of quays forms the eastern boundary of the Victualling Office, and its southern extremity terminates in a pier. The slaughter houses connected with this department, are on the Devil's point, and the brewery and cooperage on the western shores of Hamoaze.

The Borough of Plymouth returns two members to parliament, who at present are Thomas Bewes, Esq. of Beaumont, and John Collier, Esq. Plymouth contains the parishes of St. Andrew and Charles the Martyr, the latter parish having been formed in the reign of Charles I. St. Andrew is a vicarage, value 12*l*. 15*s*. 5*d*., in the patronage of the mayor and burgesses of the town. The church is large and ancient, having a tower erected in 1440; the following are the principal monuments within its walls; in memory of Sir John Skelton, governor of the citadel, ob. 1672; rev. John Samuel Northcote, the father of the Painter, ob. 1791; John Mudge, M.D., ob. 1793; of Mrs. Rosdew of Beechwood, the daughter of Dr. Mudge; and a cenotaph by Chantry, to William Woolacombe, M.D. ob.1822. Charles the Martyr is a vicarage, value 12*l*. 15*s*. 5*d*., in the patronage of the Corporation; the church was erected in 1658. St. Andrew's Chapel was built in 1828. The Royal Hotel and Theatre, erected in 1811, is 275 feet in extent upon its northern front, in the centre of which is a portico of the Ionic order. It was raised by the exertions of Edmund Lockyer, esq., and built from the designs of *John Foulston*. A Public Library in Cornwall Street, near the entrance to the market, was built in the same year from designs by the same architect. The Royal Union Baths, on the sound side of Union Street, were designed by *Roger Hopkins*, and were founded in 1828. The Athenæum adjoining the theatre, was erected in 1818, from designs by *Foulston,* and Freemasons Hall in Cornwall Street, founded in 1827, was designed by *J.E. Adams.* A road over Plymouth March, opened in 1815, leads to Stonehouse and Devonport, on the western side of the town.

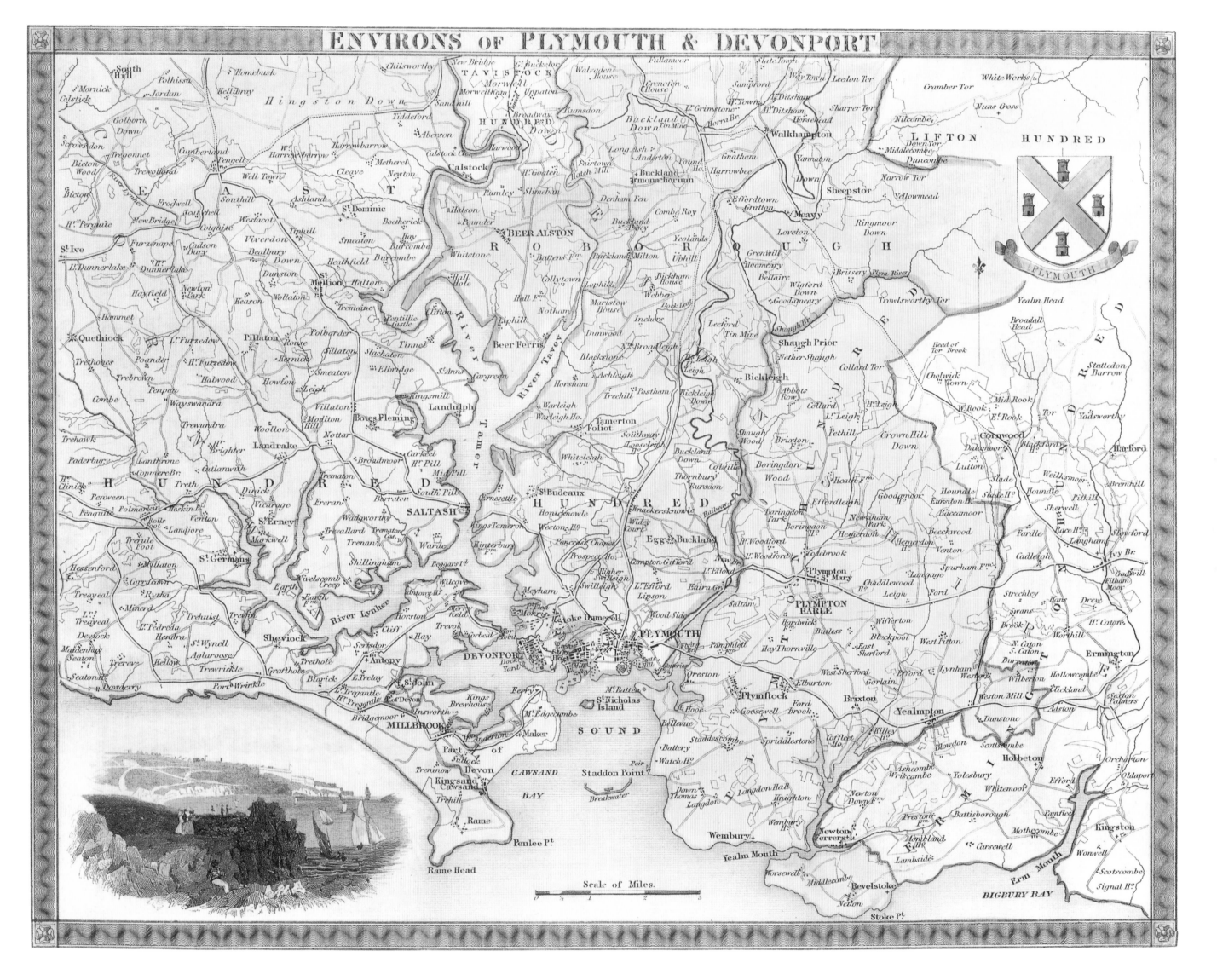

ENVIRONS OF PLYMOUTH & DEVONPORT

PLYMOUTH

Scale of Miles.

PLYMOUTH

DORSETSHIRE

THIS county is bounded on the north by Somersetshire and Wiltshire, on the east by Hampshire, on the south by the English Channel, and on the west by Devonshire. Its extent from east to west is about fifty-five miles, and from north to south, thirty-five miles, and it is in circumference about one hundred and sixty miles. Before the arrival of the Romans, Dorsetshire was inhabited by the Durotriges, or Morini, names which import the dwellers on the sea shore. On the division of the island into Roman provinces, it became part of Britannia Prima; and on the establishment of the Saxons, was included in the Kingdom of Wessex, to which it continued attached till the union of the states under Egbert. The county was then styled Dorsetta, and many of the Anglo-Saxon kings appear to have lived here; Kingston Hall and Corfe Castle are pointed out as their residences. The principal British antiquities in Dorsetshire are the Agglestone near Studland, Portisham Cromlech, Winterbourne and Pokeswell circles of stones, Badbury Rings, and Maumbury. The Roman stations appear to have been Londinis, Lyme Regis; Canca Arixa, Charmouth; Durnovaria, Dorchester; Vindo Gladia, Wimborne; Clavinio, Weymouth; Morinio, Wareham; and Bolclaunio, Poole. The Icening Way enters this county near Woodyates, and takes a course to Seaton in Devonshire: there are several smaller Roman ways proceeding from Dorchester, Wimborne, and other places in the county.

The fine downs which extend in an easterly and westerly direction, from the extremity of the Isle of Purbeck to Abbotsbury, are in many parts thickly covered with tumuli, more especially in the space between the villages of Preston and Upway. In the midst of these barrows may be traced the foundations of buildings, particularly on the hill above Pokeswell, on Charlbury, between Bindon and Preston, on Bindon Down, and on Blackdon, in the parish of Long Bredy. This last forms the highest point of land in the chain, and unlike the rest, is covered with heath instead of a fine turf. These buildings, of which the foundations only remain, are supposed, from their very elevated situations, not only to have served the purposes of defence, but to have been used as watch towers, with means of communication, by signal, with the great Roman stations of Maiden Castle, Woodbury Hill, and Eggerdon Hill. Stilicho, who was lieutenant in Britain, under the Emperor Honorius, is supposed to have been the founder of this line of defence on the southern coast, according to an original communication to the Gentleman's Magazine for Nov. 1822.

The castles of the ancient lords of Dorsetshire, were at Brownsea; Castleton, near Sherbourne; Chedric, near Blandlord; Chidiock; Corfe Castle; Lullworth; Newton, near Sturminster; Pillesdon; Portland; Sherbourn; and Weymouth. There were formerly abbeys in the county, at Abbotsbury, Bindon, Cerne, Cranbourn, Horton, Milton, Shaftesbury, and Sherbourn: priories at Bridport, Dorchester, Frampton, Loders, Spetbury, and Wareham: and a nunnery at Tarent.

Dorsetshire contains twenty-two market towns, two hundred and forty-eight parishes, 25,926 houses, and 144,499 inhabitants. It returns fourteen members to parliament, two for Bridport, two for Dorchester, one for Lyme Regis, two for Poole, one for Shaftesbury, one for Wareham, two for Weymouth and Melcombe Regis, and three for the county, who at present are the Hon. Anthony Ashley Cooper Lord Ashley, the Hon. William Francis Spencer Ponaonby, and William John Bankes, Esq.

The form of this county is every where irregular: its long northern side has a considerable angular projection in the middle: the sea shore on the south runs out into numerous points and headlands, till it stretches to the Isle of Portland; thence, westward, the coast is not so deeply indented, but inclines obliquely towards Devonshire. The county, in its general appearance is uneven, and in many parts is very hilly; its most striking features are the open and unenclosed parts, covered with numerous flocks of sheep, which feed on the verdant produce of the downs.

In the natural division of this county, the greater proportion of the land is appropriated to pasture: great numbers of sheep and oxen are fed in the vale of Blackmore, which is distinguished for its rich pasture, and extends from north to south, about nineteen miles, and from east to west, about fourteen miles: here are also some orchards, which produce excellent cyder. The greatest extent of waste land is on the south-eastern side of the county, from below Beer Regis, southward towards Lullworth and the sea, extending beyond Corfe Castle to the Hampshire border. The growth of flax and hemp, and particularly the former, is of great agricultural importance, especially about Bridport, the village of Bradpole, and towards Beminster, where it is chiefly grown: the best seed is annually imported from Riga; the inferior seed, not good enough to be sown, is valuable from its oily quality. It is first bruised in a mill, and then put into hair cloths, and afterwards pressed, when it produces oil used by painters; when all the oil is extracted, the husk is formed into oil cakes, and used for feeding cattle.

The fish obtained on the coast of Dorsetshire, are of various descriptions, but the mackerel fishery is the most considerable; vast quantities are taken near Abbotsbury, and along the shore from Portland to Bridport.

The chief products of Dorsetshire, are corn, cattle, butter, sheep, wool, timber, flax, and hemp. Barley affords great produce, and a large portion of malt is made for the internal consumption of the county. The strong beer of Dorsetshire is famous, and the ale is also particularly celebrated, and is in some respects unequalled. A principal manufacture of the county is flax and hemp. At Shaftesbury and Blandford are manufactories of shirt buttons. Flannels, spinning silk, and worsted stockings are also made in the county.

DORSETSHIRE.

DORCHESTER

DEO NON FORTUNA

SEAL OF THE ABBEY OF ABBOTSBURY

SEAL OF St EDWARD'S ABBEY SHAFTESBURY

SHAFTESBURY.

Scale of Miles
0 2 4 6 8 10

WILTSHIRE

SOMERSETSHIRE

DEVONSHIRE

HAMPSHIRE

ENGLISH CHANNEL

SHAFTESBURY

MELBORNE PORT

Sherborne

Yeovil

Crewkerne

Chard

Axminster

LYME REGIS

BRIDPORT

DORCHESTER

WEYMOUTH

MELCOMBE REGIS

Portland Bill

Bere Regis

WAREHAM

POOLE

Poole Harbour

WIMBORNE MINSTER

Cranborne

CORFE CASTLE

Swanage

St Albans Hd

Durlston Hd

DURHAM

This county is bounded on the north by Northumberland; on the east by the German Ocean; on the south by Yorkshire; and on the west by Cumberland and Westmorland. Its greatest length from east to west is forty-five miles; its breadth thirty-six miles, and in circumference it is about one hundred and seventy-eight miles. Durham was included in the country of the Brigantes, the most populous of the whole province, according to Tacitus; and on the conquest of Britain by Romans was included in the division named Maxima Caesariensis. In the time of the Anglo-Saxons it became part of kingdom of Northumberland, with which it remained connected till the union of the states under Egbert. This county termed the Bishopric, from the power which the Bishop of Durham formerly possessed. It is a county Palatine, and derived many advantages from a grant made to St. Cuthbert the Apostle of the North, by Egfrid King of Northumberland in the year 685, of all the land between the rivers Wear and Tyne, to hold in as full and ample manner as the King held the same. The county of Durham arose gradually out of Northumberland, together with the increasing patrimony the church, and besides, the main body of the county lying betwixt Tyne, Tees and Darwent, includes several scattered members of that patrimony, viz., Norhamshire and Islandshire including Holy Island and the Farne Isles, and a portion of the main land extending from the Tweed north and north-west, to the sea on the east, and separated from Northumberland on the south partly by the course of the Till, and partly by an imaginary line; – Bedlingtonshire, lying in the heart of Northumberland betwixt the rivers Blyth and Wansbeck; these are usually termed the North Bishopric;– and the insulated territory of Crake in the wapentake of Bulmer in Yorkshire. On the western side of the county a wild and irregular line of demarcation is indicated only by crosses and other boundary stones; it commences at Blanchland on Bolden Beck, and passing northward of Boltslaw, by Sheriffstone, Shorngate Cross and Stoggle Cleugh Head, to Kilhope Law, and hence runs by Kilhope Cross, Short's Cross and Headstones, to the head of Tees, which rising in Yade Moss, here forms the boundary of the county on the western side of Harwood Common.

The Roman stations of most note in this county were Vindamora, Ebchester; Vinovia, Binchester; Glanoventa, Lanchester; Gabrocentum, Gateshead; Ad Tinam, South Shields; Magae, Presbridge; Maiden Castle, near Durham; and on the banks of the Tees is an intrenchment. The castles of the early lords were at Brancepeth, Raby, Durham; Lumley, Witton, Staindrop, Hilton, Eden, Barnard Castle, Evermond Ravensworth, Dalden Tower, &c.; besides the ancient manorial houses of the Bishops usually termed castles at Auckland, Middleham, and Stockton. There were Benedictine monasteries at Monk Wearmouth, Finchall and Jarrow; and collegiate churches at Auckland, Chester, Darlington, Lanchester, Norton, and Staindrop; and hospitals at Gateshead and Shehburn. This county, besides the city of Durham, includes ancient boroughs,– Hartlepool, Barnard Castle, Auckland, Darlington, Sunderland, Stockton and Gateshead, and four other market towns, 120 parishes, 32,793 houses and 207,678 inhabitants; and according to the Reform Bill of 1832, returns ten members to Parliament: two for the city of Durham, one for Gateshead, one for South Shields, two for Sunderland and four for the county. Henry Lambton, Esq., and Sir Hedworth Williamson, Bart., of Whitburn, are members the northern division, including Chester and Easington Wards; Joseph Pease, Jun. and John Bowes Esq. are members for the southern division including Darlington and Stockton Wards.

The general aspect of the eastern coast of Durham is bare and dreary, and the soil, excepting where improved by culture, generally a cold harsh clay, intersected by chains of limestone, whose monotonous forms, destitute of wood, and ploughed to their summits, exclude the romantic grandeur of a mountainous region, and the softer features of the grazing district. There are beauties which the observing eye will not fail to discover; betwixt the swells of the country lie numerous dales, or denes, almost entirely concealed from the higher grounds. Every brook which falls to the sea has banks adorned with a profusion of wild and varying scenery: the vales commencing imperceptibly together with the course of the streamlets, sometimes contract themselves into narrow glens, sometimes open into irregular amphitheatres of rock, covered with ash or hazel, or deepen into ravines resembling the bed of a rapid river, terminating on the coast either in wide sandy bays or in narrow outlets, where the stream winds its way under crags of the wildest appearance. The western side of the county is crossed by a ridge of hills, termed the English Apennines. Tees dale here presents a long and winding strip of fertility, surrounded by one of the wildest districts in the kingdom.

This valley is more than thirty miles in length from the source of the river to Barnard Castle at its eastern extremity; and here the principal lead mines of the county are situated. Wear dale is also a wild and romantic district, and Tyne dale, on the northern border, may vie with either in natural beauty, while it is greatly superior in its cultivation. The central parts of the county include some beautiful and fertile valleys, and are pleasantly varied with hill and dale, alternately appropriated to the growth of corn and of pasturage. The principal eminences in the county are Beacon, Billy, Bail, and Brandon Hills; Teesdale Forest hills, Cock Fell and Gateshead Fell, Bolt Law, Butterby Hill south from Durham, and Merrington church. The natural curiosities are High Force and Cauldron Snout, falls on the river Tees, Marston and Black Halls rocks, Hell Kettles cavities in the earth at Oxen hall, and Hartlepool Promontory. The rivers of Durham are the East Allow, the Aurish, the Bolder, the Burdop the Cockburn, the Darwent, the Done, the Gaunless, the Hude, the Kellop, the Langdon, the Lune, the Skern, the Team, the Tees, the Till, the Tweed, the Tyne, and the Wear. The Wear crosses the central part of the county, passes Bishops Auckland, the city of Durham and Lumley Castle and falls into the sea at Sunderland. The Derwent rises northward of the Wear, in the same range of moors which border on Northumberland, and falls into the Tyne near Swalwell. The Tyne forms the northern boundary of the county from its mouth till it receives the Stanley Burn on the east of Prudhoe Castle; and the Tees, rising on the borders of Westmorland, forms the southern boundary, till it falls into the ocean below Stockton. The Hartlepool canal is the principal inland navigation. The manufactures of this county are numerous and important: the southern side of the river Tyne abounds with manufactories and coal staiths. At Swalwell and Winlaton are large iron works; and at Lumley is a manufactory for converting cast metal into malleable iron. Steel works are established at Shotley Bridge, Swalwell and Gateshead. Carpets are manufactured at Durham; and at Darlington is a machine for spinning flax into yarn. There are cotton works at Castle Eden, Stockton, and Bishops Auckland; and sail cloths made at Stockton, Sunderland and South Shields. Raby Castle is the seat of the Duke of Cleveland, Lord Lieutenant of County; and Bishop Auckland, of the Bishop of Durham, *ex officio* Custos Rotulorum of the county.

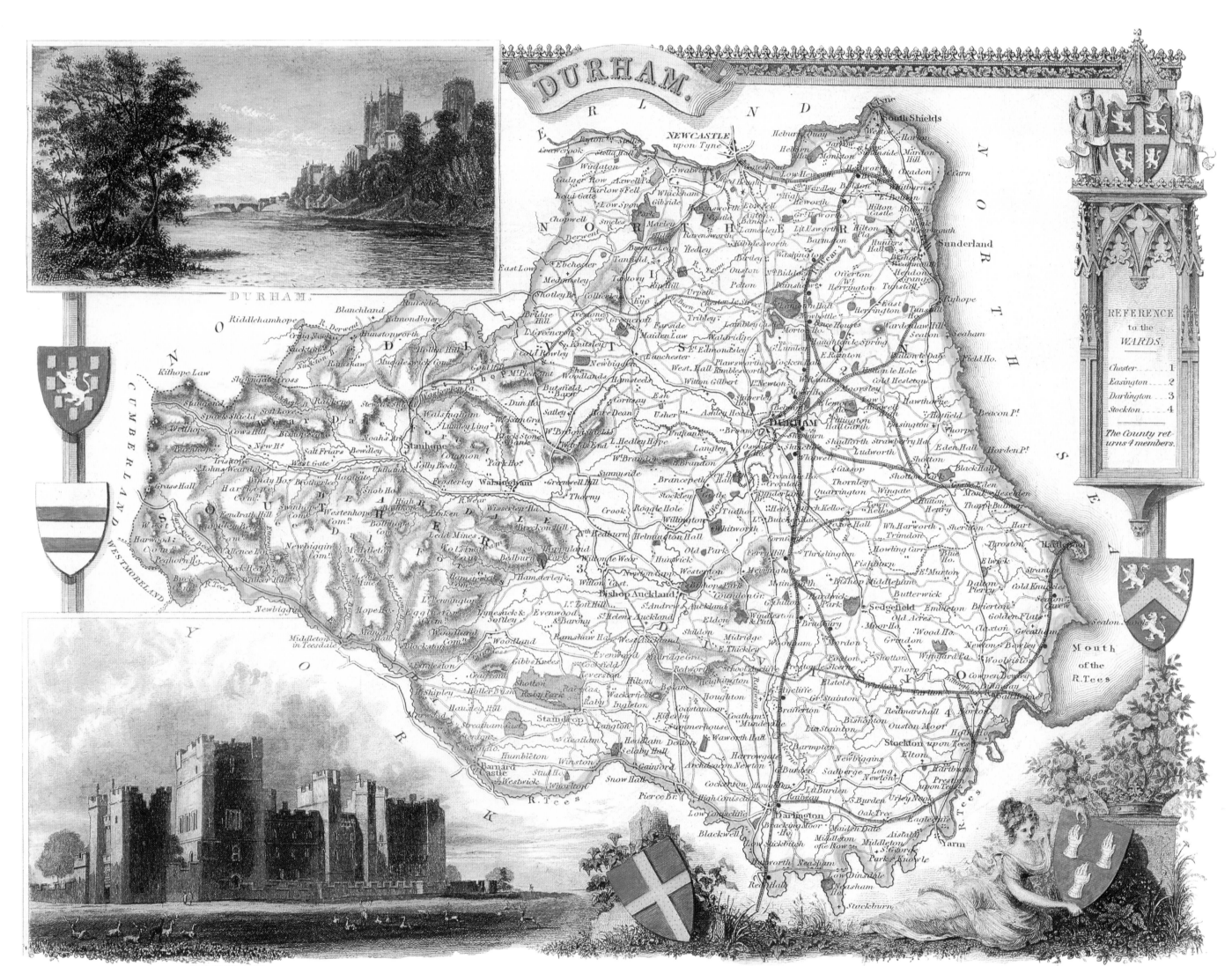

DURHAM.

REFERENCE
to the
WARDS.

Chester 1
Easington 2
Darlington 3
Stockton 4

The County returns 4 members.

DURHAM.

RABY CASTLE.

ESSEX

THIS county is bounded on the north by Cambridgeshire and Suffolk; on the east by the German Ocean; on the south by the river Thames; and on the west by Middlesex and Hertfordshire. The length from east to west is about sixty miles, the breadth from north to south fifty, and its circumference about two hundred and twenty-six miles. The British inhabitants were called by the Romans Trinobantes, a name indicative of the situation of the country on the border of broad waters. The county formed part of the Roman province Flavia Cæsariensis, and five principal stations were situated within its boundary :—Durolitum, Leyton; Cæsaromagus, Dunmow; Canonium, Canudon; Camelodunum, Colchester; and Ad Ansam, Knights Tolles-hunt. Essex formed during the Saxon Heptarchy the separate kingdom of East Seaxa, and the county now contains twenty-four market-towns, four hundred and three parishes, 49,978 inhabited houses, and 289,424 inhabitants. It is in the province of Canterbury, and diocese of London. There were formerly abbeys at Bileigh, Barking, Chiche St. Osyth, Coggeshall, Colchester, Saffron Walden, Tiltey, Waltham, and Stratford Langthorne or West Ham: also priories at Berdon, Bicknacre, Blackmore, Dunmow, Earls Colne, Hatfield, Hockesley, Latton, Lees, Malden, Panfield, Prittlewell, Tackley, Thoby, and Tiptree. The castles of the early lords were at Hadleigh, Colchester, Hedingham, Stansted, Montfitchet, Ongar, Pleshey, and Walden. The forests of Epping and Hainault still retain the name, and supply a number of deer.

Essex is part of a tract of the eastern side of the kingdom, considered the largest connected space of level ground in the whole island, but the surface is not altogether flat. Towards the north-west, where most of the rivers rise, it presents a continued inequality of surface. The most level parts are the southern and eastern hundreds, which lie under a proverbial imputation of being unhealthy. The sea-coast is broken into inlets and peninsulas deeply cut in by arms of the sea. Extensive salt marshes border most of the coast, the greater part of which is protected by embankments. The farms in these parts are very large and productive, being manured with chalk brought by sea from Kent. The northern part of the coast between the Stour and the Colne is more elevated, and the middle is in general a fine corn country, varied with gentle inequalities of surface, and studded with woods. Although not highly celebrated for its dairies, those of Epping and its vicinity are famous for the richness of their cream and butter. More calves are fattened here than in any other county. Fish are extremely plentiful on the coast, and in the various creeks; some of the last, near Colchester and the Mersey island, are celebrated for remarkably fine oyster-beds. The most considerable rivers of this county are the Colne, the Blackwater, the Chelmer, the Crouch, the Ingrebourn, the Roding, and the Cam: others of less importance are the Lea, Stort, and Stour. The river Colne rises near Ridgewell, on the northern side of the county, and after passing Castle Hedingham, Halstead, and Colchester, expands into

a wide estuary, where it is navigable to the sea. The Blackwater, called also the Pont, has its source on the borders of Cambridgeshire, passes Bocking and Coggeshall, and near Witham receives another stream. It unites with the Chelmer below Malden, and then forms an extensive estuary. The river Chelmer springs near Thaxted, and passing near Dunmow, at Chelmsford receives other streams; it then flows through a pleasant valley, and joins the Blackwater near Malden. The Crouch and Ingrebourn are small rivers rising in the southern part of the county, and pass through a short course to the Thames. The Roding, another small stream, has a circuitous course, visiting Ongar, and several villages in its progress to Wanstead, Ilford, and Barking, and is navigable from Ilford Bridge. The Cam takes a different direction from the other rivers; rising from three springs near Newport, it passes Audley End Chesterton, &c., and pursues a northern course to Cambridgeshire. The Lea and Stort constitute the western boundary of the county, separating it from Middlesex and Hertfordshire, and the Stour divides it from the county of Suffolk in the north. Essex returns eight members to Parliament; viz. two for Colchester, two for Harwich, two for Maldon, and two for the county — who at present are Charles Callis Western, Esq., and the Hon. W.P.T. Long Wellesley, Esq. Easton Lodge, near Dunmow is the seat of Viscount Maynard, Lord Lieutenant of the County.

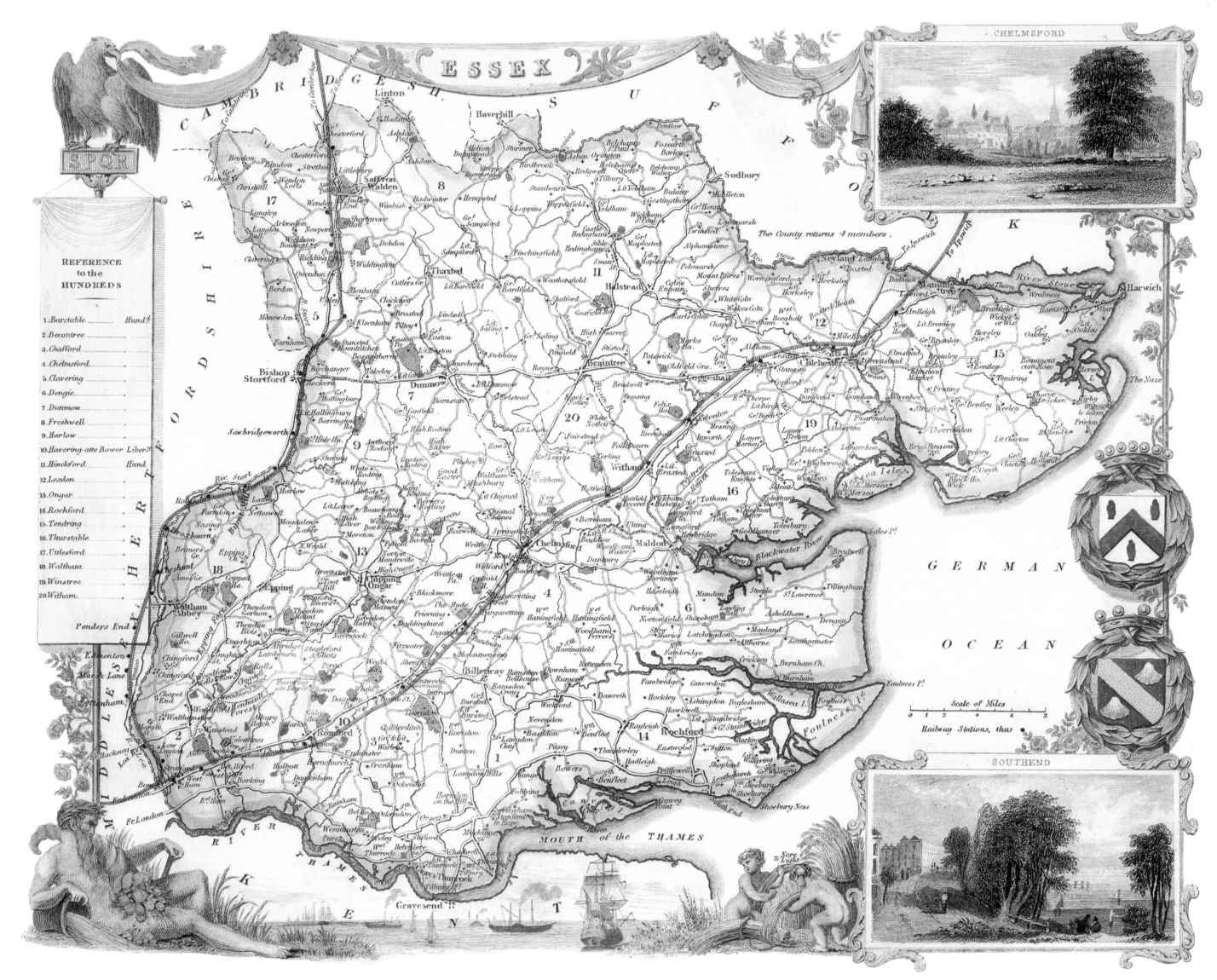

ESSEX

CHELMSFORD

SOUTHEND

REFERENCE to the HUNDREDS

1. Barstable _____ Hundred
2. Becontree _____
3. Chafford _____
4. Chelmsford _____
5. Clavering _____
6. Dengie _____
7. Dunmow _____
8. Freshwell _____
9. Harlow _____
10. Havering-atte Bower Liberty
11. Hinckford _____ Hundred
12. Lexden _____
13. Ongar _____
14. Rochford _____
15. Tendring _____
16. Thurstable _____
17. Uttlesford _____
18. Waltham _____
19. Winstree _____
20. Witham _____

The County returns 4 members.

Scale of Miles

Railway Stations, thus

CAMBRIDGESH. SUFFOLK

HERTFORDSHIRE

MIDDLESEX

GERMAN OCEAN

MOUTH of the THAMES

KENT

GLOUCESTERSHIRE

This county is bounded on the west by Monmouthshire and Herefordshire; on the north by Worcestershire and Warwickshire; on the east by Oxfordshire and a small part of Berkshire, and on the south by Wiltshire and Somersetshire. It extends in length from Clifford Chambers in the north-east to Clifton in a south-western direction, about seventy miles; in breadth from Leachlade south-east to Preston north-west about forty miles; and in circumference is about one hundred and sixty miles. It was included in the Roman province Flavia Cæsariensis, inhabited by the Dobuni, and received the present name of Gloucestershire from the Anglo Saxons. At Woodchester and Cirencester considerable Roman remains have been discovered, and there are encampments at Norbury and Sodbury. The county contains two cities, Bristol and Gloucester, and had formerly four mitred abbeys, at Gloucester, Tewksbury, Winchcombe, and Cirencester. It is in the province of Canterbury and diocese of Gloucester, excepting the city of Bristol, which is in its own diocese, and two chapelries in that of Worcester. There are in this county 26 market towns and 280 parishes; containing at the last census 60,881 houses, and 335,843 inhabitants. It returns ten members to Parliament; viz. two for the county, the Right Hon. Lord Robert Edward Henry Somerset. K.T.S., and Sir Berkeley William Guise, Bart.; two for Gloucester city, two for Bristol, two for Cirencester, and two for Tewksbury. The general aspect of the county is greatly diversified, by a natural division into hill, vale, and forest. The hill district, comprehending the Cotswold and Stroudwater Hills, may be regarded as a continuation of the central chain proceeding from Derbyshire, through this county towards Wiltshire and the Land's End. The extent of the Cotswold Hills from Broadway to Tetbury is thirty miles; the climate considering the natural elevation of the land, is unusually mild: the sides of the hills abound with springs, and almost every dip has its rill and every valley its brook. The downs, which formerly lay open, are now with few exceptions converted into arable inclosed fields, with roads forming an easy communication between the villages: here the

crops of grain and the breed of sheep have long been famous. The Stroudwater Hills partake both of the Cotswold and Vale character; the soil on the hills is principally adapted to the cultivation of turnips and barley: the woodlands are chiefly beech and here is the chief seat of the woollen manufacture. The Vale district includes the entire tract bounded by the Cotswold Hills and the river Severn on the west, and is subdivided into the vales of Evesham, Gloucester and Berkeley. The Vale of Evesham, highly famed for its fertility and beauty, and comprehending a portion of Worcestershire, extends south to Campden and Moreton, and following the

course of the river Avon east to Stratford in Warwickshire, in its climate, produce, &c. may be considered as a continuation of the Vale of Gloucester. The latter is in extent from north to south about fifteen miles, and about eight miles from east to west; the land is appropriated to arable, meadow and pasture. Cattle purchased in the neighbouring counties are here fattened for the London markets; the dairies are not large but the cheese and butter are of a very superior quality. The Vale of Berkeley extends from Aust Cliff to the foot of Matson Hill about twenty-five miles, but is in width not more than four miles; the soil is principally appropriated to grass, and the dairies produce cheese of the best quality. The Forest district, separated from the rest of the county by the river Severn, comprehends the Forest of Dean, the soil of which is peculiarly favourable to the growth of the styre apple; its principal minerals are iron and coal. The rivers of Gloucestershire are the Upper, Lower and Little Avon, the Badgworth, the Carron, the Chilt, the Churn, the Colne, the Evenlode, the Frome, the Isborne, the Leach, the Leden, the Severn, the Stour, the Stroud, the Swilly, the Thames, the Windrush, and the Wye. The navigation is composed of the Thames and Severn canal, the Hereford and Gloucester canal, the Thames, the Stroudwater navigation, and the Gloucester and Berkeley canals. The staple commodities of this county are its woollen cloth and its cheese: at Stroud, Dursley, Wotton-under-Edge, Painswick Minchinhampton, &c. cloths are made for the army and the Turkey and India trade. The cheese has been considered the best in the kingdom, excepting the Cheshire; but the cloth of this county has been successfully rivalled; in Yorkshire, and its cheese in North Wiltshire. The forests of Dean and Kingswood abound in mines of iron and coal. The Cotswold games were of great celebrity in the reigns of James and Charles I., and have been commemorated by Ben Jonson, Drayton, and other poets of that age, collected and published under the title of "Annalia Dubrensia" in 1636.

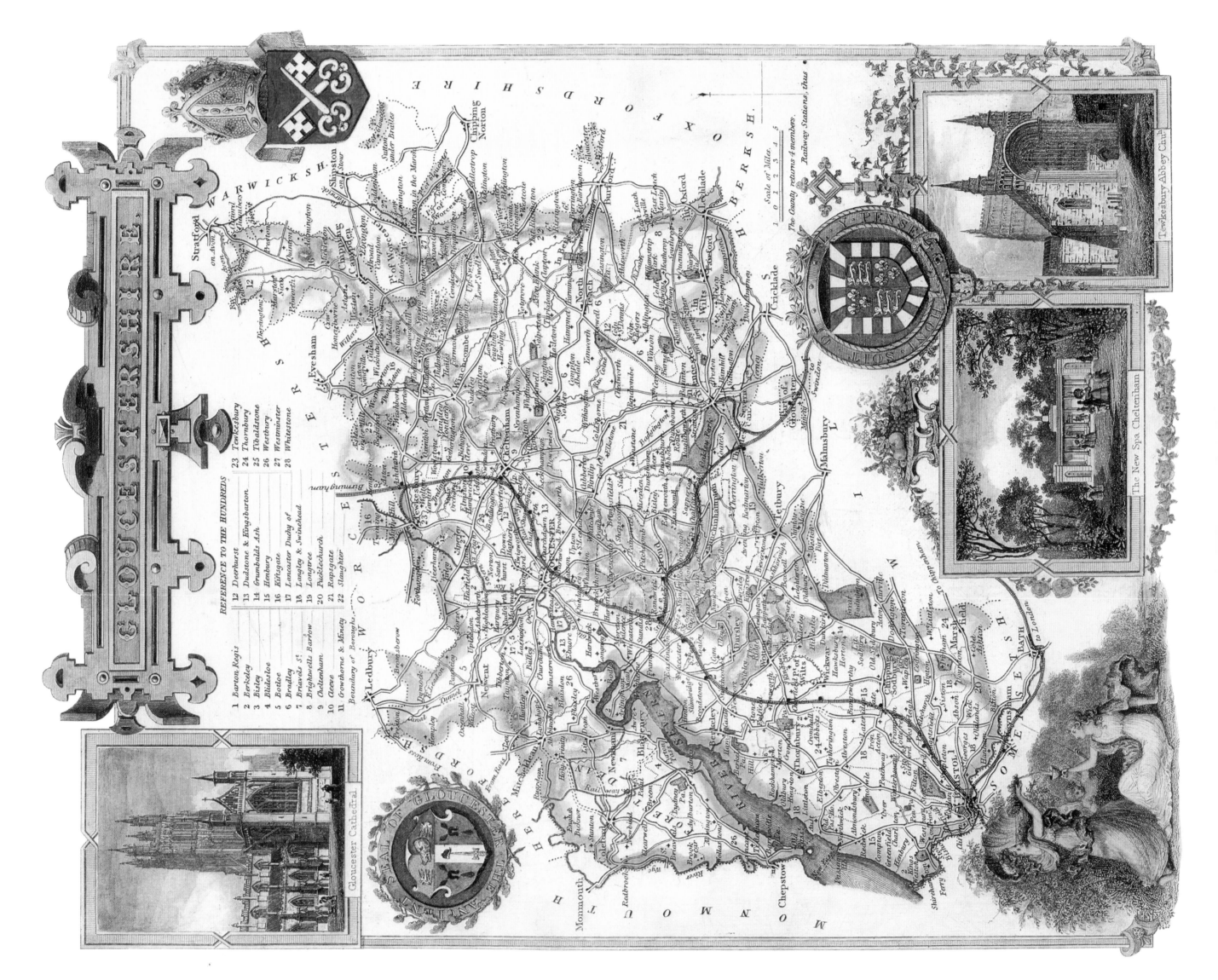

GLOUCESTERSHIRE

REFERENCE TO THE HUNDREDS

1 Barton Regis
2 Berkeley
3 Bisley
4 Bledisloe
5 Botloe
6 Bradley
7 Briavels St.
8 Brightwell Barrow
9 Cheltenham
10 Cleeve
11 Crowthorne & Minety

12 Deerhurst
13 Dudstone & Kingsbarton
14 Grumbalds Ash
15 Henbury
16 Kiftsgate
17 Lancaster Duchy of
18 Langley & Swinehead
19 Longtree
20 Pucklechurch
21 Rapsgate
22 Slaughter

23 Tewkesbury
24 Thornbury
25 Tibaldstone
26 Henbury
27 Westminster
28 Whitestone

—— Boundary of Boroughs

Tewkesbury Abbey Church

The New Spa Cheltenham

Gloucester Cathedral

SEAL OF GLOUCESTER THE CAPITAL

WARWICKSH.

OXFORDSHIRE

BERKSH.

WORCESTER

HEREFORDSHIRE

MONMOUTH

SOMERSETSH.

BATH

Scale of Miles.

The County returns 4 members.

Railway Stations, thus

HAMPSHIRE

THE County of Southampton is bounded on the north by Berkshire, on the east by Surrey and Sussex, on the south by the English Channel, and on the west by Wiltshire and Dorsetshire. It extends from north to south about 55 miles, and from east to west about 40 miles; in circumference it is about 150 miles. Anterior to the Roman invasion, this county belonged to the Regni, a tribe of ancient Britons, and the Belgæ, who emigrated from Germany and settled here: they are said to have been the first of the inhabitants who submitted to the Romans; when the district was included in the province of Britannia Prima, the Segontiaci inhabited the northern extremity of the county, and the adjoining part of Berkshire bordering on the river Kennet. Under the Anglo-Saxon government, this county formed the central portion of the kingdom of Wessex, when its original name of Gwent or Y went, descriptive of its open downs, was changed to Hanternscyre, whence comes its present name of Hants or Hampshire. The Roman stations in this county were, Venta Belgarum, Winchester; Vindonum, Silchester; Clausentum, Bittern; Brigæ, Broughton; and Andaoreon, Andover. The Isle of Wight was called Vectis: There are ancient

encampments at St. Katherine's hill, near Winchester; King's Clere; Bere hill, near Andover; Danbury hill, eastward of Quarley hill; Bere hill, near Edgebury; Quarley hill, near Stockbridge; Gads hill, near Fordingbridge; Dunbal, near Stockbridge; Norbury, near Winchester; near Broughton; Dunwood, near Rumsey; Tuckbury, near Redbridge; near Lyndhurst; Egbury, near Whitchurch; Barksbury, near Andover; and a Roman amphitheatre at Silchester. The castles of the early lords of Hampshire were at Portchester, Christchurch, Southampton, Carisbrook in the Isle of Wight, Winchester, Bishops Waltham, Odiam, Warblington, Smallwood, Wolversley, and Titchfield. There were formerly abbeys at Beaulieu, Hyde, Netley, Quarre, and Titchfield. Priories, at Andover, Appledurcombe, Breamere, Carisbrook, Christchurch, St. Dennis, St. Helens, Mottesfont, Portchester, Selbourn, and West Shireburn: and nunneries, at Rumsey, Wherwell, and Wintney. Hampshire contains one city, 21 market towns, 253 parishes, 49,516 houses, and 283,298 inhabitants. The county returns sixteen members to parliament: two for Andover, one for Christchurch, two for Lymington, one for Petersfield, two for Portsmouth, two for Southampton, two for Winchester, and four for the county, who at present are Charles Shaw Lefevre, Esq., of Heckfield Place, and James Winter Scott, Esq., of Rotherfield Park, members for the northern division; and the Right Hon. Viscount Palmerston, of Broadlands, and Sir George Thomas Staunton, Bart, of Leigh Park, near Havant, members for the southern division of the county.

The surface of Hampshire is varied with gently rising hills and fruitful vallies, interspersed with extensive woodlands. The chief part of the county is enclosed, although large tracts of open heath and uncultivated land remain on the borders of Dorsetshire. A ridge of downs or chalk hills may be traced across the county in the parallel of Winchester. On the northern side, bordering on Berkshire, the land is very productive; here great quantities of corn are annually grown, and the elm and oak flourish greatly. On the acclivities of the hills, towards Basingstoke, the land is chalky; but round Whitchurch, good crops of corn and sanfoin are produced. From Overton, towards Stockbridge, and thence to Redbridge, the valley of the Test is divided into well-watered meadows, and the vicinity of Redbridge is distinguished for its salt marshes. Around the town of Andover the land is high and downlike, but favourable to the growth of barley; and towards Rumsey it is more fertile and well cultivated, being interspersed with woods

and fine hedgerow timber. Southward the county is principally occupied by the New Forest. The parishes bordering on Surrey are chiefly appropriated to the growth of hops, the plantations of which have been greatly increased of late years. Towards Petersfield the country is open, with a considerable quantity of downs; but near Portsmouth it is more enclosed, and interspersed with timber and underwood. Round Fareham and Warnford the hills are chalky, and partly covered with beechwood: here are also extensive downs, and on the banks of the Itchin are some valuable meadows. A considerable portion of the county is occupied by the forest of Alice Holt and Wolmer, the forest of Bere, and the New Forest. Some of the finest prospects in the county are obtained from West Lodge, in Bere forest, and on the road from Lyndhurst to Lymington, in the New Forest; there are also fine views on the road from Winchester to Southampton, and from Portsdown hill. Other eminences affording views are Wey hill near Andover, Danebury hill near Stockbridge, Sidon hill in High Clere Park, Eaglehurst Cliff, St. Katherine's hill in the Isle of Wight, Culver Cliffs, and Carisbrook Castle. The following may be considered as natural curiosities: Hurst Castle Causeway, the Shingles, Portsea and Hayling Islands, Hengistbury Head, the Needles, Blackgang, Luccombe, and Shanklin Chines in the Isle of Wight, Hermit's-hole in Culver Cliff, Freshwater Cave, and Dunnose promontory, Alresford Pond, Alverstoke and Sowley Lakes. The principal rivers of Hampshire are the Alne, Anton, Avon, Auburn, Boldrewater, Exe, Hamble, Itchin, Loddon, Stour, Test or Tees, Tillhill, and the Wey. In the Isle of Wight are the rivers Medina and Yare. Several small streams rise in the north western county, but soon leave it in their passage to the Thames. The inland navigation of the county consists of the Basingstoke, Andover, Southampton, and Salisbury Canals. The manufactures of this county are but few, and those are chiefly of cloth, as shalloons and coarse woollens, checks, and bed-ticking: large quantities of malt are also made. For its breed of hogs Hampshire is proverbially famous, and this breed is of the largest kind, the farmers encouraging it as the most profitable; those in the vicinity of the forests are principally fed on acorns and beechmast, which give them a superiority over most others in the kingdom.

Strathfield Say is the principal seat of his Grace the Duke of Wellington, K.G., Lord Lieutenant of the County.

VIRTUTIS FORTUNA COMES

DUKE OF WELLINGTON

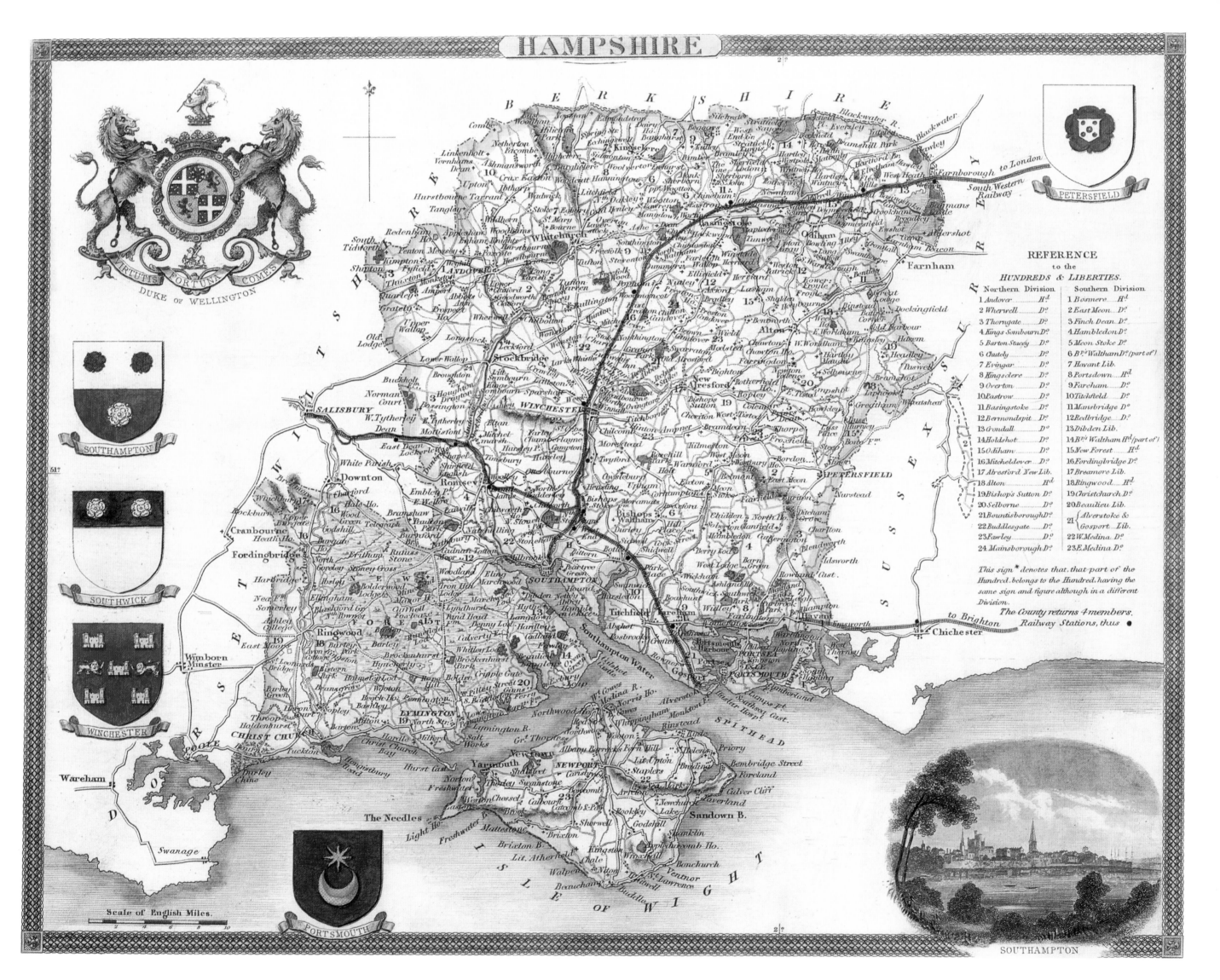

HAMPSHIRE

DUKE OF WELLINGTON

VIRTUTIS FORTUNA COMES

SOUTHAMPTON

SOUTHWICK

WINCHESTER

PORTSMOUTH

PETERSFIELD

REFERENCE
to the
HUNDREDS & LIBERTIES.

Northern Division		Southern Division	
1 Andover	Hd	1 Bosmere	Hd
2 Wherwell	Do	2 East Meon	Do
3 Thorngate	Do	3 Finch Dean	Do
4 Kings Somborn	Do	4 Hambledon	Do
5 Barton Stacey	Do	5 Meon Stoke	Do
6 Chutely	Do	6 Bps Waltham Do (part of)
7 Evingar	Do	7 Havant	Lib
8 Kingsclere	Do	8 Portsdown	Hd
9 Overton	Do	9 Fareham	Do
10 Pastrow	Do	10 Titchfield	Do
11 Basingstoke	Do	11 Mansbridge	Do
12 Bermondspit	Do	12 Redbridge	Do
13 Evendall	Do	13 Dibden	Lib
14 Holdshot	Do	14 Bps Waltham Hd (part of)
15 Odiham	Do	15 New Forest	Hd
16 Micheldever	Do	16 Fordingbridge	Do
17 Aresford New Lib.		17 Breamore	Lib
18 Alton	Hd	18 Ringwood	Hd
19 Bishop's Sutton	Do	19 Christchurch	Do
20 Selborne	Do	20 Beaulieu	Lib
21 Bountisborough Do		21 Alverstoke & Gosport Lib.
22 Buddlesgate	Do	22 W. Medina	Do
23 Fawley	Do	23 E. Medina	Do
24 Mainsborough Do			

This sign * denotes that, that part of the Hundred belongs to the Hundred, having the same sign and figure although in a different Division.

The County returns 4 members.

Railway Stations, thus ●

Scale of English Miles.

SOUTHAMPTON

PORTSMOUTH

PORTSMOUTH, on the sea coast, at the entrance of the harbour of the same name, 72 miles from London, contains 1100 houses and 7269 inhabitants. This borough is situated near the south western extremity of the Island of Portsea, and is divided from the town of Gosport, only by the strait, which forms the entrance to Portsmouth harbour. The principal street, called High Street, extends southward from the London road, and divides the town nearly in the centre, and from this other streets diverge in different directions. Near the entrance of the town is the governor's house, a handsome edifice, which has been the occasional residence of the sovereign: the houses of the lieutenant governor, in St. Thomas's Street, and of the port admiral, in High Street, are also handsome buildings. One of the most frequented parts of the town is the Point, consisting principally of Broad Street, a continuation of High Street, the grand line of communication with Spithead, the Harbour, and Gosport. The part where the merchant vessels lie, is called the Camber, where is an excellent quay. The foreign trade of Portsmouth is principally confined to timber from the Baltic, and eggs imported from France; an extensive coasting trade is carried on, and packet boats sail hence every day, for Southampton and the Isle of Wight. The Portsmouth and Arundel canal affords the means of inland navigation to London. The market days are Tuesday, Thursday, and Saturday, every week, and there is an annual fair on the 10th of July, and fourteen following days. Under a charter of King Charles I. the town is governed as to civil affairs, by a mayor, recorder, twelve aldermen, an indefinite number of burgesses, a town clerk, a chamberlain, and other officers. The mayor is chosen annually, by the aldermen and burgesses; the aldermen are elected by the mayor and aldermen, from amongst the burgesses, and the former also elect the town clerk, recorder, &c. The mayor, his predecessor, and three of the aldermen, are justices of the peace. Sessions are held quarterly, before these magistrates, for the trial of offences not capital; a court of record for the recovery of debts, is held every Tuesday, and there is an annual court leet for the appointment of constables. The arms of the borough is *Azure, a crescent or, surmounted by an etoile, of the last.*

The borough of Portsmouth, and parish of Portsea, return two members to parliament, the present members are John Bonham Carter, Esq., of Fair Oak, near Petersfield, and Francis Thornhill Baring, Esq.

The church, dedicated to St. Thomas of Canterbury, is a vicarage, value 6*l.* 13*s.* 4*d.*, in the patronage of Winchester College. It is a spacious edifice, and is said to have been erected by Peter des Roches, Bishop of Winchester, in the reign of Henry III., but the nave was rebuilt in 1693, when the chancel underwent alteration. Over the altar is a cenotaph for George Villiers, Duke of Buckingham, who was assassinated at Portsmouth, in August, 1628, whilst surrounded by his officers, and engaged in hastening the embarkation to relieve Rochelle, which at that time was invested by the French army. The house wherein this happened, is situated at the upper end of High Street. In the church are also many monuments of distinguished naval and military officers, amongst which are those of Sir Hugh Willoughby, Sir George Kempthorn, and Sir Charles Blunt. In Portsea, and the suburbs of this great seaport, are also St. George's Church, St. George's Square, erected in 1753. St. John's Church, in Prince George Street, erected in 1789; St. Paul's Church in Southsea, built in 1822, and All Saints Church, Mile-end, Southport.

The fortifications of Portsmouth extend in a semicircle around the town on the land side, forming a terrace in some parts shaded with trees, and affording a variety of extensive and beautiful views. The ramparts have grand entrance gate-houses, one erected in the reign of James II., of Corinthian architecture; St. Thomas's Gate of the Doric order, and one built in the reign of George III., in a rustic style. There are four guard-houses within the town, and near the principal gate-house are Coleworth Barracks. On the platform battery over the Magazine, a semaphore was erected in 1823, by which intelligence is transmitted to the Admiralty, in London. The town of Portsea stands upon what was formerly Portsmouth Common, and is more extensive than Portsmouth itself. The fortifications, commenced in 1770, are unequalled in point of strength and appearance. The lines stretch from north to south, defended on the eastern side by strong bastions and outerworks, with batteries of heavy ordnance: there are large and deep dykes, connected with the Portsmouth works by the Mill Pond, over the mouth of which, is the King's Mill. The entrance to the Royal Dockyard, is from the Common Yard, by a handsome gate-house. The Dockyard occupies one hundred and twenty acres of ground, and contains extensive naval and military storehouses, and numerous establishments for the supply of every thing requisite for the equipment of ships' service. Amongst the buildings most conspicuous is a residence of the commissioner, consisting of a centre, with a portico and wings, erected in 1773. A great basin covers an area of thirty-three thousand yards square, and communicates with four dry docks: there is also a double dock for frigates. The works include an anchor forge, where anchors are constructed, that weigh more than four tons and a half; a rope house, where cables are made, thirty inches in circumference; a copper foundry; rigging and mast houses, on a most extensive scale, and block machinery worked by steam, with improvements introduced by *Brunel.*

The Royal Naval College was founded in 1720. Over the college is an observatory, in which is a model of the Victory, a ship which was lost, in 1764, near the Race of Alderney. There is also another observatory, of more recent erection, over the central arch of the western storehouses, affording a prospect of the coast from the Needles, in the Isle of Wight, to the shore of Sussex. A school for the study of naval architecture, projected in 1809, was incorporated with the Naval College in 1816.

The gun wharf, situated without the dockyard, between Portsmouth and Portsea, contains the space of fourteen acres. A spacious building, occupying three sides of a quadrangle, with a gate house on the fourth side, is appropriated to the reception of an immense quantity of guns, carriages, &c., with ammunition of all kinds, for naval and military service. In the armoury are small arms for twenty-five thousand men, arranged in order. Here is likewise a laboratory and offices, belonging to the ordnance department, with residences for the officers. Opposite to them are the offices of the royal engineers, store-rooms, and a depôt of ammunition.

The port extends from the opening of Southampton water on the west, to Emsworth on the east, including within its jurisdiction, Langston, St. Helens, and Portsmouth Harbours, and Spithead. Stations for the preventive service are at Southsea Castle, Cumberland Fort, the Island of Hayling, Stokes Bay, and Hill Head. The harbour of Portsmouth, which is at the entrance narrower than the Thames at London, expands into a broad lake, stretching several miles towards the north, and affording secure shelter for the largest ships of the royal navy. The Isle of Wight forms a natural breakwater; and various headlands yield additional protection in stormy weather, while the great depth of water and admirable anchoring ground, enable ships to ride here in safety in all seasons. From the western side of the entrance extends a sandbank, called the Spit, about three miles in length, at the head of which a ship of war is always stationed; and the Roadstead, between Portsmouth and the Isle of Wight, hence named Spithead, is indicated by buoys, fixed at regular intervals, and is the rendezvous of the royal navy in war time. The opening of the harbour is defended on both sides by forts and batteries, besides those immediately connected with the town. The works for the defence of Portsmouth, extended and improved by additions of various descriptions, have rendered the united towns of Portsmouth and Portsea, one of the principal naval arsenals of the kingdom.

PORTSMOUTH.

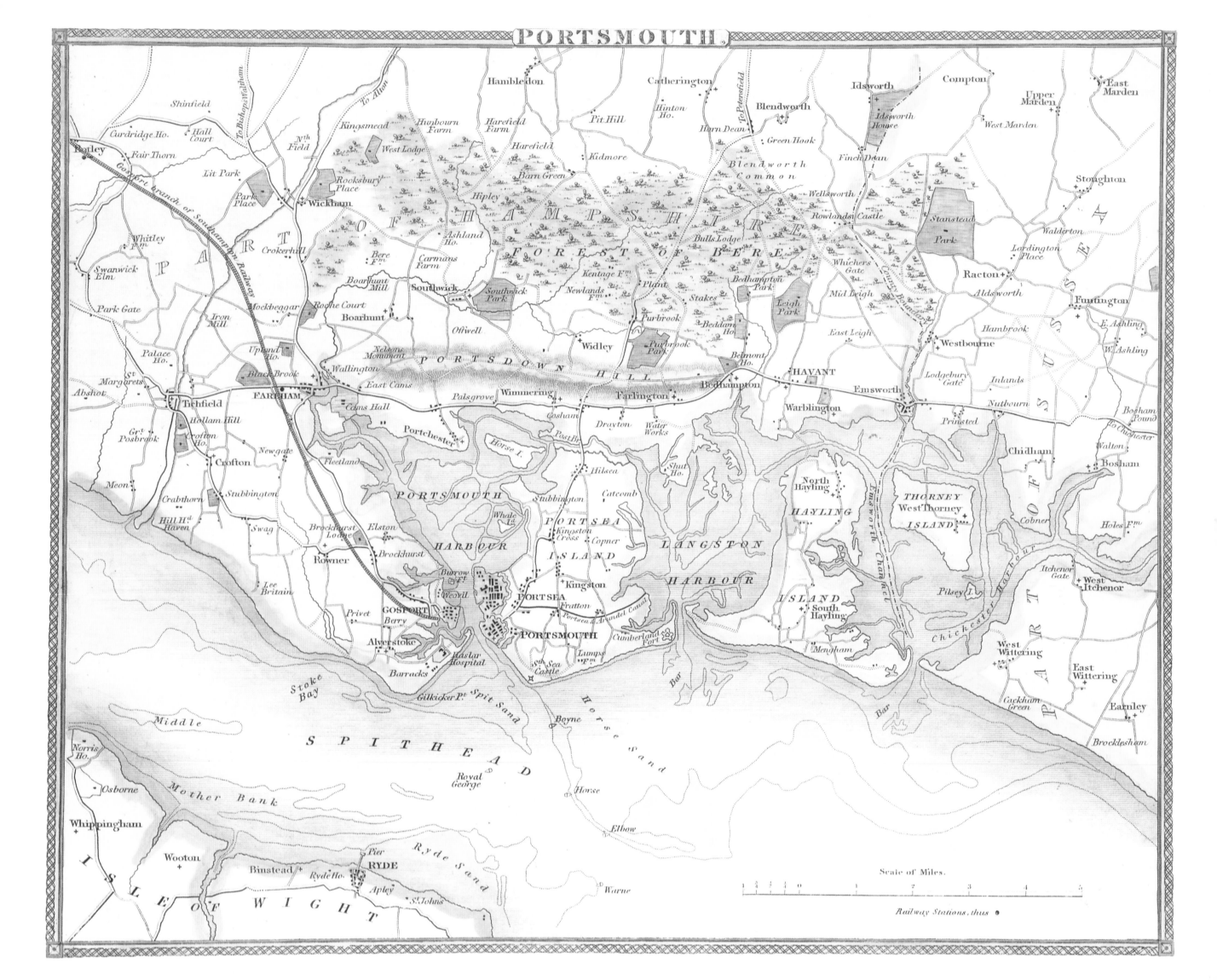

Shinfield
Hambledon
Catherington
Idsworth
Compton
Upper Marden
East Marden

Curdridge Ho.
Hall Court
N°th Field
Kingsmead
Hunbourn Farm
Harefield Farm
Pit Hill
Hinton Ho.
Blendworth
Idsworth House
West Marden

Botley
Fair Thorn
To Bishopswaltham
West Lodge
Harefield
Kidmore
Hurn Dean
Green Hook
Finch Dean
Stoughton

Lit Park
Rooksbury Place
Hipley
Barn Green
Blendworth Common
Wellsworth

Park Place
Wickham
Ashland Ho.
Stansted Park
Walderton

Whitley F.
Crokerhill
Bere F.
Carmans Farm
FOREST OF BERE
Rowlands Castle
Lordington Place

Swanwick Elm
O F   H A M P S H I R E
Kentage F.
Plant
Whichers Gate
Racton
Aldsworth

Park Gate
Iron Mill
Boarhunt Mill
Southwick
Southwick Park
Newlands F.
Stakes
Bedhampton Park
Mid Leigh
Westbourne
Funtington
E. Ashling

Mockbeggar
Roche Court
Boarhunt
Offwell
Purbrook
Beddam Ho.
Leigh Park
East Leigh
W. Ashling

Palace Ho.
Upland Ho.
Nelsons Monument
Widley
Purbrook Park
Belmont Ho.
Lodgebury Gate
Inlands

Margarets
St
Black Brook
Wallington
PORTSDOWN HILL
HAVANT
Emsworth
Bosham Pound

Abshot
East Cams
Palsgrove
Wimmering
Farlington
Bedhampton
Warblington
Prinsted
To Chichester

Titchfield
FAREHAM
Cams Hall
Cosham
Drayton
Water Works
Nutbourn
Bosham

Hollam Hill
Portchester
Post Br.
Chidham
Walton

Gr. Posbrook
Horse I.
Shut Ho.
Bosham

Crofton Ho.
Newgate
Fleetland
Hilsea
Catcomb
North Hayling
THORNEY WEST Thorney ISLAND
Holes F.

Meon
Crofton
Stubbington
PORTSMOUTH
P O R T S E A
Stubbington
HAYLING
Cobner

Crabthorn
Swag
Brockhurst Lodge
Elston
Whale Is.
ISLAND
Itchenor Gate
West Itchenor

Hill Hd Haven
Lee Britain
Brockhurst
HARBOUR
Kingston Cross
Copner
LANGSTON
Pilsey I.

Rowner
Weovil
PORTSEA
Kingston
HARBOUR
ISLAND
South Hayling

GOSPORT Berry
Burrow Ft
Fratton
Portsea & Arundel Canal
West Wittering

Privet
PORTSMOUTH
Cumberland Fort
Mengham
East Wittering

Alverstoke
Haslar Hospital
Sth Sea Castle
Lumps Fm

Barracks
Gilkicker Pt
Spit Sand
Bar

Stoke Bay
Boyne
Horse Sand
Bar
Cackham Green
Earnley

Middle
SPITHEAD
Royal George
Horse
Brocklesham

Norris Ho.
Mother Bank
Elbow
Warne

Osborne

Whippingham
Wooton
Binstead
Pier
RYDE
Ryde Sand

ISLE OF WIGHT
Ryde Ho.
Apley
St Johns

Scale of Miles.

Railway Stations, thus ⊙

HEREFORDSHIRE

This county is in form nearly circular, and is bounded on the north by Shropshire; on the east by Worcestershire; on the south by Gloucestershire and Monmouthshire; and on the west by Brecknockshire, and Radnorshire. Some detached parishes and townships are situated beyond the general outline: of these, Farlow is entirely surrounded by Shropshire, Rochford is included in the county of Worcester, and Lytton in that of Radnor. The Futhog, a considerable tract of land, and a few acres on the Devauden Hill, are insulated by Monmouthshire. The greatest extent of the county, from Ludford on the north to the opposite border near Monmouth on the south, is thirty-eight miles; its greatest width, from Clifford on the west to Cradley on the east, is thirty-five miles, and its circumference is one hundred and eighty miles. Herefordshire, inhabited by the Silures, was included by the Romans in the district named Britannia Secunda. Two of the principal stations of the Itinerary of Antoninus, viz. Magna, now Kenchester and Ariconium, near Ross, together with the smaller post of Bravinium, or Brandon Camp, are situated within the limits of the county. Upon the decline of the Roman power Herefordshire became incorporated with the Saxon kingdom of Mercia. The county has one city, Hereford, seven market towns, and 221 parishes; containing at the last census 20,061 houses, and 103,243 inhabitants. It returns eight members to Parliament; two for the county, viz. Sir John Geers Cotterell Bart,. of Garnons, and Robert Price, Esq., of Foxley; two for the city two for Leominster, and two for Weobly. The whole county is in the province of Canterbury, and diocese of Hereford. The general aspect of the county is extremely beautiful, its surface being finely diversified, and broken by swelling heights; from many of these elevations the prospects are fine; but are peculiarly so from the Malvern Hills, on the east, and the Hatterel or Black Mountains on the west: on every side a luxuriant vegetation is exhibited in widely extended corn-fields, teeming orchards, expansive meadows, and flourishing plantations. The courses of rivers and brooks may be traced from many of the adjacent eminences by the rich lines of wood skirting their margins, and every part is uniformly productive, excepting on the northern and western boundaries of the county. Herefordshire is particularly famous as a cider county, and plantations of fruit trees are found in every aspect. To Philips's Poem on Cider, written in imitation of the Georgics, is given this peculiar praise, that it is grounded in truth; that the precepts it contains are exact and just; and it is therefore at once a book of entertainment and of science. The orchards are of various sizes, from four or five to thirty and forty acres, and in years of abundance twenty hogsheads of cider have been made from the produce of a single acre of orchard ground. The Herefordshire cattle are equal, if not superior, to any breed in the kingdom, and the breed of sheep is almost equally as celebrated as that of its cattle, principally for the fineness of its wool, of which Leominster is noted as the place of sale. The cultivation of hops forms a very considerable branch of the rural economy of the county. The principal cultivated lands of Herefordshire are under tillage, and the wheat grown in the vicinity of Hereford, and thence through the clays towards Ledbury, is remarkably fine; but Herefordshire may be properly termed a woodland county, many species of trees growing up spontaneously, and becoming strong and vigorous in a very short period. The rivers of the county are the Arrow, the Dore, the Eskle, the Frome, the Gamar, the Garran, the Hothney, the Leddon, the Loden, the Lugg, the Monnow, the Olchron, the Pinsley, the Teme, the Tatnell, the Wadel, the Worme and the Wye. The navigation is composed of the Hereford and Gloucester canal, and the Kington and Leominster canal. The Right Hon John Earl Somers is Lord Lieutenant and Custos Rotulorum of the County, and Chief Steward of Hereford.

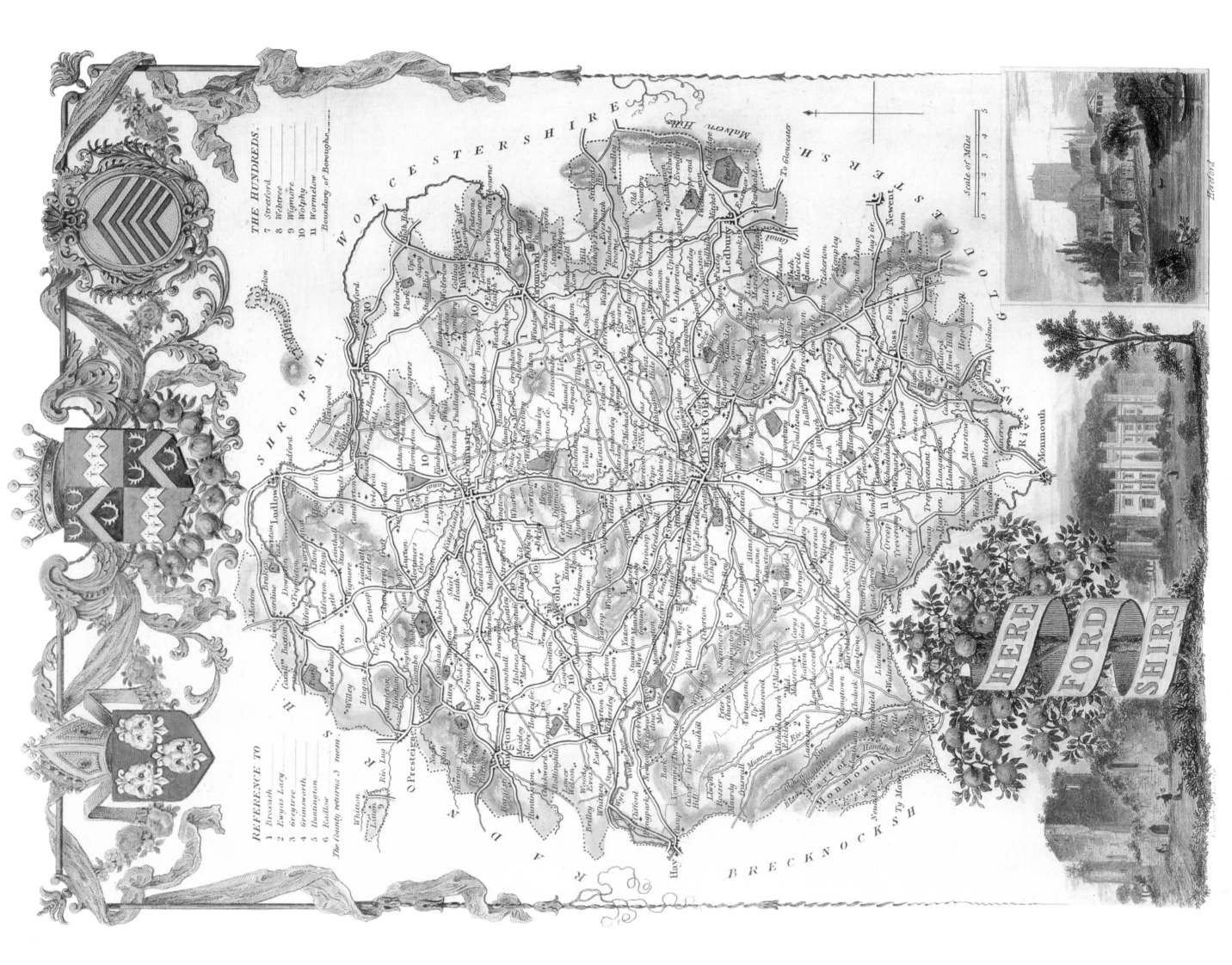

THE HUNDREDS.

7 Stretford
8 Webtree
9 Wigmore
10 Wolphy
11 Wormelow
— Boundary of Boroughs.

REFERENCE TO
1 Broxash
2 Ewyas Lacy
3 Greytree
4 Grimsworth
5 Huntington
6 Radlow
The County returns 3 mem.

Scale of Miles
0 1 2 3 4 5

WORCESTERSHIRE

SHROPSHIRE

GLOUCESTERSHIRE

RADNORSHIRE

BRECKNOCKSHIRE

HEREFORD

Hereford

Monmouth

Wye Rive

HERE FORD SHIRE

HERTFORDSHIRE

THIS county is bounded on the north by Bedfordshire, Cambridgeshire, and Buckinghamshire; on the east by Essex; on the south by Middlesex; and on the west by Buckinghamshire. It was inhabited by the British tribes of Catteuchlani, or Cassii and Trinobantes, and afterwards became a part of the Roman province Flavia Cæsariensis. There were three Roman roads leading through this county, which cannot be said of any other, and the principal stations were Verulam, St. Albans; and Durolitum, Cheshunt. During the Saxon Heptarchy it formed part of the kingdom of Mercia, when the royal palace was at Bennington. In length this county extends about thirty-six miles; its general breadth is about twenty-six, and in circumference it is about one hundred and forty miles. It contains one county town, nineteen market towns, one hundred and twenty parishes, 23,178 houses, and 129,714 inhabitants. It is in the province of Canterbury, and dioceses of Lincoln and London. The abbey of St. Albans, founded in 791 by Offa, then king of Mercia, was a mitred abbey, and by a grant from Pope Adrian IV., a native of this county, and the only Englishman who had the honour of sitting in the papal chair, the abbots of St. Albans were authorized to take precedence of all others in England. There were also priories at Cheshunt, Flamstead, Hertford, Hitchin, Langley, Rowney, Royston, Sopewell, Ware, and Wymondley. The castles of its earlier lords were at Hertford, Berkhampstead, and Stortford. The county now returns six members to Parliament, two for Hertford; two for St. Albans; and two for the county, who at present are Sir John S. Sebright, Bart. of Beechwood, and Nicolson Calvert, Esq. of Hunsdon House. The general aspect of this county is extremely pleasant; and although its eminences are not sufficiently elevated, nor its vales sufficiently depressed and broken to afford a decisive character of picturesque or romantic beauty, yet the surface is in many parts richly diversified with hill and dale, clothed with noble woods, and thickly studded with numberless parks attached to the seats of the nobility and gentry. The northern part is the most hilly, and a range of high ground stretches out from the neighbourhood of King's Langley, towards Berkhampstead and Tring, which in many parts commands a great extent of country. Another elevated ridge commences at St. Albans, and proceeds in a northern direction towards Markyate–street; while several other ranges of elevated ground run nearly parallel with the first, from the vicinity of Sandridge, Wheathampstead, Whitwell, &c. The southern line is also sufficiently high to include some extensive prospects. The most remarkable scenes and situations in the county are Bushey Heath, Little Gadesden, Kensworth, Essenden, Brookman's Park, and Knebworth. Most of the county is inclosed; and the hedges, intermixed with flourishing timber, have a verdant and pleasing effect. Independent of the wood thus distributed in hedge–rows, large quantities of very fine timber are grown in parks spread over every part of the county. The prevailing soils in Hertfordshire are loam and clay; the farmer is met with in almost all its gradations, and is more or less intermingled with flint or sand: a chalky soil prevails generally on the northern side of the county, and extends from the neighbourhood of Barkway and Royston through all the contiguous parishes to Baldock, Hitchin, King's Walden, &c. The basis, indeed, of the whole county is chalk, either more or less pure, although the depths at which it is found are very different. As the principal part of the land in this county is under tillage, the produce in wheat, barley, and oats is very considerable. Chauncy, writing in 1700, says, "This county yields the choicest wheat and barley, such as makes the best mault that serves the King's court, which caused Queen Elizabeth often to boast of her Hitchin grape." Large quantities of turnips are also grown, and artificial grasses are cultivated to a very great extent. The grass lands, compared with those under tillage, are extremely small, although a tract of grass, rendered artificially productive at a great expense, may be found connected with almost every estate in the county. The meadows on the river Stort, extending from Hockeril to Hertford, are very productive, as are those in the vicinity of the Lea, and in the neighbourhood of Rickmansworth. The many streams which intersect the land are extremely favourable to irrigation, although that system is not carried to any great extent. In the south-western angle of the county, near Rickmansworth and Watford, are many orchards, the apples and cherries from which find a ready market in London. The chief manufactures of this county are those of cotton and silk; the first is principally carried on near St. Albans and Rickmansworth, and the last in the vicinity of Watford. The rivers of this county are the Ver or Muse, Colne, Gade, Bulbourne, Lea, Mineram or Marran, Kime, Beane, Rib, Quin, Ash, and Stort, besides the Thame, Pirre, Hiz, Oughton, and Rhee, which rise in this county, but soon leave it; and the New River, the springs which constitute its source having their rise in the neighbourhood of Ware. The Lea rises near Luton, in Bedfordshire, and entering the county at Hide Hill proceeds through Wheathampstead, Brocket, and Hatfield Parks to Hertford and Ware, and after its confluence with the Stort quits the county near Waltham Abbey. The Rib has its rise near Cornybury, above Buntingford, and is joined by the Quin, which rises near Biggin: it passes Standon, and falls into the Lea between Hertford and Ware. The Beane rises near Cromer, and flows through Watton and Woodhall Park, meeting the Lea at Hertford. The Gade has its source on the borders of Buckinghamshire, and gives name to the villages of Great and Little Gadesden; thence proceeding by Hemel Hempstead, it is joined near Two Waters by the Bulbourne, and flows through the parks of the Grove and Cashiobury to the Colne near Rickmansworth. The Colne is formed by the union of several small, streams, and gives name to London Colney, Colney Park, and Colney Street, whence it enters Middlesex. The Mineram, or Marran, has its source in the vicinity of King's Walden, and is soon enlarged by the Kime; after which it passes Welwyn, and joins the Lea at Hertford. The Grand Junction canal enters this county above Berkhampstead, and follows the course of the Gade to Rickmansworth, and thence the course of the Colne till it leaves the county. The medicinal springs are chiefly chalybeate, and are confined to the southern part of the county. The principal is near the race-ground on Barnet Common; others rise on Northaw Common, and in that parish. Some incrustatory springs may be noticed near Clothall, in the northern part of the county. Gorhambury, near St. Albans, is the seat of the Earl of Verulam, Lord Lieutenant of the county.

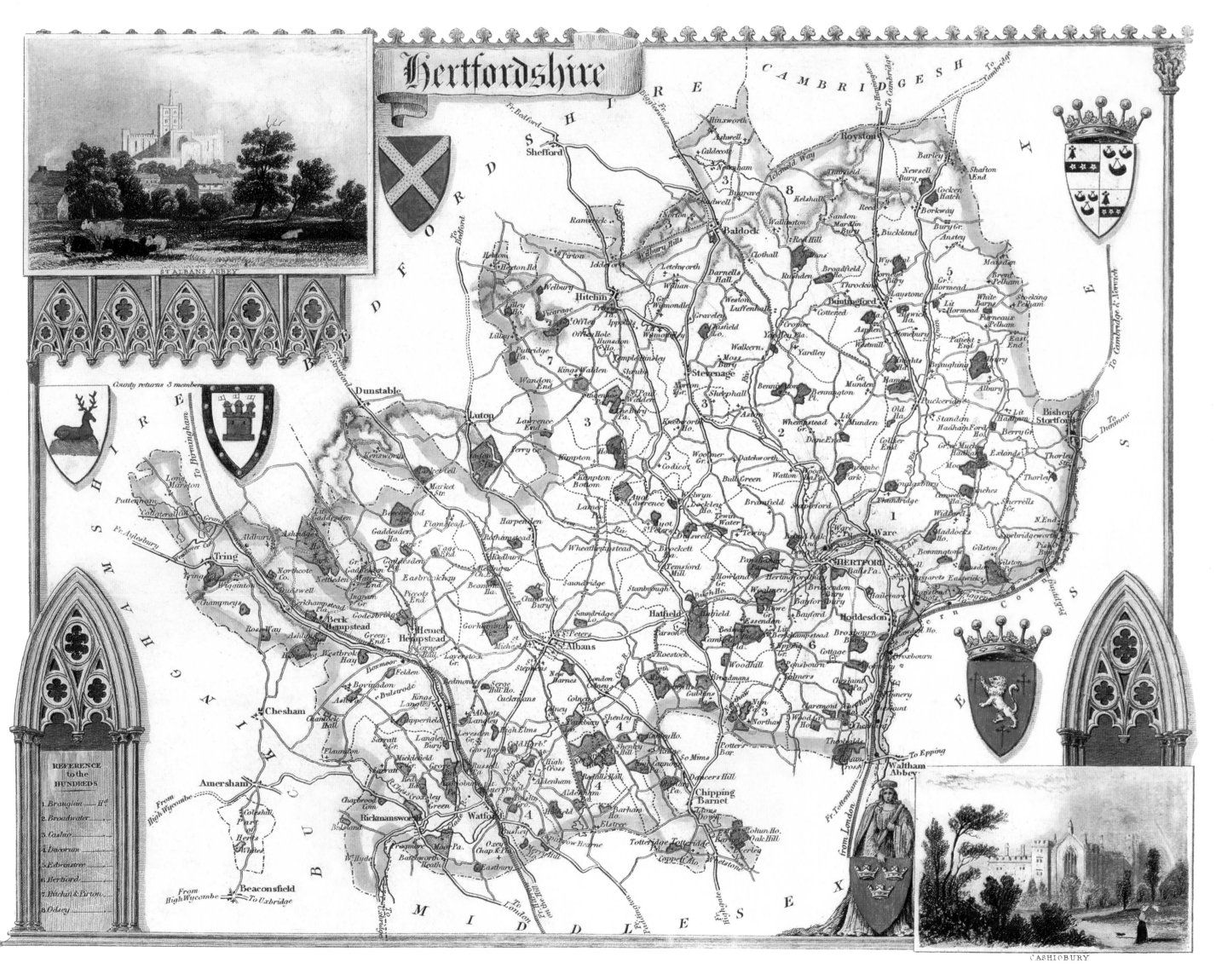

Hertfordshire

ST ALBANS ABBEY

REFERENCE to the HUNDREDS

1. Braughin _____ Hd
2. Broadwater
3. Caslao
4. Dacorum
5. Edwinstree
6. Hertford
7. Hitchin & Pirton
8. Odsey

County returns 3 members

CASHIOBURY

HUNTINGDONSHIRE

THIS county, one of the smallest in the kingdom, is bounded on the north by Northamptonshire and Cambridgeshire; on the east by Cambridgeshire; on the south by Bedfordshire; and on the west by Northamptonshire: its greatest length is about thirty miles, its breadth about twenty-three miles, and in circumference it is about one hundred miles. The British inhabitants of this tract were the Iceni, and under the Romans this part of Britain was included in the province denominated Flavia Cæsariensis. The principal Roman roads were the Ermine Street, which enters Huntingdonshire near Papworth Everard in Cambridgeshire, passes through Godmanchester, Huntingdon, and Stilton, and crosses the Nen at Durobrivæ, or Castor, in Northamptonshire, which was a considerable Roman station. A road called the Via Devana ran from Fenny Stanton to Godmanchester, and left this county for Clapton in Northamptonshire. A third road entered Huntingdonshire southward of St. Neots, and passing Paxton and the Offords, proceeded to Godmanchester, the Durolipons of Antoninus's Itinerary. Another Roman station of importance was at Chesterton, near Water Newton, on the banks of the Nen. There are ancient encampments at Dornford, Stanground, St. Neots, and at Knutyff's Dyke at Bushmead. Roman coins have been found at Godmanchester and at St. Neots, and Roman urns at Sawtry. During the Anglo-Saxon Heptarchy this county originally formed part of East-Anglia, and afterwards part of the kingdom of Mercia: in the survey made upon the Norman Conquest it is called Huntedunscire. The castles of its early lords were at Connington, Kimbolton, Buckden, Somersham, Earith and Bruck. There were formerly abbeys at Ramsey and Sawtry; and priories at Huntingdon, St. Ives, St. Neots, Stonely, and Hinchingbrook. Above a fourth part of the county is said to have been in the possession of the monks, who proverbially chose the richest land to fix their abode upon; and on the dissolution of monasteries a great many new families were established in Huntingdonshire. This county is in the diocese of Lincoln, and province of Canterbury. Besides the county town, Huntingdon, there are six market-towns, 107 parishes, 8879 houses, and 48,771 inhabitants. Huntingdonshire sends four members to Parliament, two for Huntingdon, and two for the county, who at present are Viscount Mandeville, son of the Duke of Manchester, and John Bonfoy Rooper, Esq. of Abbots Ripton.

The whole upland part of this county is said to have been anciently a forest, the haunt of deer and other animals of the chase, whence the original name Hunter's Down, and was not disafforested till the reign of Edward I.: the face of the county now presents much variety. The borders of the Ouse consist of a tract of fertile and beautiful meadows, of which Port-holm, near Huntingdon, is the most celebrated. The middle and western parts of the county are finely diversified in their surface, fruitful in corn, and sprinkled with woods; the north-eastern part consists of fens, joining those of the Isle of Ely: the fens were in early times not only richly cultivated, but produced all the necessaries of life, and grapes, of which excellent wine was made. The historians Bede and William of Malmsbury, in particular, describe their verdure and fertility, the rich pastures and wholesome air: the sea breaking in upon the land destroyed this fruitful valley; trunks of trees, hard, black, and close-grained, are now frequently found when digging in the fens. The fens of Huntingdonshire constitute nearly a seventh part of the Great Bedford Level, and consist of about forty-four thousand acres, exclusive of nearly five thousand acres of skirty lands which border on the fens, and partake of the properties of moor, combined with the soil prevalent in the adjacent uplands, and generally afford luxuriant grazing. The woodland of the county is but of inconsiderable extent, and timber is scarce, owing to the very great demand for it in the fens. The principal rivers of Huntingdonshire are the Ouse and the Nen, or *Nene*. The Ouse has its source at Ousewell in Northamptonshire, and enters this county from Bedfordshire, between St. Neots and Little Paxton; after passing Huntingdon it takes an easterly direction, and flowing by St. Ives, becomes, near Holywell, the boundary between this county and Cambridgeshire, till it enters the Great Level of the fens near Earith. The Ouse is navigable along its whole line across this county. The Nen also rises in Northamptonshire near Catesby, and after flowing through a beautiful and fertile valley, enters Huntingdonshire near Elton, where it forms the division of the counties; and meandering northward, passes Yarwell and Wansford; and winding towards the east, through a more level country, pursues a devious course to Peterborough, below which city it traverses the fens to its outfall at the sea. The greatest part of the county is well watered by springs and rivulets, and it also contains several meres or lakes, the principal of which are Whittlesey Mere, Ramsey Mere, Ugg Mere, &c. The markets and fairs for live cattle in this county are some of the greatest in England. The breed of sheep upon the enclosed pastures is of a mixed description, partaking of the Leicestershire and Lincolnshire kinds; but those bred in the open and common lands are much inferior. The neat cattle are of the Lancashire, Leicestershire, and Derbyshire breeds, being usually purchased for grazing, without any particular choice, and are never used in husbandry. No manufactures are carried on in this county, unless wool stapling and spinning yarn may be so considered, in which women and children are employed in the winter season. Kimbolton Castle, where Katherine of Arragon, the divorced wife of Henry VIII., ended her days, is the seat of the Duke of Manchester, Lord Lieutenant of the County.

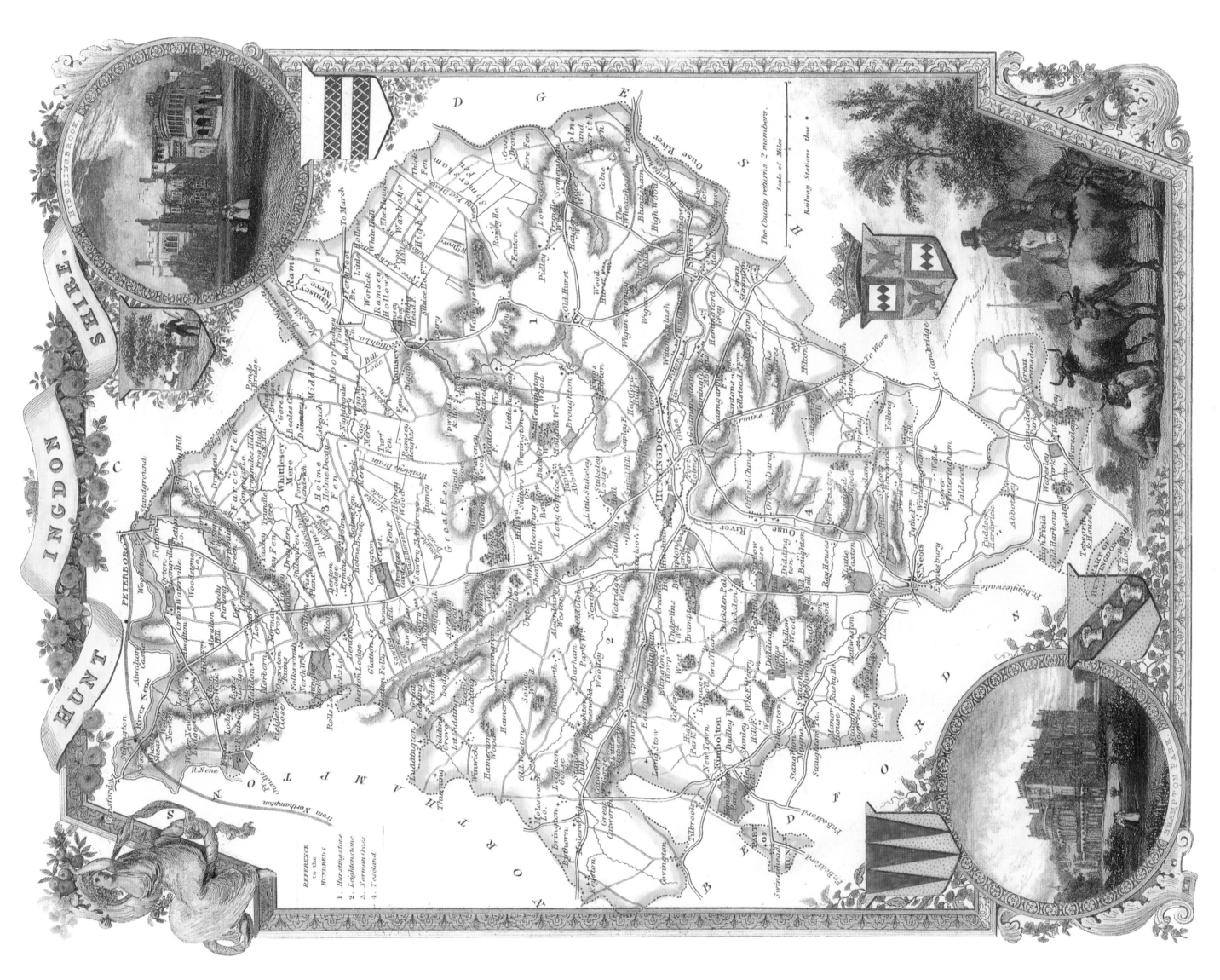

HUNTINGDONSHIRE.

HINCHINGBROOK.

BUGDEN PARK.

REFERENCE to the HUNDREDS
1. Hurstingstone
2. Leightonstone
3. Norman Cross
4. Toseland

The County returns 2 members.
Scale of Miles
Railway Stations thus •

PETERBORO'

To March

Ramsey

Whittlesey Mere

Holme Fen

Great Fen

HUNTINGDON

Ermine Street

S. Neots

To Cambridge

To Ware

F. Biggleswade

F. Bedford

NORTHAMPTONSHIRE

BEDFORDSHIRE

CAMBRIDGESHIRE

KENT

THIS county is bounded on the north by the county of Essex and the mouth of the river Thames; on the east by the German Ocean and the Straits of Dover; on the south by the county of Sussex; and on the west by Surrey. It was inhabited by the British Cantii, and afterwards became a part of the Roman province Britannia Prima, when the principal stations were Anderida, Newenden; Dubris, Dover; Durobrivis, Rochester; Durovernum, Canterbury; Lemanis, Lymne; Regulbium, Reculver; and Rutupium, Richborough. The Roman Watling-street passed through the county from Dartford to Dover. Under the Saxon Heptarchy it formed the kingdom of Kent. In length this county extends about sixty-six miles, in breadth about thirty-six, and in circumference it is about one hundred and seventy-four miles. It contains two cities, Canterbury and Rochester, and one county town, Maidstone, thirty-six market towns, four hundred and fourteen parishes, 70,507 houses, and 426,016 inhabitants. It is in the province of Canterbury, and dioceses of Canterbury and Rochester. There were anciently numerous monasteries in Kent, as abbeys at Canterbury, Boxley, Feversham, West Langdon, Lesnes, and Dover. Priories at Aylesford, Badlesmere, Bilsington, Cumbwell, Davington, Dartford, Dover, Leeds, Mottenden, Minster, Rochester, Malling, and Tunbridge. The castles of its earlier lords were also considerable in number, remains of which are at Allington, Canterbury, Chilham, Cooling, Dover, Eynesford, Hever, Leeds, Leybourne, Lullingstone, Lymne, Mereworth, Otford, Queenborough, Richborough, Rochester, Romney, Sandgate, Sandown, Shoreham, Starborough, Stone, Tunbridge, Upnor, and Walmer. The county now returns eighteen members to Parliament, two for Canterbury, two for Dover, two for Hythe, two for Maidstone, two for Queenborough, two for Rochester, two for Romney, two for Sandwich, and two for the county, who at present are Thomas Law Hodges, Esq., and Thomas Rider, Esq. The county has long been divided into East and West Kent: the eastern division contains the Lathes of Sutton, Aylesford, and part of Scray; the western, Shepway, St. Augustine, and the remaining part of Scray. In each of the great districts of East and West Kent a court of session is held four times every year; and the justices, although appointed for the whole county, generally confine their attention to that particular district in which they reside. The descent of landed property in this county is regulated by peculiar customs, which are comprehended under the term Gavelkind, or the joint inheritance of all the sons to the estate of their fathers, &c. &c. The general aspect of Kent is very beautiful, arising from the inequality of the surface, the diversity of the scenery, and the variety of the verdure. The whole county, excepting the Marshes and the Weald, is a general cluster of small hills, two chains of which, higher than the rest, run through the middle of the county, from east to west, and extend from Surrey to the sea; these are called the upper and lower hills, and are mostly covered with coppice and woodland. The northern range is chiefly composed of chalk and flints, and the southern range chiefly ironstone and ragstone. The Weald of Kent is a considerable tract, stretching along the south side of the county, from Romney Marsh to Surrey, and is bounded on the north by a range of hills which command the whole extent. Romney Marsh is an extensive level tract of rich land connected with Welland Marsh and Denge Marsh, and is defended against the sea by an immense wall of earth, called Dimchurch Wall, which extends in length more than three miles. These marshes are appropriated to the grazing and fattening of sheep and cattle, which are bred here in immense numbers, perhaps exceeding that of any other district in the kingdom. The rivers of this county are the Bewle, Cray, Darent, Dour or Idle, Len, Medway, Nailbourne, Nethergong, Ravensbourne, Rother, Scray, Great and Little Stour, Swale, Thames, Theyse, Tun, and Wantsume. The river Cray has its source at Newell, in Orpington parish, gives name to the following villages by which it takes its course: St. Mary's Cray, Paul's Cray, Foot's Cray, North Cray, and Crayford, and falls into the Darent, a river which rises in Sussex, on the borders of this county, near Westerham, whence it passes Valence, Brastead, Chipstead, Riverhead, Shoreham, Eynsford, Farningham, South Darent, and proceeds to Dartford, where it becomes navigable, and enters the Thames near Long Reach. The Medway enters this county near Edenbridge, flows by Hever Castle and Tunbridge, through a very beautiful country: thence proceeding to Twyford Bridge and Yalding, it is joined by the Bewle and Theyse, and proceeds to Maidstone, Rochester, Chatham, and Sheerness, and enters the Thames between the Isles of Graine and Sheppey, having first united its waters with those of the Swale. The Ravensbourne rises on Keston Downs, and flowing near Hayes and Bromley to Lewisham, and near Lee is joined by the Leebourne, it becomes navigable at Deptford, and falls into the Thames. The Rother rises at Gravel Hill, near Rotherfield, in Sussex and flowing eastward, becomes the boundary of the county, below Sandhurst and Newenden, after which it skirts the southern side of the Isle of Oxney, and forms Rye Harbour. The river anciently flowed round the northern side of the Isle of Oxney to Appledore, and thence to Romney, but its channel was altered by a tempest in the reign of Edward I., and it took a new course to Rye. The Great Stour rises near Lenham, and after being increased by several rivulets near Ashford, flows by Spring Grove to Wye, and thence to Canterbury, and proceeds to the Isle of Thanet, by Sarre to Richborough and Sandwich and falls into the British Channel at Pepperness. From Sarre, a branch called the Nethergong, flows into the sea at Newhaven. The Little Stour rises near Liminge, is increasedby the Nailbourne, skirts Barham Downs, and falls into the Great Stour at Stourmouth. The inland navigation of the county consists of the Croydon Canal, the Grand Surrey Canal, the Shorncliffe and Rye Canal, and the Thames and Medway Canal. Wilderness, near Sevenoaks, is the seat of the Marque of Camden, K.G., Lord Lieutenant of the County.

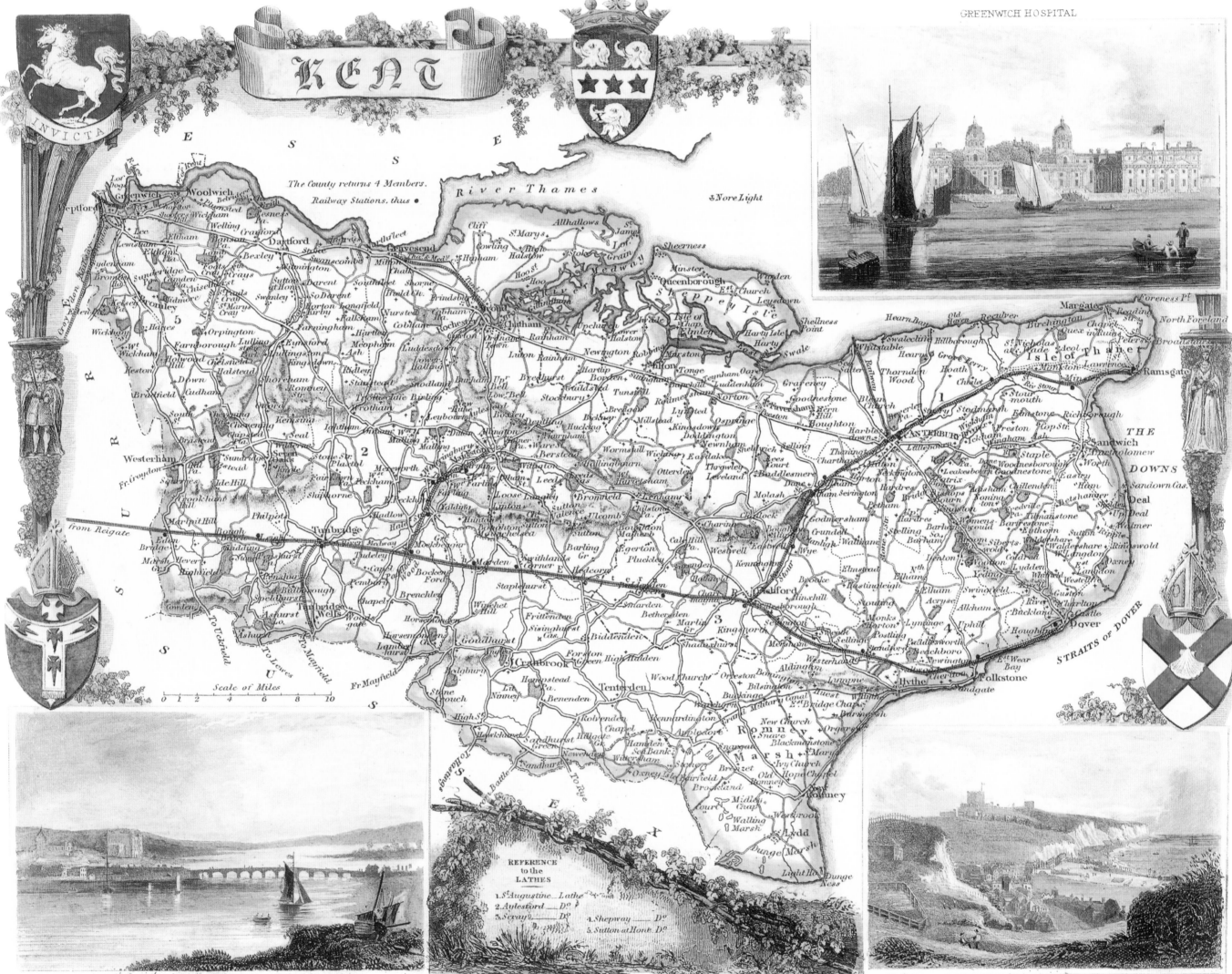

KENT

INVICTA

GREENWICH HOSPITAL

The County returns 4 Members.
Railway Stations, thus ●

River Thames

Nore Light

E S S E X

R I V E R

S U R R E Y

S U S S E X

Woolwich
Greenwich
Deptford
Lewisham
Eltham
Bexley
Dartford
Gravesend
Rochester
Chatham
Sheerness
Minster
Queenborough
Isle of Sheppey

Bromley
Orpington
Farnborough
Westerham
Sevenoaks
Tunbridge
Tunbridge Wells

Maidstone
Canterbury
Faversham
Whitstable
Herne Bay
Margate
Ramsgate
Isle of Thanet
North Foreland

THE DOWNS

Sandwich
Deal
Walmer

Ashford
Charing
Wye

Dover
STRAITS OF DOVER

Hythe
Folkestone

Cranbrook
Tenterden

Romney Marsh
Dunge Ness
Light Ho.

Scale of Miles
0 1 2 4 6 8 10

To Uckfield
To Lewes
To Mayfield
from Reigate

REFERENCE to the LATHES
1. St. Augustine Lathe
2. Aylesford Do.
3. Scray Do.
4. Shepway Do.
5. Sutton at Hone Do.

ROCHESTER

DOVER

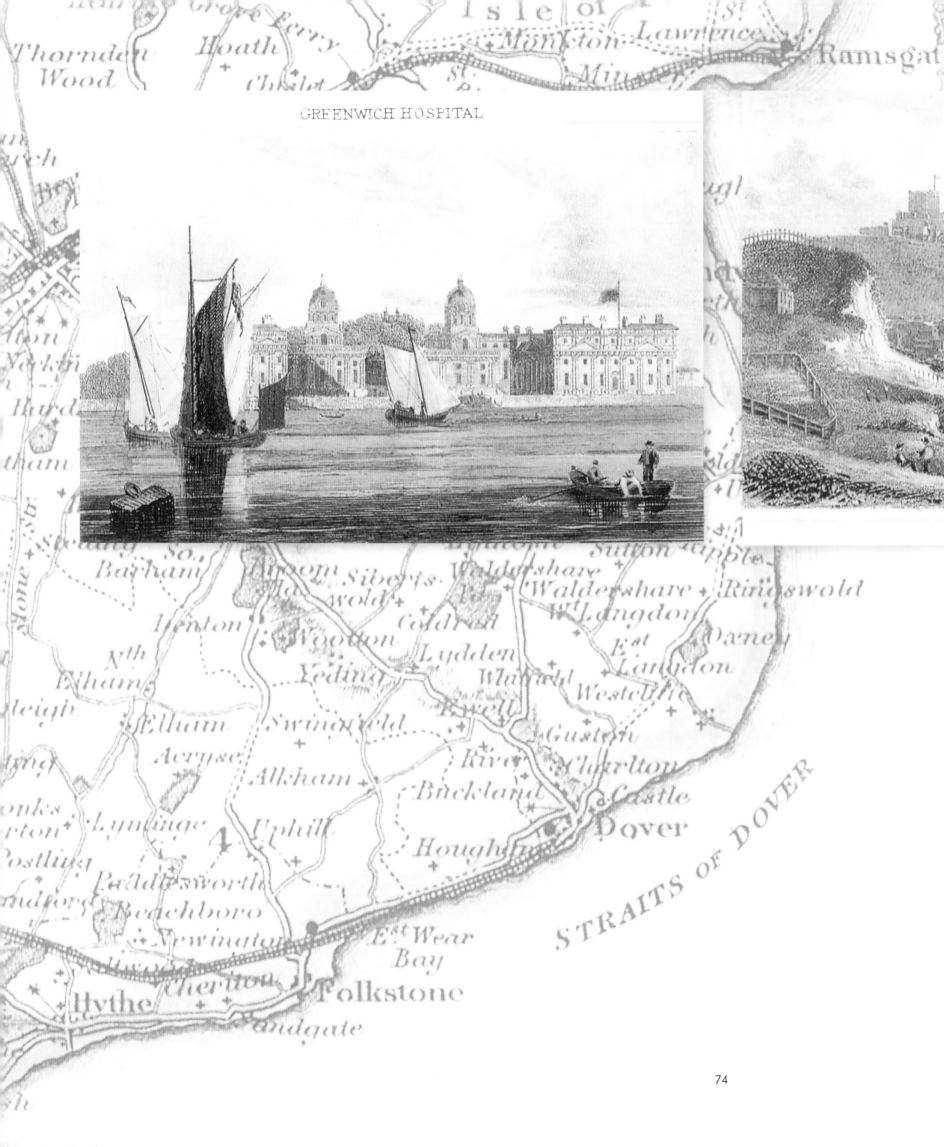

GREENWICH HOSPITAL

DOVER

ABOVE LEFT: A view of Greenwich Hospital from the Isle of Dogs. The building, which would later become the Royal Naval College, was designed by the celebrated architect Christopher Wren who was assisted by Nicholas Hawksmoor. Admiral Lord Nelson's funeral procession departed from the hospital and sailed up the River Thames to St. Pauls Catherdral in January 1806.

ABOVE: Dover Castle atop the famous white cliffs in Kent. The main motivation behind Moule's decision to commission and to include vignette views in his maps was to increase their commercial appeal. Even in the early 19th century, following many years under threat of French invasion, this view enjoyed iconic status amongst the English.

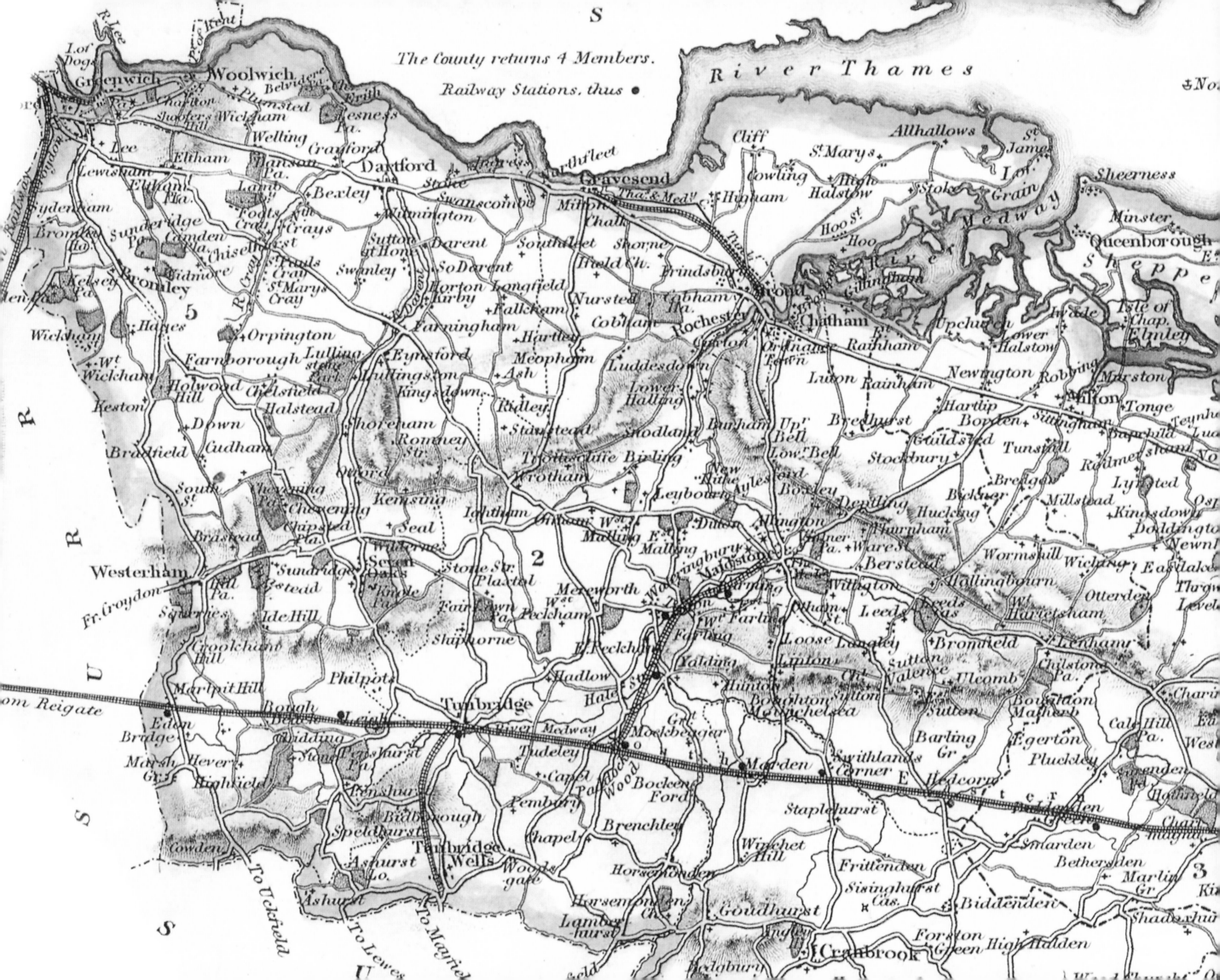

S

R. Lee
R. Kent

I. of
Dogs
Greenwich
Woolwich
Belvidere
Charlton
Plumsted
Erith
Shooters Hill
Wickham
Jesness

The County returns 4 Members.

Railway Stations, thus •

River Thames

Cliff
St Marys
Allhallows
St James
I.
Sheerness
No.

Lewisham
Lee
Welling
Cranford
Northfleet
Gravesend
Cowling
High Halstow
Stoke
Grain
Minster

Sydenham
Eltham
Pa.
Bexley
Swanscombe
Stone
Dartford
Milton
Chalk
Tha. & Medy
Hynam
Hoo St
Medway
Queenborough

Bromley
Sunridge
Camden
Pa.
Foots
Cray
Crays
Sutton
at Hon
Darent
Southfleet
Shorne
Field W.
Frindsbury
Strood
Hoo
Gillingham
Isle of
Chap. Elmley

Keston
Wickham
Widmore
Bromley
St Pauls
Cray
St Marys
Cray
So Darent
Horton
Longfield
Kirby
Fackham
Nursted
Cobham
Ha.
Rochester
Chatham
Upchurch
Lower Halstow
Wade

5
Wickham
Orpington
Eynsford
Hartley
Meopham
Luddesdown
Ordnance
Town
Rainham
Newington
Robying
Marston

Farnborough
Lulling
stone
Park
Lullingston
Ash
Lower
Halling
Upr
Bell
Luton
Rainham
Hartlip
Borden
Sittingham
Iwade
Tonge
Teynham

Holwood
Hill
Chelsfield
Kings down
Ridley
Snodland
Burham
Low. Bell
Brenhurst
Guildsted
Stockbury
Tunstall
Bredgar
Milstead
Kingsdown
Doddington

Keston
Halstead
Stansted
New
Tube
Aylesford
Boxley
Detling
Huckling
Bicknor
Wormshill

Bradfield
Cudham
Down
Shoreham
Romney
Str.
Trottescliffe
Birling
Wrotham
Leybourne
Maidstone
Thurnham
Wichling
Eastaker
Newn

Chevening
Oxford
Kemsing
Ightham
Malling E.
Ditton
Allington
Bersted
Wormshill

Brasted
Chevening
Pa.
Chipsted
Seal
Wilderne
Malling
Wateringbury
Maidstone
Wares
Pa.
Wrotham
Otterden
Thurgh

Westerham
Fr. Croydon
Squerries
IdeHill
Sundridge
Oak
Stone Str.
Plaxtol
Mereworth
Wrotham
Turning
Willaton
Leeds
as
Hollingbourn
Harietsham

To Uckfield
Idle Hill
Knole
Pa.
Fair
Lawn Pa.
Peckham
West
West Farling
Thorn St.
Leed
Chilston
Pa.

Croolehand
Hill
Marlpit Hill
Shipborne
Hadlow
E. Peckham
Yalding
Farling
Loose
Lunsley
Bromfield
Lenham

Philpot
Tunbridge
Hale St.
Hintoy
Linton
Sutton
Valence
Ulcomb
Boughton
Malherb

From Reigate
Bidborough
Leigh
River Medway
Mockbegar
Sutton
Barling
Gr.
Egerton
Pa.

Eden
Bridge
Bough
Chidding
Tudeley
Capel
Morden
Swithland
Corner
E. Hedcorn
Charin

Hever
Penshurst
Pembury
Wood
Bocken
Ford
Marden
Staplehurst
Pluckley

Marsh
Gr.
Highfield
Brenchley
Winchet
Hill
Frittenden
Bethersden
Smarden

Cowden
Speldhurst
Tunbridge
Wells
Ashurst Lo.
Woods
gate
Chapel
Horsemonden
Sisinghurst
Cas.
Biddenden
Shadorh

S
Ashurst
To Mayfield
To Lewes
Bidborough
Lamberhurst
Goudhurst
Forston
Green
High Halden
Cranbrook

U

LANCASHIRE

This county is bounded on the north by Cumberland and Westmorland; on the east by Yorkshire; on the south by Cheshire; and on the west by the Irish Sea. The greatest length of the county is seventy-four miles, and the greatest breadth forty-five miles: its circumference is three hundred and forty-two miles. The name is derived from the ancient town of Lancaster, but in the earlier periods of history it was inhabited by the Setantii, a tribe of the Brigantes, who were subdued by Julius Agricola, A.D. 79. Under the Romans, it was included in the province of Maxima Cæsariensis and the stations are supposed to be Ad Alaunum, Lancaster; Bremetonacæ, Overborough; Colunio, Colne; Coccium, Blackrode; Rerigonium, Ribchester; and Mancunium, Manchester. After the establishment of the Saxons this county was incorporated with the kingdom of Northumberland. The castles of its ancient lords were at Clithero, Gleaston, Holland Castle, Hornby, Lancaster, Peel Castle in Furness, and Thurland Castle. There were formerly abbeys at Cokersand, Furness, and Whalley; and priories at Burscough, Cartmele, Coningshead, Holland, Hornby, Lancaster, Lytham, and Penwortham, besides the collegiate church at Manchester. Lancashire is a county palatine, is in the province of York and diocese of Chester, and contains one county town, Lancaster, 27 market-towns, 95 parishes, 176,449 inhabited houses, and 1,052,859 inhabitants. It returns twenty-six members to Parliament, agreeably to the Reform Bill of 1832, viz. one for Ashton-under-Lyne, two for Blackburn, two for Bolton, one for Bury, one for Clitheroe, two for Lancaster, two for Liverpool, two for Manchester, two for Oldham, two for Preston, one for Rochdale, one for Salford, one for Warrington, two for Wigan, and four for the county, the present members for the Northern division of which, including the hundreds of Lonsdale, Amounderness, Leyland, and Blackburn, are the Right Honourable Edward Geoffery Smith Stanley, grandson of the Earl of Derby, son-in-law of Lord Skelmersdale, and chief Secretary for Ireland, and John Wilson Patten, Esq.; the members for the Southern Division, including the hundreds of Salford and West Derby, are George William Wood, Esq., and Viscount Molyneux, eldest son of the Earl of Sefton.

On the coast of Lancashire the shore is generally flat. The low lands are highly fertile, especially the Fylde; the district between the rivers Ribble

and Mersey is well adapted for cultivation. Near the sea, northward of Liverpool, appear the roots and trunks of trees at low water, although at present that part of the county is nearly destitute of wood. Lancashire abounds in mosses, which are generally named from places in their vicinity, as Chat Moss, Trafford Moss, Riseby Moss, and Pilling Moss. Eastward of the county, and dividing it from Yorkshire, is a ridge of hills called "The Backbone of England," which from their great elevation screen the county from the severity of the eastern winds. The principal eminences in the county are Pendle Hill, Billinge Hill, Cartmele, Coniston, Furness, and Longridge Fells, Clougho, Grindleton, Twist Castle, and Waddington Hills; Blackstone Edge; Rivington and Hartshead Pikes; Ashurst and Warton Beacons; Sun Low; Royton, and Lancaster Castle. The rivers of Lancashire are the Alt, the Beil, the Blakeburn, the Brown, the Calder, the Charnock, the Chor, the Crake, the Darwen, the Douglas, the Dudden, the Ellerbrook, the Fosse or Leven, the Greta, the Hodder, the Hyndburne, the Irk, the Irwell, the Kew, the Lostock, the Loyne or Lune, the Medlock, the Mersey, the Ribble, the Roch, the Roddlesworth, the Savock, the Spodden, the Swinnel, the Tame, the Taud, the Wenning, the Winbume, the Winster, the Worsley, the Wyer, and the Yarrow. The river Lune rises in the moors of Westmorland and after passing Kirby Lonsdale forms a delightful district, environed by every charm of picturesque landscape below Hornby to Lancaster, in sight of which making some great curves, it falls into the sea. Few vales in England can vie with Lonsdale with the town and castle of Hornby in the centre, finely intersected by the Lune winding between hills clothed with wood, and backed by the high mountain of Ingleborough in Yorkshire. That part of Ribblesdale where the river encompasses the town of Presion is very fine; after which its estuary forms a noble arm of the sea, pervading a great level after it issues from its dale. Few counties are so materially benefited by inland navigation. The Sankey canal was the first complete artificial canal in the kingdom, formed in 1761. Other canals in this county are the Ashton-under-Lyne canal; the Bridgewater, the Haslington, the Lancaster, the Leeds and Liverpool, the Mersey and Irwell, the Manchester, Bolton and Bury, the Rochdale and Ulverston canals. The Manchester and Liverpool railway was opened 15th September 1830. Stone of almost every description is found in this county; the productions of the mineral and fossil kingdom are not very numerous, but are rich and valuable. Coals are excellent and abundant, chiefly in West Derby and Salford hundreds. The first potatoes said to have been cultivated in England were grown in Lancashire. Manchester is the great centre of the cotton trade. Bolton also is a great mart for cotton goods, but particularly for cambrics and fancy muslin; spinning is carried on in this county to an almost incredible extent, the inventions of Sir Richard Arkwright having given an impulse to manufactures to which they were before entire strangers. The neighbourhood of Bolton abounds with extensive factories, bleaching-grounds, &c. Liverpool, as a commercial sea-port, is second only to London, and it has been estimated that one twelfth part of the shipping of Great Britain is navigated by Liverpool; that it has one fourth part of her foreign trade, one sixth part of the general commerce of the kingdom, and one half of the trade of the city of London.

Knowsley Park, near Prescot, is the seat of the Right Honourable the Earl of Derby, Lord Lieutenant of the County.

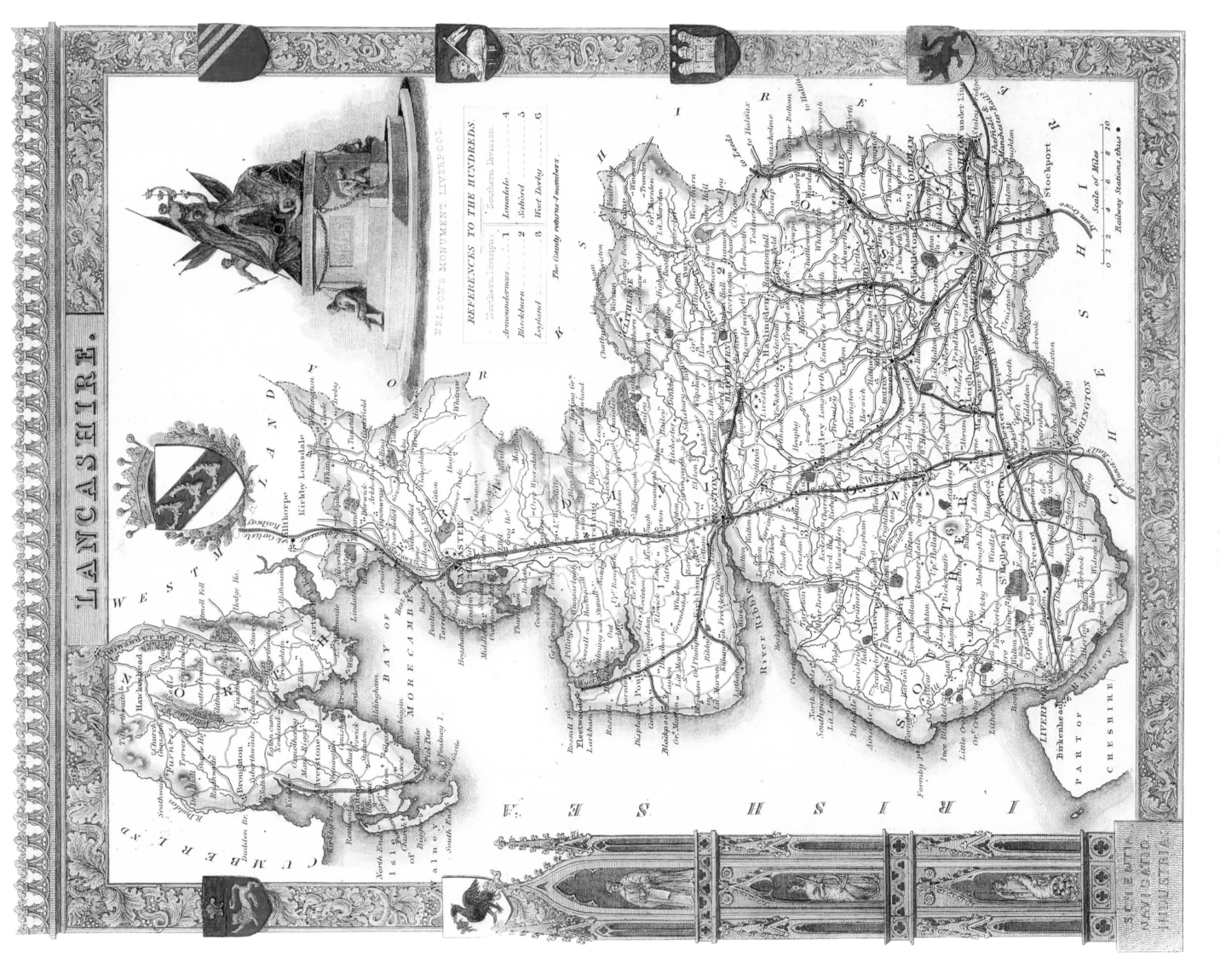

LANCASHIRE.

NELSON'S MONUMENT, LIVERPOOL.

REFERENCES TO THE HUNDREDS:

Northern Division.		Southern Division.	
Amounderness	1	Lonsdale	4
Blackburn	2	Salford	5
Leyland	3	West Derby	6

The County returns 4 members.

Scale of Miles

Railway Stations, thus

SCIENTIA
NAVIGATIO
INDUSTRIA

LIVERPOOL

LIVERPOOL on the Mersey, 36 miles W. from Manchester, and 205 miles from London, contains 19,007 houses, and 118,972 inhabitants. This borough formerly constituted part of the parish of Walton-on-the-Hill, from which it was severed by Act of Parliament in 1699, and it now has separate jurisdiction. The great increase and prosperity of Liverpool have been occasioned by the enterprise and skill of its inhabitants, by its local advantages commanding the trade of Ireland and America, and by the wisdom of the corporation in abolishing all exclusive laws, and encouraging by an entire freedom every species of industry and commercial talent. Liverpool was incorporated by King John, and is governed by a mayor, recorder, an unlimited number of aldermen, two bailiffs, a common council of forty of the principal inhabitants, a town-clerk, and other officers. Whoever has borne the office of mayor is afterwards styled an Alderman. The town-hall, one of the finest edifices of its kind in the kingdom, stands at the north end of Castle-street, a very spacious and beautiful street: it was originally constructed for an exchange in 1749 after designs by *Wood* of Bath, but was never used for that purpose. The whole of the interior being destroyed by fire in 1795, great alterations were afterwards made in the building, and it was then appropriated to offices for the general business of the corporation, a mansion for the mayor, and assembly-rooms. As a specimen of civil architecture this structure affords a striking example of the wealth and spirit of the opulent corporation, whose resources have been nobly employed in the improvement of the town to an extent scarcely credible. The principal entrance to the town-hall is by a portico, of the Corinthian order, on the southern front, facing Castle street. The principal story of the building is raised on a rustic substructure, and is formed by a range of attached columns and antæ designed in a bold and masculine style. On the northern front, where the principal alterations were made after the fire in 1795, a projecting centre is enriched by a colonnade, surmounted by statues, emblematical of the four quarters of the globe. The town hall is crowned by a light and elegant dome, above which is a pedestal and statue of Britannia, seated. From the gallery, which surrounds this dome, is a most interesting panoramic view of the whole town and environs; Everton and Edgehill on the east; the Cheshire shore on the west; and the Mersey, in its course, to the Irish Sea, on the north.

The entrance by the portico on the south front of the town-hall opens upon a vestibule leading to a grand staircase, immediately under the dome, which rises one hundred and six feet above the pavement below. A suite of rooms on the principal story is adorned with a splendid collection of royal portraits: King George III., by *Sir Thomas Lawrence* P.R.A.; King George IV. when Prince of Wales, by *John Hoppner*, R.A. ; His Royal Highness Frederick Duke of York, K.G., by *Thomas Phillips* R.A.; and His present Majesty when Duke of Clarence, by *M.A. Shee* P.R.A. The arms of the borough of Liverpool are *Argent, a cormorant table beaked and legged gules, holding in the beak a branch of laver vert*. Motto, "Deus nobis hæc otia fecit." The general sessions for the peace are held four times a year, and by adjournment every Monday. A court of requests is also held every Wednesday.

The borough of Liverpool returns two members to Parliament; the mayor and two bailiffs are the returning officers; the present members are William Ewart, Esq., and Viscount Sandon, eldest son of the Earl of Harrowby.

The town-hall, in conjunction with the Exchange Buildings, forms a noble quadrangle, in the centre of which is the monument to Nelson. Blome's Geographical Description of the Kingdom, published in 1673, notices the foundation of a mercantile exchange, in consequence of the rising importance of Liverpool. This structure has been replaced by a splendid building, one of the principal ornaments of this town, and which may even be ranked amongst the first commercial edifices in Europe. The New Exchange Buildings were founded in 1803, and in plan complete a quadrangle of greater extent than that of the Royal Exchange in London, the area being one hundred and seventy-eight feet from east to west, and one hundred and ninety-seven feet from north to south.

The style of architecture, being intended to correspond with the northern elevation of the town-hall, is of rather magnificent character. On a rusticated basement, forming a spacious arcade upon each front to protect the merchants from the weather, is raised a Corinthian order, surmounted by a balustrade. The centre division is enriched by eight coupled columns, each formed of one entire stone, and on the entablature are four statues of the elements. The entrance to the Exchange from Old Hall-street is by a vestibule, divided into three avenues, by columns of the Doric order; and the northern front of this building, towards the same street, is also of the Doric order of architecture. The whole edifice is of stone, from the quarries

in Toxteth Park, and was erected from designs by *John Foster*, architect to the Corporation. The monumental group, in bronze, in memory of Nelson, placed in the centre of the quadrangle, was designed by *Matthew Wyatt*, and erected in 1813: it displays a variety of composition. On a circular pedestal are sculptured bassi-relievi of the naval actions of St. Vincent, the Nile, Copenhagen, and Trafalgar: on the frieze, supported by captive figures, in allusion to his signal victories, is inscribed the emphatic words ENGLAND EXPECTS EVERY MAN TO DO HIS DUTY. The principal figure, Nelson, crowned by Victory is represented meeting death in the arms of his country and her navy.

The intimate connexion of Liverpool with the rising empires of the American continent, its vicinity to Ireland, its increasing commerce with the north of Europe, its colonial relations, the participation of the out-ports in the trade to the East Indies, of which Liverpool has extensively availed itself, together with its own local advantages, its important staple commodities of coal, salt, and earthenware, the unrivalled cotton manufacture of the county in which the town is situated, and its connexion with the inland navigation of the kingdom, hold out a prospect of permanent and increasing prosperity. As a proof of the present opulence of the town, and how rapidly it has advanced in a very short space of time, it is only necessary to notice the extensive ranges of houses, and the numerous public buildings which meet the eye in every direction, and mark the spirit of the inhabitants and abundance of their resources. The space at present covered with buildings may be estimated as forming an area of more than six million square yards within the liberties of the borough, and not including the suburbs.

On the banks of the Mersey is a quay of about two miles and a half in extent, presenting an uninterrupted succession of docks, and piers, and towering warehouses. At high water the river affords the most interesting prospects, particularly if a westerly wind favours the arrival of the vast fleets destined to the port. Steam-boats are here also constantly plying to Birkenhead, Tranmere, Woodside, and Seacombe on the opposite coast, whence coaches start for Chester at stated hours every day. The docks are of three kinds:— The principal are the wet docks, which chiefly receive ships in the foreign trade; in them ships are afloat at all times of the tide, the water being retained by the dock gates. The next are the dry docks, which generally receive the vessels that are employed coastwise, and are left dry when the tide is out. The others are the Graving docks, which admit or exclude the water at pleasure, and in which ships are laid dry for the purpose of caulking or repair. The Old Dock was constructed in 1710, and at the east end is the Custom house; this dock receives Irish traders and vessels from the Mediterranean. The dry dock is chiefly occupied by sloops from the northern coast. Salt House Dock derives its name from a salt work, afterwards removed to Garston, higher up the river. The upper end is chiefly occupied by ships which are laid up, and the lower part by the Levant, Irish, and coasting vessels. George's Dock extends from the corner of St. Nicholas's churchyard to Moor street. This dock is chiefly occupied by West India ships, but communicates by a basin at the northern end with Prince's Dock. On the western side of these docks, towards the river, are stairs for the accommodation of passengers embarking by the numerous steam-boats bound to North Wales, the Isle of Man, Scotland, and Ireland;– a mode of conveyance which has in no small degree increased the political and commercial importance of Liverpool.

The King's Dock, contiguous to the King's tobacco warehouses, receives all the vessels from Virginia and other parts laden with tobacco, this being the only place where they are allowed to discharge their cargo. This dock communicates with a dry dock or basin to the south, which is connected with the Queen's Dock, the largest in the harbour, chiefly occupied by timber vessels, and by Dutch and Baltic shipping; at the southern end it communicates with the Queen Half-tide Dock, southward of which is the site of Brunswick Dock.

The Prince's Dock was opened in 1821, and is exceeded in size by the Queen's Dock only. Along the western side, next to the river, runs the royal parade, whence the most delightful views of the river, the shipping, &c., are obtained; it is consequently a place of great resort. The boundary of the port of Liverpool, as fixed by commissioners 28th November, 1723, is from the Redstones in Hoylake on the point of the Wirral southerly, to the foot of the Ribble water in a direct line northerly, and so upon the southern side of the same river to Hesketh Bank easterly, and to the river Astland and Douglas, and all along the sea coast of Meols and Formby into the river Mersey, and all over the rivers Mersey, Irwell, and Weever.

Goree Buildings, at the bottom of Water-street, were erected on the site of remarkably lofty and spacious warehouses, that were destroyed by a tremendous fire on the night of the 14th of September, 1802, which consumed property estimated at more than 200,000*l.* in value. The present very extensive range of buildings, in two divisions, are chiefly designed as storehouses for corn, and have for a basement a convenient arcade for transacting business in unfavourable weather. Between these warehouses and the river Mersey is St. George's Dock.

The two water communications by which goods have been conveyed between Liverpool and Manchester, are the Mersey and Irwell navigation, consisting alternately of the two rivers Mersey and Irwell, and canals, and of the Duke of Bridgewater's canal. The Act of Parliament incorporating the Old Quay Company for the formation of the first was obtained in 1733; that for the Duke's canal was procured in 1760. The immense amount of traffic had first to be shipped at Liverpool, then conveyed up the river to Runcorn, a distance of twenty miles, and was then forwarded by canal to Manchester, the whole distance between the towns being nearly fifty miles. The average time of the passage was thirty-six hours, and the cost fifteen shillings per ton. The canals were undoubtedly a great improvement on the old mode of conveyance; and such was the increase in their value to the proprietors, consequent on the increase of the intercourse between the two towns, that the shares which were originally bought for 70*l.* have been sold for 1250*l.* each.

The Liverpool and Manchester railway, which has superseded every other mode of conveyance between the towns, is unquestionably the finest enterprise the nation has for a long time witnessed: it passes through a rich and extensive coal district in full working. The railway commences at the port of Liverpool, at a point in direct communication with the King's and Queen's docks, and passes under the town by a tunnel and inclined plane. The archway, lighted with gas is sixteen feet high, and twenty-two feet wide, and is cut through a solid rock for two thousand two hundred and forty-eight yards, rising one foot in forty nine. The road is thus continued for about a mile and a quarter, nearly from west to east, and comes into day-light at the top of Edgehill, where the road is one hundred and twenty three feet higher than at its commencement in Wapping. The rails used on the road are made of wrought iron, in lengths of five yards each; every three feet the rails rest on blocks of stone let into the ground, but on the embankments, where the road was expected to subside, the rails are laid on oak sleepers. The double line of rails for the carriages is laid down with mathematical correctness, and consists of four equi-distant rails, four feet eight inches apart, about two inches in breadth, and rising about one inch above the surface.

About half a mile from the tunnel the railway crosses Wavertree Lane, and there is then a descent for five miles and a half. About half a mile northward of Wavertree, at Olive Mount, there is an excavation, two miles in length. The railway is there carried by means of an embankment, over a valley at Roby, or *Broad Green*, two miles in length and crosses the Huyton

NELSON'S MONUMENT, LIVERPOOL.

turnpike-road a little beyond Roby. At the distance of six miles and three quarters from Liverpool there is a junction railway for the conveyance of coals from the mines on the south; and at seven or eight miles from Liverpool is the Whiston inclined plane, one mile and a half in length, where an engine is stationed to assist the carriages in their ascent. Beyond this point, for nearly two miles, the road is an exact level; and it was here that the contest of locomotive carriages for a premium of 500*l.*, given by the Company, took place in October, 1829. At Rainhill, half a mile from the Whiston plane, the railway crosses the Liverpool and Manchester turnpike-road. On leaving the level at Rainhill the railway crosses the Sutton inclined plane, which is of the same extent as that at Whiston, and descends in the tame proportion that the other rises; here is another stationary engine. A little beyond Rainhill several collieries communicate with the lioe of road by means of railways, and the Runcorn Gap railway here crosses the line to St. Helen's.

The next object of interest is Parr Moss, the road over which was formed principally of the clay and stone dug from the Sutton inclined plane, and extends about three quarters of a mile. The railway is then carried over the valley of Sankey, by means of a massive viaduct, consisting of nine arches of fifty feet span each, the height of the parapet being seventy feet above the Sankey canal in the valley beneath. The viaduct is built principally of brick, with stone facings, and the foundation rests on piles driven into the ground.

The viaduct is approached by an embankment of extraordinary magnitude, formed principally of the clay dug from the high lands surrounding the valley. The appearance of the vessels in the canal beneath has a striking effect. Southward of the town of Newton the railway crosses a narrow valley by the lofty embankment of Sandy Mains, and a bridge of four arches, each forty feet span under one of which passes the turnpike road from Newton to Warrington. The Wigan and Newton branch here enters the railway. A few miles beyond Newton is the Kenyon excavation. The Kenyon and Leigh junction railway here joins the Liverpool and Manchester line, and as that also joins the Bolton and Leigh line, brings Bolton into direct communication with Liverpool.

The railway then passes successively under three bridges, and a little beyond Culcheth over the Broxley embankment, which is about a mile and a half in length: it then passes over Bury Lane and the river Gless, or *Glazebrook,* and arrives at Chat Moss. The line extends across the Moss, a distance of about four miles and three quarters. On leaving Chat Moss the railway passes over the lowlands at Barton, extending about a mile between

the Moss and Worsley canal, by means of an embankment: it is carried over the canal by a stone viaduct of two arches, and proceeds through Eccles and a portion of Salford, under six bridges. The railway is carried over the Irwell by a stone bridge of sixty-three feet span, thirty feet from the water, and then over twenty-two brick arches, and over a bridge to the station in Water-street, Manchester, a distance of thirty-one miles from the Liverpool station. Along the line of road, there are at every mile and quarter of a mile, posts showing the distance from Liverpool to Manchester.

Most of the carriages used as public coaches consist, like the French diligences, of two or three bodies joined together; some are intended to accommodate four persons in each body, and others six; between the sittings is a rest for the arms, and each passenger has a cushion, with back, &c., covered with fine cloth, like a private carriage.

The ceremony of opening the railway took place on 15th September, 1830: a procession left Liverpool, drawn by eight locomotive engines, the first of which was the Northumbrian, with the directors of the Railway Company and numerous distinguished visitors including the Duke of Wellington; the other engines were the Phœnix, the North Star, the Rocket, the Dart, the Comet, the Arrow, and the Meteor. The Northumbrian drew three carriages, the first containing a band of music, the second the Duke of Wellington and the visitors, and the third the Directors. The Phœnix and the North Star drew five carriages each. The Rocket drew three; and the Dart, Comet, Arrow, and Meteor, each four. The total number of persons conveyed was seven hundred and seventy-two. The carriages did not proceed at a particularly rapid pace, scarcely fifteen miles an hour. On the arrival of the procession at Parkside, about nineteen miles from Liverpool, the carriages stopped to take in a supply of water. It was here that Mr Huskisson met with the melancholy accident which caused his death the same evening. The procession went on to Manchester, and returned to Liverpool in the order previously arranged, but the public dinner was of course postponed. In the year 1822 Mr. James, an engineer of London, suggested the idea of the railway to Mr Joseph Sanders, and a preliminary survey was made, upon which a prospectus of the plan was issued, and application made to Parliament for a bill to incorporate the Company. A second bill was presented to Parliament in 1826, and the Company being established the work was completed in four years.

In literary institutions Liverpool sets a noble example. The Athenæum, in Church-street, was the first of the kind established in the kingdom; and its library contains the collection of MSS., &c. made by the late William Roscoe, for his Lives of Lorenzo de Medici and Leo X. The Lyceum, in Bold street, was erected from designs by *Harrison,* of Chester; the library is deposited in a circular room, adorned with numerous busts. The Union News-room, in Duke-street, erected from designs by *Foster,* is of the Ionic order, and was founded on January 1st, 1800, the day on which the Union with Ireland took place: an emblematical picure by *Fuseli,* R.A., adorns the room. The Exchange News-room occupies part of the lower story of

the Exchange Buildings, and the underwriters' room is immediately over it. The Liverpool Royal Institution is a spacious edifice, in Colquitt-street; the Society was formed in 1814, and incorporated by charter in 1822: within the building is a large room appropriated to the use of the Literary and Philosophical Society of Liverpool, and other rooms for a library and museum, as well as an exhibition room for the use of the members of the Liverpool Academy; another room for casts of the Elgin marbles, a drawing-school, laboratory, &c.

The museum contains specimens of natural history, a collection of minerals, &c., and the exhibition room contains a series of pictures, designed to illustrate the early history and progress of the arts, formerly belonging to William Roscoe. Besides the casts from the Elgin marbles presented by King George IV., here are also casts from the Phigalian frieze, and casts from marbles discovered on the site of the Temple of Jupiter Panhellenius in the island of Egina. A school of arts was founded in 1825.

The Botanic Garden is situated near Edgehill, and is of considerable extent, inclosed by a wall, with lodges at the entrance, and a spacious conservatory. The mount on St. James's Walk, at the top of Duke-street, is an elevated situation, commanding an extensive and interesting prospect: it belongs to the Corporation; and the terrace, shrubbery, and walks are supported by them, for the accommodation of the public. The market of Liverpool are supplied from a great distance. Ireland and Scotland furnish grain, cattle, sheep, hogs, bacon, and butter. The Isles of Man and Anglesey, and many parts of North Wales, send live poultry of all sorts, eggs and fresh butter. From Cheshire, and especially the hundred of Wirral, poultry, fruit, butter, and other articles, are regularly brought over in the steam-boats, which are continually passing and repassing the river. The same articles are also brought over from Ireland, the steam-boats affording much facility to the Irish dealers to attend the markets. Potatoes are brought from the neighbouring parts of this county. The farms in the vicinity of Liverpool are devoted to the production of milk. Vegetables are here found very early in the season, as well as native and foreign fruits. The New Market, designed by *John Foster, Jun.*, was completed in February, 1822: it is situated in the centre of the town, in the neighbourhood of Queen-square, Clayton-square, and Williamson-square; its principal front is in Great Charlotte-street; the length of the building is five hundred and forty-nine feet, its breadth one hundred and thirty-five feet, forming a covered square of nearly two acres of ground. The market-place forms a large and lightly painted hall, divided into five

avenues, there being four rows of cast-iron, pillars, twenty-three feet high, supporting the conjoined abutments of the roof along the entire building; the pillars are one hundred and sixteen in number, but are so lightly formed, as greatly to improve the general appearance by their regular arrangement. The great body of the market is occupied by four lines of stalls, tables, &c., ranged in a line with the pillars from end to end, and the whole is lighted by gas every night. The principal market-days are Wednesday and Saturday, but there is a considerable market every day. St. James's market is for the convenience of the south end of the town and Harrington, and there are also seven others held in the open air; viz. the Old market in Derby-square Castle street; one in Cleveland-square; one in Islington; one in Pownall-square; the cattle and hay market in Lime street; and the pig market in Great Howard-street. Liverpool was made a distinct parish in 1699, before which it was considered a township of Walton. St. Nicholas's, or the old church, is a curacy, with the rectory of St. Peter's, in the patronage of the Corporation. It is situated on the banks of the river Mersey, at the northern end of St. George's Dock; the body of the church was rebuilt in 1774, and the tower and spire were rebuilt, from a design by *Harrison* of Chester, in 1811. In the church are a few monuments; amongst which is one in memory of William Clayton Esq., of Fulwood, who represented the borough in six Parliaments; he died in 1715. From his family Clayton-square, in the town, derives its name.

St. Peter's church in Church street was built in 1704, and is a rectory, in the patronage of the Corporation: in the chancel are monuments of Foster Cunliffe, Esq., and of William Lawley, Esq.

The other churches in the town are properly chapels-of-ease, and are all modern. St. George's church, originally consecrated in 1734, has been rebuilt under the direction of *J. Foster, Jun.,* architect to the Corporation: it is of the Doric order of architecture, rusticated, having above the entablature a panelled attic. On the side of the church is a terrace, raised upon an arcade, beneath which is a market for vegetables and fruits, the growth of the open garden, produced here earlier and in greater abundance than in many other parts of the kingdom. Octangular buildings on the southern side of the church contain offices for the clerk of the market, &c. The bate of the tower, thirty feet square, in plan is rusticated Doric; the next story is of the Ionic order of architecture, and of an octangular form; between the columns are belfry windows, and a clock. Over this is a Corinthian peristyle, surmounted by a balustrade, forming a gallery round the base of the spire, which is quite plain, with oval openings for lights, and finished with a Composite capital; the whole height, to the top of the spire, it about two hundred and fourteen feet. At this church the mayor, aldermen and common council usually attend divine service. St. Thomas's church was consecrated in 1750: the nave has a rusticated base, upon which is raised an Ionic order, with a balustrade and vases; the chancel is octangular in plan.

St. Paul's church, founded in 1763, is situated a short distance northward of the town hall. Owing to its great elevation, and being erected on rising ground, it is rendered an attractive object in a distant view of the town: it was built from designs by *T. Lightoler*. The west front consists of a hexastyle portico, of the Ionic order, elevated on a platform, with an ascent of seven steps; the entablature is continued from the portico round the entire building, surmounted with a balustrade, and vases at the angles: there are no monuments within the church.

St. Anne's church, at the northern end of St. Anne-street Richmond, was built about 1770; it is in the pointed style of architecture, and the east window is of painted glass.

St. Michael's church is situated in Kent-street, and is of the Corinthian order of architecture, from the temple of Jupiter Stator at Rome.

The Church of the School for the Blind is situated in Duncan-street: it was founded in 1818, and was erected from designs by *John Foster, Jun.*, in the Doric order of architecture. Over the altar is a picture of Christ restoring the Blind, by *Hilton*, presented to the church by Thomas Wilson, Esq.; and in the chancel is a monument to the memory of Pudsey Dawson, Esq. one of the earliest patrons of the institution.

Trinity church, on the eastern side of St. Anne-street was built in 1792. St. Stephen's church is in 13 Byrom-street; and St. Matthew's, in Key-street.

Christ church, situated in Hunter-street, was erected at the expense of John Houghton, in 1797, and endowed by him with 105*l.* per annum, as a salary for a minister. The view of the town from a circular gallery which surrounds the cupola of this church, is more perfect than can elsewhere be obtained, excepting from the town hall.

St. Mark's church, at the upper end of Duke-street, was consecrated in 1815: in the chancel is a large painted window. All Saints' church, situated in Grenville-street, was formerly a tennis-court, to which a tower has been added. St. Andrew's church, in Renshaw-street, was erected at the expense of John Gladstone, Esq., and was consecrated in 1815. St. Philip's church, situated in Hard-man-street, near Rodney-street, was built by John Craggs, in the pointed style of architecture, and was consecrated in 1816.

St. Luke's church in Berry-street, at the top of Bold-street, was founded in 1811: it was built by the Corporation, in the pointed style of architecture. There is a spacious public cemetery at Low Hill; besides which, the excavation near the mount on St. James's Walk, at the top of Duke street, whence the stone used in the erection of many of the public buildings of Liverpool was cut, has been converted into a public cemetery, in imitation of the celebrated Père la Chaise at Paris, in which is a chapel of Doric architecture. The late Right Hon. William Huskisson was here interred, 24th September, 1830, agreeably to his own request; the funeral was public; the place of his interment is at the bottom of a dell, about sixty feet below the ordinary level of the streets of the town. On the west the bank rises gradually till it comes to a double tier of terraces, and is then surmounted by the cluster of trees in St. James's Walk.

On September 30, 1822, an equestrian statue of King George III. was placed on its pedestal in the open space at the junction of London-road and Pembroke-place. The statue is of bronze, by *Westmacott*; it is of heroic size, and is in the Roman costume.

About the middle of the 17th century, the site principally covered with buildings in Liverpool, or *Lyrpoole,* appears to have been for the most part confined to the elevated ground on which Castle-street now stands, and to a few streets running short distances from the ancient Town-house. The castle built by Roger de Poitiers, was taken down in 1721. Towards the river side there appears to have been only three streets—Moor-street, Water-street, and Chapel-street and these were but scantily covered with buildings. Eastward, Duke-street appears to have been a few straggling houses, with crofts and barns. Between this street and Tithe-Barn street there would seem to have been no communication; for Sir Edward Moor, (whose name is perpetuated by Moor-street,) in a MS. description of his property in Liverpool, recommends his son to open a passage from Dale-street to Tithe Barn-street, through a petty croft where Hackinsley now stands. On the south-east, towards the Pool, there were several houses, but with wide interstices between them. The inlet along Whitechapel was the natural boundary of the town, and on the banks boats were kept. This inlet had a communication with the water in Moss-lake fields, the site of the present Abercrombie-square, adjacent to the botanic garden, its course being down Pembroke-place, across London-road, to the end of Byrom-street. The only public structures were the Town-house, St. Nicholas's church, and the old tower in Water-street, near the river, built it is supposed in 1252 and embattled by Sir John Stanley, by permission from King Henry IV. The remains of this building were replaced by warehouses in 1819. A few specimens of the dwelling-houses of the period still remain in Moor-street, Lancelot's Key, and Moor-fields. The Old Hall, the residence of the family of Moor, in Old Hall-street and Cross Hall, the seat of the Cross family, whence the present name of Cross Hall-street, were the two principal mansions of the time. The Old Hall occupied all the space between Chapel-street and Rosemary-lane now Fazakerley-street, and between Old Hall-street and Lancelot's Key. On the site of the present King's Arms in Castle-street was New Hall, belonging to the Mayhulls of Mayhull, or *Maghull*. The rapid advance of the Port of Liverpool in commercial importance will be found detailed in the histories of the town. Liverpool is almost the creation of yesterday, with nothing on the score of antiquity to illustrate it. The recent elevation to the rank of the second commercial town in the British empire, is the proudest pillar of her fame, at once her glory and her boast.

MANCHESTER

MANCHESTER, on the river Irwell 18 miles E. from Warrington, and 186 miles from London, contains 16,653 houses and 108,016 inhabitants; but the great enlargement of the town of Manchester, in consequence of its manufactures, has caused the townships of Ardwick, Chorlton Row, and Hulme, to become constituent parts of the town, which so taken, contains 149,756 inhabitants. Salford also contains 25,772 inhabitants, and the entire parish contains 186,942 inhabitants. As a commercial and manufacturing town, Manchester has of late years become distinguished by its importance beyond any other in the kingdom; the liberal and public-spirited inhabitants having attained great opulence in consequence of their superior talents and industry. Its public buildings, particularly the modern ones, are all erected on a proportionate scale of size and elegance. The architectural improvements of Manchester commenced about the year 1776, by widening some of the streets near the centre of the town. Old Millgate, Cateaton-street, and St. Mary's Gate, were the first altered: the present Exchange-street was formed soon afterwards. The Exchange itself, which had not for some time before been used for its nominal purpose, was removed in 1792. The houses in Market-street, the principal street in the town, have all been rebuilt within the last seven years. The cotton trade, an inconsiderable branch of commerce previously to the first enlargement of the streets of the town, had been greatly increased by the ingenious inventions of Sir Richard Arkwright; its subsequently rapid progress was chiefly owing to the energy and abilities of Sir Robert Peel, whose more recent improvements of the machines conferred a greater degree of practical utility, by abridging the labour of manufacturing the various articles of commerce. The great factories receive their motion from that valuable discovery the steam-engine which consumes a vast quantity of coal: of this Lancashire possesses an abundance, as well as plenty of pure water,— a necessity of the first importance to the manufacturer. The energetic exertions of the principal inhabitants of Manchester soon enabled them to produce superior articles to accommodate the wants of most foreign nations; the effect of this vast addition to our export trade conduces highly to the prosperity of this country, adding to our maritime strength an increasing number of ships, required in a commercial intercourse of great extent. The trade of Manchester extends through every part of Europe. The rivers Irk, Medlock, and Irwell, together with several canals, afford prodigious advantages of communication with all the towns and ports of Great Britain, and particularly with Liverpool, Hull, and London.

The river Irwell rising in the moors which divide this county from Yorkshire, flows westward through Rosendale Forest below Haslingdon, whence it takes a southern course to Bury; a little below this town it receives the Roch, and reaching Manchester is incorporated with the Irk and Medlock, and afterwards joins the Mersey at Flixton, seven miles southward from Manchester. The bridges over the Irwell are five:— the old bridge, built in the reign of Edward III., was improved in the year 1778; Blackfriars bridge was opened in 1820; the erection of this light and elegant bridge, in a line with the principal street and forming a spacious communication with Salford, was a long desired improvement of the town. The bed of the river Irwell is here very narrow, and liable to floods, which rise suddenly, and to a great height; these sometimes made the former bridge impassable; it was

of wood, and for foot passengers only. The road is now carried straight over three semicircular arches, the two piers adorned with coupled Ionic columns, and the entablature crowned with a handsome balustrade. The New Bayley bridge, over the Irwell derives, its present name from its situation near the New Bayley prison in Stanley-street, Salford; the bridge is of stone, and the road over it leads to Liverpool, Preston &c., through Bridge-street, the upper end of which was widened to render it more convenient: it was opened in 1785, two years prior to the erection of the prison, the foundation stone of which, inscribed with the name of Howard, was laid in 1787 by Thomas Butterworth Bayley. The Regent's-bridge of two arches, was built in 1806, and leads to Ordsall; and the Waterloo-bridge, of iron, near Strangeways, was erected in 1817. There are seven bridges over the Irk; one, leading from Miller-street, is extremely ornamental. Over the river Medlock there are several bridges, but of inconsiderable magnitude, as well as others over the different canals that intersect the town.

The commercial-rooms, one of the principal ornaments, of Manchester are situated nearly in its centre. The building was erected from designs by *Harrison* of Chester, and was opened on the 2nd January 1809. It forms a bold semicircular projection, of the Doric order, correct in its proportion and pleasing in effect; the attic is enriched with panelled compartments, sculptured with festoons of foliage. In the principal room is a portrait by *Sir Thomas Lawrence*, with this inscription "Thomas Stanley, Colonel of the Royal Lancashire Militia, and one of the Representatives of this County. This Portrait presented to the Merchants and Manufacturers of Manchester by Thomas Jackson and James Ackers, Esqs., is placed here as a testimony of regard for the ability and zeal with which he has uniformly promoted the commercial interests of this town during eight successive Parliaments: 1809." Nearly adjoining the commercial-rooms is the post-office, which produces a very large revenue, Manchester being amongst all other towns only inferior in population to London and Glasgow, and still in a state of rapid progress.

The market-places at Manchester are not remarkable, like those of Liverpool, for their appearance and accommodation; but a covered market in the London-road and another in Brown-street, as well as the shambles in Deansgate, are abundantly supplied; a market is held on Tuesday for manufactured goods from the country, and on Thursday and Saturday for provisions. There are fairs on Easter Monday for toys and ale, and 1st October for horses, cattle, and hogs. The municipal government of the town is vested in a borough-reeve and two constables, chosen annually by a jury of the

inhabitants; a magistrate, who is a barrister presides over the police, and sits every day. The town hall, situated in King-street, is a building of the Ionic order, having on each side of the portico statues of Solon and Alfred. The petty sessions are held quarterly; and here also are held a court-leet and court-baron, the hundred court of Salford, the county court, and a court of requests. The arms of the town of Manchester are *Gules, three bendlels enhanced or*. The several townships of Manchester, Chorlton Row, otherwise Chorlton-upon-Medlock, Ardwick, Beswick, Hulme, Cheetham, Bradford, Newton, and Harpur Hey, return two members to Parliament, according to the Reform Bill of 1832; the present members are Mark Philips, Esq., and the Right Hon Charles Poulett Thomson, Treasurer of the Navy, and Vice President of the Board of Trade. The collegiate church of Christ, in the patronage of the Crown, was originally founded in 1422 by Thomas West Lord De La Warr: it was dissolved in 1547, but refounded by Queen Elizabeth, and again by King Charles I. in 1636, when it was incorporated in the name of the warden and fellows of Christ-church in Manchester, although its original dedication was to the Virgin Mary. It was during the wardship of Sir James Stanley, brother to the Earl of Derby, that the present church was erected in the reign of Henry VII. On the north side is the Derby chapel, named after his family. The chapter house was erected at the expense of various persons, whose arms remain. Chetham's chapel, at the east end of the choir, was built by Sir George West, lord of the manor, and was originally dedicated to St. Michael. The chapel belonging to Strangeways was built by "Hulton of the Park," but is now the property of Lord Ducie. The interior of this church is very interesting; the windows have rich remains of the painted glass with which they were once filled. The ceiling, of fretwork, is enriched with carved figures of angels playing upon different musical instruments. The choir, if a few cathedrals are excepted, is one of the finest in the kingdom; the tabernacle work, particularly over the warden's stall, is peculiarly beautiful, and, fortunately, is in good preservation. The east end of the stalls on the north side bears the arms of Beck impaled with those of the Mercers' Company. At the east end of the south stalls are the arms of Stanley, with the usual quarterings; at the entrance of the choir on the north stall are the arms of West, the founder of the church; and on the south side the arms of Stanley, with the badge of Latham, the eagle and child, curiously carved. Over several of the stalls are inscribed the names of the proprietors;— as the warden, the fellows, the chaplains, the singing men, and the parish clerks, the head master and the under master of the grammar school; they are ornamented with carvings of the most grotesque kind, particularly under the seats: the badges of the Stanley family and the arms of the Isle of Man are also introduced. On the floor are three slabs, inlaid with brass, in memory of the members of the Ratcliff family; and one to Lady Barbara Fitz Roy, daughter of the Most Noble Charles Duke of Cleveland and Southampton, who died 4th January 1734. The organs here are considered particularly fine; the choir organ was built in 1684, and the large organ in 1724; both as well as the swell, are supplied by the same bellows, and may be played from the same point upon three rows of keys. Cathedral service is here performed every morning and afternoon. St. Ann's church, situated on the south side of St. Ann's-square, is a rectory, in the patronage of the Bishop of Chester: it is of the Corinthian order, and was consecrated in 1712. St. Mary's church, situated between Deansgate and the river Irwell, was built in the year 1756, and is a rectory, in the patronage of the warden and fellows of the collegiate church: the edifice is of the Doric order, with a tower and taper spire, one hundred and eighty-six feet high, which is admired for its pleasing effect. St. Paul's church, situated at the cast end of Turner-street, is a brick building, with a stone tower, consecrated in 1765; it is a perpetual curacy, in the presentation of the warden and fellows of the collegiate church. St. John's church, situated between higher and lower Byrom street, was built in 1769: it is a rectory, in the patronage of the heirs of the founder Edward Byrom, Esq., and the warden and fellows of the collegiate church. The east window, by *William Peckett of York*, represents St. John, St. Peter, and St. James. One of the southern windows of ancient glass, represents the entrance of Jesus Christ into Bethlehem; it was brought from a convent at Rouen. St. James's church in George-street, was built in 1788 by the Rev. Cornelius Bayley D.D., in whose heirs the presentation is vested for sixty years, and afterwards

with the warden and fellows of the collegiate church. St. Michael's church, in Angel-street, was built in 1789 by the Rev. Humphrey Owen, M.A., in whose family the presentation was fixed for sixty years, and afterwards in the warden and fellows of the collegiate church. St. Peter's church, at the end of Morley-street, was built in 1788 by subscription; *James Wyatt* was the architect: it is of the Doric order. St. Clement's church, in Lever street, was built in 1793. St. George's church, near Oldham road, was opened in 1798. St. Matthew's church, in Camp field near Deansgate, is in the pointed style by *Barry*, and was completed in 1825; the light lantern tower is much admired. The grammar-school, situated near the college gates in Long Mill-gate, was founded and munificently endowed by Hugh Oldham Bishop of Exeter in 1519; he was a native of Oldham, and was chaplain to Margaret Countess of Richmond, mother of King Henry VII. This school is still in high repute, and has eight exhibitions for the University of Oxford. The blue-coat hospital was founded and endowed by Humphrey Chetham of Clayton Hall near Manchester, and Turton Hall near Bolton, who died in 1658. The building was formerly the residence of the warden and fellows of the collegiate church, and was purchased for the use of this school. It stands upon the edge of a rock, which overhangs the river Irk, and at its foundation was romantically situated. In addition to the school, the founder erected a public library, of which a catalogue was published by the Rev. John Radcliffe, librarian, in 1791. In the library is a portrait of the founder, and of several eminent divines and natives of this county.

Besides its consequence in the commercial world, Manchester has been hardly less distinguished by its Literary and Philosophical Society, established in 1781; the Memoirs or Transactions of which body hold a high rank in literature. The Royal Manchester Institution, in Morley-street, is a handsome building; and the Portico, a building of the Ionic order, also situated in Morley-street, contains a library and news-room, on a large scale. The Natural History Society, in King-street, has a museum attached to

the building. Manchester has also its Anatomical theatre, Agricultural and Horticultural Societies, and its Mechanical Institution. In Water-street is the station of the Manchester and Liverpool railway, which crosses the Irwell to Salford and proceeds through Eccles, &c.

Manchester must be taken in conjunction with its contiguous townships of Ardwick, Chorlton Row, Hulme, and Salford, which now constitute part of the actual town, and are not distinguishable to the eye of a stranger.

Ardwick adjoins Manchester on the S.E., and contains 617 houses, and 3545 inhabitants. The chapel, dedicated to St. Thomas, was erected in 1741, but has been since enlarged: the curacy is in the presentation of the warden and fellows of the collegiate church of Manchester. Ardwick Green, three miles from Market-street, forms a pleasant approach to Manchester, being planted and adorned with handsome houses on the border of an ornamental canal.

Chorlton Row, adjoining Manchester, on the south contains 1630 houses, and 8209 inhabitants. St. Luke's chapel was built in 1805; and All Saints church, in the centre of Grosvenor-square, a building of the Doric order, was erected in 1820.

Hulme adjoins Manchester on the south-east, being divided from the town by the river Medlock. This township contains 749 houses, and 4234 inhabitants. St. George's church, erected under the recent Acts of Parliament, in the pointed style of architecture, is a curacy, in the presentation of the warden and fellows of the collegiate church of Manchester. Here are large barracks for horse soldiers.

Hulme Hall, an ancient seat of the Prestwich family, stands on the banks of the Irwell: it is singularly curious, being built of timber and plaster, with carved panels in some of the rooms, but has long been in a state of dilapidation.

Salford, only separated from Manchester by the river Irwell, contains 4503 houses, and 25,772 inhabitants. The Crescent commands a rich view of rural scenery, through which the Irwell meanders, and from its peculiar site the prospect can never be interrupted by buildings. Salford forms the north-western part of Manchester, and was a populous suburb as early as the reign of James I. Salford returns one member to Parliament, according to the Reform Bill of 1832; the present member is J. Brotherton Esq. Trinity church, the oldest ecclesiastical structure in the township, was founded in the year 1635 by Humphrey Booth, Esq., who endowed it with lands in

Pendleton, and a certain sum arising from the Ancoats estate. This church was rebuilt in 1752, in the Doric style of architecture: it is situated in Chapel-street, and is a perpetual curacy, in the presentation of Sir Robert Gore Booth, Bart. St. Stephen's church, situated in a street of the same name, near Bank Parade, was built in the year 1794: it is a perpetual curacy, in the presentation of the heirs of the Rev. N. Cheek for sixty years, and afterwards of the warden and fellows of the collegiate church in Manchester. St. Philip's church at Whitecross Bank, was erected in 1825, from designs by *Smirke*: the tower, circular in plan, presents an elevation of some elegance in three stories. A bold portico is carried round the tower, above which rises a peristyle, having between the columns arched-headed windows: this story of the tower supports a circular lantern and an hemispherical dome. The details of the whole of the enrichments employed in this building are derived from pure Grecian models, with which the architect is known to be familiar.

The market house is ornamental as well as useful: the market is held weekly, on Saturday; and there are annual fairs on Whit Monday for horses, cattle, and pigs; and on the 17th of November: the last is usually called Dirt Fair. The cloth-hall is resorted to, during Whit-Monday fair, by the Yorkshire dealers.

The New Bayley prison for the hundred of Salford is spacious; its walls form a square, the sides of which are each one hundred and twenty yards, guarded by iron chevaux de frize. This entrance to the prison is by a rusticated stone gatehouse, giving an idea of its great strength and perfect security. Over the entrance is a large room in which the sessions are held, with other rooms for magistrates, counsel, jurors, and witnesses. Behind this lodge, in the midst of a large area, stands the prison, erected on the plan of a cross, three stories high. In the centre of the second story is the prison chapel. All the prisoners who can work at any trade are employed, none being suffered to acquire habits of idleness within the walls; an indiscriminate confinement in a prison where industry is not insisted upon, being considered as only affording the means for completing a vicious education. The New Bayley prison is entirely free from this evil; the spirit of benevolence which directed the humanity of Howard and Beccaria has amply provided against it. The infantry barracks, in the Regent's-road, Salford, will afford quarters for a thousand men, and are in other respects extremely convenient.

Beswick adjoins Manchester on the east and contains 9 houses; and 35 inhabitants.

Cheetham is one mile N.E. from Manchester, and contains 369, houses and 2027 inhabitants. St. Mark's church, on Cheetham Hill, was founded in 1794. This neighbourhood abounds with handsome residences of the opulent manufacturers of Manchester. Smedley Hall, an ancient mansion, was the residence of Edward Chetham, the last of his family, who died in 1768.

Bradford, 2 miles E. from Manchester, contains 18 houses and 95 inhabitants. In this township coal is procured, which is most valuable for manufacturing purposes.

Newton, 2 miles N.E. from Manchester contains 421 houses, and 2577 inhabitants. Culcheth Hall, in this township, is the seat of Robert Keymer, Esq.

Harpur Hey, 2½ miles N.E. from Manchester contains, 55 houses, and 297 inhabitants. In this township, which is remarkable for its pleasant views, is Hendham Hall, the seat of J. Andrew, Esq.

The parish of Manchester is extensive, and contains fifty square miles in surface, including within its boundary the following townships, in addition to those already described:—

Blackley, or *Blakeley*, 4 miles N.E. from Manchester, containing 472 houses, and 2911 inhabitants.

Broughton, 2 miles N.W. from Manchester, containing 146 houses, and 880 inhabitants. Broughton Hall, the seat of the Rev John Clowes, was rebuilt about 1780.

Burnage, 4½ miles S.E. from Manchester, containing 92 houses and 513 inhabitants.

Chorlton on the borders of Cheshire, 4 miles S.W. from Manchester, containing 110 houses, and 624 inhabitants, including the hamlet of Hardy.

Crumpsall, 2 miles N. from Manchester, containing 139 houses, and 910 inhabitants. Crumpsall Hall is the seat of J.H. Waklyn, Esq.

Denton, on the river Tame, and borders of Cheshire, 3 miles S.W. from Ashton-under-Lyne, and 7 miles from Manchester, containing 323 houses and 2012 inhabitants. This village possesses an extensive manufacture of hats. Denton Hall was long the seat of a family of the same name.

Didsbury, on the borders of Cheshire 5½ miles S. from Manchester, containing 156 houses, and 933 inhabitants. Park Field, in this township, is

the seat of George Withington, Esq.; and Parr's Wood Hall is the seat of Mrs. Farrington.

Droylsden, 4 miles E. from Manchester, containing 389 houses, and 2855 inhabitants, including Moss Side, on the western edge of Ashton Moss. The Clock House is the seat of Samuel Burton, Esq.

Failsworth, 4 miles N.E. from Manchester, containing 509 houses, and 3358 inhabitants.

Gorton, on the borders of Cheshire, 3½ miles S.E. from Manchester, containing 261 houses and 1604 inhabitants. Here is a reservoir for the supply of water to the town of Manchester.

Heaton Norris, on the borders of Cheshire and banks of the Mersey, 6 miles S.E. from Manchester, and 1½ mile from Stockport, containing 1050 houses and 6958 inhabitants. This township is a suburb to Stockport, from which it is only separated by the river Mersey. The chapel, dedicated to St. Thomas, is a perpetual curacy, in the presentation of the warden and fellows of the collegiate church of Manchester.

Houghton, or *Haughton*, 6 miles S.E. from Manchester, on the borders of Cheshire, containing 133 houses, and 2084 inhabitants. The village contains numerous hat manufactories.

Levenshulme, 4 miles S.E. from Manchester, containing 133 houses and 768 inhabitants.

Moss Side, 2 miles S. from Manchester containing 25 houses and 172 inhabitants.

Moston 4 miles N.E. from Manchester, containing 89 houses and 593 inhabitants, including the hamlet of Street Fold. Morton House is the seat of Samuel Taylor, Esq.

Openshaw, 3 miles E. from Manchester, containing 86 houses and 497 inhabitants.

Reddish, 5 miles S.E. from Manchester, containing 91 houses, and 574 inhabitants.

Rushulme 2½ miles S.E. from Manchester, containing 148 houses and 913 inhabitants. Rushulme House is the seat of Richard Entwistle Esq.; Platt Hall is the seat of Richard Clegg, Esq.; and Slade Hall, an ancient mansion, is the seat of John Suddal, Esq.

Stretford, 4 miles S.W. from Manchester, containing 378 houses, and 2173 inhabitants. Withington, 3½ miles S, from Manchester, containing 143 houses and 892 inhabitants.

LEICESTERSHIRE

This county is bounded on the north by Derbyshire and Nottinghamshire; on the east by Lincolnshire and Rutlandshire; on the south by Northamptonshire and Warwickshire; and on the west by Derbyshire Staffordshire and Warwickshire. Its limits are in some places marked by nature; on the north the rivers Trent and Soar form part of its boundary. The old Roman road called Watling-street, and the river Anker are its limits on the Warwickshire side, and the rivers Avon and Welland separate the county from Northamptonshire. Its greatest length is about forty-five miles, and its breadth thirty-five, being about one hundred and fifty miles in circumference. The inhabitants were distinguished by the Romans as Coritani, the British name being Guritani, and it formed part of the Roman province Flavia Cæsariensis. The Roman roads which pass through this county are the Watling-street, the Foss, and the Via Devana, a road which led across the island from Colchester to Chester. The known and fixed Roman stations are Ratæ, Leicester; Benonæ, High Cross near Hinckley, Vernometum, on the borders of the county, near Willoughby in Nottinghamshire; and Manduessedum, Manceter, also on the borders of the county, near Atherstone in Warwickshire. These stations are mentioned in the first, fourteenth and eighteenth Itineraries of Richard of Cirencester, and in the second, sixth and eighth of Antoninus. Part of a large Roman military with an inscription was found in 1791, near Thurmaston, about three miles from Leicester on the Foss road; this singularly curious column has been carefully removed to the Belgrave Gate, Leicester. The Jewry wall, or Temple of Janus, at Leicester is another very remarkable Roman remain in this county. During the Saxon Heptarchy Leicestershire formed part of the kingdom of Mercia; and according to the fabulous Geoffrey of Monmouth, Leir, a British monarch, the King Lear of Shakspeare, was the founder of Leicester, 844 years before Christ and was buried there. The castles of the earlier lords of this county were at Leicester, Ashby, Belvoir, Grooby, Hinckley, Mountsorrel, Seagrave, Saubey, and Whitwick; and there were formerly monasteries at Grace Dieu, Launde, Charley, Ulvescroft, Belvoir, Croxton, Garendon, Bredon, Ouston, Hinckley, Bradley, Kirkby Bellers, and Leicester. This county contains one county town, Leicester, eleven market-towns, 192 parishes, 34,775 houses and 174,571 inhabitants. It returns four members to Parliament,—two for Leicester; and two for the county: the present members for the county are Lord Robert Manners, brother of

the Duke of Rutland, and George Anthony Legh Keck, Esq. of Stoughton Grange. Leicestershire is in the province of Canterbury, and in the diocese of Lincoln. The soil of this county is various, and affords a great extent of rich grazing land, and is peculiarly fitted for the culture of beans and wheat, for which it is proverbially noted. The proportion of pasture and meadow land through the whole county much exceeds that of arable; there are few open fields now left, and the quantity of waste ground is proportionably very small; the surface is in most parts varied and uneven. Towards the north-west the Bardon hills rise to a considerable height and in their neighbourhood is Charnwood or Charley Forest, a rough and open tract: further to the north-west are valuable coal-mines, which supply the country round to a great distance. The north-eastern part of the county feeds great numbers of sheep, a principal article of the wealth of its inhabitants. The Leicestershire sheep are of a very large size without horns, and covered with thick long flakes of soft wool, particularly suited to the worsted manufactory. The eastern and

south eastern is a rich grazing tract, which breeds numbers of cattle of large size to supply the London and other great markets. The county indeed has long been famous for its large black horses and horned cattle, as well as its sheep. The new Leicester breed of sheep, created by Mr. Bakewell at Dishley near Loughborough, is now dispersed through most parts of the kingdom. A great quantity of cheese is made on the western side of the county, about Leicester Forest, and in some other parts: the rich kind, called Stilton, is made at the villages round Melton Mowbray. Leicestershire is an agricultural county, and manufactures have comparatively made but little progress in it, excepting one connected with its great product of wool, the stocking trade; the chief seat of which is the county town; where, and at Loughborough, the manufacture of lace by machinery has also of late years been carried on to a considerable extent. The principal rivers of Leicestershire are the Soar and the Wreke: the first rises on the south-western border of the county and flows to Leicester, after which it receives the Wreke from the north-east, and then turns to Mountsorrel and Loughborough, watering in its course meadows of uncommon beauty and fertility, and falls into the Trent near Cavendish-bridge on the borders of Derbyshire. The Soar has been made navigable by art from Leicester to Loughborough, and thence to its junction with the Trent; and the Wreke has been also made navigable to Melton Mowbray. The other rivers of less note in the county are the Anker, Avon, Blackbrook, Deane, Eye, Scalford, Sence, Snite, Swift and Welland. The last rises in a range of hills between Lutterworth and Market Harborough, and divides this county from Northamptonshire, where it traverses a fine plain between Market Harborough and Rockingham, and after meeting the Glen from Bourne, the mouths of those two rivers form Fossdyke Wash. The inland navigation of the county, besides the rivers already mentioned, are the canals of Ashby De La Zouch, the Grand Union, the Leicester and Melton Mowbray, the Leicestershire Union, Loughborough and Oakham. The principal eminences are Bardon Hill, the highest in the county, Markfield Knoll, Beacon Hill, Old John in Bradgate Park, Belvoir Castle, Bredon Church, Billesdon Coplow, Carlton Spinney, Mountsorrel Hill, Barrow Hill, and Croft Hill. The limestone obtained from Barrow forms an excellent cement in water and was used in the building of Ramsgate Pier. Belvoir Castle is the seat of the Duke of Rutland K.G., the Lord Lieutenant of the County.

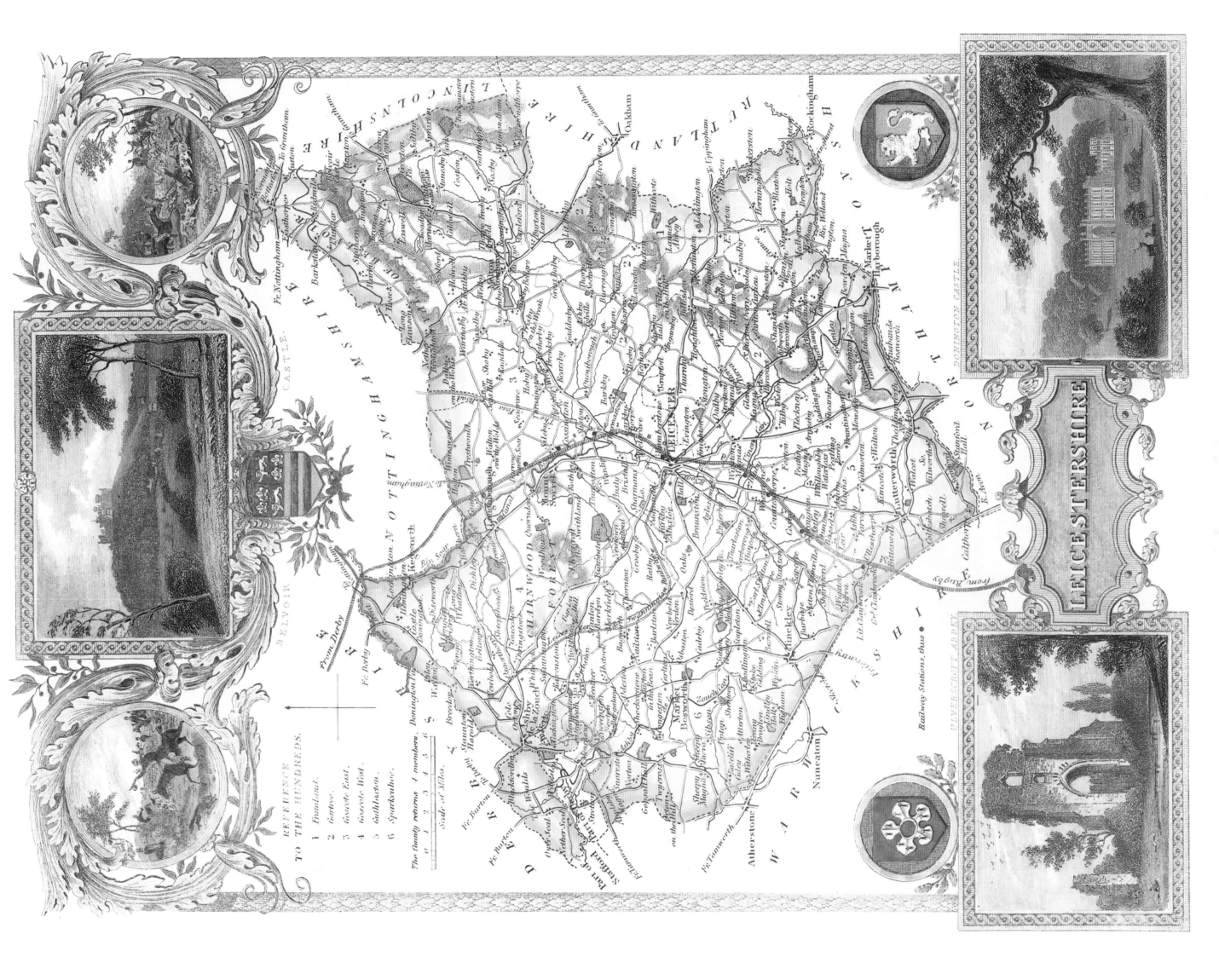

LEICESTERSHIRE

REFERENCE
TO THE HUNDREDS.

1 Framland.
2 Gartree.
3 Goscote East.
4 Goscote West.
5 Guthlaxton.
6 Sparkenhoe.

The county returns 4 members.

Scale of Miles.

Railway Stations, thus ....

ULVERSCROFT ABBEY.

DONINGTON CASTLE.

LINCOLNSHIRE

This county is bounded on the north by Yorkshire; on the east by the German Ocean; on the south by Cambridgeshire, Northamptonshire, and Rutlandshire; and on the west by Leicestershire, Nottinghamshire, and Yorkshire. Its greatest length is about seventy-five miles, and its breadth forty-five miles, being in circumference about two hundred and sixty miles. The inhabitants were called Coritani by the Romans, and it formed part of the province Flavia Cæsariensis. The Roman stations are considered to have been Ad Abum, Winterton; Aquis, Aukborough; Bannovallium, Horncastle or Ludford; Causennæ, Ancaster, or Great Ponton; Lindum, Lincoln; and Vainona, Wainfleet. A Roman road to Wragby and Newcastle ran through the north-western part of the county. During the Saxon Heptarchy, Lincolnshire formed part of the kingdom of Mercia. The castles of its earlier lords were at Bourne, Bolingbroke, Caistor Horncastle, Scrivilsby, Somerton, Sleaford, Stamford Tattershall and Torksey. This county contains one city and county town. Lincoln; thirty-one market towns; six hundred and thirty parishes 53,813 houses, and 283,058 inhabitants; and returns twelve members to Parliament; two for Boston, two for Grantham, two for Grimsby, two for Lincoln, two for Stamford, and two for the shire; the present members for which are Sir W.A. Ingilby, Bart., and C. Chaplin, Esq. of Blankney Hall. Lincolnshire is in the province of Canterbury, and in the diocese of Lincoln. It is divided into three separate districts called Lindsey, Kesteven, and Holland; of these Lindsey is much the largest, and occupies nearly one half of the county; extending from the sea, on the east to Nottinghamshire on the west; and from the river Witham, which intersects the county from east to west, to the river Humber on the north. The soils are much varied, and its geographical features marked by many inequalities. High lands, called the Wolds, occupy a long ridge of the county from Spilsby to the Humber, having a rich tract of marsh-land to the east, between it and the sea; Lincoln Heath, another ridge of high land, extends up the western side of this division from Lincoln to Brigg. The greater part of the last district, formerly appropriated almost solely to the breeding of rabbits, has within the last few years been enclosed and brought into profitable cultivation. At the north western extremity of the county is the river island of Axholme, a low tract of land, which by the operations of embanking and draining has been made one of the most fertile spots in the kingdom. The river Trent bounds the eastern side of this island, whilst the rivers Idle, Don and Torn, environ the southern and western sides. The district of Kesteven is bounded on the north and north-east by the river Witham, which separates

it from Lindsey; on the east by the division of Holland; on the south by the river Welland, which divides it from Northamptonshire; and by parts of Nottinghamshire, Leicestershire, and Rutlandshire, on the west. The features of this district are very diversified, and the soils greatly varied: the western part is fine arable, as well as grazing land, and parts of it are well wooded. The variations of soil are nearly all in a longitudinal direction from north to south. The south-western part contains some fine parks, abounding with woods and was at a former period denominated a forest, in which state it continued till the time of King Henry III., when it was disafforested. The eastern side of the division is low land, partaking of the nature of the adjacent marshes in the district of Holland. Kesteven having been enclosed, drained and cultivated, contains much rich and valuable land. Holland constitutes the south-eastern side of the county, and is bounded by parts of Cambridgeshire and Northamptonshire on the south; the division of Lindsey on the north; on the east by the German Ocean; and on the west by part of Kesteven. Nearly the whole of this tract of country appears to have been once inundated by the sea, being preserved solely by its vast embankments: the pools also have been drained by means of deep canals with sluices. Most of the drains or dykes of this district communicate with, and empty themselves into the rivers Welland and Witham; the channels of which have been widened and altered in various places. Holland is divided into Upper and Lower; both of the divisions consisting entirely of fens and marshes, intersected by numberless dykes and canals, and crossed by raised causeways called Droves. The lower or southern division is only preserved by its mounds from constant inundations. The air of these tracts is not considered wholesome, and the water is of a brackish nature; whence the inhabitants are obliged to make reservoirs for rain-water; yet their industry has produced comfort and opulence by forming excellent pasture-land out of the marshes, which are found capable of yielding large crops of corn. Prodigious flocks of geese are bred in the fens, and here the principal decoys in England for wild ducks, teal, widgeon, and other aquatic birds, which afford the chief supply to the metropolis. Wild geese, grebes, godwits, whinibulls, coots, ruffs and reeves, avosets or yelpers, knots and dottrels, and a great variety of other species of water fowl, breed here in amazing numbers. The general period for working in the decoys lasts from October to February. Lincolnshire may be said to present four great natural features, each of which has a specific and nearly uniform character: these are the heaths and sandy lands, the wolds, the marshes and the fens. The heaths, north and south of Lincolnshire, are

calcareous hills, which from their brows command many very fine views. Lincoln heath, now almost entirely enclosed is a tract of high country, in which the soil is a good sandy loam, and excellent turnip and barley land. This hill slopes sharply to the west, the declivity of the same nature, but generally good: and this extends some distance in the valley, where the soil is rich loam containing much pasturage. Between Gainsborough and Newark, for twenty-five miles, is a large tract of flat sandy soil, which has been enclosed and drained. The wolds extend from Spilsby, in a north-westerly direction, for about forty miles to Barton on the Humber. They are, on an average, nearly eight miles in breadth and consist of sand and sandy loam, upon flinty loam, with a substratum of chalk, particularly about Louth, and in the extensive rabbit warrens between Gayton and Tathwell; but rich upland pastures are seen, pleasingly intermixed.

From Binbrook to Caistor, with the interruption of Caistor Moor, a sandy soil prevails; and thence sand, with an inter-mixture of clay, till they change into the rich loam, of which Barton Field, a space of 6000 acres, principally consists. Beneath this line, and parallel with the eastern shore, lies an extensive tract of land at the foot of the wolds, reaching from Barton to Wainfleet, of various breadth, from five to ten miles, called the Marsh, which is secured from the encroachments of the sea by embankments of earth, and is agriculturally divided into north and south marshes, by a difference in the soil, called Middle Marsh. The first occupies a large extent of rich salt lands; the second clay of inferior value; and the intervening land is a rich brown loam. stretching across from Beelsby to Grimsby. The Fens form one of the most prominent features of this county, and consist of lands, which, at a distant period, have been inundated by the sea, and by human art have been recovered from it. In the summer season they exhibit immense tracts, chiefly of grazing land, intersected by wide deep ditches, which answer the end both of fences and drains. These are accompanied generally by parallel banks, upon which the roads pass, and are intended to keep the waters, in flood time, from overflowing the adjacent lands. They not only communicate with each other, but also with larger canals, called dykes and drains, which in some instances are navigable for boats and barges. At the lower end of these are sluices, guarded by gates, termed Gowts. During the summer, numerous flocks and herds are seen grazing over this scene, where the pastures afford a rich and luxuriant herbage. Many of the fens actually lie below the level of the sea; some are lower than the beds of the rivers; and all are beneath the high water of their respective drains. In winter these fens are mostly covered

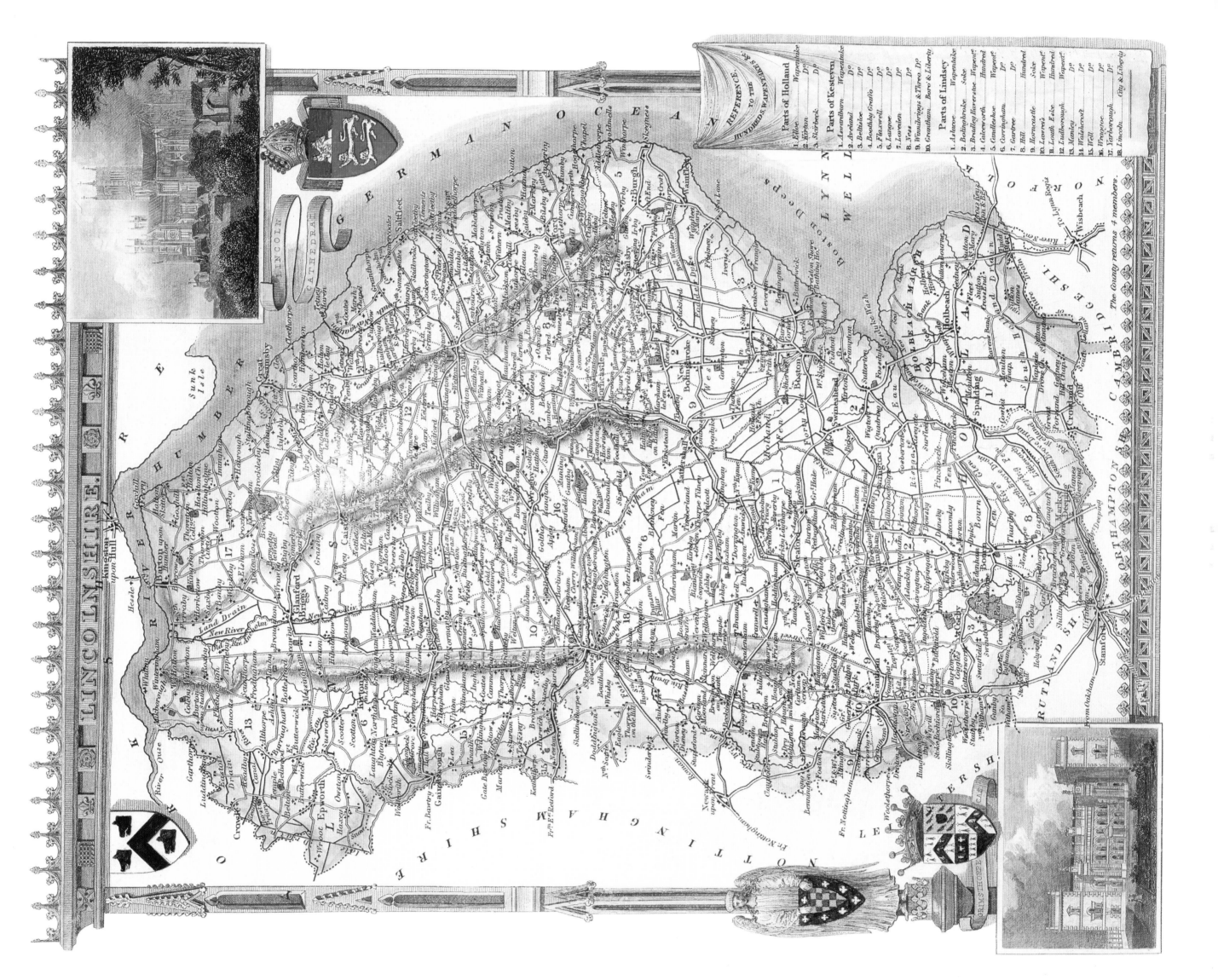

LINCOLNSHIRE.

LINCOLN CATHEDRAL

GERMAN OCEAN

NORFOLK

CAMBRIDGESHIRE

NORTHAMPTON SHIRE

RUTLAND SH.

LEICESTERSH.

NOTTINGHAMSHIRE

YORKSHIRE

RIVER HUMBER

The County returns 4 members.

BOSTON

with water; but during the summer the inhabitants are greatly distressed for it. Some of what are called the fens are in a state of waste, and serve for the breeding and rearing of geese, which are considered the fenman's treasure, a highly valuable stock. They breed numerous young, which quickly become saleable; the feathers and quills of a large flock amount to a very considerable sum. The rabbit-warrens of this county were formerly much more extensive than at present, and have gradually yielded to the plough. Lincolnshire has been long famous for a fine breed of horses, although the adjoining county, York, has now the credit for rearing many really bred in this county. The neat cattle are remarkably large, but not peculiarly famed for their fine symmetry The sheep are also very large and perhaps the most profitable stock; as vast numbers are bred and fattened, and large quantities of wool are obtained to supply the demand of the manufacturing districts. Within these few years great numbers of spinning schools have been established. Rabbits are esteemed highly advantageous in situations unfit for the plough. Few manufactures are in this county; but rabbits' fur and goose feathers are objects of considerable merchandize. The eminences and views most remarkable in the county are Aukborough Cliff, Yarborough Camp, Brocklesby Mausoleum, Lincoln Cathedral, Belmont Tower, Boston Church Tower, Gonerby, Thunnington, Leadenham, Skirbeck and Tathwell Hills. The principal rivers in the county are the Ancholme, Bain, Don, Glen, Humber, Idle, Limb, Lud, Mowbeck, Nen, Rasen, Slea, Torn, Trent, Waring, Welland, and Witham. The Ancholme is a small river rising in the Wolds near Market Rasen, and flowing northward by Brigg, whence it is navigable to the Humber, and falls into it some miles below the junction of the Trent. The Witham derives its source near South Witham, a village about ten miles north of Stamford, and pursues a line deviating but a little from the north by Grantham to Lincoln; it then turns eastward, and joined by a stream from the wolds in the north, proceeds southward through the Fens to Tattershall, where it is met by the Bain from Horncastle, and afterwards to Boston, soon falling into the great bay between Lincolnshire and Norfolk, at the mouth of Foss Dyke Wash. Foss Dyke is an artificial trench, extending about seven miles in length, from the Great Marsh, near the city of Lincoln, to the river Trent in the vicinity of Torksey. This, which is the first canal of its kind in England, was made by King Henry I. in 1121, for the purpose of bringing vessels from the Trent to the city, as well as for making a general drain for the adjacent level; but it has since that period been many times altered and improved. The other canals are those of Caistor, Grantham, Grimsby, Horncastle, and Louth. Belton Park near Grantham, is the seat of Earl Brownlow, the Lord Lieutenant of the County.

BOSTON, the chief town of Holland division, 34 miles S.E. from Lincoln and 117 miles from London, contains 2176 houses, and 10,330 inhabitants. It is situated near the mouth of the river Witham, over which is an elegant iron-bridge erected by *Rennic*, in 1806 and is a large well-built town. The market place is spacious. Markets are held on Wednesday and Saturday, which are well supplied with all kinds of provisions, especially sea and river fish. The fairs are 4th May, for sheep chiefly; 12th Aug. the town fair; 30th Nov. for horses, lasting four days; and 11th Dec. for beasts. All the neighbouring country is marsh land, which is extremely rich, feeding vast numbers of sheep and oxen. The port of Boston, anciently famous as a staple of wool, has a considerable foreign and coasting trade in corn, particularly oats. Barges navigate the Witham as far as Lincoln; and the enclosure of the waste lands, which are extra-parochial, has very much contributed to the prosperity of the town. Over the Market Cross is a chamber, appropriated to the purposes of the public business, where the petty sessions for the Wapentakes of Kirton and Skirbeck are held every Wednesday. The Corporation consists of a mayor, who is chief clerk of the market and admiral of the liberties, a recorder, deputy recorder, 12 aldermen, 18 common councilmen, a town clerk, judge advocate, coroner, and other officers. Arms, crests and supporters were allowed and confirmed to the Corporation, 1st Dec. 1568. Arms, *Sable, three ducal crowns in pale, or.* Crest, *on a woolpack a ram couchant, argent.* Supporters, *two mermaids ducally crowned, proper.*

The borough of Boston returns two members to Parliament, a privilege conferred upon it in the reign of Edward VI., and is vested only in the mayor, aldermen, common council, and freemen of the borough resident therein, paying scot and lot, and claiming their freedom by birth or servitude. The present members are J. Malcolm, Esq. and J. Wilks, Esq. The church dedicated to St. Botolph, is a vicarage value 33*l.* 6*s.* 8*d.*, in the patronage of the mayor and burgesses. The edifice is supposed to be the largest parochial church, without cross aisles, in the kingdom; being 300 feet long within the walls, and 100 feet wide. The ceiling is of oak. The chancel has stalls on each side, the seats of which are enriched with grotesque carvings. The altar-piece, of the Corinthian order, contains a copy of Rubens' celebrated picture "The Descent" from the Cross by *P. Mequignon*, the gift of Richard Smith, Esq. The tower of this church may be considered as one of the most lofty and highly decorated in England. It is stated to have been begun in 1309, on the authority of Dr Stukeley, and the first stone of the edifice to have been laid by Dame Margery Tylney. The architectural style, however, does not correspond with that of the period to which it is ascribed; a circumstance which has been accounted for by supposing that the edifice

was many years in progress, and that the superstructure was much posterior to the foundation, and that the style corresponds with that prevailing when the building was completed. It is also said to have been designed on the model of that of the great church at Antwerp; but the arrangement of the different stories more resembles that of Louth, which was erected at the commencement of the 16th century. The tower is divided into four stories above the basement. In the lower story is the arch, opening into the body of the church, and the great west window. The next story has two pointed windows, in each face, with ogee caps and finials; and in the story above is a single window in each face. This part of the tower is surmounted by an embattled parapet, and the whole is terminated by an octangular lantern, connected with the square portion of the tower by flying buttresses. The parish library is over the south porch of the church; it was founded by Anthony Tuckney. There were formerly several guilds at Boston, as those of St. Botolph, Corpus Christi, the Blessed Mary, St. Peter and St. Paul, St. George, and the Holy Trinity. The guild of the Blessed Mary was the most flourishing, and had a chapel in the church. In 1510 it supported a grammar-school. The possessions of this guild were granted to the Corporation in 1554, who now use its Guildhall for their corporate and judicial proceedings. A Dominican or Black friary was founded here in 1221; a Carmelite friary in 1301; an Augustine friary, by one of the Tylney family, about the year 1 307; and a Franciscan or Gray friary, by the Easterling merchants in 1332; but of a priory said to have been dedicated to St. Mary, nothing certain is known. The commercial importance of Boston was much reduced at the Dissolution of monasteries by Henry VIII., who, however raised the town to the rank of a free borough. Queen Mary endowed a grammar-school in 1554 and it was erected by the mayor and burgesses in 1567. In 1643, Boston being a place of considerable importance, was strongly fortified for the King, from whom it was soon wrested, when it was styled by Fairfax, the Key of the Associated Counties, and made the headquarters of Cromwell's army. John Fox, the martyrologist, was born here in 1517,— the very year that Luther began to oppose the errors of the Church of Rome. Kyme Tower, about 2 miles eastward from Boston, is sometimes called Richmond Tower, from its being situated on land belonging to that honor; and has the name of Rochford Tower from having belonged to that family. The estate appears to have passed to the Kyme family in the 15th century, and the tower does not seem from its style of architecture to be older than the reign of Elizabeth. The whole is of brick, and quadrangular, having an octagonal turret at the south-east angle. It was formerly moated; the remains of which may be traced but the fine avenue of trees on the road to Boston has been destroyed.

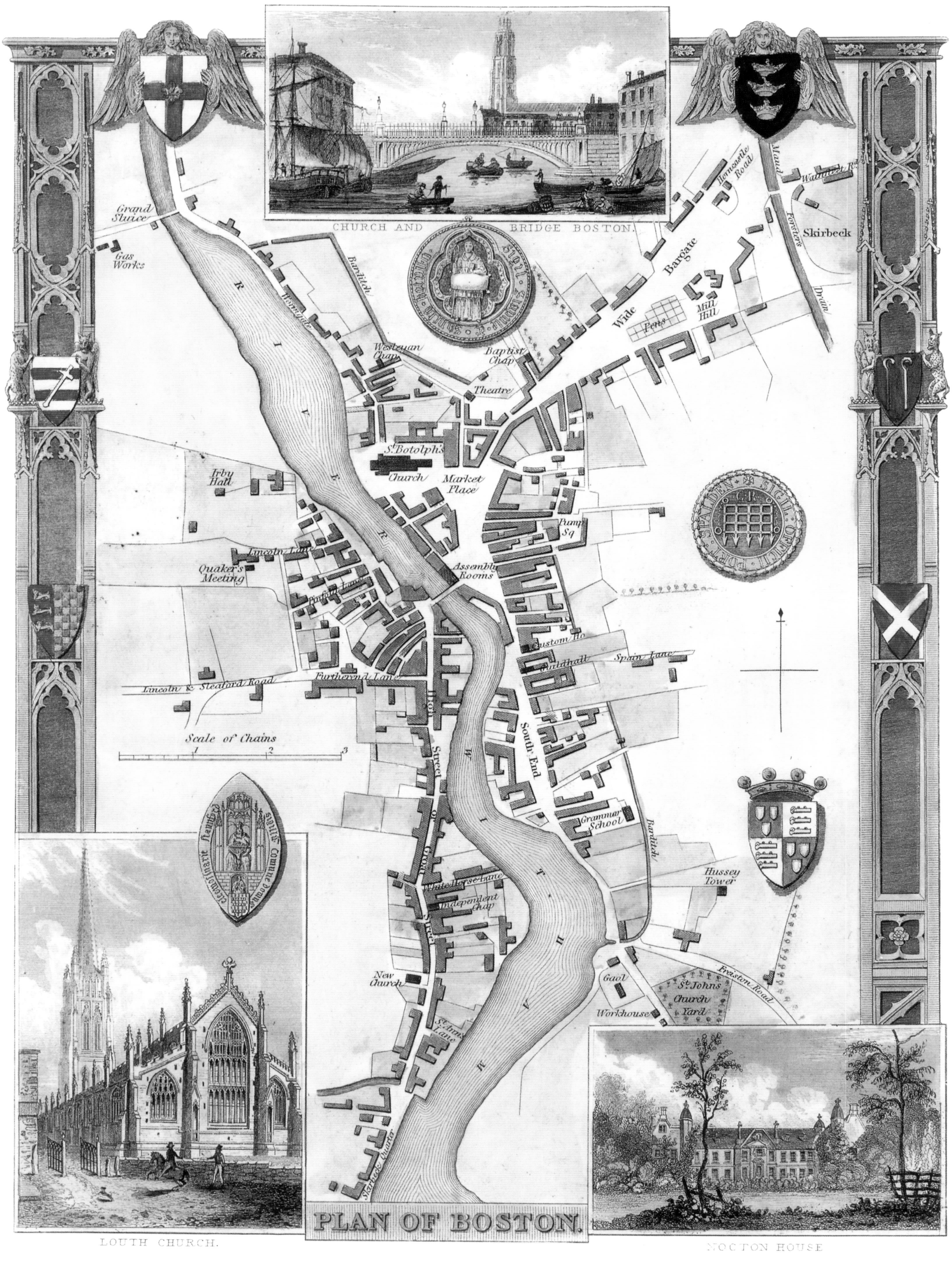

PLAN OF BOSTON.

NOCTON HOUSE.

LOUTH CHURCH.

Waterwell

Skirbeck

Forster's

Drain

Maud

Hermondike Road

Mill Hill

Wide Bargate

BRIDGE BOSTON.

CHURCH AND

SIGILL. OFFICII. SPALDEN

Baptist Chap

Theatre

St Botolphs Church

Market Place

Wesleyan Chap

Barditch

Warmgate

Fry Hall

Quaker's Meeting

Grand Sluice

Glass Works

RIVER

Scale of Chains

Lincoln & Stamford Road

Pump Sq

South End

Assembly Rooms

Spain Lane

Barditch

Grammar School

Hussey Tower

Gaol

Workhouse Yard

St Johns Church Yard

Froston Road

WITHAM

Street

Methodist Meeting Independent Chapy

New Church

St Anns Lane

Sigillú Comune domus Gremontanim Familia

Sigill Comune

ISLE OF MAN

The Isle of Man is very centrically situated between England, Ireland and Scotland, nearly opposite to the western coast of Cumberland, from which it is distant thirty miles. The extent of the island from the north-west to the south-east is about thirty miles; its breadth is about ten miles in the widest part, and its circumference between seventy and eighty miles. The name of MAN or *Mann* is supposed to refer to its situation with regard to the surrounding kingdoms, from the Saxon word *Mang,* signifying "among". Its ancient ensign was a ship, but the present heraldic bearing is *Gules, three legs conjoined in the fesse point in armour proper garnished and spurred or.* The kings of Man are often mentioned in history: a succession of kings of the Danish line were sovereigns of the island in the tenth century, and in the eleventh century the sovereignty was in the Norwegian line. These were succeeded by a line of Scottish Monarchs till the year 1344, when Sir William Montacute, afterwards Earl of Salisbury, was crowned by order of King Edward III., having enabled him to conquer it. In 1393 the island was sold to Sir William Scrope, on whose attainder it was granted by King Henry IV. to Henry Percy Earl of Northumberland, in sovereignty by the service of bearing before the King at his coronation the Lancaster sword. In the year 1400 a grant was made to Sir John Stanley, ancestor of the Earls of Derby, of the island, Castle Peel and lordship of Man, and all the islands, lordships, regalities &c. with the patronage of the bishopric, and all ecclesiastical benefices in as full and ample a manner as they had been possessed by any former kings or lords of Man, to be holden by homage, and the service of presenting to His Majesty and to his successors at their coronation a cast of falcons, by which ancient tenure the manor is still held. The Stanley family continued to be the sovereigns of the island till the year 1504, when Thomas Earl of Derby voluntarily resigned the regal title and assumed that of Lord of Man.

The British Government making overtures of purchase, John, third Duke of Athol, agreed to resign the Island in 1765 for £70,000; and by the Revestory Act it became annexed to the British Crown. Parliament

afterwards granted an annuity of £2000 to the Duke and Duchess of Athol by way of additional compensation. The kings of England always claimed sovereignty over the island as lords paramount; but they interfered not with its government. The lord's power was ample; he coined money, punished delinquents, &c.

The western isles divided into two clusters, were in the Norwegian language, called Sudor and Nordor, signifying "southern and northern" and Man was included in the Sudor. The two bishoprics of Sodor and Man were united under the Norwegian kings, and continued so until the island was conquered by the English: since which time the Bishop of Sodor and Man

has retained the united title; and the Scottish bishops were styled Bishops of the Isles. By an Act of King Henry VIII. the bishopric of Sodor and Man was declared to be in the province of York. The diocese contains only twenty-one parishes, 6627 houses, and 40,081 inhabitants.

A high ridge of mountains runs nearly through the whole length of the island, and occupies a considerable portion of the centre. This mountainous tract gives rise to many springs and rivulets, and likewise affords pasturage for sheep, besides supplying heath and peat for fuel. The two extremities of the island consist of good arable and pasture land.

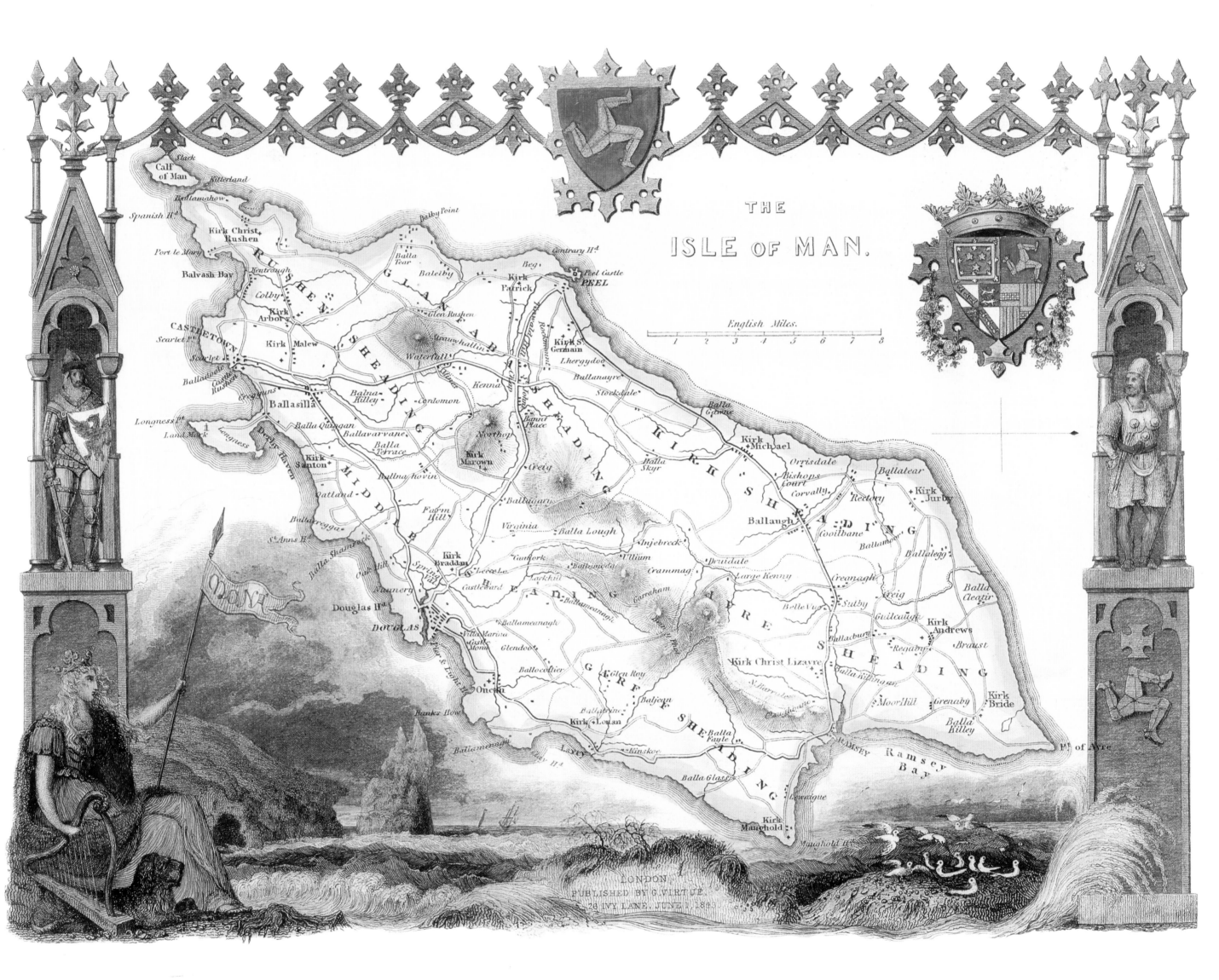

THE
ISLE OF MAN.

English Miles.
1 2 3 4 5 6 7 8

LONDON
PUBLISHED BY G. VIRTUE.
26 IVY LANE, JUNE 1, 1840

MIDDLESEX

THIS county is bounded on the north by Hertfordshire; on the east by Essex; on the south by Surrey; and on the west by Buckinghamshire. Previously to the Roman invasion, Middlesex was included in the district inhabited by the Trinobantes, or Trinovantwys; and after the subjugation of the island, was included in the division named Flavia Cæsariensis, when Londinium became a principal station, and Sullonicæ, on Brockley, was also a Roman station. The Roman roads in this county appear to have concentrated in London, whence they branched off as from a centre, nearly in the direction of the principal points of the compass. The Watling-street from Dover is presumed to have continued along Stone-street in Southwark to Dowgate and the present Watling-street; quitting the city at Aldersgate, it skirted the station of Sullonicæ towards Verulam. Another road, by some called Ikenild-street, is supposed to have led eastward down Old-street, and crossed the river Lea at Old Ford to Duroleiton, or Leyton in Essex. The Hermen-street passed under Cripplegate, and led northwards through Islington and Highbury to Enfield and Hertfordshire. Another Roman road from London went through Brentford, Hounslow, and Staines, in the same course as the present turnpike road to Bath. The county derives its present name from its relative situation to the three ancient surrounding kingdoms of East, West, and South Saxons. Its greatest length is twenty-three miles, and its greatest breadth about seventeen miles; in circumference it is about one hundred and fifteen miles. It contains two cities, London and Westminster, eleven market towns, two hundred and thirty-four parishes, 152,969 houses, and 1,144,531 inhabitants. It is in the province of Canterbury, and diocese of London. Besides the monasteries in London, there were priories at Kilburn, Hounslow, and Sion. Hampton Court, and Holland House at Kensington, are ancient residences. Middlesex returns eight members to Parliament, four for the city of London, two for the city of Westminster, and two for the county, who at present are George Byng, Esq. of Wrotham Park, and Joseph Hume, Esq. Middlesex is a well cultivated county: the least productive parts, as Hounslow Heath, Finchley Common, and Enfield Chase, are now inclosed; and the quantity of manure procured from the metropolis is of great service in improving the land, from which cause the produce is always earlier within a few miles of London than at a more considerable distance. In the art of hay-making, the Middlesex farmers are superior to those of

any other part of the kingdom : the districts near London usually afford two crops of hay every year; those in the more remote parts yield but one. The corn grown in this county is nearly confined to wheat and barley; rye and oats are cultivated only in small quantities. The fruit-gardens of this county, exclusive of those attached to private houses, are supposed to occupy about three thousand acres, and are principally situated in the parishes of Hammersmith, Brentford, Isleworth, and Twickenham. Besides the quantity of fruit raised from these gardens, the London markets receive additional supplies from gardens on the Surrey side of the Thames; and much is also brought from Kent, Essex, Berkshire, and other counties. The nursery-grounds lie in the neighbourhood of Chelsea, Brompton, Kensington, Hackney, Dalston, Bow, and Mile End. The taste for elegant and rare plants has become so prevalent, that the rearing them for sale forms a considerable object of commerce; and the English gardeners have attained such celebrity for the cultivation of exotics, that a great exportation is made to France, Spain, Portugal, Italy, Russia, and other countries. The kitchen-gardens in the vicinity of the metropolis are estimated to comprise above ten thousand acres. The rivers of this county are the Brent, the Colne, the Crane, the Lea, the Exe, or *Echel*, the Moselle, and the Thames, besides the artificial stream called the New River. The Thames enters Middlesex at the point where it receives the waters of the Colne, a short distance above Staines, and forms the southern boundary of the county in a devious course of about forty-three miles; and being navigable the whole way adds to the convenience and wealth of the numerous towns and villages situated on its banks. At Hampton, the Thames makes a bold reach round the park and gardens of Hampton Court; hence passing Teddington, (said to be a corruption of Tide End Town,) the majestic stream flows onward to Twickenham, Isleworth, and Brentford. At Isleworth it receives the Crane; and at Brentford, the river, contracted by a line of islands, is also enlarged by the Brent and the Grand Junction canal. Chiswick, Hammersmith, and Fulham, and the populous village of Chelsea, border the river in its course to Westminster and the port of London, whence the Thames rolls onward to the sea, between the shores of Kent and Essex. The tides flow up the river to the distance of between seventy and eighty miles from its mouth, and occur twice in every twenty-four hours nearly. The fall of water from Oxford to Maidenhead is about twenty-five feet

every ten miles; from Maidenhead to Chertsey twenty-two feet every ten miles; from Chertsey to Chiswick sixteen feet every ten miles; and from Chiswick to London, about one foot per mile : afterwards the fall diminishes gradually till the river unites with the sea. The Colne river enters this county in several channels at its north-western extremity, and flowing along the western border, passes Harefield, Uxbridge, and Cowley, towards Colnbrook and Longford, being divided into six or seven branches, the principal of which flow into the Thames at Staines. The river Brent enters Middlesex near Finchley, takes a circuitous direction by Hendon, Kingsbury, Twyford, Greenford, and Hanwell, to the town of Brentford, where it unites with the Thames. The Crane rises near Pinner, and assuming a winding course, flows under Cranford Bridge, and crossing Hounslow Heath falls into the Thames at Isleworth. The Lea river bounds the whole eastern side of Middlesex, and falls into the Thames at Bow. The Serpentine River in Hyde Park is chiefly supplied by a stream which rises near West End, Hampstead, and passing Kilburn and Bayswater, through Kensington Gardens to Hyde Park, flows by Knightsbridge into the Thames at Chelsea. This county is intersected by the Grand Junction, Paddington, and Regent's canals. The first joins the Thames at Brentford, and passing Sion Hill and Osterley Park, is carried through a rich corn district to West Drayton, Cowley, Uxbridge, and Harefield, beyond which it quits the county. By means of collateral cuts, this canal has become the most important inland navigation in the kingdom, affording a direct communication between London and the manufacturing towns of Warwickshire, Staffordshire, Lancashire, Derbyshire, and other counties. The Paddington canal branches off from the Grand Junction near Cranford, and is of very great importance from its connection with the trade of London. The sides of the basin at Paddington are occupied with warehouses, a quay, and market-places for hay, straw, and cattle. The Regent's canal also connects the Grand Junction with the Thames. After passing through the Regent's Park, where it supplies the ornamental lakes, it crosses the Hampstead and Kentish-town roads to a tunnel under the hill at Pentonville; after which it passes near the Rosemary Branch, where a branch is carried across the City Road, and the canal crosses the Kingsland and Haggerstone roads to the Cambridge Heath road, crossing Mile End and Commercial roads to Limehouse. The Duke of Portland is Lord Lieutenant of the County.

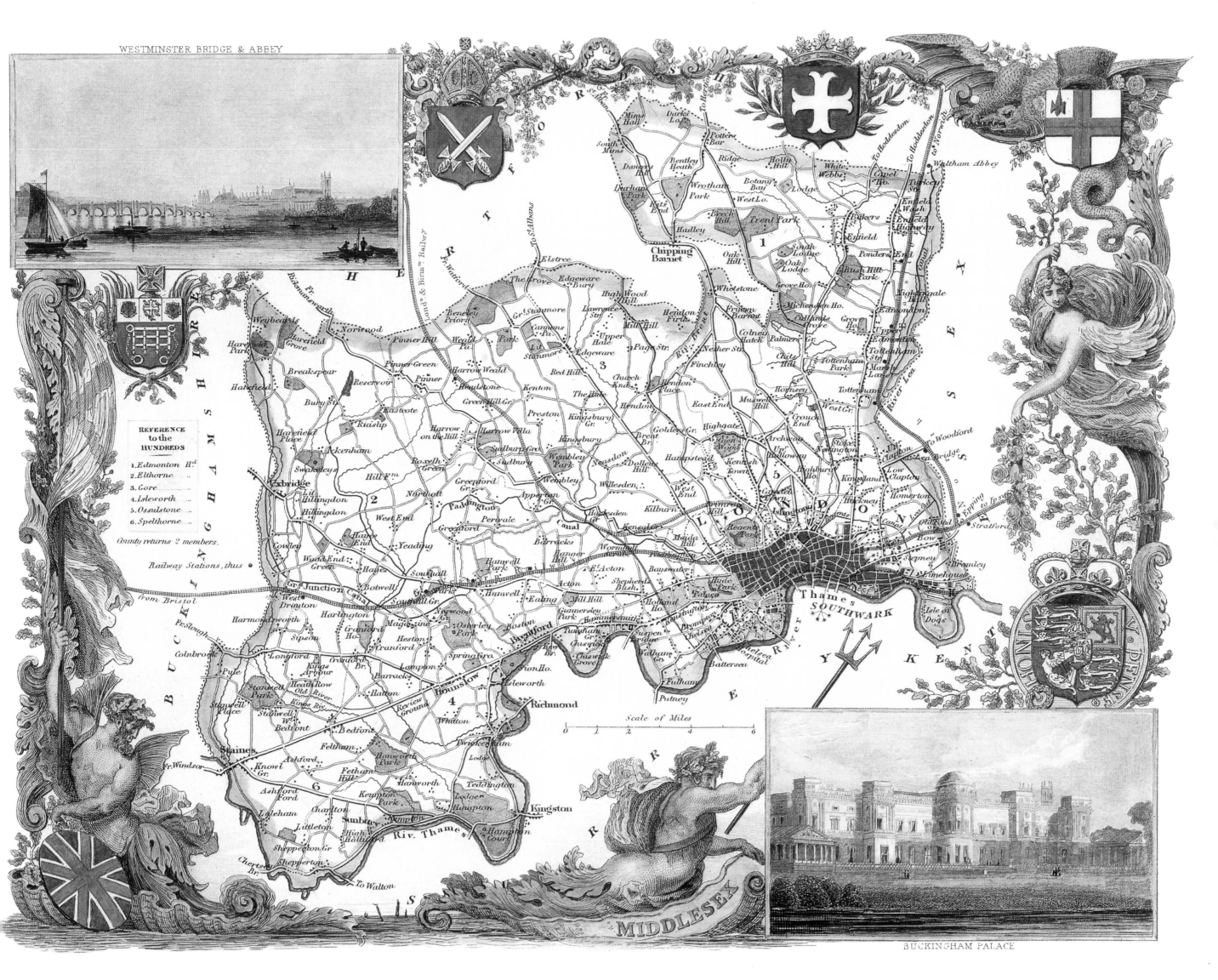

WESTMINSTER BRIDGE & ABBEY

REFERENCE
to the
HUNDREDS

1. Edmonton Hd.
2. Elthorne   "
3. Gore   "
4. Isleworth   "
5. Ossulstone "
6. Spelthorne "

County returns 2 members.

Railway Stations, thus •

MIDDLESEX

BUCKINGHAM PALACE

THE CITIES OF LONDON AND WESTMINSTER

LONDON

THE situation of London, defined by its cathedral, is in the latitude of 51° 30′ 49″ north: its longitude is 5′ 47″ west from the Royal Observatory at Greenwich. Its population, according to the Census of 1821, was found to be in the city of London, within the walls, 7,938 houses, and 56,174 inhabitants; without the walls 9,232 houses, and 69,260 inhabitants. The immediate site of London is about sixty miles westward from the sea, in a pleasant and spacious valley, stretching along the banks of the Thames, which river, as it flows through the city, forms a bold curve. On the northern side the ground rises with a quick ascent, and then more gradually, but unequally, heightens to the north-west and west, which are the most elevated parts. On the southern side the ground is nearly level, and was anciently a morass of several miles in extent, but was reclaimed by means of the artificial embankment of the river. The average breadth of the stream in this part of its course is from four to five hundred yards, its general depth, at low water, is about twelve feet, but at spring tides it rises sometimes to fourteen feet above that level. The tides commonly flow to the distance of fifteen miles above London-bridge.

From the neighbourhood of Tothill-fields on the south, to that of the Tower on the east, the buildings following the natural bend of the river, rise in a sort of amphitheatrical form, and are defended from the winds of the north by the rising grounds about Islington and Highbury, and the hills of Highgate and Hampstead. Below the Tower, and extending to the extremity of the county of Middlesex, along the river Lea, in the vicinity of Wapping, Limehouse, Poplar, &c., the ground is in general flat, and the houses are exposed to the easterly winds. The western and higher parts of the metropolis stand pleasantly open to the genial breezes of that quarter. The southern or Surrey side lies low and level, particularly in the neighbourhood of Lambeth and St. George's Fields.

The extent of what is generally called London from west to east, or from Knightsbridge to Poplar, is seven miles and a half; its breadth from north to south is very irregular, but may be described as varying from two to four miles. The outward line or circumference is at least thirty miles, and the area of the whole metropolis comprehends about nine square miles. The principal mercantile streets range from west to east, and in that direction London is intersected by two great thorough-fares; the one, which may be called the southern line, commences at Hyde Park Corner, and under the successive names of Piccadilly, Regent-street, Waterloo-place, Pall Mall East, Trafalgar-square, Duncannon-street, Strand, Fleet-street, Ludgate-hill, the southern side of St. Paul's churchyard, Watling-street, Cannon-street, Eastcheap, and Tower-street, and thence to East Smithfield, Ratcliff Highway, Upper and Lower Shadwell, &c., extends to Limehouse. The northern line begins with Oxford-street, and under the different appellations of High-street St. Giles's, Broad-street, Holborn, Skinner-street, Newgate-street, Cheapside, Cornhill, Leadenhall-street, Aldgate, and Whitechapel, extends to the Mile-End-road into Essex. At Church-lane, Whitechapel, the Commercial-road branches off south-eastward, and continues to the West India Docks,—a distance of about two miles.

The principal thoroughfare which crosses London from north to south enters it at Kingsland, and continues along Shore-ditch, Norton Falgate, Bishopsgate-street, Gracechurch-street, King William-street, London-bridge, Wellington-street, the Borough High-street, Blackman-street, and Newington Causeway. There are other roads into Surrey and Kent over the several bridges, which meet at the Obelisk in St. George's Fields, and again diverge near the Elephant and Castle,—a well known site. Regent-street, leading from Portland-place on the north, to Waterloo-place on the south, is perhaps one of the finest streets in Europe. London, independently of its various local and judicial divisions, may be considered as comprehending three great districts, viz. the West end of the town, the City, and the East end of the town. The west end of the town, in its general acceptation, extends from the vicinity of the Strand to Brompton, Hyde Park, Paddington, and the Regent's Park: it is the most uniform part of the metropolis, and contains the town residences of the nobility and gentry, the seats of Legislature, the offices of Government, and the Court. The city, which includes some portion of its liberties, forms the centre of the metropolis and trading part of the town, excepting the silk manufacture, which is chiefly confined to the vicinity of Spitalfields. The east end of the town is a large district, comprising the warehouses and residences of the comercial and shipping interest; and the immediate banks of the river in this quarter are occupied by docks, wharfs, timber-yards, &c.

London is computed to contain more than sixty squares, many of which are extremely spacious; and the central area of most are enclosed by palisades, and laid out in walks and shrubberies, for the recreation of the inhabitants. In short, London, according to Dr. Colquhoun, is not only the first commercial city that is known at present to exist, but is also one of the greatest and most extensive manufacturing towns perhaps in the universe, combining in one spot every attribute that occasion an assemblage of moving property, unparalleled in point of extent, magnitude, and value, in the whole world.

BRITISH AND ROMAN LONDON

As the metropolis of the kingdom, a brief account of its origin is necessarily inserted, and the following statement will explain its relative importance. Amongst the Britons were ninety-two cities, of which thirty-three were more celebrated and conspicuous. Two municipal, Verulamium, St. Alban's; and Eboracum, York: these municipia were towns whose inhabitants possessed in general all the rights of Roman citizens, excepting those which could not be enjoyed without an actual residence at Rome. Nine cities were colonial, namely, Londinium, London; Camalodunum, Colchester; Rhutupis, Richborough in Kent; Thermæ, Bath; Isea, Caerleon; Deva, Chester; Glevum, Gloucester; Lindum, Lincoln; and Camboricum, Cambridge. These were different kinds of colonies, each entitled to different rights and privileges: but we have no criterion to ascertain the rank occupied by those of Britain. Ten cities were under the Latian law, which consisted of privileges granted to the ancient inhabitants of Latium. These are not distinctly known, but appear principally to have been the right of following their own laws, an exemption from the edicts of the Roman Prætor, and the option of adopting the laws and customs of Rome. Twelve were stipendiary, a class which paid their taxes in money in contradistinction from those of lesser consequence, which gave a certain portion of the produce of the soil,

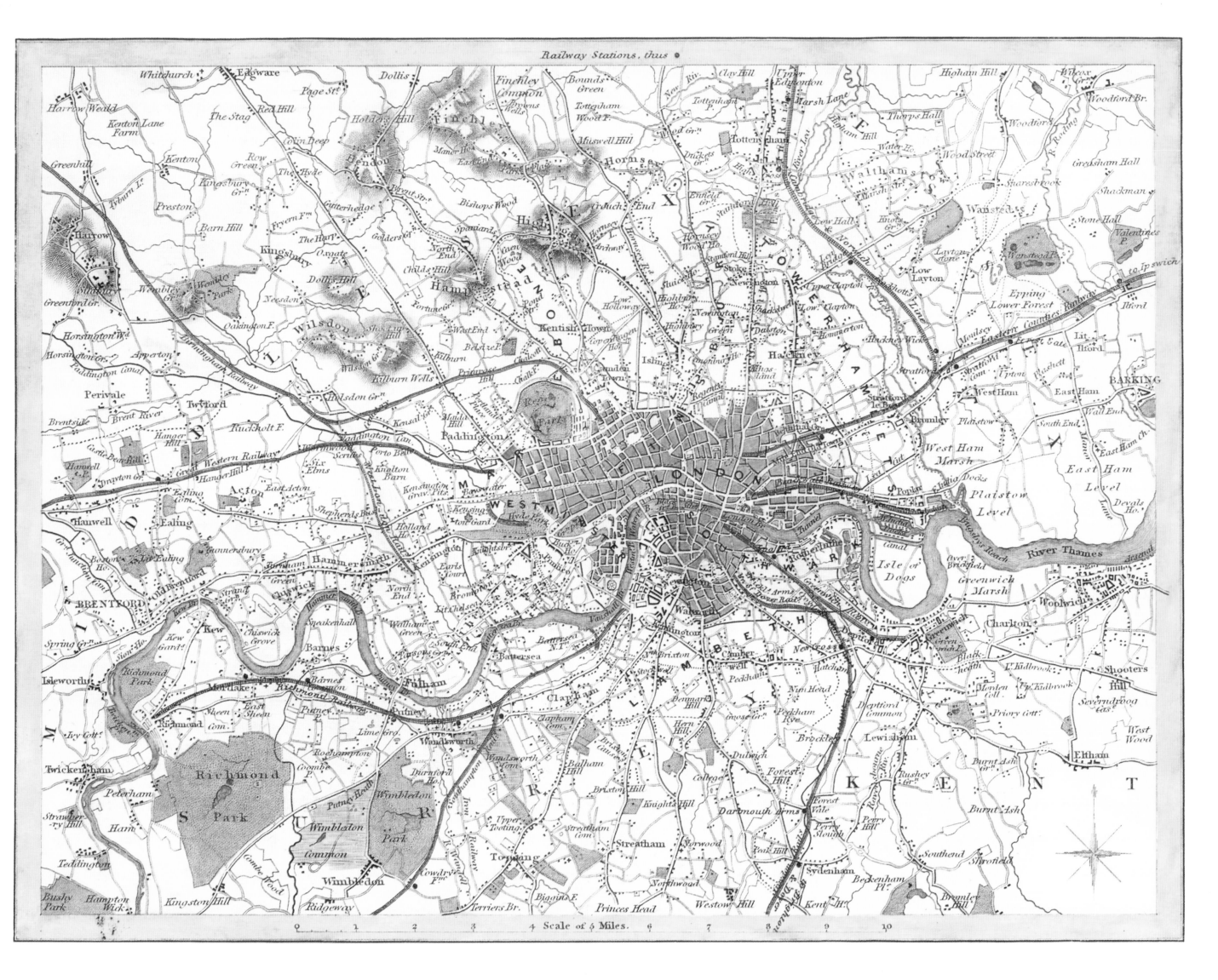

Railway Stations, thus •

and were called Vectigales; these included the more celebrated cities of Britain. There is every reason to suppose that the Romans possessed themselves of London in the reign of Claudius, about a hundred and five years after the first invasion of our island by Cæsar; but there is no mention of the place till the reign of Nero, when Tacitus speaks of it as not having been distinguished as a colony, but famous for its great concourse of merchants and its commerce. There is known to have been a great trade carried on with the Gauls in the days of Cæsar; that celebrated invader assigning as his reason for attempting the conquest of this island, the vast supplies given to his Gaulish enemies, and which interrupted his conquests on the continent. When the Romans became masters of London, they enlarged the precincts and altered its form. The time in which the wall was built is very uncertain. Maitland, the historian of London, ascribes its foundation to Theodosius, who was governor of Britain A.D. 369 : the ancient course of the wall began with a fort near the present site of the Tower, was continued along the Minories and the back of Houndsditch, across Bishopsgate-street, in a straight line by London Wall to Cripplegate, then returned southward by Crowder's-well-alley to Aldersgate, thence along the back of Bull-and-Mouth-street to Newgate, and again along the back of the houses in the Old Bailey to Ludgate; soon after which it probably finished with another fort near the former site of the King's printing-house in Black-friars; hence another wall ran near the river side along Thames-street, quite to the fort on the eastern extremity. The walls were three miles and one hundred and sixty-five feet in circumference, guarded at certain distances on the land side with fifteen towers, some of which were remaining within these few years. The walls when perfect are supposed to have been about twenty-two feet high, and the towers forty. London-wall, near Moorfields, was the last entire part left of that ancient precinct. A barbican stood a little without the walls, north westward of Cripplegate. The gates which received the great military roads were four; the Anglo-Saxon Watling street passed under one on the site of Newgate: vestiges of the road above Holborn-bridge have been discovered in its course to Dowgate, *Durgate*, or the Watergate, where there was a ferry to connect the road on the Surrey side of the river, whence it was continued to Dover. The Hermen-street passed under Cripplegate, and a vicinal way led through Aldgate by Bethnal-green to Oldford, over the river Lea to Duroleiton, the modern Layton in Essex. A plan of Roman London is given by Dr. Stukeley, whence it has been frequently copied; there is also an improved plan in the Gentleman's Magazine for 1829. The Prætorium and its adjuncts are supposed to have occupied the whole space between the Poultry and the eastern end of Cornhill. The present diverging streets show that this part has been completely un-Romanized. The vicinity of the Prætorium is proved by the discovery of Roman tessellated pavements, and other remains at the Lothbury-gate of the Bank, at St. Mary Woolnoth's church, Lombard-street; in and near Birchin-lane; near Sherborne-lane; the site of the Old Post-office, and along Lombard-street. Concerning the ancient streets of London, the best mode of conjecture is by taking those for the oldest which are of the greatest continuity and advance into the adjacent country. Thames-street from Blackfriars to the Tower is one; Lothbury seems to have been formed for the convenience of passing from the British part of the town by Ludgate, Cripplegate, or Aldersgate to Bishopsgate, without interfering with the Via Prætoria; and in nearly a parallel line it answers on the north side to Watling-street on the south, Finsbury-marshes interrupting any direct progress outside the walls; Holborn, Gray's-Inn-lane, and St. John-street, are other ancient ways. White-chapel, Mile-end, Bow, &c. are unquestionably primæval continuations from Aldgate.

There were doubtless other communications unnoticed in any plans extant, for it is to be remembered that there were formerly two distinct sorts of roads, Viæ Patriæ, and Viæ Militares, and that this distinction originated with the frequent Roman practice of cutting the latter parallel with the former, when an old Via Patria was not converted into a Via Militaris,—a change which seems to have taken place with the Watling-street, the apparently principal thoroughfare of all Great Britain.

ANGLO-SAXON LONDON

The history of London during the Anglo-Saxon era is scanty: being a walled town it was of course a place of importance, our ancestors holding those which were open in less estimation. The very fact of its having been walled in at the decline of the empire by the Romans, shows that it was then a place of consequence, no doubt as an emporium of commerce. There are two desiderata attached to the history of London during the Anglo-Saxon era; one is the historical silence as to the period when the possession of it was permanently vested in the Northern invaders; the other is connected with Canute's ditch. It is presumed that the first is not mentioned because it was simply evacuated by the Britons, when their communication with the circumjacent country was cut off. At the end of the sixth century it was a confirmed part of the Anglo-Saxon dominions, under Ethelbert King of Kent, who in the year 604 appointed Mellitus to the see of London.

During the wars between Edmund Ironside and Canute, in the latter in the year 1016 having fitted out a considerable fleet to reduce London, the chief support of his competitor, found on his arrival that he could not pass the bridge, the citizens having strongly fortified it; he therefore set about cutting a canal through the marshes on the southern side of the river Thames, that he might invest the city on all sides, and by preventing supplies from entering to facilitate its reduction. This canal is presumed to have commenced at Deptford, proceeded to Newington Butts, and joined the Thames at Lambeth, or Vauxhall, or Chelsea. The Saxon Chronicle states, that the Danish ships advanced from Greenwich to London, and that the Danish dug then a great ditch on the south half of it, and dragged their ships to the west half of the bridge, and *after that* besieged the city; so that no one could go in or out, anno 1016. With this account other Chronicles agree, but the historians of London have omitted an important point. It was impossible that London could be invested by merely cutting a canal from Deptford to Vauxhall. This trench was only intended for the purpose of getting the ships up to Westminster; and having so done, Canute landed his army, and invested the city by digging a second foss on the land side, supposed by Leland to be in the suburb of St. Giles's; the ships were reserved for retreat under disaster.

In Castle Baynard ward was an ancient residence of the Anglo-Saxon Kings of England, situated on the southern side of St Paul's Cathedral, and extending to the river. This palace was erected either by Alfred, Edward, or Athelstan; probably by the last, whose name of Adelstan, as it was called by an imperfect Norman utterance, is still preserved in the corrupted pronunciation of Adel-hill, near the spot where the palace stood. The windows of one of the southern apartments opened upon the river Thames, not then confined by quays and wharfs to its present narrowed stream. Northward the palace extended as far as the close of the cathedral. The north-eastern angle of the keep-tower is supposed to have occupied the spot now King's Head-court, and No. 26 on the southern side of St. Paul's Churchyard. The city wall running in a straight line from Ludgate to the Thames, served, it is probable, as the western boundary. An undoubted allusion to this palace as the abode of royalty occurred in the reign of Canute, in whose presence the perfidious Edric, after a very summary process, expiated his treason with his life, and his body was thrown out of the window into the river Thames.

This Anglo-Saxon palace was forsaken by King Edward the Confessor, who removed his residence to the new foundation at Westminster.

It was certainly destroyed by fire with the cathedral in the year 1087, and was not rebuilt. Subsequently to the Norman Conquest, the Tower Royal, situated at the northern end of the street, now so called, was a spacious, strong, and magnificent mansion, belonging to the Kings of England, but its origin cannot now be traced; although it is supposed to have been founded by King Henry I., and was certainly inhabited by King Stephen. In Richard the Second's reign it was called the Queen's Wardrobe; according to Stowe, who says, King Richard having in Smithfield overcome and dispersed the rebels, he, his lords and all his company, entered the city of London with great joy, and went to the Lady Princess his mother, who was then lodged in the Tower Royal, called the Queen's Wardrobe. King Richard III., granted this palace to the first Duke of Norfolk.

It is a remarkable fact, that Domesday Book, which is usually so minute in regard to our principal towns and cities, is deficient in respect to London. It only mentions a vineyard in Holborn, belonging to the Crown, and ten acres of land near Bishopsgate, viz. the manor of Norton Folgate, belonging

to the Dean and Chapter of St. Paul's: yet certainly, observes Sir Henry Ellis, in his introduction to that valuable record, no mutilation of the manuscript has taken place; since the account of Middlesex is entire, and is exactly coincident with the abridged copy of the survey taken at the time, and now lodged in the office of the King's Remembrancer in the Exchequer.

The etymology of the name of London is involved in incertitude. Lundenburgh was its Anglo-Saxon appellation. Tacitus calls it Londinium, and Column Augusta. Ammianus Marcellinus mentions the city as an ancient place, once called Lundinium, but when he wrote, Augusta: the same author styles it Augusta Trinobantum. Bede calls it Londonia; and King Alfred, in his translation of the passage in Bede, Lundonceaster. According to W. Owen, the learned editor of the Welsh Archaiology, its primitive appellation was Llyn Din, or the Town on the Lake; and this appearance

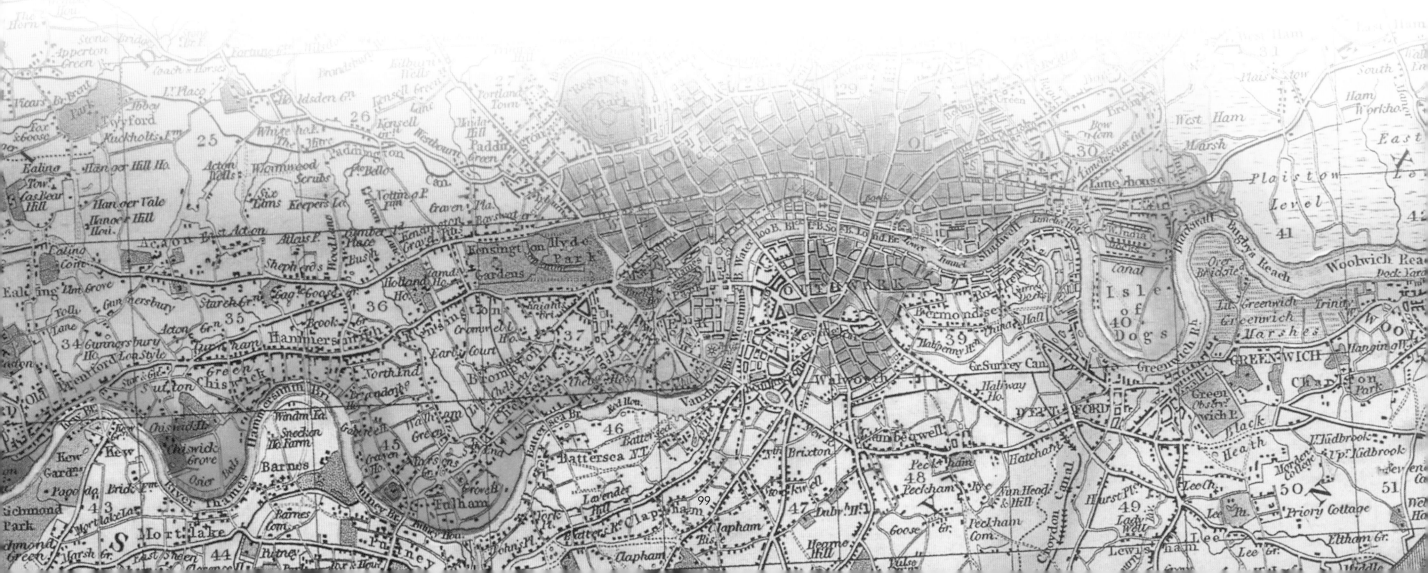

might have been exhibited when all the low grounds on the Surrey side of the river Thames were overflowed, as well as those extending from Wapping Marsh to the Isle of Dogs, and still further for many miles along the Essex shore. The transition from Llyn Din to London would be of easy growth. The name of Augusta is evidently Roman; and the opinion is, that it obtained the appellation Augusta when it became the capital of the British province, and in consequence only of its having become so. Tacitus states that London was so called from its situation, and Augusta from its magnificence.

London Stone is a remarkable fragment of antiquity, now standing against the southern wall of St. Swithin's church, in Cannon street. The earliest record of it, according to Stow, is at the end of "a fayre written Gospell Booke given to Christes Church in Canterburie by Ethelstane King of the West Saxons," where a parcel of land belonging to that church is described "to ly neare unto London Stone." It is also noticed in a record of a fire, which, in the first year of the reign of Stephen, 1135, "began in the house of one Ailwarde, neare unto London Stone," and consumed a considerable part of the city.

When Jack Cade, who headed an insurrection, and assumed the name of Mortimer, in the year 1450, had forced his way into the city, he struck his sword upon London Stone, and exclaimed, "Now is Mortimer Lord of this city;" as if, says Mr. Pennant, that had been a customary way of taking possession. Antiquaries seem, with Camden, to consider this stone as a milliary, whence the Romans began the admeasurement of their roads as from a centre. This opinion is said to be confirmed by the coincidence which its distance bears with the neighbouring stations mentioned in Antoninus's Itinerary. But Sir Christopher Wren supposed that "by reason of its large foundation it was rather some more considerable monument in the forum; for in the adjoining ground to the south, upon digging for cellars after the great fire, were discovered some tessellated pavements, and other remains of Roman workmanship and building." It was removed from the edge of the kerb-stone, where it had been placed in 1742, to its present situation against the church-wall, in the year 1798.

LONDON PRIOR TO THE REFORMATION

London, for some ages before the Reformation, contained an extraordinary number of religious edifices and churches, which occupied nearly two thirds of the entire area. Independently of St. Paul's Cathedral and the Abbey at

Westminster, the following friaries and abbeys existed immediately prior to that epoch: Black Friars, between Ludgate and the Thames; Gray Friars, near Old Newgate, now Christ's Hospital; Augustine Friars, now Austin Friars, near Broad-street; White Friars, near Salisbury-square; Crouched, or Crossed Friars, St. Olave's, Hart-street, near Tower-hill; Carthusian Friars, now the Charter House; Cistercian Friars, or New Abbey, East Smithfield; Brethren de Sacco, or *Bon Hommes*, Old Jewry.

Priories: St. John of Jerusalem, Clerkenwell; Holy Trinity, or Christ Church, on the site of Duke's-place, and near Aldgate; St. Bartholomew the Great, near Smithfield; St. Mary Overies, Southwark; St. Saviour's, Bermondsey.

Nunneries: Benedictines, or Black Nuns, Clerkenwell; St. Helen's, Bishopsgate-street; St. Clare's, Minories; Holy Well, between Holy-well-lane and Norton Folgate.

Colleges, &c.: St. Martin's le Grand; St. Thomas of Acres, West-cheap; Whittington's College and Hospital, Vintry Ward; St. Michael's College and Chapel, Crooked-lane; Jesus Commons, Dowgate.

Hospitals, having resident Brotherhoods: St. Giles's in the Fields, near St. Giles's church; St. James's, now St. James's Palace; Our Lady of Rounceval, near Charing Cross; Savoy, Strand; Elsing Spital, now Sion College; Corpus Christi, in St. Lawrence Pountney; St. Passey, near Bevis Marks; St. Mary Axe; Trinity, without Aldgate; St. Thomas, Mercer's Chapel; St. Bartholomew the Less, near Smithfield; St. Giles and Corpus Christi, without Cripplegate; St. Mary of Bethlehem, on the eastern side of Moorfields; St. Mary Spiral, without Bishopsgate; St. Thomas, Southwark; Lok Spiral, or Lazar, Kent-street, Southwark; St. Katherine's, below the Tower.

Fraternities: St. Nicholas, Bishopsgate-street; St. Fabian and St. Sebastian, or the Holy Trinity, Aldersgate-street; St. Giles, White-cross-street; The Holy Trinity, Leadenhall; St. Ursula le Strand; Hermitage, Nightingale-lane, East Smithfield; Corpus Christi, St. Mary Spiral; the same at St. Mary, Bethlehem, and St. Mary, Poultry.

The archiepiscopal and episcopal residences were, Lambeth Palace; York Place, or Whitehall; Durham House, Strand; Inns of the Bishops of Bath, Bangor, Chester, Llandaff, Worcester, Exeter, Lichfield, and Carlisle, all but one in and near the Strand; Bishop of Hereford's Inn, Old Fish-street; Ely House, Holborn; Bishop of Salisbury's, near Salisbury-square, Fleet-street; Bishop of St. David's Inn, near Bridewell Palace; Bishop of Winchester's House, Southwark, near St. Mary Overies; Bishop of Rochester's Inn, adjacent thereto, and the hostelry of the prior of Lewes, Southwark; besides the numerous residences of abbots and priors, mostly called Inns; not a vestige of any of the latter is however now known to remain.

The first Act of Parliament for the pavement and improvement of the city was passed in 1540, in the reign of Henry VIII., which described the streets to "be very foul, and full of pits and sloughs, very perilous and noyous, as well for all the king's subjects on horseback as on foot with carriages." The streets first paved under the statute were, Aldgate High-street, Shoe-lane, Fetter-lane, Gray's Inn-lane, Chancery-lane, and the way leading from Holborn-bar towards St. Giles's in the Fields, as far as any habitations on both sides of the same street.

The next Act for paving London referred particularly to Chiswell-street, Whitecross-street, Golden-lane, Grub-street, Long-lane, St. John's-street from Smithfield-bars up to the Pound; Cowcross, from the said bars; the way leading without Temple-bar westward by and to Clement's Inn gates, and New Inn gates to Drury-place, and that stretching to the sign of the Bell, at Drury-lane end; the bridge called Strand Bridge, and the way leading thither from Temple-bar; and the lane called Foscue-lane, leading

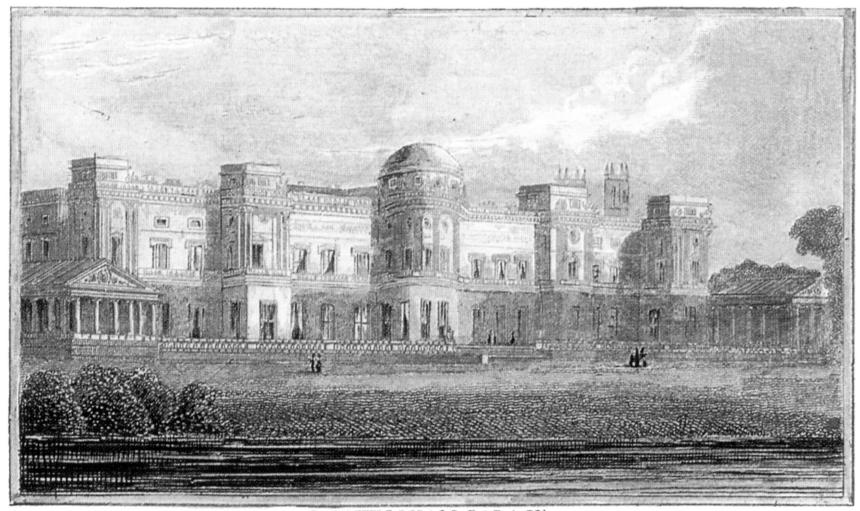

BUCKINGHAM PALACE

considerable degree, composed of detached wooden and brick houses, with trees intermingled, and standing at a distance from each other. About this era some fresh supplies of water were conveyed to the city from the springs near Perilous Pool, near the City-road, since called Peerless Pool, Hackney, Muswell-hill, Hampstead-heath, and St. Mary-le-Burne; and in 1546 new conduits were erected in Coleman-street and Lothbury.

LONDON IN THE TIME OF QUEEN ELIZABETH

From Aggas's view and plan of London, in the beginning of the reign of Elizabeth, it appears that the most crowded part of the city extended from Newgate-street, Cheapside, and Cornhill, to the banks of the Thames. Beyond Lothbury, from Basinghall-lane to Bishopsgate, with the exception of Coleman-street, a great portion of the ground was uncovered, and apparently occupied by gardens. Similar void spaces, but separated by buildings, occurred between Bishopsgate-street and the Minories; at the extremity of which, next to Tower-hill, stood a cross. Goodman's Fields was only an extensive enclosure; and East Smithfield and St. Katherine's extended but very little beyond St. Katherine's church. The north side of Whitechapel, and behind Houndsditch, was occupied by gardens and fields, lying entirely open from the back of St. Mary Spital. Houndsditch was only a single row of houses, extending from St. Botolph's, Aldgate, to Bishopsgate Without; thence a regular street extended to Shoreditch church, which terminated the avenue. Westward from Bishopsgate, besides gardens and enclosures, were a few buildings; the principal was a long range called the Dog House, where the city hounds were kept; hence a part of the City-road has been distinguished as Dog House-bar. On the site of what is now Finsbury-square stood several windmills; hence the avenue called Windmill-hill, and afterwards Windmill-street. In Old-street, from St. Luke's church to Shoreditch, there were no houses, and only two or three stood in the fields beyond. Finsbury-court, or Manor-house, stood on the south side of Chiswell-street, nearest Moorfields: the houses were not connected with Whitecross-street. Goswell-street was merely indicated by a road leading to St. Alban's; and Islington could hardly be seen. Clerkenwell was mostly occupied by the precincts of the monastery and the church, with the exception of some large houses in St. John's-lane, St. John's-street, and Cow-cross; at the back of which, towards the Fleet river, running on one side of Saffron-hill, and towards Ely House, the ground was entirely vacant, or filled

ABOVE: The rear, west facade of Buckingham Palace designed by John Nash, was widely criticised at the time for its central 'egg cup' dome. The building would have been under construction in the early 1830s as the London section of *The English Counties Delineated* was being compiled. Later versions of Moule's Middlesex map would include Edward Blore's short-lived east front which was completed in 1847 and caused the removal of Marble Arch to the top of Park Lane.

from the garden and tenement of the Bishop of Lichfield, called the Bell and Proctors, down to Strand-bridge. It is evident from this Act, that the streets afterwards named Butcher-row, Holywell-street, and St. Clement's, were not then built. Holywell-street must have been so denominated from its proximity to St. Clement's Well, at which many miraculous cures were supposed to have been performed. Some writers consider this well to have been in St. Clement's-lane, which at least must have been one of the avenues to it. At this time Golden-lane was literally a green avenue, between cottages and gardens. Whitecross-street derived its name from a conduit which stood there, surmounted by a white cross. Chiswell-street was an open road, between detached wooden houses, shaded with trees, as was probably also the case with Beech-lane. Bishopsgate-street Without was also in a with gardens; a great part of which, including the site of Red Lion-street, Clerkenwell, remained in this state until the commencement of the reign of George I. The precincts of the monastery of St. John of Jerusalem occupied ten acres in this vicinity. At that time there were houses on both sides of the way, from Holborn-bridge to Red Lion-street; but further up, to about Hart-street, the road was entirely open. A garden wall commenced there, and ran almost as far as Broad St. Giles's, and the end of Drury-lane, where a small cluster of houses, mostly on the right, formed the principal part of the village of St. Giles, which, in process in time, was called "The Ruins of St. Giles," and were taken down upwards of sixty years since, to make room for Bedford chapel, and the new streets adjacent. The precincts of the old hospital at St. Giles's were spacious, and surrounded with trees.

Beyond this, both to the north and west, all was country. From Oxford-road southward to Piccadilly, and thence along the highways named the Haymarket and Hedge-lane, not a house was standing, excepting three or four near the site of Carlton House. St. Martin's-lane had only a few houses beyond the church, abutting on the Covent garden, which extended quite into Drury-lane. No houses then stood in Drury-lane from near Broad St. Giles's, to Drury house at the top of Wych-street. Nearly the whole of the Strand was a continued street, mostly formed of spacious mansions, the residence of noblemen and prelates, with their large grounds and gardens extending towards the Thames, which have since given names to the streets built upon their sites; as Howard-street, Norfolk-street, Essex-street, Durham-yard, York-street, &c. Spring Gardens were literally gardens, reaching as far as where the Admiralty Office now stands. Along King-street, to St. Margaret's church and the Abbey, the houses stood closely; and from Whitehall to Palace-yard they were also thickly clustered on the banks of the Thames. Adjacent to Abingdon-street were several buildings, and some others stood opposite to Lambeth Palace. On the Surrey side, the plan exhibits only a single house at a small distance from the Archbishop's residence; but more northward, near a road that took the same direction from Westminster as the present Bridge-road, were six or seven buildings; nearly opposite to which was a stage landing-place. All beyond these, to the banks of the Thames opposite to White-friars, was entirely vacant; there a line of houses, with garden, and groves behind them, commenced, and was continued with little intermission beyond Bankside, to the vicinity of Winchester House, Christ church, and the next parish, then occupied by the theatre and gardens, called Paris Gardens. Further eastward, but behind the houses, and nearly opposite the Broken wharf and Queenhithe, were

the circular buildings and enclosures appropriated to bull-and-beat-baiting, amusements to which Queen Elizabeth seemed partial, Southwark, down the Borough High-street, was tolerably clustered with houses, and London-bridge was completely encumbered with them. Along Tooley-street to Battle-bridge, the houses stood thickly; but were much thinner from Horsleydown to where the plan ends, nearly opposite to St. Katherine's, below the Tower of London. Such was London about the period of Queen Elizabeth's accession to the crown of England. In the time of King Edward III, the shops in London appear to have been detached and separate tenements, or at least separate properties unconnected with houses. The shops, or rather stalls or stands, in Cheapside, St. Lawrence Jewry, the Old Jewry, and those, next to those of the goldsmiths', are reputed to have been the most splendid in London. The domestic conveniencies, however, had but little correspondence with this outward appearance: the general use of woollen was unfavourable to cleanliness, and the want of chimneys both inconvenient and prejudicial. The fires were made in the halls, against a reredoss or screen; and the smoke generally found a passage through the openings of the roof. The windows, also, were principally latticed; the use of glass was generally confined to religious houses, churches, and palaces.

THE PLAGUE AND FIRE OF LONDON

The year 1665 became memorable in London by the direful ravages of the great plague, the most dreadful that ever infested this kingdom, and which swept away sixty-eight thousand five hundred and ninety-six persons. Its virulence was most rife between the months of May and October, yet its appearance was noticed as early as December 1664, and it had not entirely ceased till January or February 1666.

This was soon followed by the most important event, perhaps, that ever happened in the metropolis, whether it be considered in references to its immediate effects, or to its remote consequences, the great fire of 1666, which broke out about one o'clock in the morning of the 2nd of September, and being impelled by strong winds, raged with irresistible fury nearly four days and nights, nor was it entirely mastered till the fifth morning after it began. This destructive conflagration commenced in Pudding-lane, near New Fish-street, and within ten houses of Thames-street, into which it spread within a few hours; nearly all the contiguous buildings being of timber, lath, and plaster, and the whole neighbourhood presenting little else than

confined passages and narrow alleys. There not being either a sufficient aid of engines or water, the flames soon reached Grace-church-street, towards the north-west, and the Three Cranes in the Vintry towards the south-west, including Cannon-street and the lanes and courts in the way; and either by communication of the flakes from such a vast body of fire, or by any of the other means which have been suspected, the flames burst out in divers and distant places; and the conflagration became so general that there was not a building left standing from the west end of Tower Wharf, in the east, to the Temple church, in the west; nor from the north end of Mincing-lane, in Fenchurch-street, from the west end of Leadenhall-street, and from the south-west end of Bishopsgate-street, as far as the entrance into Threadneedle-street, to Holborn-bridge on the west in a direct line; besides the damage done in Throgmorton-street, Lothbury, Coleman-street, Basinghall-street, Cateaton-street, Aldermanbury, Addle-street, Love-lane, Wood-street, Staining-lane, Noble-street, and Silver-street; at length it stopped at Pye-corner, near West Smithfield. This dreadful fire, within the walls, consumed almost five sixths of the whole city; and without the walls, it cleared a space nearly as extensive as the one sixth part left unburnt within. Scarcely a single building that came within the range of the flames was left standing. Public buildings, churches, and dwelling-houses, were alike involved in one common fate; and making an allowance for irregularities, it may be fairly stated, that the fire extended its ravages over a space of ground equal to an oblong square, measuring upwards of a mile in length, and half a mile in breadth. The ruins of the city comprised four hundred and thirty-six acres in extent; of the twenty-six wards fifteen were utterly destroyed, and eight others left shattered and half burnt; four hundred streets were consumed, thirteen thousand two hundred dwelling-houses, the cathedral church of St. Paul, eighty-eight churches, besides chapels, four of the city gates, Guildhall, the Royal Exchange, Custom House, and Blackwell Hall, many public structures, hospitals, schools, and libraries, fifty-two of the Companies' halls, and a great number of other edifices; together with four bridges, and the prisons of Newgate and the Fleet, and the Poultry and Wood-street compters. Notwithstanding all this destruction, only six persons lost their lives. The loss occasioned by the fire of London, as this tremendous conflagration has been emphatically denominated, amounted to the vast sum of 10,730,500*l.* sterling. A great loss was sustained by the stationers and booksellers; the immediate vicinity of St. Paul's was then, more particularly than at present, the chief seat of the trade; and when the fire was making its approaches, all those who dwelt near flew with their stock of

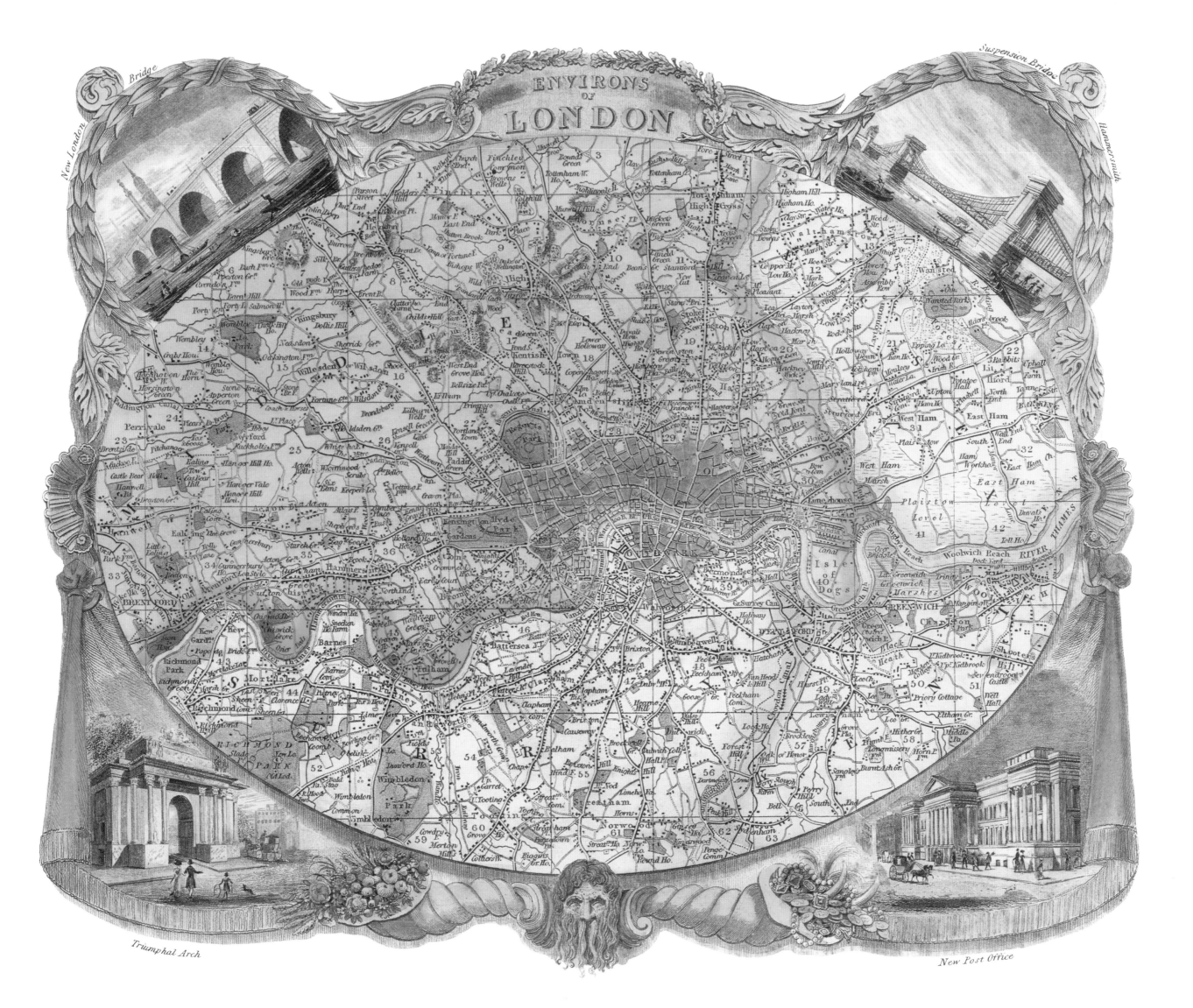

ENVIRONS OF LONDON

New London Bridge

Suspension Bridge

Hammersmith

Triumphal Arch

New Post Office

books, MSS., &c., and placed them in the vaults under the cathedral: the church was consumed, but the treasure in the crypts remained untouched, until the stationers, too eager to ascertain the state of their property, caused an aperture to be made into the glowing pit; a stream of wind consequently rushed in, and with explosive rapidity consumed the whole.

"Heavens, what a pile! whole ages perish'd there;
And one bright blaze turn'd learning into air."

The following is a list of those churches destroyed by the fire, which have not been rebuilt. Allhallows, Honey-lane; the church was situated where part of Honey-lane market now is.

Allhallows the Less was situated in Thames-street, near Cole harbour, now a buying-ground.

St. Andrew Hubbard was situated where the King's Weighhouse now is.

St. Anne, Blackfriars, was situated in Ireland-yard, now a burying-ground.

St. Benet Sherehog was situated in Pancras-lane, near Bucklers-bury, now a burying-ground.

St. Botolph Billingsgate, was situated in Thames-street, over against Botolph-lane, late a burying-ground, now built on.

St. Faith was under the late cathedral of St. Paul, where the parishioners have now a place to bury in.

St. Gabriel, Fenchurch, was situated in Fenchurch-street; the ground where it stood laid into the highway or street.

St. Gregory was situated in St. Paul's churchyard, near where Queen Anne's statue now stands.

St. John the Baptist was situated on Dowgate-hill, the corner of Cloak-lane, now a burying-ground.

St. John the Evangelist was situated in Watling-street, the corner of Friday-street, now a burying-ground.

St. John Zachary was situated at the corner of Noble-street, now a burying-ground.

St. Lawrence Pountney was situated on Lawrence Pountney-hill, now a burying-ground.

St. Leonard Eastcheap was situated near Eastcheap on Fish-street-hill, now a burying-ground.

St. Leonard, Forster-lane, was situated on the west side of Forster-lane, late a burying-ground, now part of the site of the present Post-office.

St. Margaret Moses was situated in Passing-alley, near Friday-street, late a burying-ground, now Little Friday-street.

St. Matgaret, New Fish-street, was situated where the Monument now stands.

St. Martin Pomeroy was situated in Ironmonger-lane, on a part of the ground now the churchyard.

St. Martin Orgars was situated in Martin's-lane, where there is now a French church.

St. Martin Vintry was situated at the lower end of College-hill in Thames-street, now a burying-ground.

St. Mary Bothaw was situated in Turnwheel-lane, now a burying-ground.

St. Mary Colechurch was situated in the Old Jewry, where the Mercers' school was, and Frederic-place now is.

St. Mary Magdalene, Milk-street, was situated where part of Honey-lane-market now is.

St. Mary Mounthaw was situated on Labour-in-vain-bill, now a burying-ground.

St. Mary Staining was situated on the north side of Oat-lane, now a burying-ground.

St. Mary Woolchurch was situated where the Mansion-house now stands.

St. Michael le Quern was situated in Paternoster-row, in the High-street of Cheapside, where a conduit formerly stood.

St. Nicholas Acon was situated in Nicholas-lane, now a burying-ground.

St. Nicholas Olave was situated on Bread-street-hill, now a burying-ground.

St. Olave, Silver-street, was situated on the south side of Noble-street, now a burying-ground.

St. Pancras, Soper-lane, was situated in Pancras-lane, near Queen-street, now a burying-ground.

St. Peter Cheap was situated at the corner of Wood-street, Cheap-side, now a burying-ground.

St. Peter, Paul's Wharf, was situated at the bottom of Peter's-hill, in Thames-street, now a burying-ground.

St. Thomas the Apostle was situated in the street or highway near the burying-ground the corner of Cloak-lane.

The Holy Trinity was situated where there is now a Lutheran church.

Whilst the city lay in ruins, various temporary edifices were raised for the public accommodation; and as soon as the general consternation had subsided, the rebuilding of the city became the first object of consideration. On the 13th of September the King held a court of Privy Council at Whitehall, in which many judicious regulations were determined on for the immediate re-edification of the city. The proclamation that was issued in consequence, provided for an increased breadth in the streets, for the erection of all new buildings either with brick or stone, for an open wharf by the river side, for the removal of noisome trades, and for various other circumstances that the nature of the business required. One of the first Acts that was passed was for erecting a Court of Judicature, consisting of the Justices of the Courts of King's Bench, Common Pleas, and Barons of Exchequer, for settling all differences that might arise between landlords and tenants in respect to any of the destroyed premises. Shortly afterwards the Parliament passed an Act for the expeditious rebuilding of the city; some of the principal clauses enacted that all the new buildings should have party-walls, and be erected within three years; that the Corporation should have full power to widen streets, passages, &c., and make new ones; and that the conflagration should be commemorated by a column. Various orders and regulations were afterwards made both by the Common Council and the Privy Council for making improvements in the city. Amongst the several plans that were proposed at this time for improving the capital, were two that acquired much celebrity: the first was designed by Sir Christopher Wren, and the other by John Evelyn, Esq., neither of which however was adopted. The city was principally rebuilt within little more than four years after its destruction.

The Monument, erected from designs by Sir Christopher Wren, on the site of St. Margaret's church, New Fish-street, is a fluted column of the Doric order. It is built of Portland stone, and stands upon a pedestal forty-feet in height and twenty-one feet square; the attitude of the whole is two hundred and two feet, being the exact distance westward from the precise spot where the fire began. Over the capital is an iron balcony encompassing a cone thirty-two feet high, supporting a blazing urn of gilt brass. The diameter of the shaft or body of the column is fifteen feet, and the ground plinth or lowest part of the pedestal is twenty-eight feet square. Within is a staircase of black marble containing three hundred and forty-five steps. The western front of the pedestal is enriched with an allegorical alto relievo by *Gabriel Cibber*, denoting the destruction, and restoration of the city under the superintendence of King Charles II. On the northern front is a Latin inscription relating the extent of the conflagration; on the southern front is one concerning the rebuilding of the city, and on the eastern front is the following:—

This pillar was begun. Sir Richard Ford, Knt., being Lord Mayor of London, in the year 1671;—carried on in the mayoralties of Sir George Waterman, Knt., Sir Robert Hanson, Knt., Sir William Hooker, Knt., Sir Robert Viner, Knt., Sir Joseph Sheldon, Knt., Lord Mayors;—and finished, Sir Thomas Davies being Lord Mayor, in the year 1677.

Round the pedestal was an inscription, which, upon James II.'s accession to the crown, was immediately erased, but soon after the Revolution it was again restored. However, on December 6, 1830, it was decreed by the Court of Common Council that the objectionable inscription should be expunged, which was accordingly done.

THE CITY OF WESTMINSTER

The Metropolis is formed by the union of the Cities of London and Westminster, and the Borough of Southwark. Westminster on the northern bank of the Thames, received its name from its Minster situated westward of London, and is so called in a charter of sanctuary, granted by King Edward the Confessor, in the year 1066. For a considerable period it was entirely distinct from London, although it now forms an integral part of it. The Abbots of Westminster had archiepiscopal jurisdiction within their liberties, and had the keeping of the regalia; performing also a chief service in the coronation of the Kings of England, and had a seat in Parliament. The ancient arms of the Abbey were *Azure, on a chief indented or, a crosier on the dexter side, and a mitre on the sinister, both gules.* After the dissolution of monasteries, King Henry VIII. erected the abbey into a deanery, and in 1541 established it as a Bishopric, appointing John Thirlby the first bishop: upon this occasion it became a City; he having wasted the revenue allotted by the King for the support of the See, was translated to Norwich, and with him ended the Bishopric of Westminster, the dignity continuing only nine years, when Middlesex, which was the diocese, was restored to London. The dean continued to preside until the accession of Queen Mary, who restored the abbot; but Queen Elizabeth displaced the abbot, and erected the Abbey into a collegiate church, as it still continues. The arms of the Deanery of Westminster, are *Azure, a cross patonce between five martlets or, on a chief of the last a pale quarterly of France and England, between two roses gules.* The dean of Westminster being invariably Dean of the Order of the Bath, bears the ribbon of the order with the badge pendant. When the Bishopric was dissolved by King Edward VI., the right of Westminster to the name of City was lost with it, although custom has retained the epithet ever since. Westminster is governed by a high steward, who is usually a nobleman, and is appointed by the dean and chapter, a deputy steward, sixteen capital burgesses, sixteen assistants, a high bailiff, high constable, town clerk and other officers. The quarter sessions for the peace are held in the Court House in King-street. The arms of the City, granted the 1st October, 1601, are *Azure, a portcullis with chains pendant Or, on a chief of the last, the arms of King Edward the Confessor, in pale, between two roses of York and Lancaster. (See page 100).*

MONMOUTHSHIRE

This county is bounded on the north by Breconshire and Herefordshire; on the east by Gloucestershire; on the south by the river Severn and the Bristol Channel; and on the west by Glamorganshire. In extent it is considered to be about thirty-three miles long, and twenty-six broad, being in circumference about one hundred and ten miles. The district including Monmouthshire, Glamorganshire, and the Forest of Dean, was anciently known by the name of Gwent or Went (from Gwen, *fair*), and afterwards of Essyllwg (from Syllt, *aspect)*, whence the Roman name Siluria. Under the Romans Caer Went became Venta Silurium, when the county was included in the province Britannia Secunda. Other Roman stations were Blestium, or Monmouth, Burrium, or Usk, Gobannium or Abergavenny, and Isca Silurium, the head-quarters of the second legion, and seat of government for Britannia Secunda at Caerleon. This county was not included in the Saxon Heptarchy. It was formerly a part of South Wales, but was separated from Welsh jurisdiction in 1535, and has been regarded as a part of England ever since. There were abbeys at Grâce Dieu, Lantarnam, Lanthony and Tintern, and priories at Goldcliff, Kynemark, Monmouth and Usk. The principal castles in the county were at Abergavenny, Caerleon, Caldicot, Castell Glas, or Green Castle, Chepstow Dinham, Grosmont, Lanfair, Iscoed, Langibby, Monmouth, Newport, Pencoed, Penhow, Ragland, Skenfreth, Usk, and White Castle or Landeilo. The county contains seven market-towns, one hundred and twenty-seven parishes, 13,211 inhabited houses, and 71,833 persons. It is in the province of Canterbury, and the diocese of Landaff, excepting three parishes, Welsh Bicknor, Dixton and St. Mary's, in the diocese of Hereford, and three, Cwmyoy, Lanthony and Oldcastle, in the diocese of St. David's, and returns three members to Parliament; two for the county, who at present are Charles Henry Somerset, Lord Granville, and Sir Charles Morgan Bart.; and one for the town of Monmouth. Nearly one-third of the county is a rich plain on the shores of the Severn, one-third consists of beautifully variegated ground, watered by considerable rivers, and the hills cultivated or wooded; and one-third assumes the mildest character of mountain, abounding with lovely valleys. The air is mild, temperate, and healthy generally, even in the lower parts of the county; and it has been remarked that the southern situations, bordering upon the sea, are less humid than the western mountainous districts, probably owing to the frequent breezes arising from the ocean, and the attractive influence of the mountains over clouds that float low in the atmosphere. Upon the hills it is bleak and cold in winter, the snow continuing here a considerable time; while in the valleys it soon melts away. Almost every necessary article of life is to be found in the different districts of this charming county, and so contiguous to each other that all parts are in general equally well supplied; the hills feed great numbers of cattle and sheep, and the vales produce plenty of corn, pulse, and grass. Coals and wood abound, and are distributed at very reasonable rates; lead and iron ores, with limestone and quarries of stone for building, &c., are also plentifully found within this luxuriant county; particularly a fine quarry a few miles from Newport. The principal rivers are the Severn, which washes the southern boundary of the county; the Usk, which rises upon the western border of Breconshire, and enters Monmouthshire at a short distance from Abergavenny, by which it runs and continues its course through the heart of the county to Usk, Caerleon, and Newport, below which it finally discharges itself into the Severn. The rivers Wye, Monnow, and Rumney are the boundaries which separate it from other counties, and the streams of less note are the Avon Llwyd, Beeg, Berden, Carn, Cledaugh, Ebwy, Fidan, Gavenny, Grony, Honthy, Kebby, Lumon, Morbesk, Mythve, Nedern, Olwy, Organ, Pill, Pool Meyric, Rhyd y Mirch, Sorwy, Tilery, Troggy, Trothy, and Ystwith. The Monmouthshire canal commences on the western side of the town of Newport, having a basin connected with the river Usk; it passes between the town and the river, and crosses the Chepstow road; thence by Malpas it pursues its route parallel to and near the river Avon, by Pontypool to Pont Newidd, being nearly eleven miles, with a rise of twelve feet in the first mile, and four hundred and thirty-five feet, in the remaining ten miles. Nearly opposite to Malpas, a branch canal takes a course parallel to the river Ebwy, to a point near Crumlin Bridge, being a course of nearly eleven miles from the junction, with a rise of three hundred and fifty-eight feet making the total length of the two canals twenty-two miles: from these there are several rail-roads to different iron-works, collieries, and lime kilns. The Brecon canal unites with the Monmouthshire canal one mile from Pontypool; it crosses the river Avon, where by a tunnel two hundred and twenty yards in length it crosses the high land there, and passes the town of Abergavenny, towards the river Usk, and proceeds parallel with that river to Brecon, being thirty-three miles in length, with sixty eight feet rise to Brecon. The Abergavenny canal communicates with the Brecon canal. The county of Monmouth, throughout its whole extent, is celebrated for the beauty and sublimity of its scenery; the most noted places in this county are Gold Cliff Point, Denny Island, Charston Rock, the Severn mouth and Usk mouth, with the Hatterel, Pen y Vale, and Valire Hills; Wentwood Forest and many other situations exhibit scenes of exquisite beauty. In the hundreds of Went Lloog and Caldicot sea-walls have been erected, at a vast expense, to keep off the sea at high tides and in stormy weather; some of these walls are admirably built, to the height of twelve or fourteen feet, with a gradual slope from the sea, and a spacious embankment of earth behind the stone-work. — Troy House, near Monmouth, is the seat of His Grace the Duke of Beaufort, K.G., Lord Lieutenant of the County.

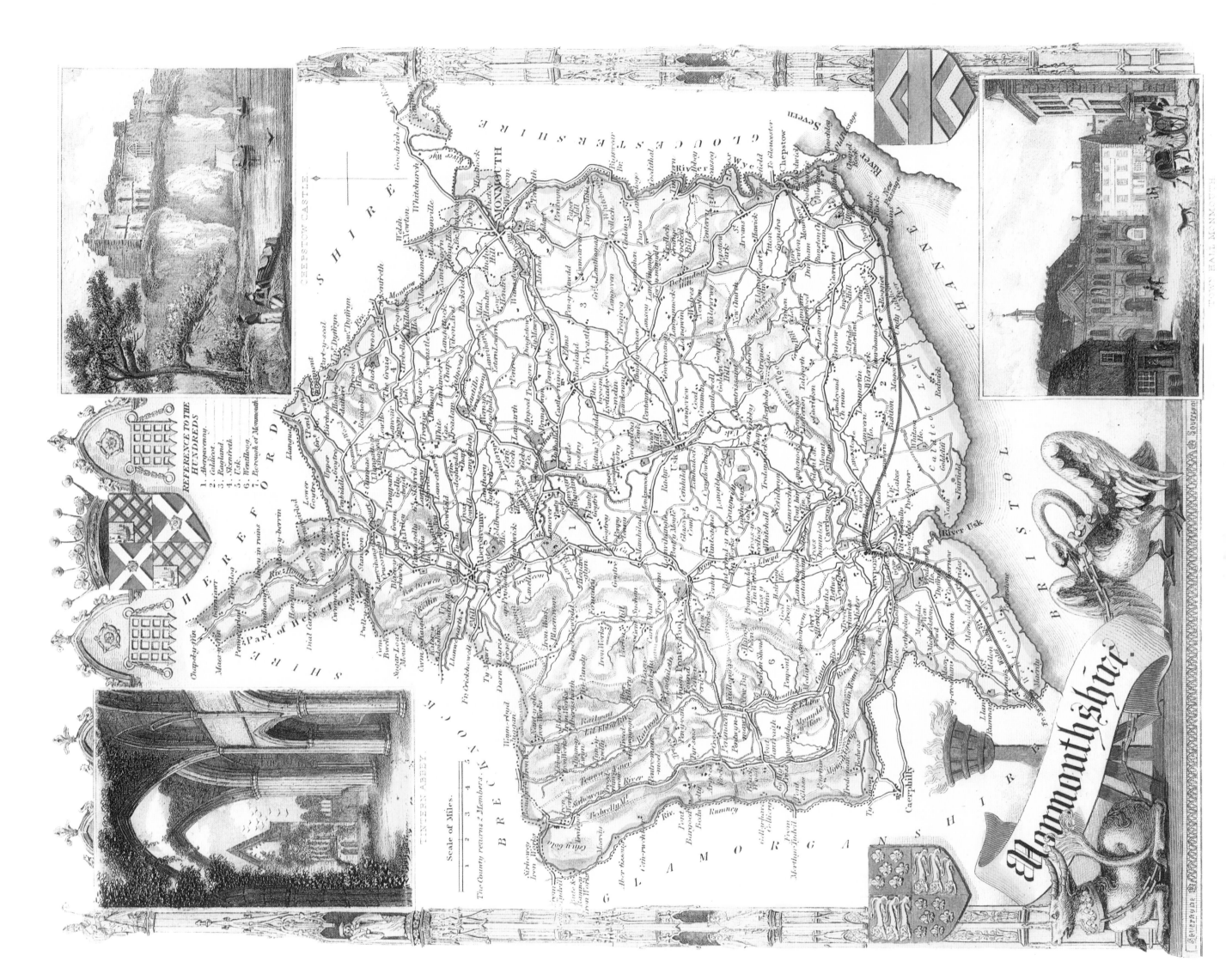

Monmouthshire.

REFERENCE TO THE
HUNDREDS.
1. Abergavenny.
2. Caldicot.
3. Ragland.
4. Skenfreth.
5. Usk.
6. Wentlloog.
7. Boxworth et Monmouth.

Scale of Miles.
1 2 3 4 5
The County returns 2 Members K.

TINTERN ABBEY.

NORFOLK

THIS county is bounded on the north and east by the German Ocean; on the south by Suffolk; and on the west by Lincolnshire and Cambridgeshire: in length it is about seventy miles, in breadth forty-five miles, and in circumference it is one hundred and forty miles. The British inhabitants were the Iceni, an extensive tribe; and the Romans had several stations of importance within this county, which formed part of the province of Flavia Cæsariensis, as Ad Taum, Tasburgh; Branodunum, Brancaster; Gariannonum, Burgh; Iciani, Ickburgh or *Oxburgh;* Sitornagus, Thetford; and Venta Icenorum, Caistor near Yarmouth. Buckenham, Castle Acre, and Elmham are also supposed to have been Roman stations. The Ermine-street terminated at Yarmouth. During the Anglo-Saxon Heptarchy Norfolk formed part of the kingdom of East Anglia, of which Thetford was the capital, and an episcopal see. There are remains of encampments at South Creake, the Foss near Weeting, Narbury and Wareham. The castles of its ancient lords were at Norwich, Castle Acre, Castle Rising, New Buckenham, Caistor and Weeting. Blickling Hall and Melton Constable are ancient residences. Norfolk is remarkable for having been more abundantly endowed with religious houses, from the earliest introduction of Christianity, than any other county of equal size in the kingdom: so extensive indeed were the temporal possessions of the religious institutions, that there were few, or probably none of the parishes in this county, numerous as they are, which were not in part claimed by the regular orders, or in which the religious had not an interest. There were abbeys at Hulme, West Dereham, Langley, Wendling and Wymondham; priories at Dele, Beeston, Binham, Bromhill, Bromholm, Old Buckenham, Castle Acre, Cokesford, Creake, Flitcham, Hickling, Horsham, Lynn, Molycourt, Mountjoy, Pentney, Shouldham, Thetford, Waburn, Walsingham, Wells, Wereham, West Acre and Yarmouth; and nunneries at Blackborough, Crabhouse and Marham. Norfolk still contains numerous early specimens of ecclesiastical architecture, with which the antiquary will be highly gratified. Stone crosses, indicating the routs of pilgrims, abound in this county; and the sites of more than eighty have been ascertained by Mr. Taylor, author of the *Index Monasticus.* Norfolk contains one city and county town, 32 market towns, 660 parishes, 62,274 houses, and 344,368 inhabitants; and returns twelve members to Parliament, two for Yarmouth, two for Norwich, two for Thetford, two for Lynn, two for Castle Rising, and two for the county, who at present are, Thomas William Coke, Esq. of Holkham Hall, and Sir William John Browne Folkes, Bart, of Hillington Hall.

The face of this county varies less than in most tracts of equal extent in the kingdom: not a single hill of more than moderate height is to be seen, but its surface is in many parts broken into gentle undulations; the chief eminences are Athill near Swaffham, Docking near Burnham, Hunstanton Cliffs, and Marum Hills. At the western extremity is a considerable tract of flat fenny land; and on the east near Yarmouth a narrow tract of marshes runs from the sea for some distance up the country; the northern coast near Cley is also marsh land: in these parts great quantities of butter are made, which is sent to London under the name of Cambridge butter. King Charles

ABOVE: Norwich Cathedral, constructed under the Normans and completed in 1145, is regarded as one of the most complete Gothic ecclesiastical buildings in Britain. It would have been held in high regard by Thomas Moule.

II. is reported to have said of this county, that "it was only fit to be cut into roads for the rest of the kingdom," considering it to be flat, stony and infertile; but by the patriotic exertions and laudable example of Mr. Coke, of Holkham, the desert has been converted to a granary. In the northern parts of the county, where wheat was almost unknown, the most abundant crops wave over the district between Holkham and Lynn; but the basis of Norfolk farming is the turnip, and it is mainly to its extensive culture that the naturally barren soil has been fertilized. Poultry, of all kinds, is very plentiful; the Norfolk turkey is in especial estimation, for the whiteness of its flesh, the delicacy of its flavour, and the largeness of its size: immense quantities are annually sent to very distant parts of the kingdom. The principal lakes are Braydon, Hickling and Rockland broads, Diss, Hingham, North Walsham and Quiddenham lakes; others abound in the southern parts of the county, and are nurseries of innumerable wild fowl of various species, but principally ducks; they are taken in great numbers on the margin of these waters. The rabbit is also an object of trade to a considerable extent: Moushold Heath was formerly a celebrated spot for the finest and best flavoured. Mackerel and herrings are taken in abundance on the coast,—the first in spring, and the last in autumn. Yarmouth is famed for curing its herrings, which are exported to the southern parts of the Continent, particularly Italy. This county is geologically situated within the London Chalk Basin, which terminates towards the north at Flamborough Head; its strata consist of the chalk series, with a superposition of diluvial debris, having the plane of their inclination nearly east. The rivers of Norfolk are the Great Ouse, the Nene, the Little Ouse, the Wensum, the Waveney, the Yare, the Bure, and the Ant: these rivers in general rise in marshy lands, and running through a level country, diffuse themselves over the lower tracts, in their course forming shallow pools, which are plentifully stocked with fish and water-fowl; and on some of them are-decoys for wild ducks. The Great Ouse crosses the western side of the county, and falls into the Wash below Lynn. The Nene forms the western boundary from Lincolnshire, and empties itself into the sea at Cross Keys Wash. The Little Ouse rises near Lopham, in the southern part of the county, and separating Norfolk and Suffolk, falls into the Great Ouse. The Wensum rises at West Rudham, thirty miles from the city, and being augmented by several rivulets, passes through Norwich, and joins the Yare below Trowse, not far from the city. The source of the Waveney is separated from that of

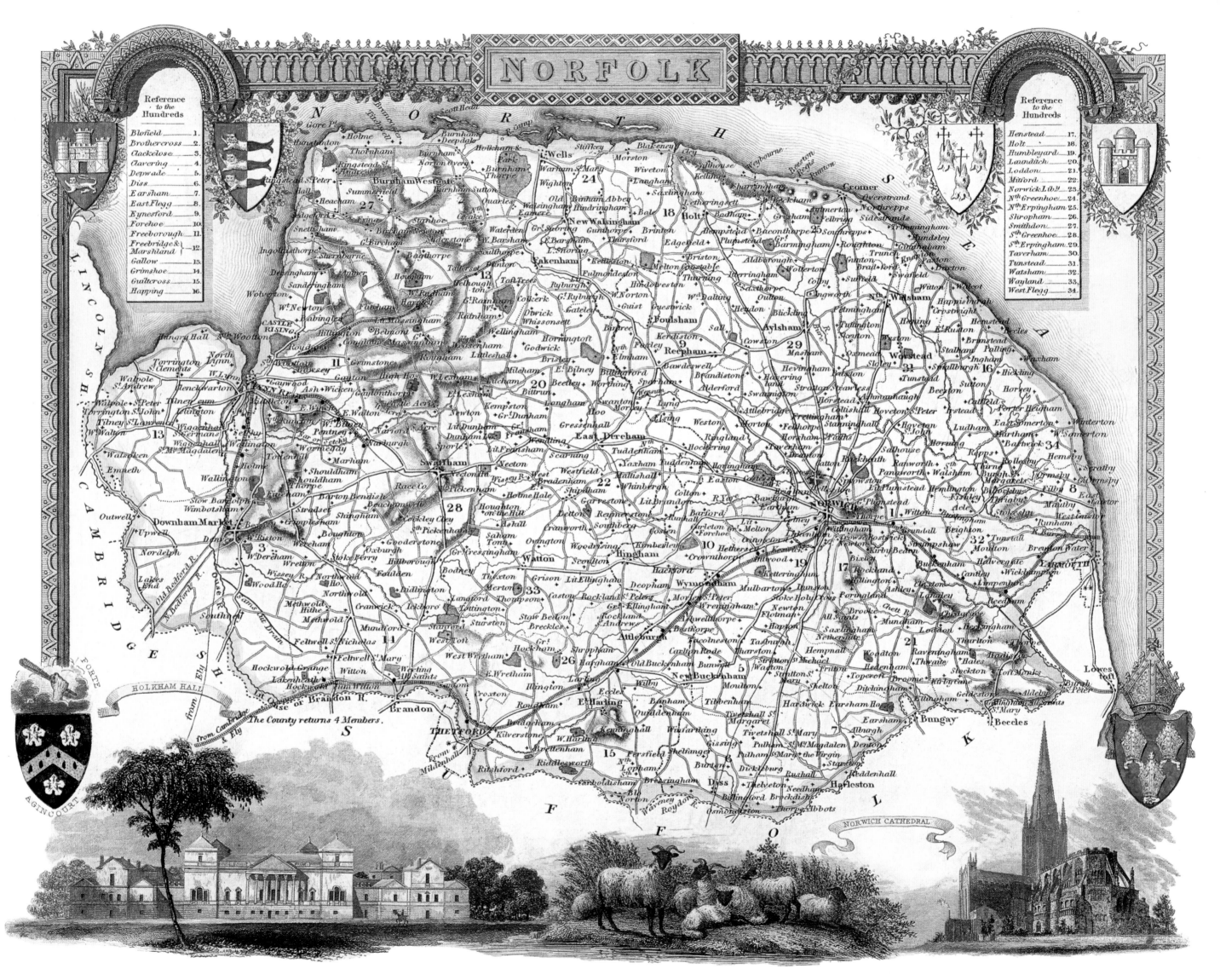

NORFOLK

The County returns 4 Members.

HOLKHAM HALL

NORWICH CATHEDRAL

the Little Ouse by a causeway only, and running in a contrary direction, forms the rest of the Suffolk boundary, and joins the Yare a little above Braydon. The Yare, rising near Shipdam, is augmented by another stream at Marlingford, which has its source near Hingham; the river joins the Wensum at Trowse Eye near the city of Norwich, and flows to Yarmouth, where having also received the waters of the Waveney and the Bure, it falls into the German Ocean below that port. The Bure, rising beyond Blickling, becomes navigable at Aylsham; after passing Wroxham-bridge, and being joined by the Ant and Thirne, it passes Acle bridge, and joins the Yare at Yarmouth.

The Ant rises at Antingham, and flowing on the east of North Walsham, is made navigable near Stalham, whence it passes to Ludham, and below that village falls into the Bure. The inland navigation is by the Thirne, Bure, and Wisbech canals. The staple articles of manufacture in this county are worsted, an appellation derived from a village of that name; Norwich stuffs, which were introduced here by Flemings who settled in the city in the year 1336; bombasins, introduced by Dutch and Walloons who fled to Norwich for refuge from the Duke of Alva, the Spanish Governor of the Netherlands, in 1566; damask, shawls, crapes, and fine camlets,—the last in great request for the East India trade: to these articles have been added cotton shawls and fancy goods; and Canada is one of the principal markets for Norwich goods. The Honourable John Wodehouse is Lord Lieutenant of the County.

BELOW: Holkham Hall in north Norfolk was originally designed by the architects William Kent and Lord Burlington in the Palladian revival style in the early years of the eighteenth century. Kent would also work on the design of a series of buildings and monuments – including obelisks, a triumphal arch and a domed temple – in Holkham's gardens and park.

NORTHAMPTONSHIRE

NORTHAMPTONSHIRE borders on more counties than any other shire in the kingdom. On the north it is separated from Leicestershire, Rutlandshire and Lincolnshire, by the rivers Avon and Welland; on the east it is bounded by Cambridgeshire, Huntingdonshire, and Bedfordshire; on the south by Buckinghamshire and Oxfordshire; and on the west, the river Leam divides it from Warwickshire. Its greatest length is about seventy miles, and its breadth thirty miles, being in circumference about two hundred miles. The British inhabitants were called Coritani by the Romans, and it formed part of the province Flavia Cæsariensis. The Roman stations were Benaventa (Daventry); Durobrivae (Castor); and Lactodorum (Towcester). During the Saxon Heptarchy, Northamptonshire formed part of the kingdom of Mercia. The Watling-street, in proceeding from the south towards the north, enters the county near Stratford, and continuing in almost a direct line leaves it at Dove Bridge. There are encampments at Arbury Hill, Barrow Dyke, Borough Hill, Castle Dyke, Chester Burrow, Guilsborough, Huntsborough, Passenham, Rainsborough, Sulgrave, and Wallow Bank. There were formerly abbeys at Northampton, Pipewell and Sulby; and the castles of its earlier lords were Barnwell, Fotheringhay, Rockingham and Drayton. This county contains one city (Peterborough), one county town, twelve market-towns, three hundred and seven parishes, 32,503 inhabited houses, and 162,483 inhabitants. It is in the province of Canterbury and in the diocese of Peterborough, excepting three parishes, Gretton, King's Sutton, and Nassington, in that of Lincoln. Northamptonshire returns nine members to Parliament; two for Brackley one for Higham Ferrers two for Northampton two for Peterborough and two for the county. The present members are

Lord Althorp, and Lord Milton. At a former period the greater portion of Northamptonshire was occupied by the forests of Salcey, Whittlebury, and Rockingham, of which there are still some considerable remains. The highest ground in the county is in the neighbourhood of Daventry; about Towcester, in the south, the ground is also hilly. It is peculiarly celebrated for grazing land, that tract especially, from Northampton towards the Leicestershire border. Horned cattle and other animals are here fed to extraordinary sizes, and many horses of the large black breed are reared: much of the arable land is still open-field; and many sheep are grazed on the high grounds. The extreme point of this county, surrounded and intersected by rivers, is very liable to inundations and forms the commencement of the Fenny tract extending to the Lincolnshire Washes. The rivers are the Avon, Cherwell, Ise, Leam, Nen, Tove, and Welland. Northamptonshire is singularly independent as to water, for all its rivers take their rise within its own boundaries; not a single stream, however insignificant, runs into it from any other districts; whilst there is not a county bordering upon it that is not in some degree supplied from its various and ample aquatic sources. The Nen, rising in the west, flows first across the county to the eastern side, and then turning more northward, accompanies the whole remaining length of it to Peterborough, where it leaves the county, and runs into Cross Keys Wash on the coast of Lincolnshire. The canals are the Grand Junction, Oxford, Leicestershire and Northamptonshire, and the Union. The manufactures are shoes, lace, woollen stuffs, whips and earthenware. Apethorp Hall, near Wansford, is the seat of the Earl of Westmorland, K.G. Lord Lieutenant of the County.

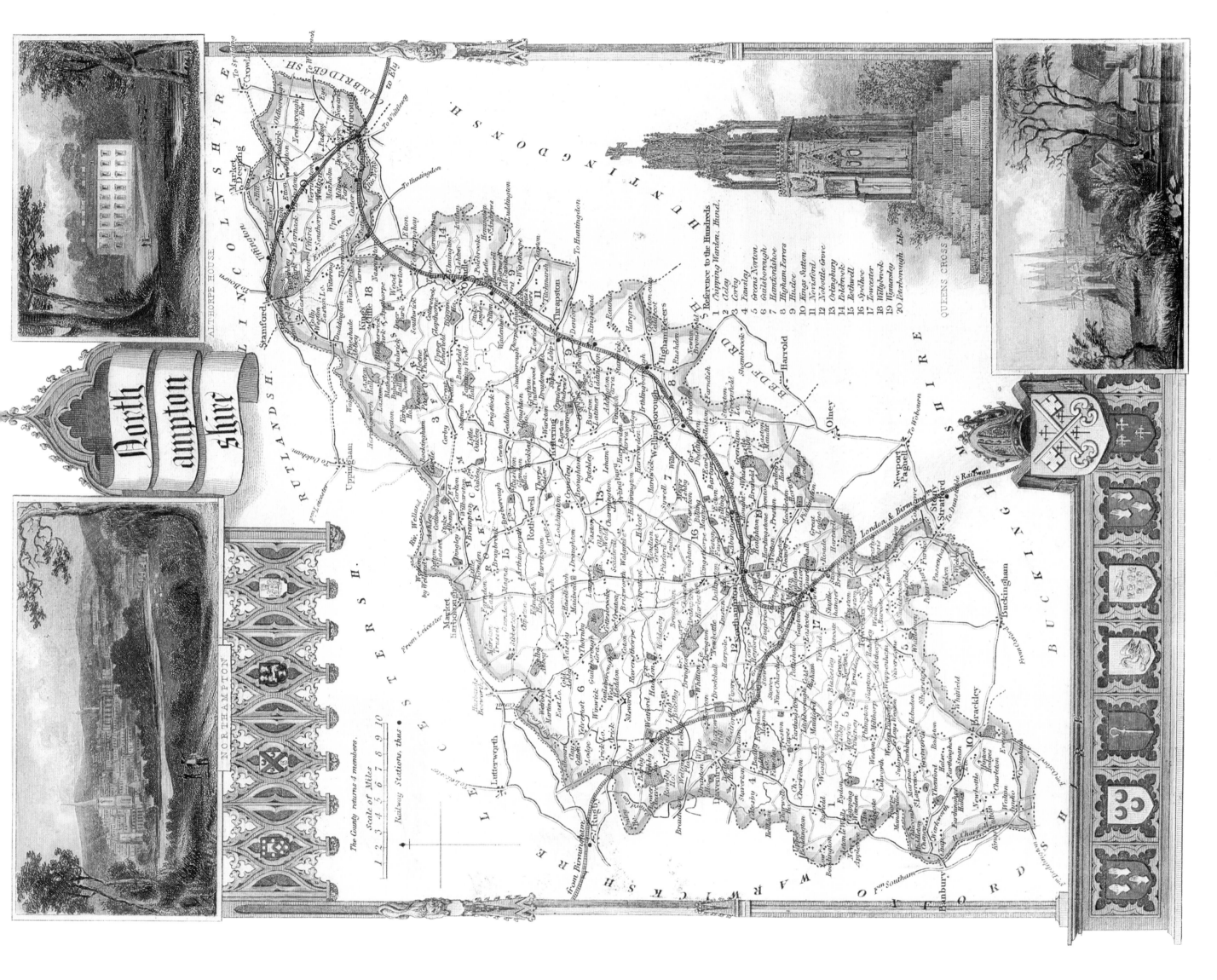

North ampton Shire

ALTHORPE HOUSE

NORTHAMPTON

QUEENS CROSS

The County returns 4 members.

Scale of Miles
1 2 3 4 5 6 7 8 9 10

Railway Stations, thus ●

Reference to the Hundreds.
1 Chipping Warden. Hund.
2 Oxley
3 Corby
4 Fawsley
5 Greens Norton
6 Guilsborough
7 Hamfordshoe
8 Higham Ferres
9 Huxloe
10 Kings Sutton
11 Navisford
12 Nobottle Grove
13 Ortlingbury
14 Polebrook
15 Rothwell
16 Spelhoe
17 Towcester
18 Willybrook
19 Wymersley
20 Peterborough Lib.ty

LINCOLNSHIRE

CAMBRIDGESHIRE

HUNTINGDONSHIRE

BEDFORDSHIRE

BUCKINGHAMSHIRE

OXFORD

WARWICKSHIRE

LEICESTERSHIRE

RUTLANDSH.

NORTHUMBERLAND

This county, the most northerly in England, is bounded on the north by Scotland, and a detached part of the county of Durham; on the east by the North Sea or German Ocean on the south by Durham and on the west by Cumberland. Its greatest length is sixty-four miles; its greatest breadth forty-eight; and in circumference it is two hundred and twenty-three miles. Its name is derived from the Anglo-Saxons, who named this district Northan Humber Land, on account of its situation northward of the river Humber; including also Yorkshire, Durham, Lancashire, Westmorland, and Cumberland, under that denomination. Previously to the Roman invasion of Britain, it was inhabited by the Ottadini, the Gadeni, and the Brigantes. Under the Romans it formed part of the province of Maxima Cæsariensis; the northern frontier of this province was protected by a wall of stupendous magnitude, built by the Romans across the isthmus, eighty miles in length, twelve feet high, and nine thick, strengthened with towers, now called the Wall of Severus. The exact site of the barrier erected by Severus against the northern tribes furnished matter of dispute to many of our antiquaries. The researches of others, particularly Horsley, have set this question at rest: from their information, joined to the scanty evidence of history, it has been proved that three walls, or ramparts, were erected by the Romans, at different times, to secure the northern frontier of their dominions in Britain. The first was a rampart of earth, from the Solway Frith to the Tyne, raised by Hadrian about the year 120, but its form and construction have not been satisfactorily ascertained; it was, however, evidently nothing more than a line intended to obstruct the passage of an enemy between the stations which constituted the real defences of the frontier. The second was raised by Lollius Urbicus under the reign of Antoninus Pius, about the year 140, between the Firths of Forth and Clyde; this was likewise of earth, though perhaps faced with stone, and, like that of Hadrian, seems to have been intended as a line connecting the chain of stations which formed a new barrier on the advance of the Roman arms; in the course of both there was a military road communicating from station to station. The last and most important is that wall begun by Severus after his expedition against the Caledonians about the year 208; it runs nearly over the same ground as that of Hadrian but is a complete and well-combined system of fortification. From an examination of its remains, it appears to have been built of stone, fifteen feet high, and nine thick; it had a parapet and ditch, a military road, and was defended by eighteen greater

stations, placed at intervals of from three to six miles; eighty-three castles, at intervals of from six to eight furlongs; and as it is imagined, a considerable number of turrets, placed at shorter distances.— *Hatcher's Notes to Richard of Cirencester*. The Roman stations in this county were Æsica, Great Chesters; Borcovicus, House Steads; Bremenium, Rochester; Cilurnum, East Chesters; Condurcum. Benwell; Corstopitum, Corchester; Habitancum, Risingham; Hunnum, Halton Chesters; Magna, Caervoran; Pons Ælii, Newcastle; Procolitia, Carrowburgh; Segedunum, Wall's End; Vindobala, Rutchester; and Vindolana, Little Chesters. The Roman roads passing through the county were the Watling-street &c.; there are also extant numerous Roman earthworks, buildings, and inscriptions at the several stations, particularly at House Steads, called by Dr. Stukeley the Palmyra of Britain. During the latter part of the Roman ascendancy, Northumberland formed a part of the province Valentia; but in the fifth century an independent kingdom was erected by the Britons, under the name of Bryneich, or Bernicia, which passed to the Angles under King Ida, about the year 547; this was subsequently united to the territory between the Humber and the Tyne, and the whole called Northumbria, or Northan Humber Land. The

Northumbrian Angles became tributary to Egbert, King of Wessex, A.D. 828 and continued to be governed by their own princes, when the kingdom was conquered by the Danes in 867: it was recovered by Edred, King of England, in the tenth century, and was subsequently governed as a dependent kingdom or earldom till the Norman conquest. There are remains of the Anglo-Saxon period, consisting of entrenchments of Black Dykes Bolam; Castel Banks; Castle Hill; Clinch and Ingram circular camps; Green Castle; Hairlaw Camp; Marden Castle; Old Rothbury; Outchester; Spindeston; Trodden Gares; Whalton Camp; Whitchester; and Whitby Castle; besides a circle of stones at Three Stone Burn. The castles of the early Lords of Northumberland were numerous; the principal were those of Alnwick, Aydon, Bamborough, Bavington, Belsay, Bellister, Bothall, Bellingham, Bywell, Beltingham, Coupland, Chillingham, Capheaton, Dale Castle, Dunstanburgh, Errington, Featherstone, Horton, Haughton, Hurst, Harnham, Cockle Park Tower, Cold Marten, Crawley, Chipchase, Ford, Harbottle, Langley, Lemington, Mitford, Morpeth, Newcastle, Ogle, Prudhoe, Simonsburn, Swinburn, Spylaw, Staward, Warkworth, Widdrington, Wark, Walltown, and Willymoteswick. There were formerly abbeys at Alnwick, Blanchland, Hexham, Hulm, and Newminster; priories at Bamborough, Brinkburn, and Tynemouth; and nunneries at Haliston, Lambley, Nesham, and Newcastle. This county is in the province of York and diocese of Durham, excepting four parishes; Allondale, Hexham, St. John Lee, and Throckington, in that of York: it contains one county town, 12 market-towns, 82 parishes, 31,526 houses, and 198,965 inhabitants; and according to the Reform Bill of 1832, returns ten members to Parliament, viz. two for Berwick-upon-Tweed, one for Morpeth, two for Newcastle, one for Tynemouth, and four for the county; the members for the Northern Division are Viscount Howick, eldest son of Earl Grey, and Lord Ossulston, eldest son of the Earl of Tankerville; and the members for the Southern Division are Thomas Wentworth Beaumont, Esq., of Hexham, and Matthew Bell, Esq.

The face of the country in this large district is various; the mountainous parts, absolutely unfit for tillage, comprise more than a third of the land; the most fertile tracts are on the east side, in the vales, through which the rivers run in their course to the sea, and the Vale of Coquet is particularly noted for its fertility. Woods are chiefly confined to the banks of rivers, but plantations are formed in various parts. The Cheviot Hills, in the northern part of the

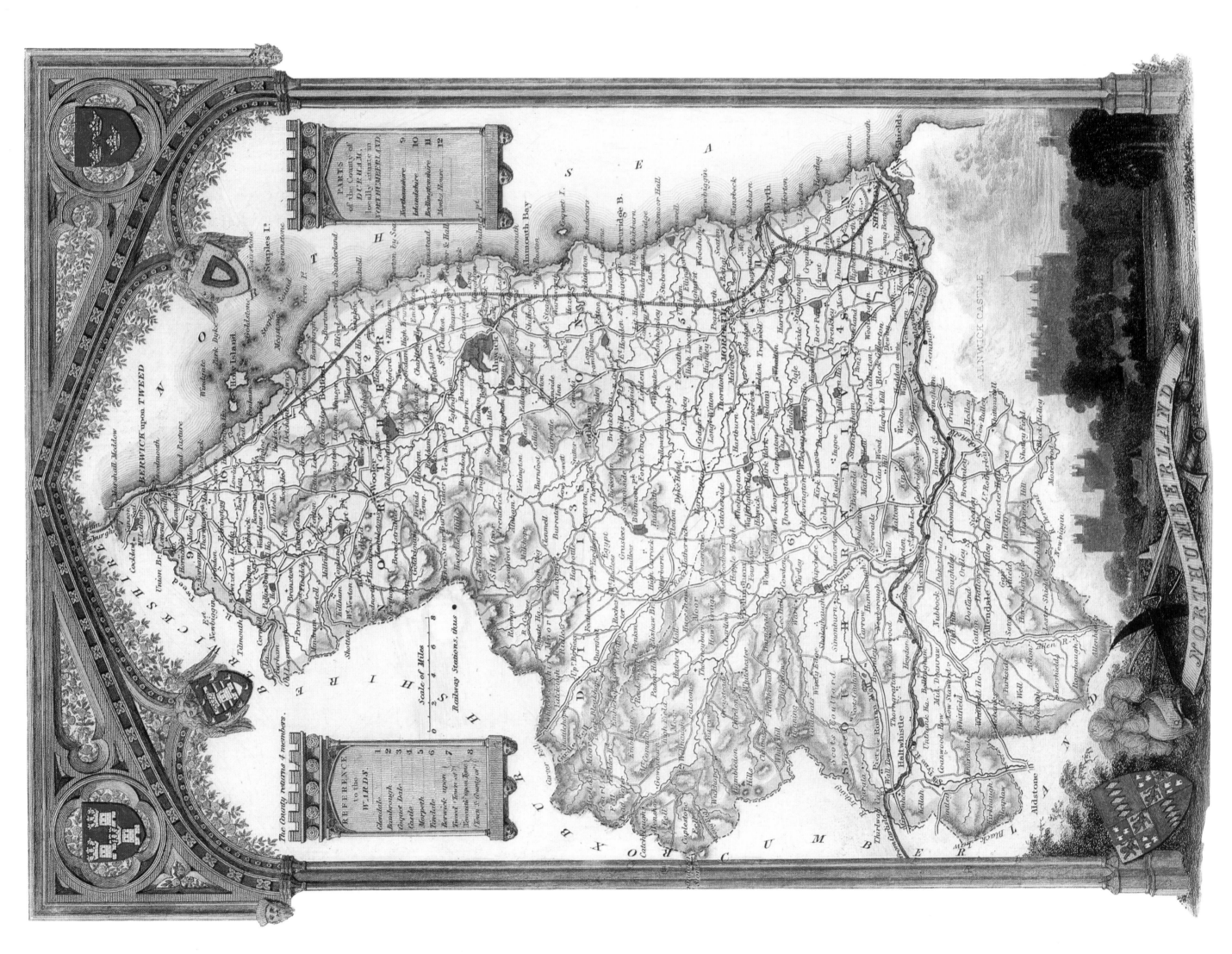

NORTHUMBERLAND

ALNWICK CASTLE

PARTS
of the County of
DURHAM
locally situate in
NORTHUMBERLAND

9 Northumberland
10 Islandshire
11 Bellinghamshire
12 Melds Mense

Scale of Miles

Railway Stations, thus

REFERENCE
to the
WARDS.

1 Glendale
2 Bamborough
3 Coquet Dale
4 Castle
5 Morpeth
6 Tindale
7 Berwick upon Tweed
8 Newcastle upon Tyne
(Newcastle upon Tyne)

The County returns 4 members.

county, are the most valuable of the mountainous tracts, being fine green hills, thrown into a great variety of forms, and feeding innumerable flocks of sheep peculiar to them. The central part of Northumberland stretches into wastes, on which arise a tew rocky hills of no great height. The principal eminences and views in the county are from the Cheviot chain, Aumond, the Bannocks, Bilden Hill, Blacktree, Borcum Hill, Byres Fell, Camp Hill, Catcleuch, Chattlehope, Clinch Hill, Cock Law, Dale Castle, Earl's Seat, Ellis Crag, Flodden Hill, Fox Crag, Glanton Pike, Glassen Hope, Harnham Hill, Hanging Shaw, Harwood Moor, Hawk Hope, Hedge Hope, Ingram Hill, Leam Beacon, Mote Law, Newton Tor, Ottercaps, Plin Meller, Red Squire, Rosedon Edge, Samyel Crag, Scotch Coltherd, Silverton Mountain, Snow Hope, Tynedale Fell, Tinney Hill, Two Pikes, Warkworth Castle, White Squire, and Yevering Bell. The principal rivers of Northumberland are the East and West Allen, the Alne, the Alwain, the Blythe, the Bovent, the Brennich, the Cherlop, the Coquet, the Cor, the Derwent, the Dill, or Devil's Beek, the Erringburn, the Font, the Glen, the Hart, the Hestild, the Hoc, the Irthing, the Knare, the Line, the Nent, the Otter, the Perop,

the Pont, the Rede, the Ridley, the Ridland, the Seaton, the Shele, the Till, the Tippal, the Tweed, the Tyne, and the Wansbeck. The products of this county are cattle, sheep, wool, corn, lead, and coals; there are still some of the original wild cattle in Chillingham Park, the seat of the Earl of Tankerville. Coal is the principal source of the immense trade and revenue that enriches this district: the coal trade has progressively increased, and at present the capital employed in it is estimated at four millions sterling. In its various branches about seventy five thousand persons find employment its produce has been calculated at 60,000*l.* per week; and the duty on coal yields to Government 600,000*l.* annually. The glassworks on the Tyne are remarkable for the elegance and beauty of their productions; and the cast-plate-glass manufactory of Newcastle rivals every similar establishment in Europe, in the size fineness and brilliancy of the plates.

Alnwick Castle is the seat of the Duke of Northumberland, K.G., Lord Lieutenant, Custos Rotulorum and Vice Admiral of the County of Northumberland and Newcastle-upon-Tyne.

BELOW: An atmospheric, distant view of Alnwick Castle, and a foreground of knightly armour and weapons, are set off against the wider Gothic decorative scheme which adorns the map of Northumberland.

Dyke Head
Hatherwick
Ewesley
Fenruther
Ulgham
Ellington
High Lincoln
Longhurst
Harrington
Codger Ft.
Low Highley
Woodhorn
Newbiggin
Long Witton
Pegsworth
Seaton
West Woodburn
Catcherside
Thornton
MORPETH
Bothal
Hepple Heugh
Hartburn
Mitford
R. Wansbeck
Whelpington
Bellingham
Fourlaws
Low Angerton
Molesdon
Hepscot
West
E. Sleekburn
Hawick
Heldon
Tranwell
Netherton
Waterfalls
Kirk Hark
Bolam
Blyth
Whalton
Bedlington
Capheaton Cas.
Hartford Ho.
Cowden
Throckington
Low Horton
Bradford
Ogle
Horton
Birtley
Twizle
Stannington
W. Belsay
Belsay Ho.
Lit. Bovington
Gramlington
Chipchase
Kirk Heaton
Black Heddon
Deer Park
Arcot
Hartley
Colwell
Seghill
Hollywell
Gunnerton
Ryal
Ingoe
Brenkley
Mason
Dinnington
E R N D I V I 4 S I O N
Earsdon
Bingfield
Stamfordham
Ponteland
Higher Gosforth
Chollerton
Pont R.
Humshaugh
Matfen Hall
Woolsington Ho.
St. Oswalds
High Callerton
L. Gosforth
SHIELDS
Clare Wood Hill
Black Callerton
Gosforth
Harlow Hill
Dewley
Long Benton
Wall
Halton
Kenton
Heddon on the Wall
Heaton Ha.
Welton
Newburn
Warden
Kip Hill
St. John Lee
R. Tyne
Blaydon
Elswick
NEWCASTLE
Hexham
Corbridge
Newton
Lemington
Buwell St. Peters
Ovingham
Oakerlands
Broomhaugh
Prudley
Houghtley
Ordley
Broomley
Stocksfield
Dotland
Hedley
Siegley
Dalton
Lt. Rotherley
New Ruller
Whitley Chap.
ALNWICK CASTLE
Whittonstall
Minster Hill
Gair Shield
Bentley
Acres

NOTTINGHAMSHIRE

This county is bounded on the north by Yorkshire; on the east by Lincolnshire; on the south by Leicestershire; and on the west by Derbyshire. It is about fifty miles in length, twenty-five in breadth and about one hundred and forty in circumference. The inhabitants were called Coritani by the Romans, and it formed a part of the province Flavia Cæsariensis. The Roman stations are supposed to have been Ad Pontem, Southwell; Crocolana, Brough; Margidunum, East Bridgford; Agelocum, Littleborough; and Vernometum, near Willoughby, on the borders of Leicestershire. Extensive remains of a Roman villa were discovered near Mansfield Woodhouse, and encampments are found at Barton Hill, Combe's Farm, Gringley on the Hill, Hexgrave. Holly Hill, and Winny Hill. During the Saxon Heptarchy, Nottinghamshire formed part of the kingdom of Mercia. The castles of its early lords were at Nottingham and Newark. A royal palace was at Clipston, and archiepiscopal palaces at Southwell and Scrooby. There were abbeys at Newstead, Rufford, and Welbeck; and priories at Blyth, Lenton, Mattersey, Worksop, Shelford, Thurgarton, and Radford. This county contains one county-town, nine market-towns, one hundred and sixty-eight parishes, 35,022 houses, and 186,873 inhabitants, and returns eight members to Parliament,— two for Newark, two for Nottingham, two for Bassetlaw hundred and East Retford, and two for the county, which at present is represented by John Evelyn Denison, Esq., and John Savile Lumley, Esq. The surface of this county, except the level through which the Trent runs, is uneven and may perhaps be said to be hilly, though none of the hills rise to any considerable degree of elevation. In point of soil, it consists of three divisions, sand or gravel, clay, and limestone and coal-land. In the first is included the ancient forest of Sherwood and the borders of it, the Trentbank land, or the level ground accompanying the Trent, from its entrance into the county, down to Sutton-upon-Trent, and also the level ground running up the river Soar from its junction with the Trent to Rempston. The clay district lies north of the Trent, and includes the hundred of Thurgarton, the Vale of Belvoir, and the Nottinghamshire Wolds,— a range of high bleak country. The lime and coal districts may be defined to lie westward of a line drawn from the river at Shire Oaks to the river Lene, near Wollaton and Radford, no lime being found eastward of the Lene. This county is well watered for different purposes. The navigable river Trent enters the county near Thrumpton, and runs through it on both sides till a little below North Clifton, whence to the northern point of the county it forms a boundary between it and Lincolnshire. The Erwash forms the boundary between this county and Derbyshire for ten or twelve miles down to its junction with the Trent below Thrumpton. The Soar forms the boundary between Nottinghamshire and Leicestershire for seven or eight miles above its junction with the Trent, near Thrumpton. On the forest side no less than five fine streams cross from east to west, almost parallel to each other, and afterwards run to the north forming the river Idle:— The Rainworth water from near Newstead Park to Inkersall Dam and Rufford, joins the Maun at Ollerton. The Maun goes from Mansfield by Clipston and Edwinstow to Ollerton. The Meden by Budby, and through Thoresby Park, joining the Maun near Perlthorp: from this junction the river is called the Idle. The Wallen, through Welbeck Park, and after receiving the Poulter, from Langwith and Cuckney, by Carburton and through Clumber Park, into the Idle near Elksley. The Ryton river runs by Worksop, Bilby, Blyth and Scrooby, into the Idle at Bawtry. Two other rivers run southward: the Lene, from Newstead Park, by Papplewick, Bullwell, Basford, and Lenton, into the Trent near Nottingham Bridge; the Dover, or Darebeck, from near Blidworth, by Oxton and Calverton, Eperston and Lowdham, into the Trent, near Caythorp. In the clay district are the Greet and many nameless streams; and in the Vale of Belvoir are the Devon, the Smite, and other smaller rills. The inland navigation consists of the Chesterfield canal, which entering this county on the western side passes Worksop and Retford, and joins the Trent near the mouth of the Idle. The Nottingham canal commences near Eastwood in the west, communicates with the Cromford and Erwash canals, and is met by the Beeston Cut two miles from Nottingham, where it unites with the Grantham canal, which after passing over the Trent leaves this county near Hickling. The productions of Nottinghamshire are coals, lead, wool, cattle, fowls, abundance of fresh-water fish, liquorice, grain of all sorts, hops and weld, "the yellow staining weed, *luteola*." Botanists find in this county ample scope for their interesting pursuit. Amongst many rare indigenous plants, the following may be mentioned:—the spring and autumnal crocus; the wild yellow tulip; the spreading bell-flower; the yellow, common, and drooping star of Bethlehem; the maiden pink; the Nottingham catchfly; *Silene nutans;* and that elegant and very rare moss the *Schistostega pennata*, with many other species less ornamental in appearance, but not less interesting to the inquisitive naturalist. A Botanical Calendar for the county, far surpassing the catalogue of Deering in scientific arrangement, and rendered entertaining by apt quotations from eminent poets, has already been printed by Mr. Thomas Jowett, surgeon of Nottingham; and it is to him, who has left no part of the county unexplored, the editor is indebted for the very slight notice of its plants to which he is necessarily confined. The commerce and manufactures of this county are extensive. The malting business is carried on at Nottingham, Newark, Mansfield, and in many other places. At Newark are breweries which vie with Burton-upon-Trent in the trade to the Baltic and other parts; and at Nottingham is a brewery established on an extensive plan. The stocking trade occupies a great many hands at Nottingham, and the villages for many miles round; as also at Mansfield, Southwell, and other places in its neighbourhood. Many cotton mills in this county prepare the thread; and large woollen mills are at Arnold, Retford and Cuckney. Frame-work knitted lace, a source of increasing wealth to the town of Nottingham is of modern origin; but in 1810 there were at least 1500 frames employed. Clumber Park, in Sherwood Forest, is the seat of His Grace the Duke of Newcastle, K.G. Lord Lieutenant of the County.

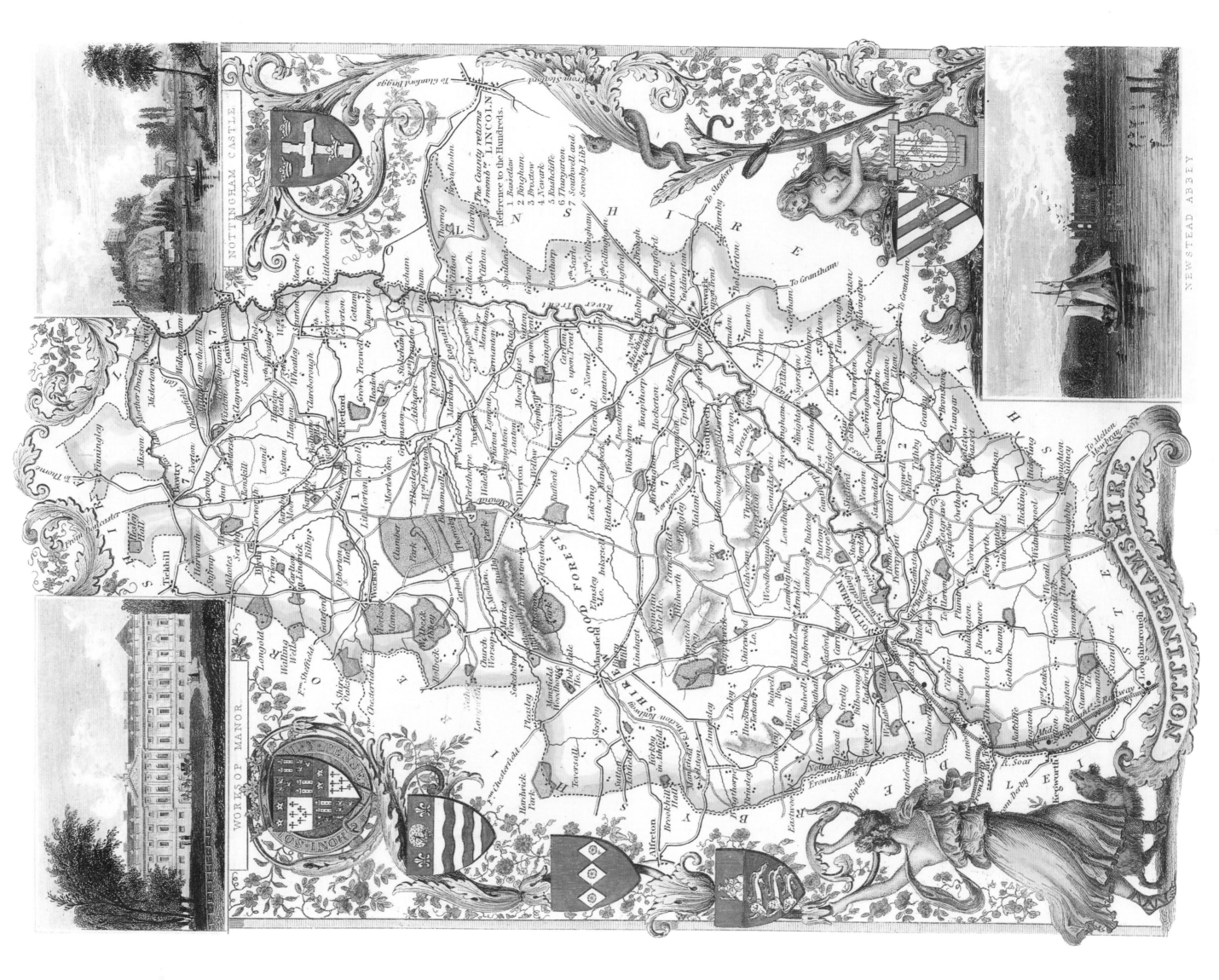

NOTTINGHAM CASTLE

NEWSTEAD ABBEY

WORKS OF MANOR.

NOTTINGHAMSHIRE.

LINCOLNSHIRE

Reference to the Hundreds.
The County returns
4 memb[rs] to LINCOLN.
1 Bassetlaw
2 Bingham
3 Brocton
4 Newark
5 Rushcliffe
6 Thurgarton
7 Southwell and
  Snooby Lib[ty]

YORKSHIRE

DERBYSHIRE

LEICESTER SHIRE

River Trent

SHERWOOD FOREST

OXFORDSHIRE

This county is bounded on the north by Warwickshire and Northamptonshire; on the west by Gloucestershire; on the south by Berkshire and on the east by Buckinghamshire. The extreme length of the county is fifty miles, its greatest breadth thirty-eight miles, and its circumference one hundred and thirty miles. It was included in the Roman province Flavia Cæsariensis, inhabited by the Dobuni, and during the Saxon Heptarchy formed a part of the kingdom of Mercia. The Akeman Street, a Roman military way, enters this county near Alchester; and Dorchester is built on the site of the station Durocornovium. Oxfordshire contains one city and university, and had formerly abbeys at Dorchester, Ensham, Oseney, and Thame; priories at Bicester, Brightwell, Burford and Minster Lovell; as well as nunneries at Godstow and Goring. It is in the province of Canterbury, and diocese of Oxford, excepting seven parishes in that of Lincoln. There are in this county twelve market-towns, and 280 parishes, containing in 1821, at the last census 25,594 houses, and 136,971 inhabitants. It returns nine members to Parliament; viz. two for Oxford, two for the University, two for Woodstock, one for Banbury, and two for the county, which at present is represented by William Henry Ashurst, Esq., of Waterstock, and John Fane, Esq., of Wormsley. The air is considered as salubrious as that of any other county in England, and the soil, naturally dry, is entirely exempt from bogs, fens, and stagnant waters, being in general fertile both in grass and corn. The northern division is chiefly strong, deep land, partly arable and partly pasture; the south-western includes the Royal Forest of Whichwood, a great part of which is woodland. On the banks of the Thames the soil is chiefly pasture. The Chiltern Hills form a wide tract of chalk, mixed with a small portion of loam and clay, but very full of flints: much of this is covered with beech wood; besides the Chiltern, there are not any hills in this county of considerable height: gentle eminences vary the landscape without obstructing tillage; on the grass farms much cheese is made of a good quality, though in general thin; the cows are chiefly of the old Gloucestershire kind, and Southdown sheep are preferred; many boars are also fed for the purpose of making brawn, a considerable article of trade at Oxford and other parts. The chief manufactures in this county are those of blankets at Witney, worsted

plush at Banbury and Bloxham, of gloves and polished steel at Woodstock, and of malt at Henley; the employment of females in the neighbourhood of Thame is lace-making, and in the northern part of the county spinning wool. The produce is that which is common to the midland counties; also artificial grasses, particularly sainfoin. The hills yield ochre, pipe-clay, and other earths; as well as lime-stone, free-stone, and rag-stone. The rivers are the Bure, the Cherwell, the Evenlode, the Glyme, the Isis, the Ray, the Thame, the Thames, and the Windrush. The Bure is a branch of the Ray,

which it joins near Bicester. The Cherwell rises in Northamptonshire, and passing Banbury discharges itself into the Isis below Oxford. The Evenlode rises in a detached part of Worcestershire, which adjoins this county, and passing Blenheim falls into the Isis near Cassington. The Glyme falls into the Evenlode. The Isis rises in the northern angle of Wiltshire, and enters this county near Lechlade, where it becomes navigable; after passing Ensham, it receives the Evenlode, and unites with the Cherwell below the city of Oxford: flowing southward it passes Abingdon, and below Dorchester is joined by the Thame, whence their united streams form the river Thames. The Thame rises near Tring in Hertfordshire, and flowing through the Vale of Aylesbury, enters Oxfordshire near Thame, and taking almost a south-westerly direction to Dorchester, unites with the Isis. The Windrush, rising amongst the Cotswold Hills in Gloucestershire, enters this county near Burford, and passing Witney falls into the Isis at New-Bridge about eight miles below that town. The Oxford Canal commences at Longford in Warwickshire, enters this county near Claydon, passes Banbury, Alderbury Somerton, Heyford Warine, Heyford Purcell, Shipton-on-Cherwell, Begbrook, and Wolvercott and joins the Isis at Oxford.

The most memorable of the military transactions in this county were the battle between the English and the Danes in the year 914 at Hook Norton, in which the former were entirely defeated; the battle of Banbury between the Yorkists and Lancastrians in 1469, in which Edward IV. was made prisoner by the Earl of Warwick; and the skirmish at Chalgrove-field, 15th August 1642, which is rendered memorable by the death of the patriot Hampden. The magnificent seat and park of Blenheim was the grant of the British Parliament to the great Duke of Marlborough, on account of his signal victory over the French at Blenheim in Germany; and Shirburne Castle is the seat of the Earl of Macclesfield, Lord-Lieutenant of the county. Broughton Castle is a remarkable structure; and the remains of the ancient mansions at Stanton Harcourt, and Minster Lovel, are particularly interesting.

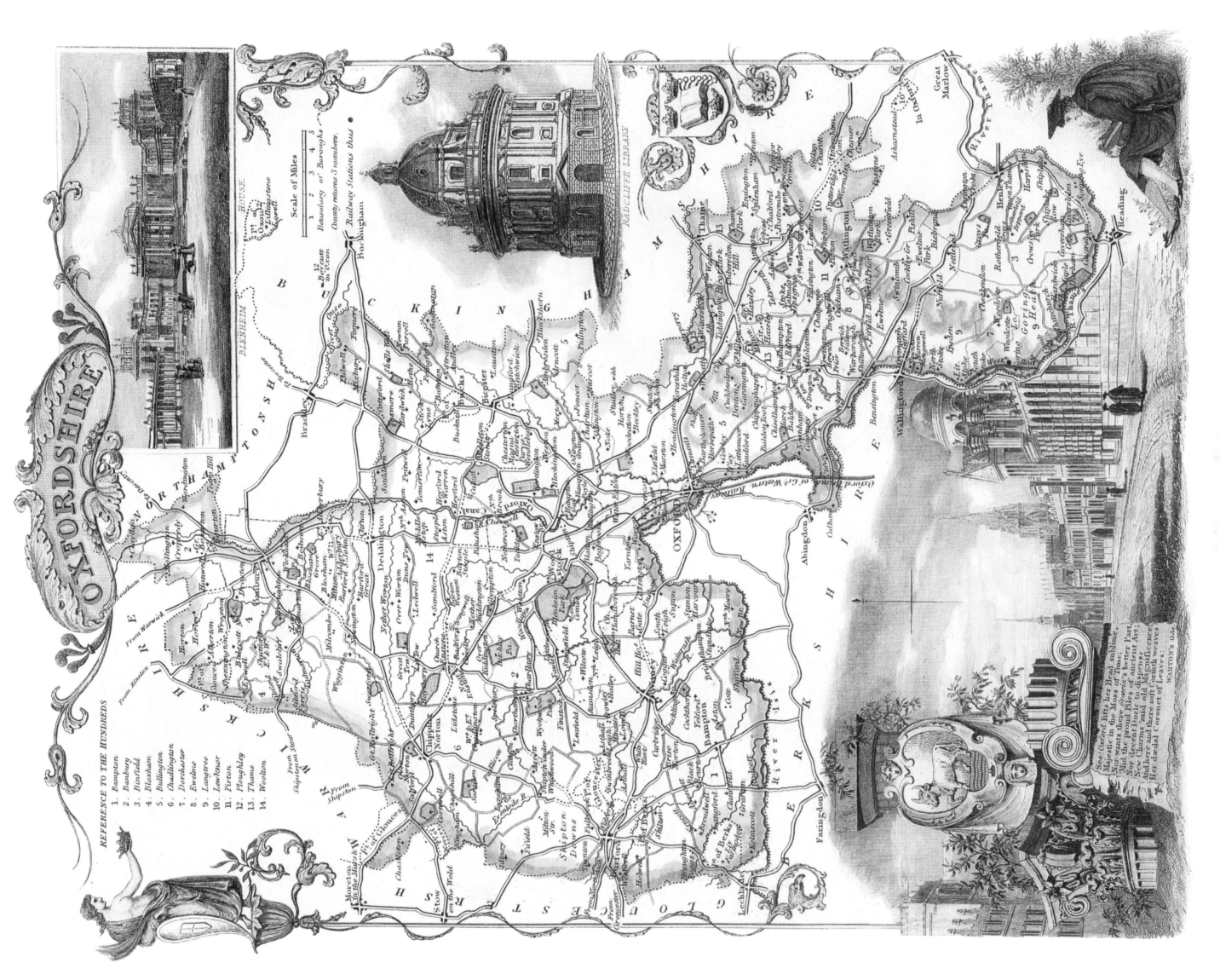

OXFORDSHIRE

BLENHEIM HOUSE.

Scale of Miles
1 2 3 4 5

Boundary of Boroughs
County returns 3 members
Railway Stations thus

REFERENCE TO THE HUNDREDS

1. Bampton
2. Banbury
3. Binfield
4. Bloxham
5. Bullingdon
6. Chadlington
7. Dorchester
8. Ewelme
9. Langtree
10. Lewknor
11. Pirton
12. Ploughley
13. Thame
14. Wooton

RADCLIFFE LIBRARY

WARTON's Ode.

See Oxford, Bits, her Head sublime,
Majestic in the Moss of Time;
Nor yet the spoil of Seasons of Thame;
And rear their proud fronts a better Part,
New Oxen! Too fit to disparage Art,
New Chance maid old Magnul,
And fire, and there soft Corinth weaves
Her dædal Coronet of Leaves.

CITY AND UNIVERSITY OF OXFORD

Oxford is locally situated in Wootton Hundred, fifty-four miles west from London by way of High Wycombe, and fifty-eight by way of Henley. The city occupies a gentle eminence, near the junction of the rivers Isis and Cherwell, and including the suburbs, is more than a mile in length from east to west, nearly the same from north to south, and about three miles in circumference. It contains 2,431 houses, and 16,364 inhabitants. The general views of Oxford, in every direction, are singularly interesting: from the north, the venerable buildings are displayed in such a remarkably picturesque group as to seem disposed entirely for effect. The eastern prospect is equally magnificent, the architectural beauties of Oxford surpassing those of any city in Great Britain; it is satisfactory also to learn from so able a critic as Mr. Dallaway, that it will find few rivals even on the continent. The south-western view of the city is considered one of the best, as affording a more distinct arrangement of the various interesting edifices without their intercepting each other, a defect rather observable in most of the other views of Oxford. Under the classical name of Isis the river Thames here flows through a valley, expanded into a spacious amphitheatre, bounded by gentle eminences, in the very centre of which the city of Oxford appears rising behind the thick shade of venerable groves. The Isis divides itself into various small channels, which reuniting, it crossed on the south side of the city by the Folly Bridge, in the road to Abingdon, after which it glides through Christchurch meadows, where a wide walk, bounded by lofty elms, is formed upon its banks. The Isis is here joined by the Cherwell, which passes on the eastern side of Oxford, through Magdalen Bridge, the two streams almost insulating the city. Oxford was formerly surrounded by a wall,

with towers at about one hundred and fifty feet distance from each other, and included an oblong space of about two miles in circumference. Magdalen College with the eastern and northern suburbs, including the parishes of Holywell, Magdalen and St. Giles, with Baliol, Trinity, St. John's and Wadham Colleges, are beyond the walls. Some part of the old walls is said to be yet remaining, as a boundary to Merton College and to New College. Of the ancient gates of the city, the East Gate, formerly in the High-street near Long Wall, was the chief; the North Gate, or Bocardo, was long used as a prison, and was memorable for the Bishops' Room, in which Cranmer, Latimer and Ridley were confined, previously to their execution in front of Baliol College; the South Gate of the city was in Fish-street, near Christ-church College; Little Gate in Blackfriars Road, near St. Ebbe's Church; and the West Gate, on the south side of the Castle. Agreeably to an Act of Parliament for improving the streets of the city, the old gates were all taken down about 1771.

The Corporation of Oxford consists of a mayor, high steward, a recorder, four aldermen, eight assistants, two bailiffs, and those who have served that office, two chamberlains, and those who have served that office, twenty four common-councilmen, a town clerk, and a solicitor. The Corporation of Oxford claim, by virtue of their charter, to serve at the Coronation of the King, in the office of the butlery, with the citizens of London, and to have for their fee three maple cups. This duty was probably assigned to the city of Oxford by Henry I.; it is acknowledged in the charter of Henry II., and confirmed in that of Henry III. The arms of the city, as represented in the heraldic visitation 1634, are: *Argent, in chief an ox gules,*

in base barry wavy argent and azure, the shield encircled with a ribbon azure, charged with roses and fleurs de lis, alternately, or: the ribbon edged with the last. Crest, a demi-lion rampant gardant or, semee of fleurs de lis azure, regally crowned of the first, and folding a Tudor rose. Supporters, dexter, an elephant ermines, armed or, eared, collared, and lined argent, sinister a beaver proper, ducally collared and lined or. Motto: FORTIS • EST • VERITAS. The magistracy of the city is subject to the chancellor or vice chancellor of the University in all affairs of moment, and an oath is annually administered to the magistrates and sheriffs to maintain the privileges of the University. No person, unless matriculated, is allowed to keep an open shop in the city except he be a freeman, and freedom can only be gained by birth, by apprenticeship, or by purchase. The city of Oxford sends two members to Parliament, a privilege granted to it 23rd Edward I., when the right of election was vested in the Corporation and freemen, who at present amount to about fifteen hundred; the mayor and bailiffs are the returning officers. The present members are John Haughton Langston, Esq., and William Hughes Hughes Esq. The assizes and petty sessions are always held here, and the markets on Wednesday and Saturday are kept in a general market-house on the north side of the High-street, designed by *Gwynn*; one of the most convenient and airy in the kingdom. The fairs are on 3rd May, Monday after St. Giles's day, and Thursday before Michaelmas-day. The city of Oxford with its suburbs consists of thirteen parishes, which with the exceptions of St. Giles's and St. John's were consolidated by Act of Parliament in 1771.

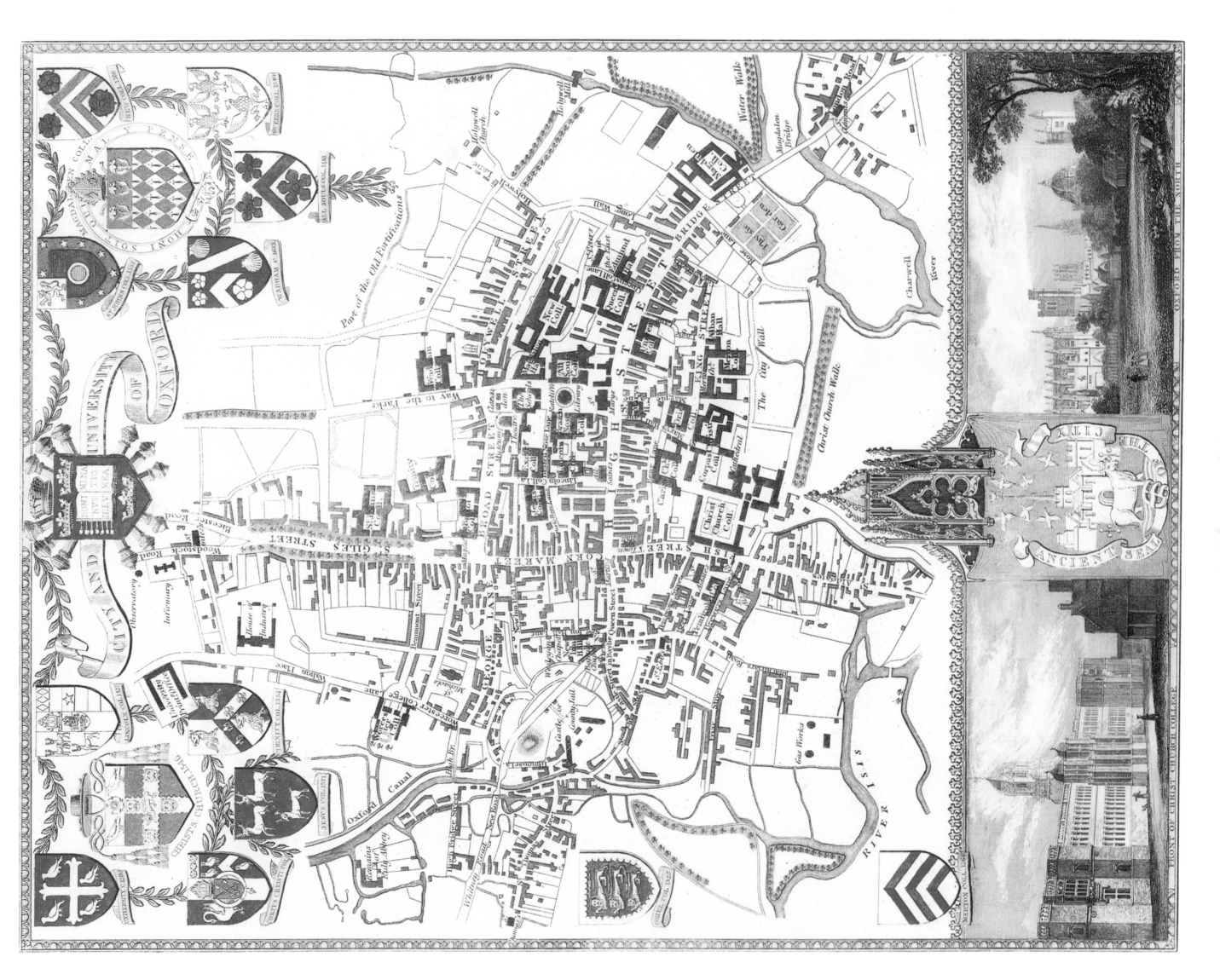

CITY AND UNIVERSITY OF OXFORD

MAGDALEN COLL.

GILES COLL. 1247

ST. GILES THE LEAST

WADHAM c. 1613

ST. JOHNS COLL. 1557

DOMINA NUSTIO ILLUMEA

UNIVERSITY COLL.

LINCOLN COLL. 1427

TRINITY COLL.

CHRIST'S CHURCH 1546

CORPUS CHRISTI COLL.

ORIEL COLL. 1326

MERTON COLL. 1264

THE ANCIENT SEAL OF THE CITY

OXFORD FROM THE NORTH

FRONT OF CHRIST CHURCH COLLEGE

Observatory

Infirmary

House of Industry

Walton Place

Woodstock Road

Bicester Road

ST. GILES STREET

Part of the Old Fortifications

Way to the Parks

HOLYWELL STREET

Holywell Church

Holywell Mill

Water Walk

Magdalen Bridge

Headington Road

Cherwell River

Magdalen Coll.

Phys. Garden

Rose Lane

BROAD STREET

St. Mary Magdalen

New Coll.

Queen's Coll.

BRIDGE STREET

KING STREET

The City Wall

Christ Church Walk

HIGH STREET

Clarendon

Bodleian Library

Radcliffe Library

All Souls Coll.

St. Mary's

St. Peter's

St. Edmund

Queen's Coll.

Magdalen Coll.

Wadham Hall

Wadham Coll.

Corpus Christi Coll.

Christ Church Coll.

Cathedral

GEORGE LANE

Beaumont Street

St. Michael's

Worcester College

Worcester Coll.

Castle

County Jail

Bridewell

Canal

Oxford Canal

Remains of Osney Abbey

Whitnell Road

High Bridge Street

New Road

St. Thomas's

Queen Street

New Inn Lane

New Coll.

St. Martin

Pembroke Coll.

St. Ebbe

St. Aldate's

Gas Works

RIVER ISIS

OSNEY COLL. 1873

RUTLANDSHIRE

This is the smallest county in England; it is bounded on the north by Leicestershire and Lincolnshire; on the south east by Northamptonshire; and on the south west by Leicestershire, from which county it is separated by the river Eye. Its greatest length is about eighteen miles, and its breadth about sixteen, being in circumference about fifty-five miles. The British inhabitants were called Coritani by the Romans, and it formed part of the province of Flavia Cæsariensis. Brigg Casterton was a station on the Roman Road, called the High Street, which formed the great line of communication between Londinium and the Humber on the eastern coast, and is supposed to be the Gausenna of Antoninus's Itinerary. During the Saxon Heptarchy, Rutlandshire formed part of the kingdom of Mercia. King Edward the Confessor by will bequeathed this county to Edith his queen, and, after her decease, to the abbot and convent of St. Peter's Westminster; but after the Conquest, this estate was resumed by the Crown. The principal antiquities of the county are Oakham Castle and church, the churches of Empingham, Essendine, Exton, Stretton, Tickencote, and Tinwell; Liddington Palace, and Preston Manor-house. The county contains one county-town, Oakham; two market-towns; fifty-three parishes; 3,589; houses and 18,487 inhabitants. It returns two members to Parliament; who at present are Sir Gerard Noel, Noel, Bart., of Exton Hall, and Sir Gilbert Heathcote, Bart., of Normanton Park. Rutlandshire is in the province of Canterbury, and in the diocese of Peterborough, excepting the parishes of Empingham, Ketton, and Liddington, which are in the diocese of Lincoln.

The air of this county is considered as pure as that of any other part of the kingdom, and the land is very productive in corn and pasture. The mode of agriculture is chiefly that pursued in Norfolk, the turnip and sheep husbandry in general forming its basis. The flocks are healthy, and the seed-corn some of the finest in the kingdom. Rutlandshire is beautifully varied in surface, with gentle swells and depressions; the rising grounds running east and west, with valleys intervening about half a mile in width. Amongst these is the rich valley of Catmose, running from the western side to the centre of the county, including within its limits the town of Oakham. The eminences and views most remarkable in the county are at Manton, Preston and Bee Hills, Beaumont Chase, Burley on the Hill, Rakesborough Hill, Teigh, the Wissendine Hills, and Witchley Common. The road from near Stamford to Uppingham is also exceedingly picturesque. The principal rivers in this county are the Eye, the Welland, Guash, and Chater. The Eye, rising in Leicestershire, takes a south-easterly course, forming the boundary of the county on that side, and empties itself into the Welland. The Welland, rising near Sibbertoft in Northamptonshire, south-west of Market Harborough, runs north-easterly, and forms the boundary of the county on that side: near Ketton it receives the waters of the Chater, and a little below Stamford those of the Guash; continuing nearly the same course, it passes the towns of Market Deeping and Spalding, and falls into the German Ocean at Foss Dyke Wash. The Guash and Chater both rise on the western side of the county, and flowing nearly parallel to each other in an easterly course, unite with the Welland, the former above, and the latter below Stamford. The south-western part of this county was formerly entirely occupied by the Forest of Leighfield, part of which still remains, including Beaumont Chase, stocked with deer. The manufactures of Rutlandshire are of little importance; but by the Oakham canal, which joins the river Wreke at Melton Mowbray in Leicestershire, a communication is formed with the Trent, whence a considerable inland trade is effected, particularly in coals and corn. The rich kind of cheese called Stilton is made in the district of Leighfield Forest, and in Catmose Vale. Timber, limestone, and building-stone are amongst the products of the county. Although the smallest of the English counties, there are perhaps more gentlemen's seats and parks in Rutlandshire, considering its extent, than in any other in the kingdom. Burghley House, the princely seat of the Marquess of Exeter, the Lord Lieutenant of the County, is in Northamptonshire, immediately on the borders of Rutlandshire.

Michael Drayton, in his Poly-Olbion, which is dedicated to his patron Henry Prince of Wales, greatly commends the peculiar beauty of the scenery of Rutlandshire.

"Love not thyself the less, although the least thou art;
 What thou in greatness want'st wise Nature doth impart
 In goodness of thy soil; and more delicious mould,
 Surveying all this isle, the sun did ne'er behold.
 Bring forth that British vale, and be it ne'er so rare,
 But Catmose with that vale for richness shall compare.
 What forest nymph is found, how brave soe'er she be,
 But Lyfield shows herself as brave a nymph as she?
 What river ever rose from bank or swelling hill,
 Than Rutland's wandering Wash a delicater rill?
 Small shire that canst produce, to thy proportion good,
 One vale of special name, one forest, and one flood."

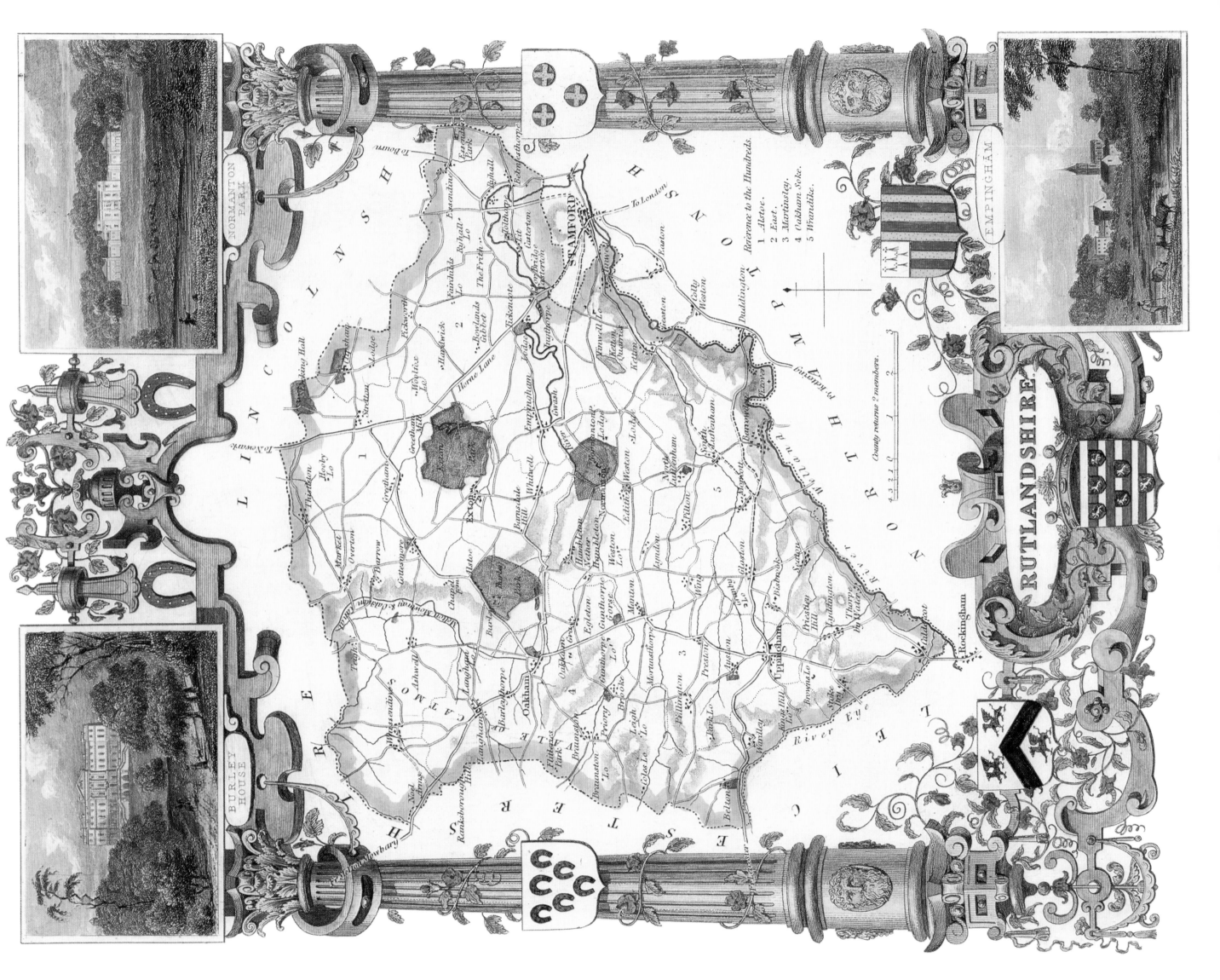

SHROPSHIRE

This county is bounded on the north by Cheshire, and a detached part of Flintshire; on the east by Staffordshire; on the south by Worcestershire, Herefordshire and part of Radnorshire: and on the west by Denbighshire and Montgomeryshire. The greatest length is nearly fifty miles, being forty miles in breadth, and one hundred and sixty miles in circumference. Shrewsbury, called by the Britons Pengwerne, was the capital of the principality of Powis, and the present county was included in the Roman province Flavia Cæsariensis, inhabited by the Cornavii and Ordovices. The ancient British and Roman road Watling-street crosses the county; and the Roman stations were Bravinium at Rushbury, Mediolanum at Drayton in Hales, Rutupium at Rowton or near Wem, Sariconium at Bury Hill, Uriconium at Wroxeter, and Usacona at Red Hill. During the Saxon Heptarchy Shropshire formed a part of the kingdom of Mercia; Offa's Dyke and Watt's Dyke are earthworks of this period. This county contains one county-town, 17 market towns, 170 parishes, 38,663 inhabited houses, and 206,153 inhabitants. It is in the province of Canterbury, and in the dioceses of Hereford, Lichfield & Coventry, St. Asaph, and a detached part, Hales Owen, &c. in that of Worcester. There were formerly abbeys at Buildwas, Hales Owen, Haughmond, Lilleshall, Wenlock, Shrewsbury and White Abbey near Alberbury; also priories at Bromfield, Chirbury, White Ladies near Boscobel, and Woodhouse near Cleobury Mortimer. The castles of its earlier lords were

at Acton Burnell, Alberbury, Bridgnorth, Cause, Clun, Hopton, Ludlow, Middle Castle, Moreton Corbett, Oswestry, Red Castle, Shrewsbury, Sibdon, Stoke, Wattlesborough and Whittington. Shropshire returns twelve members to Parliament, viz. two for Shrewsbury, two for Wenlock, two for Bridgnorth, two for Ludlow, two for Bishop's Castle, and two, Sir Rowland Hill, Bart. of Hawkestone, and John Cressett Pelham, Esq., of the Castle at Shrewsbury, for the county. By an Act of Parliament passed in the 27th of Henry VIII. 1535, the marches or intermediate border lands between England and Wales were divided into new counties, or annexed to old counties; by this Act Shropshire was augmented. Few counties are possessed of a greater variety of soil, or are more diversified in appearance. It is divided into nearly two equal parte by the river Severn: its southern portion assumes the mountainous character of Montgomeryshire and Denbighshire, whilst the northern division approaches more nearly to a level, agreeably relieved by a few single hills and romantic valleys finely wooded. The meadows on the banks of the Severn are extremely fertile, being frequently enriched by the overflowing of that river. The whole county is in general well cultivated, yielding great quantities of grain; its southern border, producing excellent hops, is agreeably varied with fine healthy orchards. The breed of cows and sheep deserves particular notice, the former giving large quantities of rich milk, and the latter some of the finest fleeces in the kingdom. The mineral productions of

the county are a vast abundance of coal, iron and lead, quarries of freestone, and limestone and pits of pipe-clay. The rivers are Bellbrook, Borebrook, Bow, Camalet, Ceriog, Clive, Clun, Coalbrook, Corve, Dee, Elfbrook, Ketley, Ledwich, Marbrook, Meolebrook, Mordabrook, Morles, Oney, Perry, Quenny, Rea, Roden, Severn, Shelbrook, Stradbrook, Teme, Tern, Vymey, Warfe, and Warren. The Severn enters the great plain of Shropshire below Welsh Pool, and making a considerable reach abruptly to the south-east, almost encircles the town of Shrewsbury; and after passing Coalbrook Dale flows southward to Bridgnorth, Bewdley and Worcester. Below Coalbrook Dale it forms an enchanting object in two great reaches, descending to the town of Bridgnorth, built on a high cliff. The Tern rises in the northern part of the county, and at the village, which derives its name from it, receives the waters of the Strine from Newport, and winding southward unites with the Roden, and falls into the Severn near Brompton Ferry. The Roden rises also in the northern part of the county, and flowing southward joins the Tern near Walcot. The canals passing through Shropshire are those of Donnington Wood, Dudley Extension, Ellesmere, Ketley, Kington, Leominster, Montgomeryshire, Shrewsbury, Shropshire, and the Marquess of Stafford's Canal. Walcot Park, near Bishop's Castle is the seat of the Earl of Powis, who has lately resigned the office of Lord Lieutenant of the county, now held by his eldest son Viscount Clive, who resides at Powis Casde near Welsh Pool.

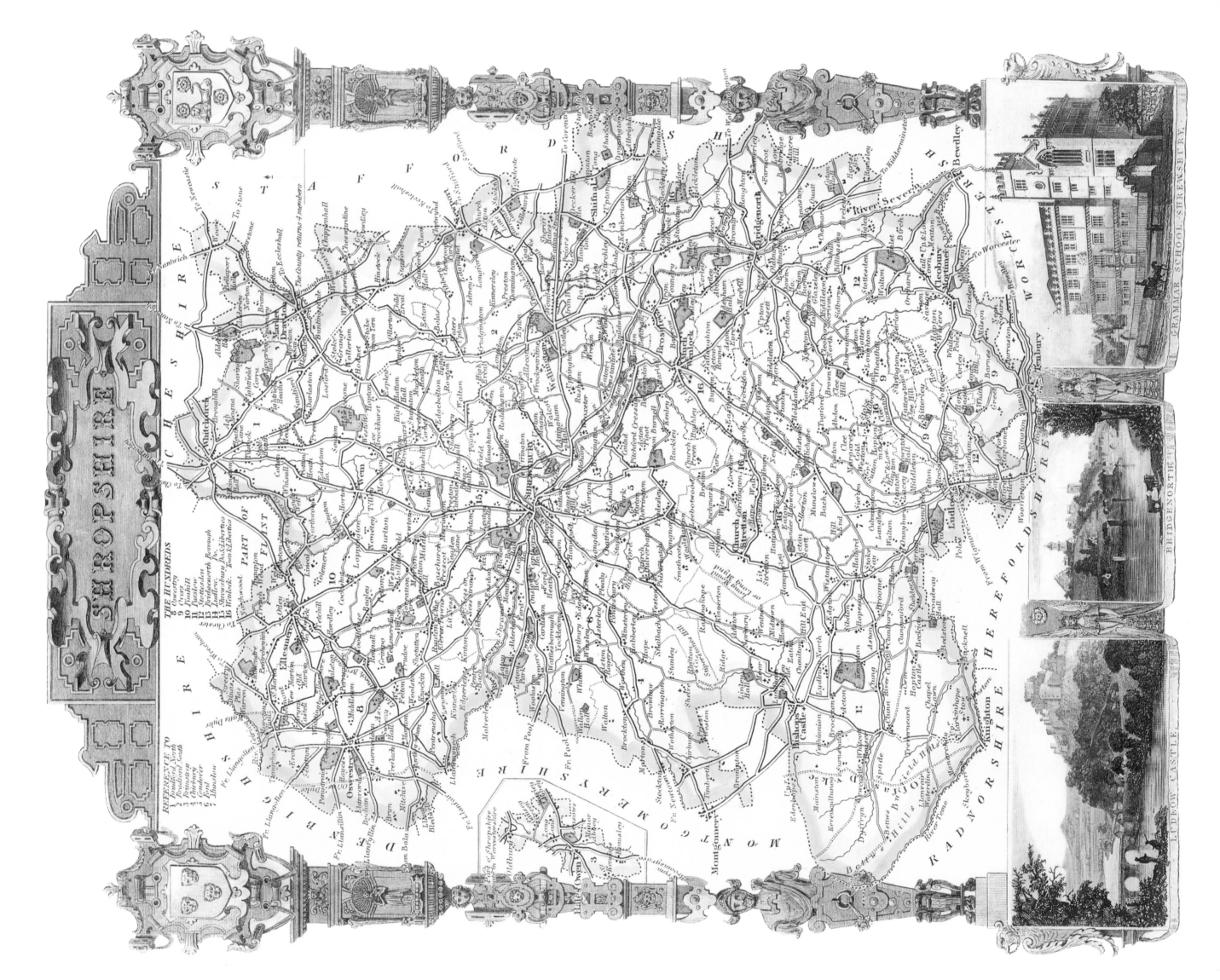

SHROPSHIRE

REFERENCE TO
THE HUNDREDS

1. Bradford North
2. Bradford South
3. Brimstry
4. Chirbury
5. Condover
6. Ford
7. Munslow
8. Oswestry
9. Overs
10. Pimhill
11. Purslow
12. Stottesden
13. Bridgnorth Borough
14. Wenlock, Pt. & Liberties
15. Shrewsbury Bor.Liberties
16. Town & Liberties

THE COUNTY RETURNS 4 MEMBERS

STAFFORDSHIRE

CHESHIRE

PART OF FLINTSHIRE

DENBIGHSHIRE

MONTGOMERYSHIRE

RADNORSHIRE

HEREFORDSHIRE

WORCESTERSHIRE

Shrewsbury

GRAMMAR SCHOOL SHREWSBURY.

BRIDGENORTH.

LUDLOW CASTLE.

SOMERSETSHIRE

THIS county is bounded by Gloucestershire and the Bristol Channel on the north, by Wiltshire on the east, by Dorsetshire on the south, and by Devonshire on the west. It is in length from east to west about 80 miles, and in breadth from north to south, about 35 miles; in circumference it is about 200 miles. Somersetshire was anciently inhabited by the Belgæ, and remains of this early period are found in the circles of stones at Chew Magna, and Stanton Drew, as well as in Wansdyke, a celebrated earthwork. Under the Romans it formed part of Britannia Prima, and there were stations at Aqua Solis, Bath; and Ischalis, Ilchester. The castles of its early lords, were at Dunster, Enmore, Henton, Ilchester, Nunney, Stoke Courcy, Taunton, Castle Cary, and Somerton. There were formerly abbeys at Athelney, Cleve, Glastonbury, Keynsham, and Michelney. Priories at Barlinch, Burgh, Bruton, Buckland, Cannington Dunster, Henton, Montacute, Stoke Courcy, Taunton, Witham, and Worspring. Somersetshire is in the province of Canterbury, and in the diocese of Bath and Wells, and contains two cities, Bath and Wells; 31 market-towns, 472 parishes, 61,852 inhabited houses, and 355,314 inhabitants. The county returns thirteen members to parliament; two for Bath, two for Bridgewater, one for Frome, two for Taunton, and two for Wells, and four for the county, who are at present Colonel Gore Langton, of Newton St. Loo, near Bath, and W. Miles, Esq. for the eastern division; and Edward Aysford Sanford, Esq. of Nynehead Court, near Wellington, and Charles John Kemeys Tynte, Esq. of Halswell, near Bridgewater, for the western division of the county. Somersetshire displays a great variety of soil and surface. The north-eastern quarter, including that part of the county between Uphill, on the Bristol Channel, and Frome on the borders of Wiltshire, bounded on the south by the Mendip Hills, is diversified by rocky eminences, declining towards the west into fertile plains, and near the sea into moorland tracts, subject to inundation. The south-eastern portion of the county on the borders of Wiltshire, and Dorsetshire,

consists of high downs, appropriated to the pasturage of sheep, or raising corn; and from Shepton Mallet to Chard is a fertile tract, interspersed with meadows and orchards. The central district, intersected by rivers, comprises extensive fens and marshy moors, where dykes form the divisions of property, and the land is often covered by water. Towards the south-west, near the borders of Devonshire, is the fruitful valley of Taunton Dean, whence the Quantock Hills extend north-westward to the Bristol Channel; more westward, is the ridge of the Brandon Hills; and, at the western extremity is the Forest of Exmoor, lying partly in Devonshire. The loftiest eminence is Dundry Beacon, in the northern part of the county; but Lansdown, near Bath, Broadfield Down, north of Wrington, Black Down, south-westward of Taunton, Glastonbury Tor, and Bratten, near Minehead, are hills of considerable altitude.

The ancient forests in this county, were Selwood, near Frome; Mendip, between Frome and the Bristol Channel; Exmoor, between the port of Watchet, and the north-western part of Devonshire; Neroche, near Ilminster; and North Petherton, near Bridgewater.

The rivers of Somersetshire are numerous, but not very considerable; most of them, through their whole course, being confined to the county. The principal are the Avon, the Axe, the Barle, the Bey, the Brent, the Brew, the Cale, the Car, the Chew, the Dunsbrook, the Exe, the Frome, the Ivel, or Ile, the Ordred, the Parret, the Severn, the Tone, the Tor, and the Yeo. The Parret, rising on the borders of Dorsetshire, flows northward, being joined near Michelney by the Ivel, and at Langport, by the Yeo, on the east; afterwards, by the Tone from Taunton, on the west; it passes the town of Bridgewater, and pursues a winding course to the Bristol Channel. The Brew has its source in Selwood Forest, on the borders of Wiltshire, passes Bruton and Glastonbury, and, after receiving a stream from Shepton Mallet and Wells, and some others, flows westward, entering the sea a short distance

northward of the Parret. The Axe, which rises in the Mendip Hills, passes Axbridge, and falls into the Bristol Channel near Black Rock. The Exe, has its origin in Exmoor Forest, soon leaves this county, and enters Devonshire. Several streams in the northern part of Somersetshire, fall into the Lower Avon, which divides this county from Wiltshire and Gloucestershire. There is a canal from Frome to Stalbridge, with branches to the city of Wells and Bradford, and a canal at the bottom of Hampton Down.

The principal mineral products of the county, are coal; found only in the hilly tract, between Mendip and the Lower Avon; lead, lapis calaminaris, manganese, copper ore, spars, and chrystals, from the Mendip Hills; from the Quantock Hills, lead and copper ore have been excavated; calamine, from the Broadfield Downs and other hills; iron ore from various places; and in the rocks near Porlock, have been found small quantities of silver. Granite has been quarried a few miles north-eastward of Taunton, and at Coombe Down, quantities of excellent free-stone for building.

The productions of this county are numerous; besides corn, barley, and oats, hemp, flax, teasels, and woad are largely cultivated. The plains afford luxuriant herbage for cattle, numbers of which are annually fattened on the moors, and the dairies furnish excellent cheese, that made at Chedder, on the borders of the Axe, being particularly famous. Great numbers of sheep, of different kinds, are fed on the hills and downs, and the Mendip breed is noted for the fineness of the wool. Abundance of fowls, in greet variety are raised in the vicinity of Bath and Bristol, for the markets of those cities, and many geese are kept in the marshy districts. Cider is made from apples, grown in several parts of the county, but the best is produced in the vale of Taunton Dean, where it is made in the highest perfection. The proprietors of orchards in this delightful vale, are supposed to possess an art peculiar to themselves of conducting the fermentation, by which a rich and delicious flavour is preserved.

SOMERSETSHIRE

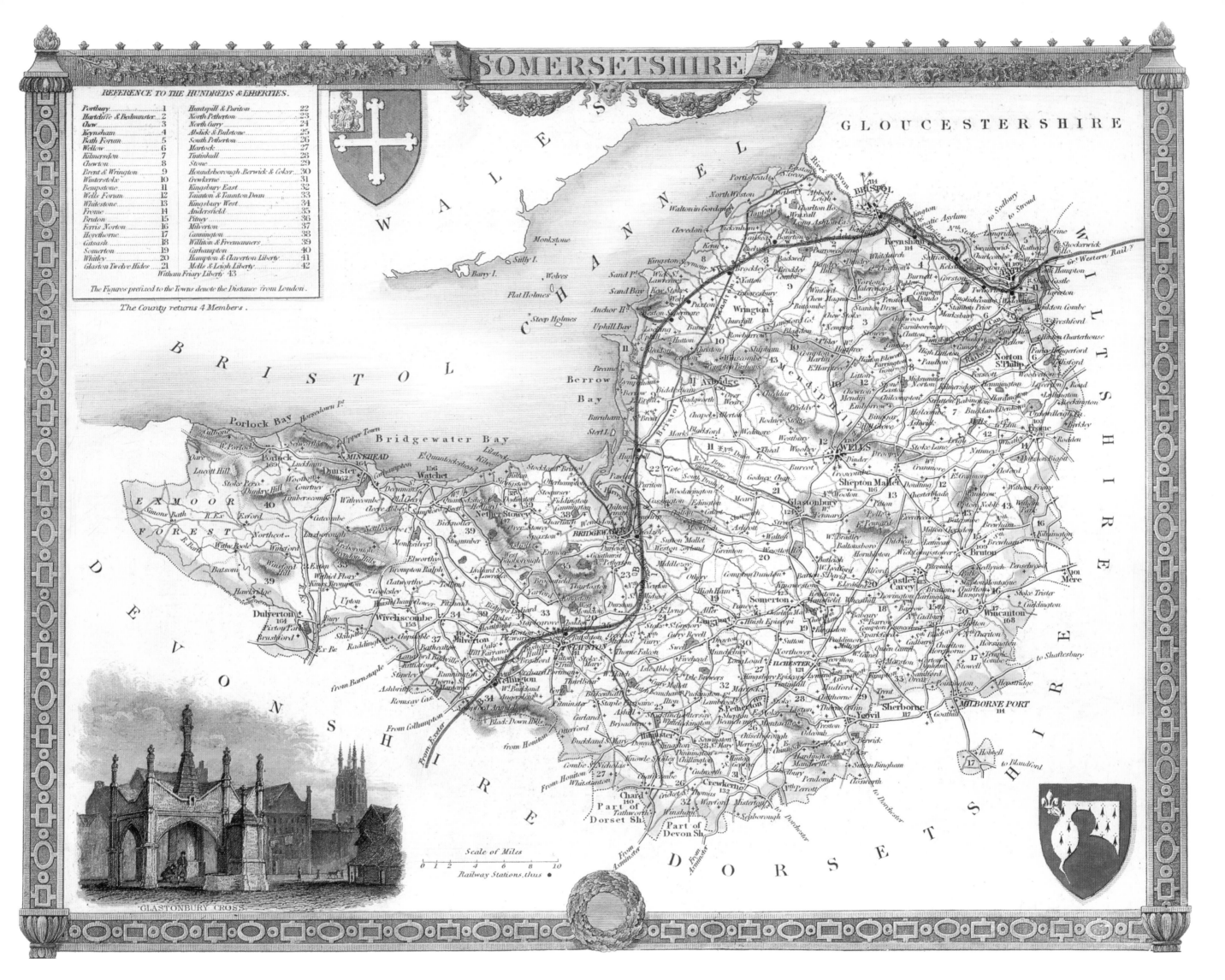

GLOUCESTERSHIRE

WALES

BRISTOL CHANNEL

REFERENCE TO THE HUNDREDS & LIBERTIES.

Portbury	1
Hartcliffe & Bedminster	2
Chew	3
Keynsham	4
Bath Forum	5
Wellow	6
Kilmersdon	7
Chewton	8
Brent & Wrington	9
Winterstoke	10
Bempstone	11
Wells Forum	12
Whitstone	13
Frome	14
Bruton	15
Ferris Norton	16
Horethorne	17
Catsash	18
Somerton	19
Whitley	20
Glaston Twelve Hides	21

Huntspill & Puriton	22
North Petherton	23
North Curry	24
Abdick & Bulstone	25
South Petherton	26
Martock	27
Tintinhull	28
Stone	29
Houndsborough Berwick & Coker	30
Crewkerne	31
Kingsbury East	32
Taunton & Taunton Dean	33
Kingsbury West	34
Andersfield	35
Pitney	36
Milverton	37
Cannington	38
Williton & Freemanners	39
Carhampton	40
Hampton & Claverton Liberty	41
Mells & Leigh Liberty	42

Witham Friary Liberty 43

The Figures prefixed to the Towns denote the Distance from London.

The County returns 4 Members.

EXMOOR FOREST

DEVONSHIRE

WILTSHIRE

DORSETSHIRE

Scale of Miles

Railway Stations, thus ●

"GLASTONBURY CROSS."

CITY OF BATH

THE CITY OF BATH, on the river Avon, in the northeastern part of the county, 107 miles from London and 13 miles from Bristol, contains 5157 houses and 36,811 inhabitants. The Lower or Somersetshire Avon rises in the hilly district of North Wiltshire, a little distance from Wootton Basset, and in some places divides this county from Wiltshire; emerging from beneath the lofty eminence on which the village of Bathford stands, this river almost surrounds the splendid City of Bath, seated amidst an immense amphitheatre of hills, and then pursues its course to Bristol. The valley in which Bath lies being too small to contain the numerous buildings which have been erected here within the last century, the sides of the hills have been gradually covered towards the north, and houses now crown the summits. In elegance of building, it is said to exceed every town in England, being constructed of a white stone, of which the surrounding soil is chiefly composed; and the houses rising in progressive order behind each other, render its appearance very picturesque.

The origin of the improvements and progress of the buildings at Bath may be ascribed to *John Wood*, an architect, by whose perseverance the plans he contemplated were brought to perfection. In January, 1729, he laid the foundation of Queen's Square. In March, 1739, the North and South Parades, Pierepoint Street, and Duke Street were begun, which Mr. Wood lived to see completed. Some time before his death, in 1754, he laid out the plan of the Circus. North eastward of the Circus is the Royal Crescent, the communication between which and the Circus is formed by Brock Street. While Mr. Wood was employed in his improvements, others profiting by his example, were raising streets and different detached works in various parts of the city; and from that time to the present, the ardour for building has not abated. Lansdown Place, a second crescent, has been erected towards Lansdown; and near it, Camden Place, a third crescent, both commanding views of the city and surrounding country. The avenues to these buildings and the downs above them have also been improved, and a new tower on Lansdown has been erected by W. Beckford, Esq.

The following critique on the buildings of Bath is derived from Dallaway's Observations on English Architecture. A visitor to this resort of wealth and elegance is disappointed on a close examination of its architects. The beautiful inequalities of ground seen from a distance might lead him to expect specimens peculiarly adapted please the eye, delight the fancy, and satisfy the judgment. The first place of public access is the Pump Room; the pediment appears to be disproportionably small, and the columns and architrave bear no analogy to the ample space contained is the breadth and height of the building, and to its large and lofty windows. Pulteney Street is long and broad, but being chiefly divided into distinct houses, is far from impressive, and being on a level, the eye feels no relief from a flat uniformity. The Crescent is grandly situated, and so beautifully formed, that the judgment is for a while suspended; but, in a nearer view, it is to be regretted that the upper parts of the buildings lose all the effect which the Ionic columns would have communicated, by the defective projection and unornamented basement story. The houses which terminate each end exhibit striking fronts. When this has been called the finest modern Ionic screen in Europe, the praise has been exaggerated. The Circus forms a dark and heavy area, although the individual structures are highly ornamental. Bath, in short, betrays that fallacy to the eye which all buildings of a theatric nature are known to do; the visionary pleasure soon vanishes, when a close inspection shows the littleness of the component parts, the slimness of the structures, and the imperfect durability of the materials. The New Crescent owes the degree of beauty it possesses to its lofty situation alone. Milsom Street, from its being built on an ascent, is very striking, and the junction in the middle of several tenements under one design is not without an appearance of grandeur; yet the ornaments are merely such as a builder uninstructed in the Palladian school might have capriciously invented. The long façade to the upper room is handsome, but the principal approach is heavy and deformed, by the jutting parts of the building, which make a dark, narrow, and deep area. The North Parade exhibits a promising front; the South Parade is inferior. Neatness of appearance, in most instances, cannot, however, exempt the architecture of Bath from the general characteristic of flimsiness and apparent want of durability. The elevation of the Baths are pretty, and the colonnades in the street leading to Bristol give that part of the city a light and airy view.

The ancient city, renowned for its mineral hot springs and baths, was called by the Britons, Caer Palladur; by the Saxons, Akemancester: and by the Romans, Aquæ Solis. In the year 1672; a book, under the title of The Bathes of Bathes aide, was published by Dr. Jones; and in 1703, the city became, in some measure, frequented by people of distinction. In 1755, on taking down the abbey house, to build the Duke of Kingston's baths, were found, at the depth of twenty feet below the ground, remains of Roman baths and sudatories, the springs and drains of which were then made use of in the new building. These baths extended above one hundred and fifty feet in length, and one hundred and twenty feet in breadth, enclosed with walls, built of stone, and lined with cement. Within these walls were square and circular baths of various dimensions, the floors of which were supported by pillars of brick, consolidated with strong mortar, about fourteen inches asunder. The floor was composed of hard tiles, about two feet square, on which were layers of cement, with brick tubes, to heat the vapour-baths and sudatories. The warm baths had tesselated pavements, and thus were formed drains to carry off the water to the river.

The Kingston Rooms, on part of the estate of the Duke of Kingston, descended to Earl Manvers, who enlarged the building, and added a portico; but the whole was destroyed by fire, December 21, 1820. A literary and philosophical institution has been built on the site.

The public baths are four in number. 1. The King's Bath, near the Abbey Church; in this is a statue of King Bladud, erected in 1699, and on which he is stated to be the discoverer and founder of the baths; a tradition long since discarded. The Queen's Bath is a department of the King's Bath, but at a greater distance from the springs. 2. The New Baths, in Stall Street, erected in 1688, by *Baldwin.* 3. The Cross Bath, near the King's Bath, is so called from a cross which was erected in the centre of it, by the Earl of Melfort, as a memorial of the queen's bathing in it, in the year 1687; but this cross is now removed. 4. The Hot Bath, deemed the hottest of all; was built from designs by *Wood.* The Great Pump Room was erected from designs by *Baldwin*, but was afterwards materially altered by *J. Palmer.* In a niche at the eastern end, is a statue of Richard Nash, formerly Master of the Ceremonies, by *Prince Hoare;* this extraordinary personage died at his house in St. John's Court, February 3, 1761, ætat eighty-seven, and the statue was placed here at the expence of the corporation. It is unquestionable that the city owes much to Nash's judicious administration of its pleasures. The room is sixty feet by fifty-six in dimension. Near the Hot Bath is a pump room, erected in 1792, by *J. Palmer*, and there is another pump room at the Cross Bath.

The New Assembly Rooms, at the east end of the Circus, were built from designs by *John Wood, junior*, in 1769, and were opened in 1771. The Ball-room is one hundred and six feet, eight inches, by forty-two feet eight

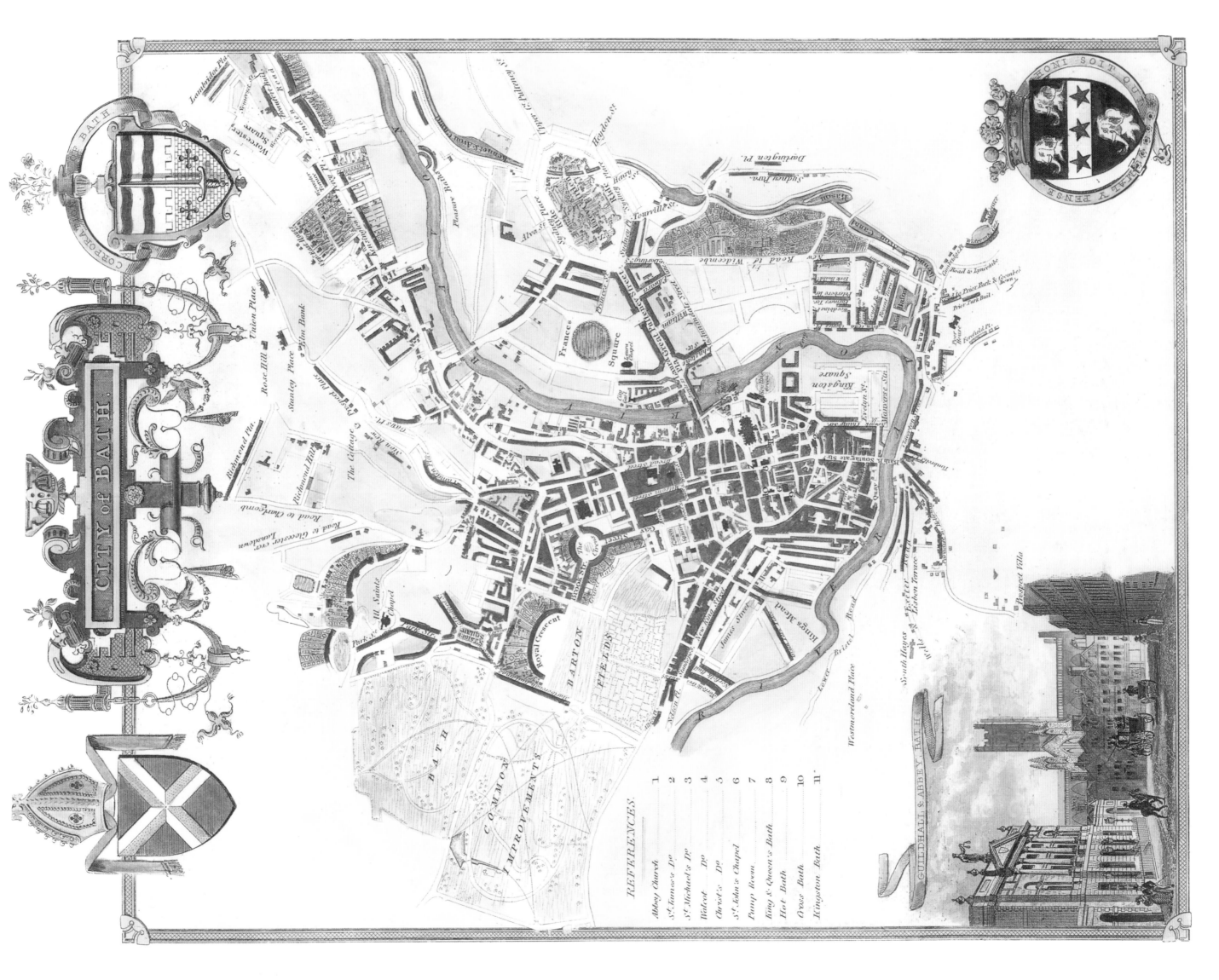

CITY of BATH.

GUILDHALL & ABBEY, BATH.

REFERENCES:

1 Abbey Church
2 St James's Dᵒ
3 St Michael's Dᵒ
4 Walcot Dᵒ
5 Christ's Dᵒ
6 St John's Chapel
7 Pump Room
8 King & Queen's Bath
9 Hot Bath
10 Cross Bath
11 Kingston Bath

HONI SOIT QUI MAL Y PENSE

inches, in dimension. In the Card-room are the portraits of Captain Wade, by *Gainsborough*, and Richard Tyson, by *James*. The Theatre, built by *Palmer*, from designs by *George Dance, R.A.*, was opened in 1805. Sydney Gardens, at the termination of Great Pulteney Street, were opened in 1795, the gardens were designed by *Harcourt*, and the Kennet and Avon Canal is carried through the grounds. Orange Grove, the former seat of all the amusements of Bath, is planted with rows of trees, in the centre of which stands an Obelisk, erected in memory of the restoration of the health of the Prince of Orange, by drinking the Bath waters, in 1734. In the centre of Queen's Square, is also an obelisk, erected in memory of Frederic. Prince of Wales, in 1737. The bridge of St. Lawrence, is at the end of Horse Street, at the southern end of the city. Sir William Pulteney, afterwards Earl of Bath, erected Pulteney Bridge, over the Avon, and Bathwick Bridge was opened September 28, 1827. This bridge is of cast iron, and was designed by *Goodridge*; the mound of stone, requisite to bring the Bathwick side of the river to a level with that of Walcot, was raised at the expence of the Marquess of Cleveland. Sion Place, and Cavendish Place, as well as Sydney Place, were designed by *Pinch*. In the year 1817, the late Queen Charlotte visited Bath, and resided in New Sydney Place; the queen was accompanied by the Duke of Clarence, now King William IV., the Princess Elizabeth, now Landgravine of Hesse Homberg, and the principal officers of the royal household. Immediately after the death of the Princess Charlotte, the queen left Bath for Windsor, but returned on November 24, and remained here about a month, during which time the queen visited Doddington, the seat of Sir Bethel Codrington, and Bailbrook House, an establishment since removed to Clifton.

Bath Park, on the north-western side of the city, is one of the latest improvements; the entrance is from the Queen's Parade, and in front of the Royal Crescent. The ornamental plantations are of great extent, and are brought in contact with the most central part of the city, forming one of the finest promenades in the kingdom.

The market days of Bath are Wednesdays and Saturdays, and there are two annual fairs, one on February 14, and the other on July 10. There is a market in Walcot Street for sheep and cattle, adjoining which is a corn market. No inland place is so well supplied with sea fish as Bath; and the supply is ample and regular. Coals are brought to the city from Timbsbury, Camerton, Radstock, Paulton, Dunkerton, and the adjacent pits.

The civil government of Bath, was, by a charter of Queen Elizabeth, vested in a mayor, recorder, ten aldermen, and twenty common councilmen, with a chamberlain, and town clerk. Two sheriffs or high bailiffs, and two

chief constables, are annually chosen from the common council. The arms of the city are. *Per fesse embattled azure and gules, the base masoned sable, with crosses botonnée of the last. In chief, two bars wavy argent; over all, in pale, a sword of the last, hilted and pommelled or; on the blade, a key.* The Guildhall, finished in 1775, was erected from designs by *Baldwin*. The banqueting-room contains portraits of King George III., Queen Charlotte, the Prince and Princess of Orange, and those of the Earls of Chatham and Camden. Bath returns two members to parliament, who at present are, General C. Palmer, and J. A. Roebuck, Esquire.

The city of Bath contains four parishes, St. James, St. Michael, St. Peter and St. Paul, and Walcot.

King Osric founded a nunnery here, in the year 676, which, being destroyed by the Danes, King Offa, about the year 775, rebuilt the church and monastery for secular canons. In the year 970, King Edgar altered the establishment to an abbey, and convent of Benedictine monks, who continued here till the dissolution. The revenues of the monastery were valued at 695*l.* 6*s.* 1*d.* The arms of the abbey are, *Gules, two keys in bend sinister, conjoined in the bows, or, and interlaced with a crosier in bend dexter,*

argent. The abbey church, dedicated to St. Peter and St. Paul, was made cathedral by a charter of William II., in 1090, who granted it to John de Vilula, Bishop of Wells, for the purpose of augmenting the see, and who removed the bishopric to Bath. This caused great discontent amongst the monks of Wells, when that city was included in the title, and it was made the alternate residence of the bishop, with the city of Bath.

The abbey church was rebuilt in 1495, by Bishop Oliver King, who was principal secretary to Prince Edward, son of King Henry VI., to the Kings Edward IV., and Henry VII.; and also registrar of the Order of the Garter. He is reported to have have built this church, in consequence of a dream or vision, but he died before the completion of the building, which did not take place till the reign of James I. The abbey church of Bath, partakes, in a very small degree of the florid ornaments of the pointed style. It was, in fact, the last building of equal magnitude, entirely in that style, and remains in the same form as when finished in 1532. Oliver King, Bishop of Bath and Wells, who died thirty years before that time, is considered the founder, and, together with Priors Bird and Holloway, gave the plan, and carried it to a certain point. It was finally completed by Bishop Montagu, and the executors of Lord Treasurer Burghley. In an age when ecclesiastical fabrics of the first degree were constructed with a vast profusion of wealth and labour, it is more pleasing to contemplate this work of a prelate, who preferred the admirable simplicity of the earlier school of pointed architecture, to the overcharged decorations which other architects of his own time were so ambitious to display.

To the western front of the church is attached a continued alto-relievo, representing Jacob's Ladder, with angels ascending and descending, as in the founder's dream. The tower, one hundred and fifty feet high, has four turrets, without pinnacles, and is an oblong of the proportion of thirty-five to twenty-five feet, north and south, being narrowed to the transept. The church was formerly called "The Lantern of England" on account of the number and size of its windows. The upper tier of windows is lofty beyond proportion, and there is no triforium; the aisles are low. The ceiling of the nave and choir, is singular in its design, and beautiful in its execution. Of the two parts, that of the nave is evidently of later construction, than that of the choir. The nave is divided from the aisles by clustered pillars, supporting flat Tudor arches. The ceiling of the choir runs higher than that of the nave, although the groins of the choir are lower, and consequently the form of the arch is more acute. The choir screen is beneath an organ gallery, in which is a fine organ. The screen was erected in 1825, from designs by *Manners*.

Near the altar is the monumental chapel, or oratory of Prior Bird, who died in 1525, it is elaborately enriched with ornaments. No church of equal size contains so great a number of monuments as the Abbey Church, one of the most conspicuous is that of James Montagu, Bishop of Bath and Wells, in 1608. On his primary visitation at Bath, his attention was directed, by Sir John Harrington, to the state of the Abbey Church, which had suffered devastation from its very origin, he immediately contributed towards its completion, and under his auspices, the church was finished, about the period at which he was translated to the see of Winchester, in 1616. He died at Winchester, on the 2nd of July 1618, and agreeably to his own desire, was buried in Bath Abbey Church, when his costly monument was erected at the expence of his four brothers. Other monuments are those of James Quin, the celebrated Richard Nash, Lady Miller, of Batheaston, who died in 1781, by *Bacon*; and that of Lieutenant General Sir Manby Power, K.C.B., by *King*. In the southern aisle is a monument of William Hoare. R.A., who died in 1792, by *Chantrey*.

The Abbey Church is now under repair, and disencumbered of the buildings which were formerly placed against it, as well as the accumulation of stone, by which its base had long been hidden. The plan extends to the removal of the houses at the bottom of the High Street, or Market Place, and thus opening a view of the whole northern side of the church. The clock has been removed from the tower, and an illuminated dial placed in the centre of the gable end of the northern transept. In the aisles of the choir an important restoration has been made. The parapet walls, have been partly removed, the blocking up of the windows taken out and replaced with glass, and the roof covered with lead. It is also proposed to lower the present roofs of the choir and transepts, which now injure the proportions of three sides of the tower. The handsome carving of the western doors, contributed by Sir Henry Montagu, Chief Justice of the King's Bench, and brother of Bishop Montagu, in 1617, has been restored by *James Jones* of Bath. The repairs of the interior of the Abbey Church, were commenced by a restoration of the oratory of Prior Bird, a very beautiful specimen of Tudor architecture, under the direction of *E. Davis*, of Bath. The arrangement of the monuments, throughout the building is to be performed in the same manner as has been effected in Winchester Cathedral.

There is some question as to the propriety of surmounting the buttresses of the church with pinnacles, and of adding a pierced parapet to the aisles. The simplicity and gracefulness of the turrets of the main tower would be entirely destroyed by pinnacles, and the square towers of the eastern front would become quite grotesque if pinnacles were placed upon them. The turrets of the western front comport remarkably well with the rest of the building, as they are, and would be only injured by the proposed addition. Bath Abbey Church, it will be remembered, is in the latest period of pointed architecture, nearly coeval with the chapels of King's College, Cambridge, St. George's Chapel, Windsor, and Henry VII.'s chapel at Westminster; but although it possesses the general features of the style in which those buildings are erected, it is itself simple and unadorned almost to plainness. The proposed pierced parapet, in conformity with the style of the period, is at variance with the plain and simple character of the architecture of this church, and for which it is valuable. The repairs are executed under the direction of *George Manners*, a gentleman every way competent to the task.

The parish church of St. James was rebuilt in 1769, from a design by *Palmer*, but the tower was erected in 1726. The church, dedicated to St. Michael, was completed in 1742, and the parish church of Walcot, which stands within the liberties of the city, was rebuilt in 1780. A new church, at Walcot, was founded in the year 1829, and built by *Pinch*. Christ's Church, in Montpelier Row, was built by voluntary subscription, on ground given for that purpose by Lord Rivers, it is in the pointed style of architecture. The church, dedicated to the Holy Trinity, in James's Street, was erected from designs by *Lowder*, without fee or reward. It is an enriched specimen of the pointed style of architecture, and is devoted exclusively to public accommodation, the service of sacramental plate was the contribution of an unknown benefactor; there are also in Bath the following chapels, one annexed to St. John's Hospital, dedicated to St. Michael erected in 1723. The Hospital, founded by Reginald Fitz-Joceline, bishop of this see, in the reign of Henry II., was rebuilt in 1728, by the Duke of Chandos. A chapel near the south-western corner of Queen's Square, dedicated to the Virgin Mary, was erected from designs by *Wood*, in 1735; and the Octagon Chapel in Milsom Street, from designs by *Lightholder* in 1767; the altar-piece, the Pool of Bethesda, was painted by *Hoare*. Margaret Chapel, in Margaret Buildings, Brook Street, so called in compliment to Mrs. Margaret Gerrard, lady of the manor, was built from designs by *Wood*, and opened by Dr. Dodd in 1770. All Saints' Chapel, Lansdown Grove, was opened in 1794. It is in the pointed style, and was erected from designs by *Palmer*, as also was Kennington Chapel, at Walcot, opened in 1795. Laura Chapel, in Henrietta Street, Laura Place, was built in 1796, from designs by *Baldwin*. There is also a chapel, dedicated to St. Mary Magdalen, under Beechen Cliff, besides several other chapels, not connected with the established church.

A Grammar School, in Broad Street, originally founded and endowed by King Edward VI., was rebuilt in 1752. The Rev. W. Robins, L.L.B. formerly master of this school, conveyed the right of patronage of the Rectory of Charlcombe, to the corporation, to be annexed to the school for ever.

One of the principal hills in the environs of Bath, is Lansdown, long famous for the number of sheep fed on its delicate herbage. On this down a fair is annually held, on the 10th of August, for cheese, horses, &c. On the summit of Lansdown, is a tower, erected from designs by *H. E. Goodridge*, by William Beckford, Esq. formerly of Fonthill. This building is square in its plan, to the height of one hundred and thirty feet from the foundation, and then assumes an octangular from, for twelve feet, and is crowned by a lantern, also twelve feet in height. From the top is a prospect of great extent, presenting the meanderings of the river Severn, Salisbury Plain, and Fonthill, at a distance of nearly thirty miles. At the extremity of the Down is also a fine and most extensive view of the vale of Gloucester, the hills of Worcestershire, part of Wales, the river Servern, and Bristol Channel, and the Wiltshire Downs. From North Stoke brow, the cities of Bath and Bristol, may be seen at the same time. The Bath and Bristol races are held on Lansdown, generally in the month of July.

On this down is a monument erected by George, Lord Lansdown, in 1720, in memory of a battle fought here between the royal and the parliamentary forces, on July 5, 1643. Claverton Down is now entirely enclosed; from it is a communication with Hampton Down, and towards Combe Down is Prior Park, a place rendered in some degree classical as the scene of "Tom Jones," the most celebrated of Fielding's works, and as the subsequent residence of Bishop Warburton, a wit and a scholar, distinguished amongst his contemporaries of the middle of the last century. In the novel of Tom Jones, Ralph Allen, the liberal-minded proprietor of this estate is said to have suggested the character of Allworthy, a name expressive of his benevolent disposition. Ralph Allen, Esq. built this seat in the year 1743, upon land which had formerly belonged to the prior of Bath, and whose grange in the immediate neighbourhood supplied venison for the convent. Although the house stands below the summit of Combe Down, it is considered to be elevated four hundred feet above the city of Bath. On Combe Down are those vast quarries of free-stone, striking objects of curiosity, whence the stone is brought down to the river side for conveyance to different parts of the kingdom by means of an inclined plane railway.

ENVIRONS OF BATH AND BRISTOL

BRISTOL

BRISTOL, 120 miles W. from London, situated on the rivers Avon and Frome, contains 7,736 houses, and 52,889 inhabitants. Its name is Anglo-Saxon *Bright stowe* or pleasant place. Robert Earl of Gloucester in the reign of Henry I. rebuilt the castle, then a strong and spacious structure, and encompassed the town by a wall. In the reign of Henry II. Bristol became a rich and flourishing place; and ever since the reign of Edward III. has been an independent county within itself, of which Bedminster in Somersetshire forms a part. The old town, within the inner wall, stood a narrow hill, the descent from which in many places was formerly very steep, but has been rendered easy by modem improvements. This hill is bounded on the S. by the Avon, on the N. and W. by the Frome, and on the E. by the fosse of the castle, now arched over at the lower end of Castle street. The valley is on the other side of the two rivers; on the N. side of it is St. Michael's Hill and King's Down, the highest ground in the city. On the W. side is College Green, a considerable eminence, and on the S. side is Red Cliff Hill: the whole of this extent is covered with buildings. The summit of St. Michael's Hill and King's Down being considerably higher than any other quarter, the houses here command a fine view of the city and surrounding country. The old town is crowded with houses; but being seated on a hill, and the streets intersecting each other, there is always a free current of air even in the lowest situations. The city on the whole is handsome and well built, and contains many structures deserving particular attention. The castle was destroyed by order of Cromwell in 1654, so effectually, that but very few vestiges of the foundation are now to be seen, incorporated with other buildings. The diocese of Bristol was one of the six Sees erected by Henry VIII. out of the revenues of the monasteries and religious houses which that monarch dissolved. The cathedral was the church of the Abbey of St. Augustine, founded by Robert Fitz Hardinge, ancestor of the Berkeleys for Canons Regular, in 1148. At the Reformation King Henry VIII. placed therein a Dean and six Prebendaries, which mode of government still continues. During a great part of Elizabeth's reign the See was held in *commendam* by the Bishop of Gloucester. This diocese was formed chiefly out of that

of Salisbury, with a small part from the dioceses of Wells and Worcester. It contains most of the city of Bristol, and all the county of Dorset. The revenue of the Abbey of St. Augustine in Bristol was valued at the Dissolution at 670*l.* 13*s.* 11*d.*, when it was erected into a cathedral by Henry VIII. by the name of the cathedral church of the Holy Trinity. The arms of St. Augustine's Abbey were *sable, three ducal coronets, in pale, or*, now used by the See of Bristol. The length of the church from east to west is 175 feet, whereof the very beautiful choir includes 100 feet; the length of the transepts from north to south is 128 feet the width of the body and side aisles is 73 feet, and the height of the tower is 127 feet. The edifice displays two distinct species of beautiful architecture. The Chapter House and elder Lady's Chapel were built towards the close of the 12th century, and the present nave and choir in the beginning of the 14th. lt is but an incomplete structure, a great part of the nave having been destroyed.

The fine painted windows are very much admired; and on the north side is an ancient monument supposed to be that of Robert de Berkeley, who died in 1219. ln the cloister is the entrance to the Chapter House and Bishop's Palace; west of the church is a magnificent Gatehouse enriched with statues. There are 18 parish churches. St. Stephen's church is remarkable for its very fine tower. The church of St. Mark, opposite the cathedral, was formerly collegiate, and is now the Mayor's chapel: that of St Mary Redcliffe, one of the finest architectural specimens in the kingdom, contains the monument of its founder, William Canninge, Mayor of Bristol, and of Sir William Penn, father of the founder of Pennsylvania. The principal hospitals in Bristol are Queen Elizabeth's and Colston's. in each of which 100 boys are educated. The Right Hon. Lord Grenville is High Steward of the city; and the government is under a mayor and 12 aldermen, who are justices, one for each ward; 2 sheriffs, 28 common-council men, a town clerk and deputy, a chamberlain, vice-chamberlain, under sheriff, &c. besides a city marshal, and other inferior officers. The mayor holds a Quarter Session, and a Court of Requests is held every Monday. Arms of Bristol:— *Gules, a castle with two towers, argent, on a mount vert, on each tower, a banner of St. George, on the dexter side of the castle a ship with three masts with waves in base, proper.* Motto— "Virtute et lndustria." Besides the Guildhall, an ancient

edifice, there is a handsome Exchange, and a Commercial Hall, built by the merchants. There are 13 city companies, several of whom have halls; that of the Merchants in Prince's-street has a curious front of stone, and Coopers' Hall in King-street has a Corinthian front of four columns. The new Commercial Rooms were opened in 1811, and the Corn Market in 1813. The several squares in Bristol are handsome; Queen-square has a spacious walk shaded with trees, with an equestrian statue of William III. by *Rysbrach* in the centre. King-square is well built on an agreeable slope: on the north-west side of the city is Brandon Hill, where the laundresses dry their linen by charter from Queen Elizabeth.

On the east bank of the Avon is Red Cliff Parade, affording a beautiful prospect of the city, shipping, and surrounding country. Over the river Frome is a draw-bridge; and the quay is above a mile in length from St Giles's to Bristol Bridge, under the names of the Back, the Grove, and the Gib: on the banks of the river below the city are several dock-yards, as well as the merchants' floating dock. The tide rises greatly, affording depth of water for any merchant ship at spring tides; and the whole trade of the city is brought to the quay, where every possible convenience is prepared for loading and unloading; but at low water the vessels lie aground, and, together with various difficulties in navigating to and from the Severn through a narrow river, were disadvantages under which the city formerly laboured, but a spirit of improvement has induced the inhabitants to amend the navigation by forming a dam near the Hotwells. In King's Road, at the Avon's mouth, vessels ride securely while waiting for the opportunity of entering the river. The principal branch of foreign commerce is to the West Indies; with the north and south of Europe it has a general trade, of which that with Spain is the most important: the trade with Portugal is likewise considerable, as well as to the continent of America, Newfoundland, the Baltic, and an extensive commerce with Ireland. This city sends two members to Parliament; Richard Hart Davies, of Mortimer House Clifton; and Henry Bright, Esq. The right of election is vested in the freemen and freeholders, about 6000 in number, the sons of freemen and the husbands of freemen's daughters being considered freemen.

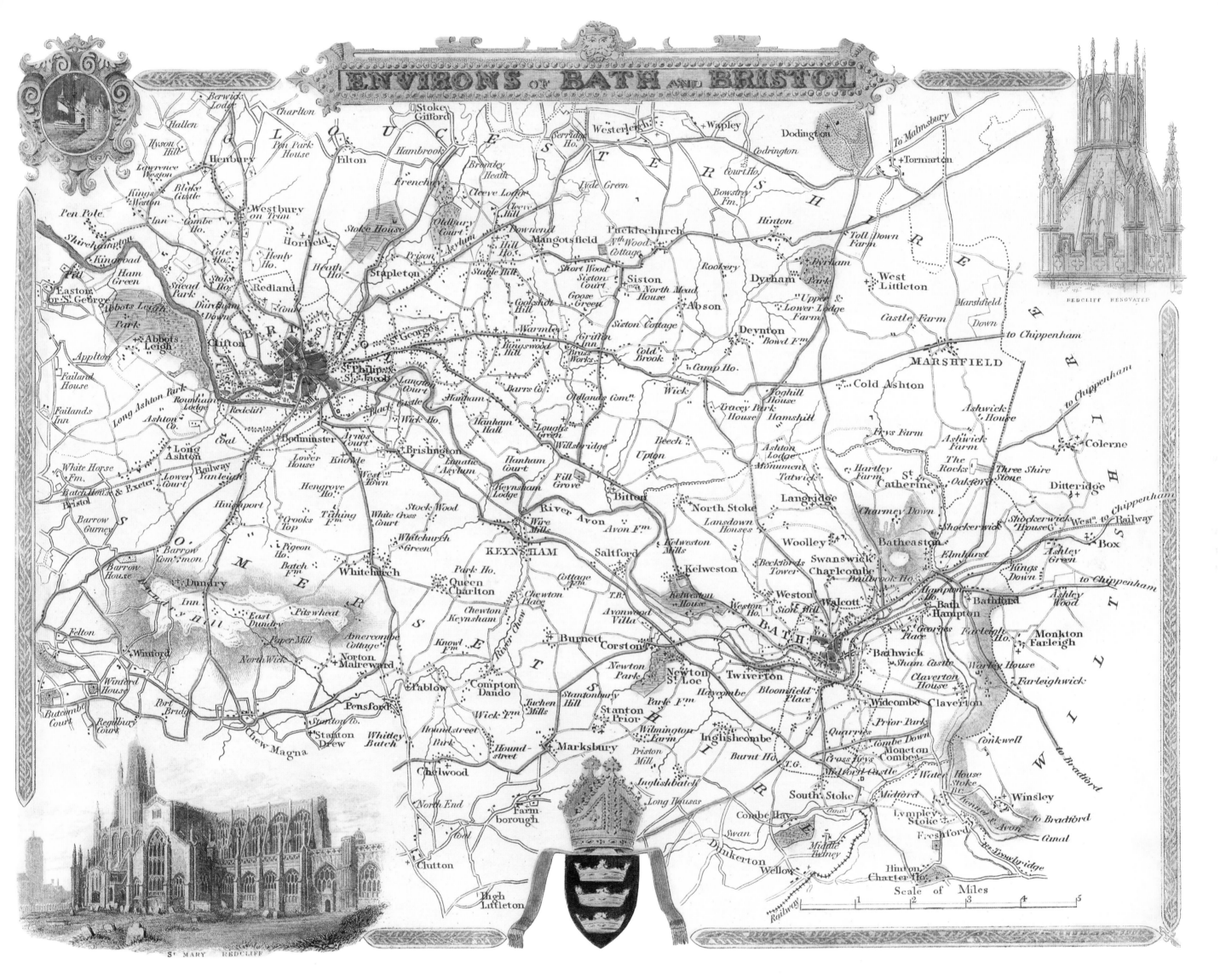

ENVIRONS OF BATH AND BRISTOL

REDCLIFF RENOVATED

Scale of Miles
1   2   3   4   5

ST. MARY REDCLIFF

STAFFORDSHIRE

This county is bounded on the north by Cheshire; on the east by Derbyshire; on the south by Warwickshire and Worcestershire, and on the west by Shropshire. The greatest length is sixty miles, being thirty-eight miles in breadth, and one hundred and eighty miles in circumference. The present county was included in the Roman province Flavia Cæsariensis inhabited by the Ordovices, afterwards the Cornavii and Brigantes. During the Saxon Heptarchy, Staffordshire formed a part of the kingdom of Mercia. The celebrated Roman road Watling Street crosses the county; and the Roman stations were Etocetum at Wall, and Penocrucium at Penkridge: there is a Roman earthwork at Morton; Roman encampments at Arleywood, Ashton Heath, Ashwood Heath, Kinner, Oldbury, Shareshill, Teddesley Park, and Wolverhampton churchyard; Roman remains at Eccleshall and Wall. There were formerly abbeys at Burton, Chotes, Croxden, Dieulacres, Hanbury, Hilton, and Radmore; also priories at Calwich, Canwell, Lapley, Lichfield, Ronton, Rocester, Sandwell, Stafford, Stone, St. Thomas, Trentham, Tutbury and Wolverhampton. The castles of its earlier lords were at Alton or *Alveton,* Audley, Bonebury, Burgh Maer, Burton, Cannock, Caverswall, Chartley, Chesterton, Croxden, Darlaston, Eccleshal, Heleigh, Lichfield, Newcastle, Stafford, Stourton, Tamworth, Tirley, Tutbury and Wednesbury. This county contains one city, Lichfield; one county town, nineteen market-towns, one hundred and fifty parishes, 63,319 inhabited houses and 341,040 inhabitants. It is in the province of Canterbury, and in the diocese of Lichfield and Coventry. Staffordshire returns ten members to Parliament; two for Stafford, two for Lichfield, two for Newcastle under Lyne, two for Tamworth, and two for the County. Sir J. Wrottesley, Bart. of Wrottesley Hall, and E.J. Littleton Esq., of Teddesley Park. The aspect of this county is various; the northern part rises gently in small hills, which, beginning here, run through the heart of England in a continued ridge, rising gradually higher and higher under different names. The Moorland is a rough, dreary, cold tract, the snow lying long on it. It is here observed that the west wind always brings rain, but the east and south winds make fair weather, unless the wind turns about from the west to the south, which then continues rainy. The middle and southern parts of the county are generally level, or with only gentle eminences; to this, however, there are some exceptions; as the limestone hills of Sedgeley, which furnish an inexhaustible supply of that material, and great part of it of excellent quality. The quartzose, or ragstone hills of Rowley furnish an excellent material for roads and pavements. The Clent Hills and Barr Beacon, besides many others of less elevation, as the high grounds on Cannock Heath, the hills of Bushbury and Essington, formed chiefly of, or at least containing, great quantities of gravel. Kinfare Edge, Tettenhall Wood, and some situations near Enville, also command extensive prospects. Staffordshire is particularly celebrated for its Potteries, now become the general name of a district in which the manufacture of earthenware is carried on in an improved manner. These manufactures give employment to nearly 20,000 people in the county; and the operations of digging and collecting the clay, flint, terra porcellana, &c. in Kent, Sussex, Hampshire, Dorsetshire, Devonshire and Cornwall, and conveying them to the different ports, are supposed to employ nearly 40,000 more, besides upwards of 60,000 tons of shipping. In the north-western part of the county considerable iron-works are established; and its southern parts are enlivened by various branches of hardware. The mineral productions of the county are iron ore, limestone, firestone, freestone, pipe-clay, ochre and a valuable clay which bears the fire very well. The rivers are Blythe, Burne, Churnet, Dane, Dove, Hamps, Ilam, Lime, Manifold, Penk, Smestall, Sow, Stour, Tame, Tern and Trent. The river Severn passes through Over Areley, and receives the tribute of some considerable brooks in this county. The Trent takes its rise from three springs or heads in the north-western extremity of Staffordshire in the Moorlands. After traversing the Potteries, it runs in a southerly direction past Trentham Park to the town of Stone, whence inclining eastward, at Great Haywood it receives the waters of the Sow; thence pursuing a south-east course is at King's Bromley further augmented by the Blythe, and at Wichnor by the Tame: here suddenly turning to the north-east it flows past the town of Burton, about two miles beyond which it is joined by the Dove; running east, it crosses the south part of Derbyshire, where it receives the Derwent; and now skirting the north-west part of Leicestershire it meets with the Soar, when it becomes a considerable river as it advances through a range of flowery meadows, bounded by high tufted hills and chequered with villages, to the town of Nottingham. After passing Newark and Gainsborough, it makes a bold junction with the Ouse, and combined with it, forms the grand estuary of the Humber. The Dove rises in the rocky hills of Derbyshire, and pursues a south course at no great distance from the towns of Ashborne and Uttoxeter; at the latter place, inclining to the east, it flows on in a south-east direction and unites with the Trent near Newton Solney. The lakes of Staffordshire are those of Aqualate, Eccleshall Pool, Latford Pool, Lush Pool, Maer Pool, and New Pool. The canals of this county are, the Birmingham, Coventry and Oxford, Dudley and Netherton, Grand Trunk, Gresley's, Staffordshire and Worcestershire, Stourbridge, Trent and Mersey, and the Wyrley and Essington. The chief manufactures are earthenware, various kinds of hardware, glass, toys, hats, shoes, buttons, ferrets, handkerchiefs, twists, sewing-silks, cotton, leather, woollen and linen.

The Clog, or Perpetual Almanack, was in common use in this county; of the word clog there is no satisfactory etymology in the sense here used, which signified an almanack made upon a square stick. Dr. Plot, who wrote the history of this county in 1686, instances a variety of these old almanacks then in use here. Some he calls Public, because they were of large size, and commonly hung at one end of the mantle tree of the chimney: others he calls Private, because they were smaller and were carried in the pocket. There were three months contained upon each of the four edges of the clog, the number of days in them are represented by notches: that which began each month had a short turned up mark upon it, and every seventh notch of a larger size stood for Sunday. Upon these ancient clogs or almanacks the symbols of the saints were carefully represented, and all the purposes of a modern almanack were obtained by the use of this log of wood, known to antiquaries by the name of the Staffordshire Clog. – Ingestrie Hall is the seat of Earl Talbot, Lord Lieutenant of the County.

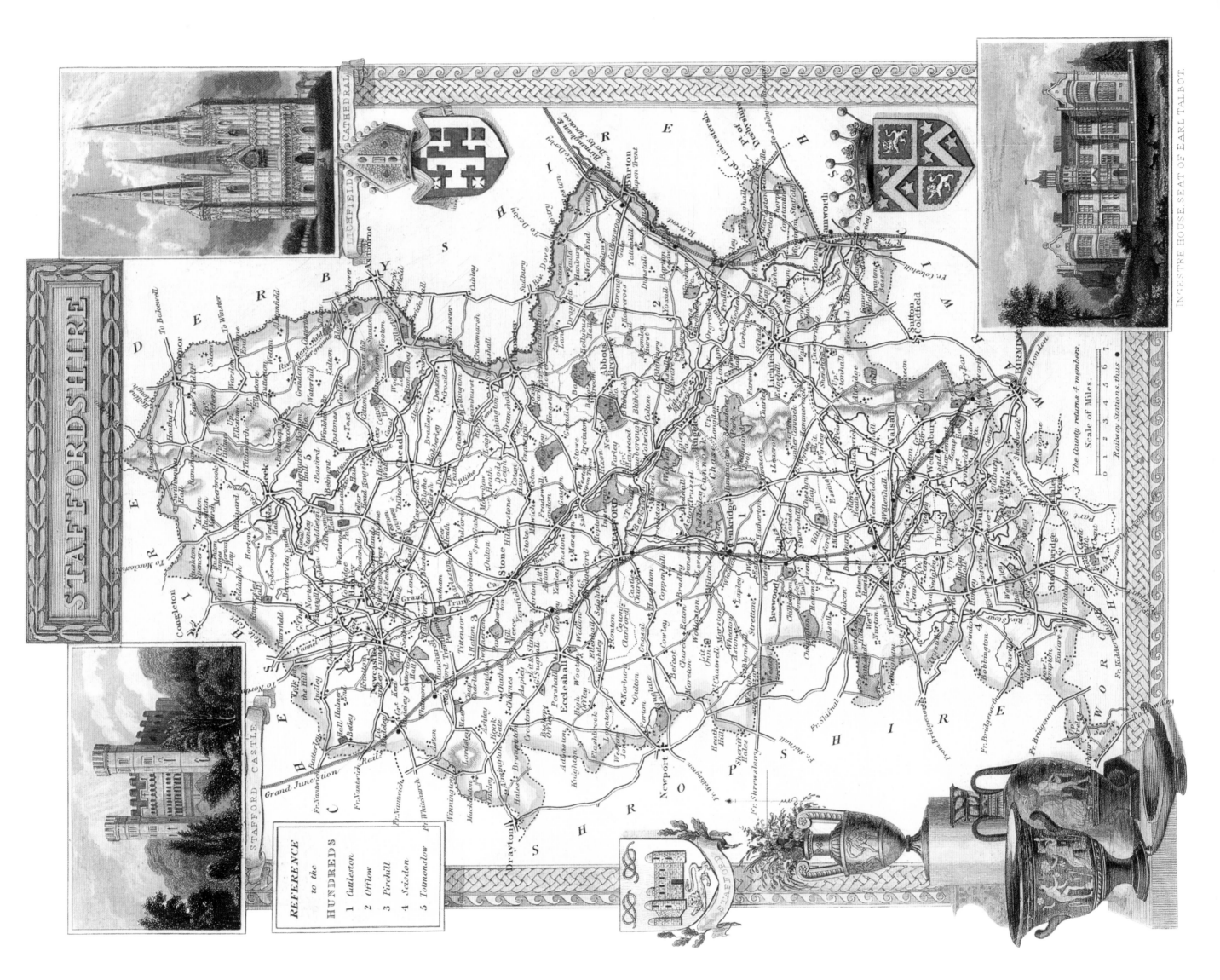

STAFFORDSHIRE

LICHFIELD CATHEDRAL

INGESTRE HOUSE, SEAT OF EARL TALBOT.

STAFFORD CASTLE

REFERENCE
to the
HUNDREDS
1 Cutleston
2 Offlow
3 Pirehill
4 Seisdon
5 Totmonslow

The County returns 17 members.
Scale of Miles.
0 1 2 3 4 5 6 7
Railway Stations thus ●

DERBYSHIRE

WARWICKSHIRE

WORCESTERSHIRE

SHROPSHIRE

CHESHIRE

SUFFOLK

THIS county is bounded on the north by Norfolk; on the east by the German Ocean; on the south by Essex; and on the west by Cambridgeshire: in length it is forty-seven miles, twenty-seven in breadth, and in circumference it is one hundred ninety-six miles. The British inhabitants of this county were the Iceni, or Cenomanni; and by the Romans it was included in the province of Flavia Cæsariensis, whose principal stations are supposed to have been Combretonium, Stratford; Extensium, Easton Ness; Garianonum, Burgh; Sitomagus, Stowmarket; and Villa Faustina, Woolpit. During the Anglo-Saxon Heptarchy Suffolk formed part of the kingdom of East Anglia, and received its present name from Sud, or Southern, folk, There are ancient encampments at Brettenham, Habyrdon near Bury, Kentfield near Icklingham, Stow Langtoft, and at Strafford on the banks of the Stour. The castles of its ancient lords were at Framlingham, Bungay, Clare, Felixstow, Haughley, Ipswich, Mettingham, Offton, Ousdon, Wingfield, and Soham Lodge. There were abbeys at Bury, Leiston and Sibton, and priories at Blithburgh, Briset, Butley, Clare, Dodnash, Eye, Felixstow, Herringfleet, Hoxne, Ipswich, Ixworth, Kersey, Letheringham, Mendham, Snape, Wanford, and Woodbridge; nunneries at Bruisyard, Bungay, Campsey, Flixton, and Redlingfield; besides collegiate churches at Mettingham, Stoke, Sudbury, and Wingfield. Suffolk contains one county town, 30 market-towns, 510 parishes, 42,773 houses, and 270,542 inhabitants. It returns sixteen members to Parliament, two for Aldeburgh, two for Bury St. Edmund's, two for Dunwich, two for Eye, two for Ipswich, two for Orford, two for Sudbury, and two for the county, who at present are Sir Henry Edward Bunbury, Bart., of Barton Hall near Bury, and Charles Tyrrell, Esq.

There is in this county a considerable variety of soil, nor is the diversity anywhere more distinctly marked; the whole may be divided into clay, sand, loam, and fen: the clay comprehends the midland part of the county, through nearly its whole extent from east to west, and forms about two thirds of the land; it consists of a stony or clayey loam, much of it high land and flat, but occasionally diversified by valleys, the sides of which are of superior quality, being in general composed of rich friable loams: this district is High Suffolk. The sand lies in opposite sides of the county; the maritime part from the Orwell to the Waveney is chiefly of this description, towards the north inclining to loam: much of this district is highly cultivated, and it is considered the most profitable. The rest of the sand division lies on the western side of the county, and comprises nearly the whole north-western angle; it contains few spots of such rich land as are found on the coast, but abounds with warrens and sheep-walks. The third division is that of loam, which is but a small portion of the county, and is chiefly confined to the hundred of Samford, with a small part of Colneis near the coast: this is not so clearly discriminated as the others, and is composed of a vein of vegetable mould of extraordinary fertility. The remaining division is fen, at the extreme north-western angle from Brandon to the conflex of the Ouse and Lark. The rivers of this county are the Alde, Breton, Blythe, Deben, Gipping, Lark, Little Ouse, Ore, Orwell, Stour, Waveney, and Yare. The Stour rises near Haverhill, on the borders of Cambridgeshire, passes to Sudbury, and thence, after being joined by the Brett near Nayland, to its mouth, dividing Suffolk from Essex, at Harwich it meets the Orwell from Ipswich, and both rivers fall into the sea beneath Landguard Fort on the Suffolk coast. The Orwell has its source in the centre of the county, near Stowmarket, whence

it pursues a south-easterly direction to Ipswich, and making a curve almost to the south, meets the Stour opposite to Harwich. The Deben, the Alde, and the Blythe are three small rivers, penetrating through this county to the German Ocean: the Deben, at Woodbridge; the Alde, at Aldborough and Orford; and the Blythe, at Southwold. The Waveney and the Yare meet in the marshes which environ Yarmouth, the first for a considerable distance dividing this county from Norfolk as it flows towards the north-east, and the last winding eastward through the heart of Norfolk. The course of the Waveney is very pleasant; but that of the Yare is not accompanied by much distinction and beauty. A canal from Stowmarket to Ipswich was opened in 1793. The produce of the county, which is purely agricultural, is wheat, beans, barley, oats, clover, turnips, &c.: it is one of the most productive and most skilfully tilled counties in the kingdom. In some parts there are extensive dairies, producing excellent butter; but the cheese is proverbially inferior. The horses of this county are the very best for agricultural purposes; the breed of cows is also very famous; the sheep are of the Norfolk breed, excepting where of late they have been changed for that of the South Down. Suffolk is almost unrivalled in productiveness of game; and for rabbits it is certainly unequalled. What woodland there is in the county may be traced from the north-eastern to the north-western side of it; but it is not a woody county. It has no mines of any kind, nor has it any manufacture, excepting that of Woolpit bricks. The Suffolk words and phrases have been collected by Edward Moor, and were published by him in 1823; and a Suffolk Garland, or a Collection of Poems, Songs, &c., relative to the county, was published in 1818. Euston Hall, near Thetford, is the seat of the Duke of Grafton, Lord Lieutenant of the County.

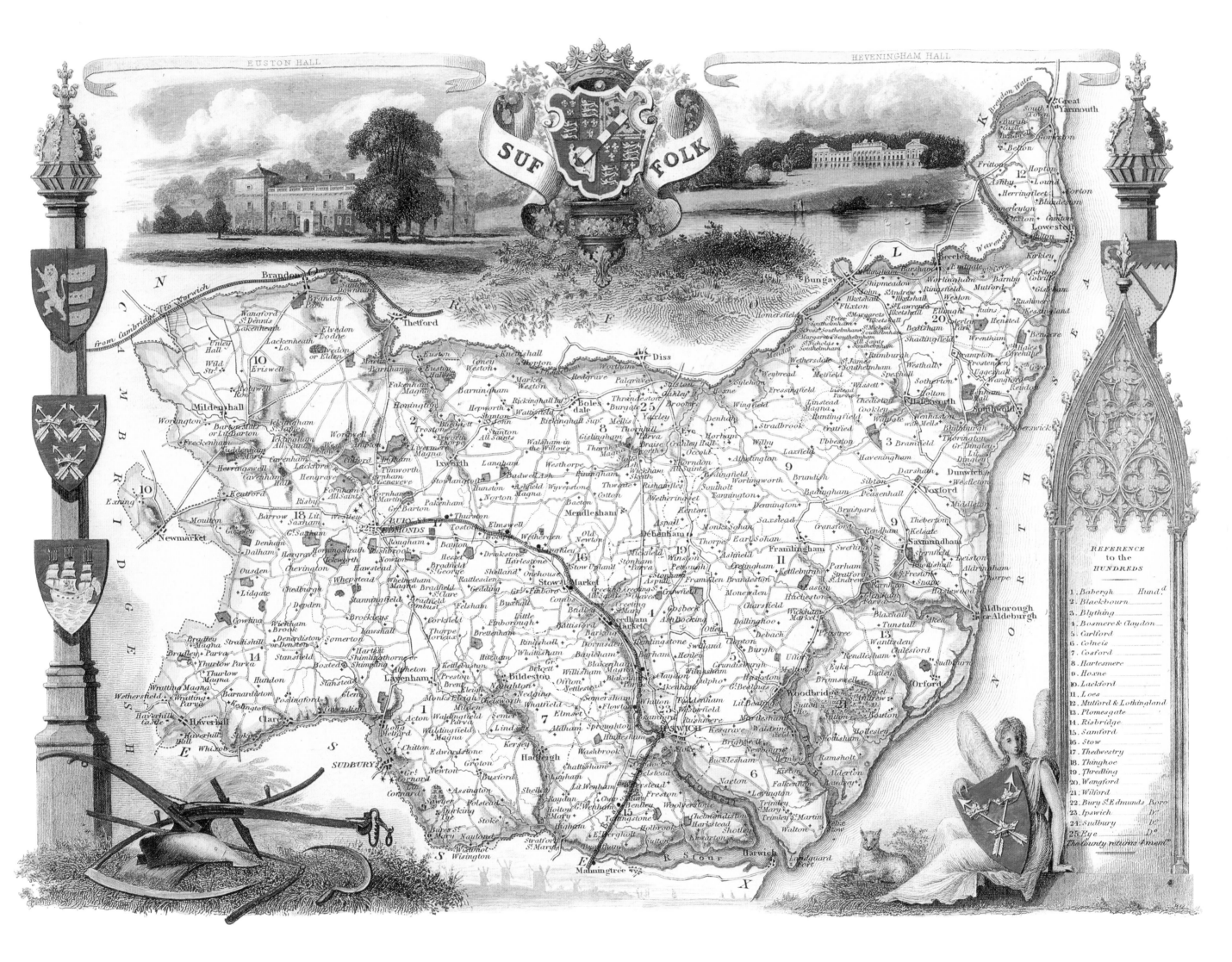

EUSTON HALL

HEVENINGHAM HALL

SUF FOLK

REFERENCE
to the
HUNDREDS

1. Babergh Hundd
2. Blackbourn
3. Blything
4. Bosmere & Claydon
5. Carlford
6. Colneis
7. Cosford
8. Hartesmere
9. Hoxne
10. Lackford
11. Loes
12. Mutford & Lothingland
13. Plomesgate
14. Risbridge
15. Samford
16. Stow
17. Thedwestry
18. Thinghoe
19. Thredling
20. Wangford
21. Wilford
22. Bury St Edmunds Boro
23. Ipswich   Do
24. Sudbury   Do
25. Eye   Do
The County returns 4 membs

SURREY

THIS county is bounded on the north by the river Thames, which separates it from Buckinghamshire and Middlesex; on the east by Kent; on the south by Sussex; and on the west by Berkshire and Hampshire. It is about twenty-six miles in length, thirty-eight in breadth, and one hundred and twelve miles in circumference. The British inhabitants were called Segontiaci by the Romans, under whom the county formed part of the province of Britannia Prima, when the people were denominated Regni, in conjunction with those of Hampshire. Woodcote, near Epsom, or Croydon, is supposed to have been a Roman station, the Novus Magus of Antoninus's Itinerary. At Walton-on-the-Hill Roman remains have been found. Under the Anglo-Saxon Heptarchy this county formed part of the kingdom of Southsex, and receives its present name of Surrey from the Saxon words Sud and Rey, the former signifying south, and the latter a river, indicating its situation on the south side of the river Thames. There are ancient encampments at Bottle Hill, Anstie Bury, Warlingham, Hascomb, Chelsham, Holmbury Hill, Ockley, Ladlands, Oatlands, and Walton-on-Thames; at the last Cæsar encamped previous to his crossing the Thames. Others are Bensbury, near Wimbledon, formed in 568, War Coppice Hill, Caterham, Beechworth Hill, Oldbury Hill near Chertsey, and one on the Common near Effingham. The Danes, after sacking London in the year 851, passed into this county, but were defeated at Ockley by Ethelwolf and his son Ethelbald: they are supposed to have been pursued to Fetcham, where, near the bottom of Hawkesworth Hill, many of them were killed. On this spot, at different times, many bones have been found; and upon Standard Hill, on the road from Leatherhead to Guildford, is a large tumulus, where bones also have been found. In the year 893 the Danes committed great depredations near Godalming, but at Farnham Alfred defeated them, and Edward the Elder was crowned at Kingston in the year 900. The castles of its earlier lords were at Guildford, Beechworth, Blechingley, Farnham, Horn, and Reigate. Esher Palace was an ancient seat of the Bishops of Winchester, and Lambeth Palace of the Bishops of Rochester and Archbishops of Canterbury, Primates of all England. Sheen, afterwards called Richmond, was a palace of the early sovereigns of the kingdom. There were formerly abbeys at Bermondsey, Chertsey, and Waverley; and priories at Merton, Newark near Ripley, Reigate, Sheen, St. Mary Overies, Tandridge, and Tooting. This county contains one county-town, Guildford, fourteen market-towns,

one hundred and forty parishes, 64,790 houses, and 398,658 inhabitants, and returns fourteen members to Parliament, viz. two for Southwark; two for Blechingley; two for Gatton; two for Reigate; two for Guildford; two for Haslemere; and two for the county, who at present are William Joseph Dennison, Esq. of Denbies, near Dorking, and John Ivatt Briscoe, of Botleys, near Chertsey. Surrey is in general a most delightful county, various parts of it being beautifully diversified with hills, valleys, and woods. In the middle of the county is an irregular ridge of hills extending from east to west; this is chiefly composed of chalk, but intermixed with sandy heaths and open downs. The northern part of the county, which is skirted by the Thames, is remarkable for the fertility of its meadows, for the excellence of its cultivation, and for the number of elegant mansions. The northwestern side is occupied by Bagshot Heath; the south-western angle of the county is noted for growing some of the finest hops in the kingdom; the south side is well watered and finely varied with wood, arable, and pasture; and the south-east side is a rough woody district, called Holmsdale, extending into the county of Kent. The principal eminences of this county are the Addington Hills, near Croydon; Albury Hill, near Guildford, whence the whole extent of the Weald, clothed with wood, appears, with an occasional glimpse of the sea through the breaks of the Sussex Downs, which form the background; Anstie Bury; Bagshot Heath; Banstead Downs,—the prospect hence is singularly diversified and pleasing; Blechingley Hill, on which the castle formerly stood, commanding an extensive view of Holmsdale in every direction; Botley Hill; Box Hill,—whence is a view of Sussex and great part of Middlesex; Dorking Hills,—the prospect here is unparalleled by that of any inland county in the kingdom; the road from Guildford to Farnham, particularly the first five miles of it; Hascomb Hill, commanding extensive views on every side; Headley Heath; Hind Head Hill; Katherine Hill near Guildford; Leith Hill, the highest ground in the county, and commanding a most extensive prospect; Norbury Park, Nunhead Hill; near London, with a fine view of the metropolis; Old Bury, or St. Anne's Hill, with a very extensive prospect; Richmond Hill; Tilbuster Hill, near Godstone; and Woodmansterne, the highest ground in the county, excepting Leith Hill. The rivers of Surrey are the Lodden, the Mole, the Thames, the Wandle, and the Wey. The Thames, forming the northern boundary to this county, first reaches it at Lion's Green on the north-west, and flowing past

Chertsey, continues its course to Kingston, Richmond, and Kew, and takes a serpentine course to Mortlake, Putney, Wandsworth, Battersea, Southwark, and Rotherhithe, where it leaves the county. The river Wey rises at Hartley, below Alton, in Hampshire, and enters this county about two miles below Farnham, whence it flows to Godalming, Guildford, and Weybridge, near which it falls into the Thames. The Wandle rises near Croydon, and passes Beddington, Carshalton, Mitcham, Merton, and Wandsworth, where it falls into the Thames. The Mole rises on the borders of Sussex, and passing Dorking, Leatherhead, and Cobham, also falls into the Thames. The canals intersecting this county are the Basingstoke, the Surrey, and the Croydon and Rotherhithe. The Surrey canal passes from Rotherhithe to Deptford, and unites with the Croydon canal, which passes Camberwell, Walworth, Lambeth, Kennington, Stockwell, Clapham, Balham, Streatham, Tooting, and Mitcham, to Croydon. Surrey, from its vicinity to the metropolis, and from the convenience of its streams for water-carriage, has numerous manufactures established in it. The course of the river Wandle from Croydon to the Thames, which is not more than ten miles in extent, supplies a great number of flour, paper, snuff, and oil mills; also mills for preparing leather and parchment, and for grinding logwood, besides affording excellent water and convenient grounds on its banks for large calico and printing works; the last are principally in the parishes of Croydon and Mitcham. The flour-mills at Merton are supposed to be amongst the largest and most complete in England, having been erected and supplied with water at a great expense. The river Mole, besides several flour-mills, turns the iron-mills near Cobham, and the flatting-mills at Ember Court. There are many paper-mills on the several branches of the Wey. A very extensive iron-work is carried on at Garrat Lane, in the immediate vicinity of the Wandle. At Godalming are some manufactories for weaving stockings, combing wool, and making worsted, blankets, sails, and collar cloths. There are several distilleries in Surrey, in the neighbourhood of London, on a very extensive scale, particularly at Battersea and Lambeth: at the last-mentioned place are manufactories of patent shot. Numerous manufactures, also, are carried on in the Borough of Southwark, and in the immediate vicinity of the metropolis.—Nork House, near Epsom, is the seat of Lord Arden, Lord Lieutenant of the County.

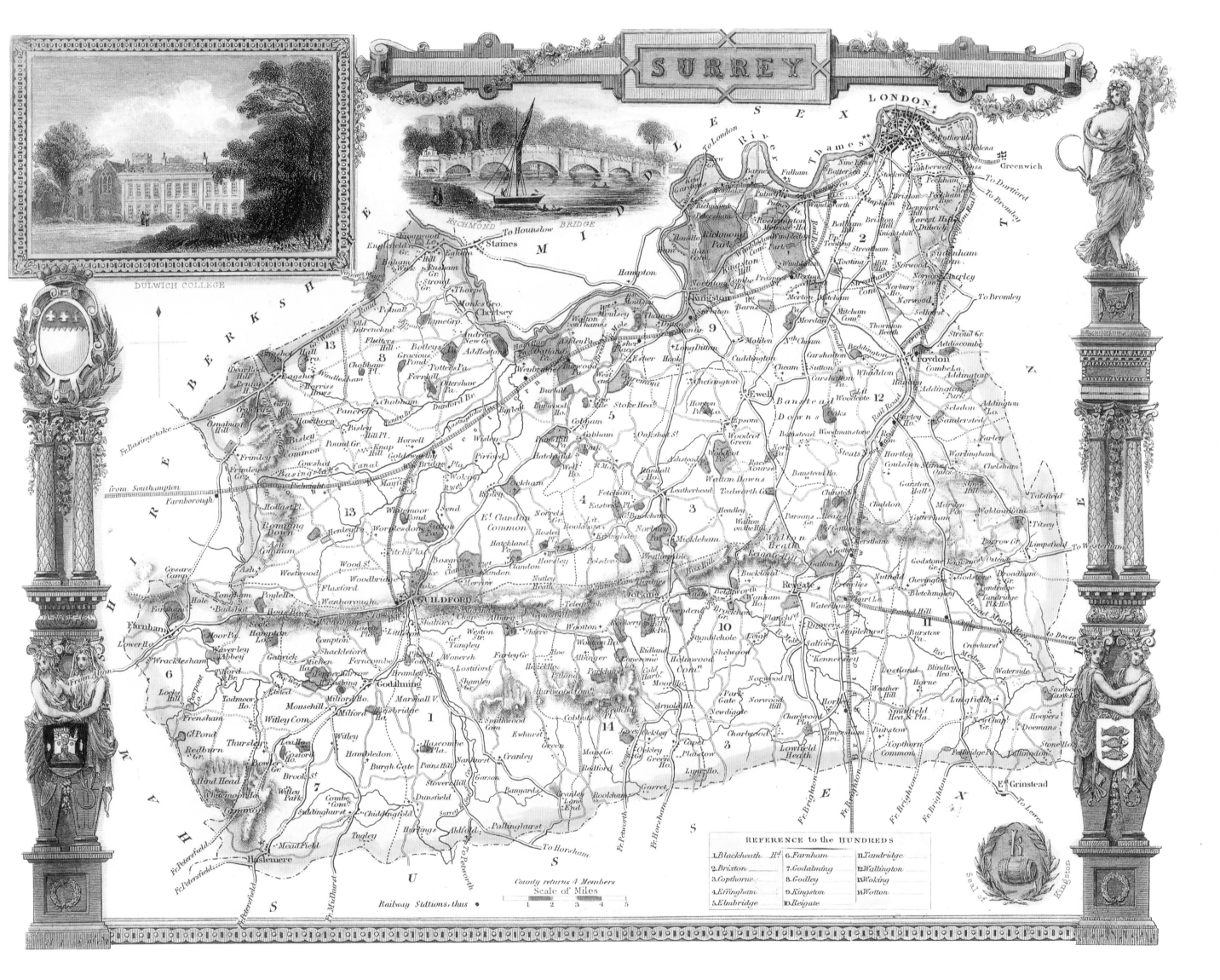

SURREY

DULWICH COLLEGE

RICHMOND BRIDGE

County returns 4 Members
Scale of Miles
1 2 3 4 5

Railway Stations, thus •

Seal of Kingston

SUSSEX

THIS county is bounded on the north by Surrey; on the north-east by Kent; on the south by the English Channel; and on the west by Hampshire. It is about seventy-six miles in length, and twenty miles in breadth. The Romans gave the name of Regni to the inhabitants, and Chichester was the Roman station Regnum. Roman remains have been found at Eastbourne, Pevensey, and Rye. Under the Anglo-Saxon Heptarchy it formed the kingdom of Southsex, whence evidently its present name originated. In the year 803, Egbert King of Wessex, or the West-Saxons, united it to his dominions, and a few years after was crowned King of England at Winchester. The castles of the early lords of Sussex were at Pevensey, Arundel, Amberley, Bramber, Hastings, Hurstmonceux, Lewes, Winchilsea, and Bodiham. Mayfield was a palace of the Archbishops of Canterbury; and other noble mansions were at Halnaker, Petworth, Stanstead, Cowdry, Laughton, and Brede. There were formerly abbeys at Battle, Bayham, Durford, and Robertsbridge; and priories at Boxgrove, Eastbourne, Hastings, Lymister, Lewes, Michelham, Pynham, Rusper, Sele, Shelbred, Steyning, Tortington, Wilmington, and Winchilsea. This county is in the diocese of Chichester and province of Canterbury, contains one city (Chichester), eighteen market-towns, 342 parishes, 36,283 houses, and 233,019 inhabitants. It sends twenty-eight members to Parliament, viz. two for each of the following boroughs: Chichester, Midhurst, Arundel, Horsham, Steyning, Bramber, Shoreham, East Grinstead, Lewes, Seaford, Hastings, Winchilsea, and Rye, and two for the county; the present members are Lord J. G. Lennox, and H. Barrett Curteis, Esq. The surface of this county is varied by several considerable hills, commencing on the borders of Hampshire on the north-west, and extending to Beachey Head on the south-east. That part running from Lewes to the sea is distinguished by the name of the South Downs, and is noted for feeding sheep, celebrated for the fineness of their wool and the goodness of their mutton. The north-western part of this ridge is composed of gritstone and lime-stone, and

abounds in iron ore, for the smelting of which this county was formerly famed. The northern and middle part of the county is woodland. Sussex is celebrated for the growth of its timber, principally oak; no other county can equal it in this respect, either in quantity or quality: it overspreads the Weald in every direction, where it flourishes with a great degree of luxuriance. The abundance of timber in this county, combined with the singular custom of planting shaws, has rendered it one of the most thickly inclosed parts of the kingdom; and if Sussex is viewed from the highlands, it appears an uninterrupted woodland. The shaws consist of tall screens of underwood and forest, around many of the fields, some of which are so wood-locked that it is surprising corn ever ripens. The rivers of Sussex are the Arun, the Adur, the Ouse, the Rother, the Lavant, the Cuckmere, the Ashbourn, the Brede, and the Asten, all of which are confined within the limits of the county. The Arun rises in St. Leonard's Forest, near Horsham, and flowing southward to Stopham, it penetrates a hollow of the South Downs to Arundel, and falls into the English Channel at Little Hampton. The Rother, a branch of the Arun, rises on the borders of Hampshire, passes Midhurst, Rotherbridge, and Stopham. In the Arun are caught quantities of mullets, which in the

season come up from the sea as far as Arundel, and feed upon a particular weed, which gives them a fine flavour:—this river is likewise famous for trout and eels. The Adur rises also in St. Leonard's Forest, and descends southward by Steyning and Bramber to New Shoreham on the coast. The Ouse rises in two springs, the higher in St. Leonard's Forest, and the lower at Selsfield, on the borders of the forest of Worth; a confluence takes place a few miles north of Lindfield. Pursuing its course south-eastward, the Ouse nearly half encircles Sheffield Park; thence it passes Isfield, Barcombe, and Hamsey, and winding round the sloping headland opposite Landport, enters Lewes levels northward of the town: after separating the cliff from Lewes, it proceeds through the marshy levels southward, and receiving several tributary streams forms the harbour of New Haven. The Rother rises near Mayfield, in a very hilly, cultivated, and thickly-wooded country, fed also in its course by various streams, from valleys similar to that which it forms : it nowhere approaches the Downs, but following a south-easterly direction till it emerges from its hills, sinks into a sandy level, and turns southward, to make a great basin eastward of the port of Rye, at the extremity of the county. The Brede, from some pleasant valleys beyond Battle, joins the Rother below Winchilsea, which is now to its exit, surrounded by a fen from the high grounds of Sussex to Romney Marsh, in Kent. The Cuckmere, rising near the foot of Crowborough Hill, passes in its course Heathfield, Warbleton, Hellingly, Arlington, Michelham; and winding through the vale of Alfreston, empties itself into the ocean below Excett Bridge, eastward of Seaford. The manufactures of this county chiefly consist of iron, charcoal, gunpowder, and paper. The iron-stone generally pervades, but its manufacture is on the decay. Charcoal is an object of importance; large quantities are sent hence to London. Gunpowder is manufactured at Battle and paper at Iping, Duncton, and other places. Potash is made at Bucksill Hill.—Petworth House is the seat of the Earl of Egremont, Lord Lieutenant of the County.

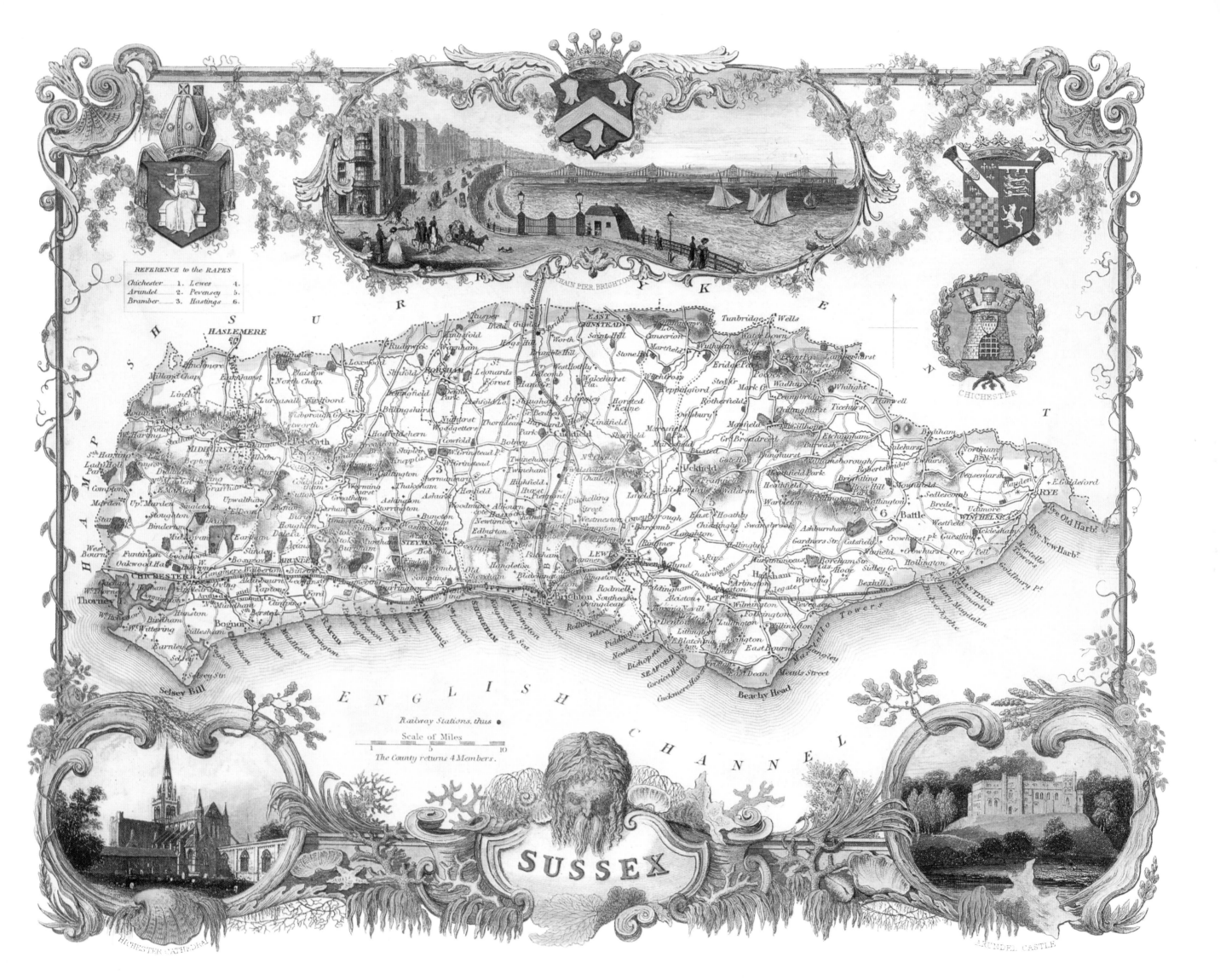

REFERENCE to the RAPES

Chichester 1.   Lewes   4.
Arundel   2.   Pevensey   5.
Bramber   3.   Hastings   6.

CHAIN PIER, BRIGHTON.

CHICHESTER

HAMPSHIRE

SURREY

KENT

HASLEMERE

HORSHAM

EAST GRINSTEAD

Tunbridge Wells

MIDHURST

PETWORTH

STEYNING

LEWES

UCKFIELD

Battle

RYE

WINCHELSEA

HASTINGS

CHICHESTER

ARUNDEL

Bognor

Brighton

Worthing

SEAFORD

Selsey Bill

Beachy Head

EASTBOURNE

ENGLISH CHANNEL

Railway Stations, thus   ●

Scale of Miles
1   5   10

The County returns 4 Members.

SUSSEX

CHICHESTER CATHEDRAL.

ARUNDEL CASTLE.

WARWICKSHIRE

This county is bounded on the north by Staffordshire and Leicestershire; on the east by Northamptonshire and Oxfordshire; on the south by Oxfordshire and Gloucestershire; and on the west by Worcestershire. The greatest length is about fifty miles, the breadth thirty-four miles, and the circumference about one hundred and sixty miles. The inhabitants were the Cornavii and Wigantes, and it formed a part of the province Britannia Secunda. During the Saxon Heptarchy Warwickshire was included in the kingdom of Mercia. The Roman stations are supposed to have been Alauna, Alcester; Benonæ, High Cross; Chesterton Manduessedum, Manceter; Præsidium, Warwick; and encampments are found at Brinklow, Chesterton, Edge Hill, Ratley, and Oldbury. At Welcombe Hills are earthworks presumed to be Saxon. The castles of its early lords were at Allesley, Astley, Baginton, Beaudesert, Birmingham, Brandon, Brinklow, Coleshill, Coventry, Hartshill, Kenilworth, Kineton, Maxstoke, Rugby, Studley, and Warwick. There were abbeys at Combe, Coventry, Merevale, and Stoneley; the priories were those of Alcester, Birmingham, Coventry, Erdbury, Kenilworth, Maxstoke, Monk's Kirby, Shortley, Studley, Thellesford, Warmington, Warwick, Wolston, and VVootton Waven; with nunneries at Coventry, Henwood, Nuneaton, Pinley, Polesworth, and Wroxall. This county contains one city (Coventry), one county-town, fourteen market-towns, one hundred and fifty-eight parishes, 55,082 houses, and 274,392 inhabitants. It is in the province of Canterbury, and in the dioceses of Lichfield and Coventry, and Worcester. Warwickshire returns six members to Parliament; two for Coventry, two for Warwick, and two for the county,— the present members for the county being Francis Lawley, Esq., and Sir Gray Skipwith, Bart. It is divided into two irregular and unequal portions by the river Avon; the south or smaller portion, called Heldon being

a champaign country of great fertility; and the north, called the Woodland, is generally highly cultivated, but interspersed with wild heaths and moors: a large part of it still bears the name of the Forest of Arden. Warwickshire is principally a feeding and dairy county: in the strong land a considerable quantity of flax is grown, and manufactured in the county. There are also large woods, and much timber of all kinds, especially oak, in that part which constituted the ancient Forest of Arden. The air is mild, pleasant and healthy. The mineral productions are freestone, limestone, marl, coal, ironstone, blue flagstone, and blue clay. The rivers are the Alne, Anker, Arrow, Avon, Blythe, Cole, Leam, Rea, Stour and the Tame. The Avon, rising near Naseby in Northamptonshire, adds great beauty to the delightful territory of Warwick Castle, as it flows beneath the cliff on which the lofty towers are situated. It then glides through a charming country to the celebrated Stratford-on-Avon, the birthplace of our immortal bard; thence it traverses the great level of Worcestershire by Evesham, having received the lesser Stour at Stratford, and turning to the south at Pershore falls into the Severn at Tewkesbury. The lakes of Warwickshire are those of Compton Verney and Hewell. The canals are the Ashby de la Zouch, the Avon (made navigable for vessels of forty tons as early as 1637), Bilston, Birmingham, Birmingham and Fazely, Coventry, Oxford and Coventry, Grand Trunk, Stratford, Warwick and Birmingham, Warwick and Napton and the Worcester and Birmingham. The manufactures are hardware, watches, horn-combs, worsted, calico and cottons, needles, flax, linen yarn, ribbons, cutlery, toys, guns, swords, brassfoundery, iron, hats, buttons, buckles, and leather. Warwick Castle is the seat of the Earl of Warwick, Lord Lieutenant of the County.

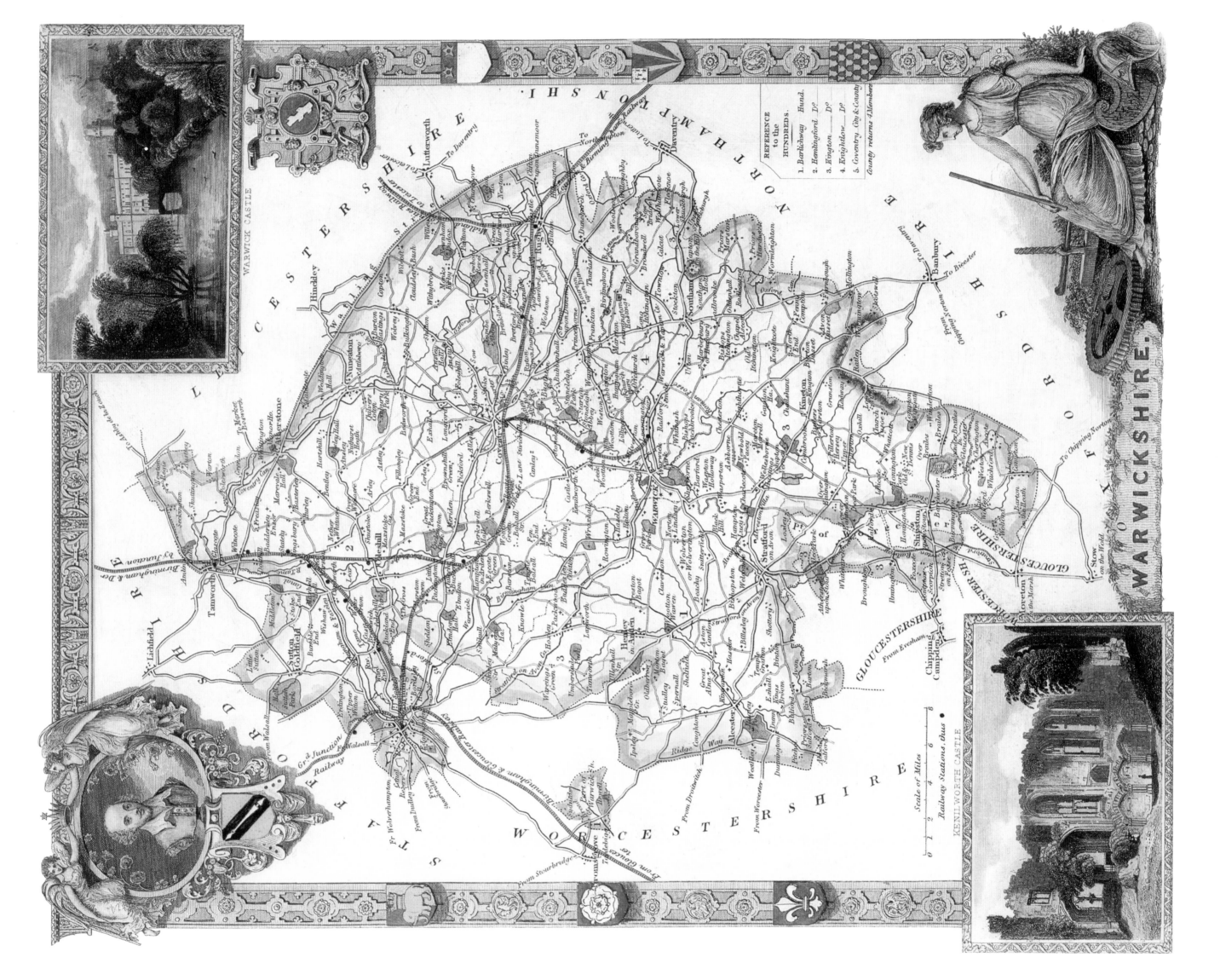

WARWICKSHIRE.

WARWICK CASTLE

KENILWORTH CASTLE

REFERENCE to the HUNDREDS.
1. Barlichway   Hund.
2. Hemlingford   D°
3. Kington   D°
4. Knightlow   D°
5. Coventry, City & County
County returns 4 Members

Scale of Miles
Railway Stations, thus •

LEICESTERSHIRE

NORTHAMPTONSHIRE

OXFORDSHIRE

GLOUCESTERSHIRE

WORCESTERSHIRE

STAFFORDSHIRE

WESTMORELAND

This county is bounded on the north by Cumberland, on the east by Yorkshire, on the south by Lancashire, and on the west by Northumberland and Cumberland. It is about forty miles in length, from sixteen to twenty-five in breadth, and in circumference it is about one hundred and thirty miles. Westmorland received its name from its westerly situation, and from the principal part having been a hilly barren district. Its British inhabitants were termed Brigantes, Voluntii, and Sistuntii, by the Romans, under whom it was made part of the province of Maxima Cæsariensis. The principal Roman stations within this county were Alone, Ambleside; Brovonacis, Brough; Brovacum, Brougham; Concangium, Natland; Gallacum, Kendal; and Voreda, Whelp Castle. There are evident remains of Roman encampments at Castle Hows, Borrowdale, Castle Steads, and Coney Beds, which last were exploratory camps to Water Crook, where it is supposed was a station. There are several encampments between Crackenthorp and Cross Fell; also at Hader Wain, Maiden Castle, and Sandford, besides a Roman temple at Levens. There are traces of two Roman military ways in this county, in one of which several antiquities have been found. It takes a south-easterly direction from Carlisle to Penrith, near which town it crossed the river Eamont into Westmorland, and, still taking the same direction, through Appleby, enters Yorkshire at Rere Cross, north-eastward of Brough under Stainmoor. The other Roman road, called the Maiden way, enters the north-eastern part of this county at Rere Cross, and thence passes to Maiden Castle, supposed to have been built by the Romans. It afterwards leads to Brough, and over Brough Fair hill, passes Sandford moor, to Coupland Beck brigg; hence the road passes to Appleby, and to the camps on Crackenthorp moor; then by Kirby Thore, through Sowerby, and takes its course by Winfell Park, to Hart Hall Tree; and hence directly westward to the Countesses Pillar and Brougham Castle, over Lowther Bridge, into the county of Cumberland.

The castles of the early lords of Westmorland were Brougham, Brough, Green castle, Kendal, Hartley, Howgill, Peel castle, Pendragon castle, Appleby, Buley, Amside Tower, Levens, Sizergh, Crakenthorp, &c. There was formerly an abbey at Shap, and priories at Appleby, Brough, and Kendal.

The county of Westmorland contains 10 market-towns, 32 parishes, 9243 houses, and 51,359 inhabitants, and, according to the Reform Bill of 1832, returns three members to parliament,— one for the town of Kendal, and two for the county; the present members for the county are the Hon. Lieut.- Col. Henry Cecil Lowther, and Right Hon. William Viscount Lowther, of Whitehaven castle.

This county is divided into two unequal portions, the baronies of Westmorland and Kendal; the former, although abounding with hills and general unequalities of surface, is comparatively an open country. The latter is extremely mountainous, containing numerous fells, or bleak barren hills. Scarcely a fourth part of the whole county is under cultivation, which is chiefly applied to the growth of oats, the proportion of wheat or barley being very small. The valleys in which the rivers run are tolerably fertile, and in the north-eastern quarter is a considerable tract of cultivated land. The rest of the county consists of narrow glens of fertility, amidst dreary hills, and extended wastes. In the valleys a great quantity of butter is made, for the London market. On the hills large flocks of sheep, and herds of black cattle, are grazed, and sent into the neighbouring counties; and on the moors great numbers of geese are bred, and sent to distant markets. The mountains are stored with prodigious numbers of grouse.

The rivers of this county are the Barrow, the Betha or Bela, the Eamont, the Eden, the Helle Beck, the Hunna, the Kent, the Lowther, the Lune or Len, the Lyvennate, the Mint, the Rothay, the Sled, the Sprint, the Tees, and the Winster, a boundary between Westmorland and Lancashire. The lakes are Ais Water, Angle Tarn, Broad Water, Elter Water, Gras Mere, Grisedale Tarn, Hawes Water, Kent Mere, Keppel Cove Tarn, Red Tarn, Rydal Water, Skeggles Water, Small Water, Sunbiggin Tarn, Ulls Water, Wastdale Beck, Winfell Tarn, and Winder Mere. The Wigan and Kendal canal is the only navigation in Westmorland. Lowther castle is the seat of the Earl of Lonsdale, K.G. Lord Lieutenant of the County.

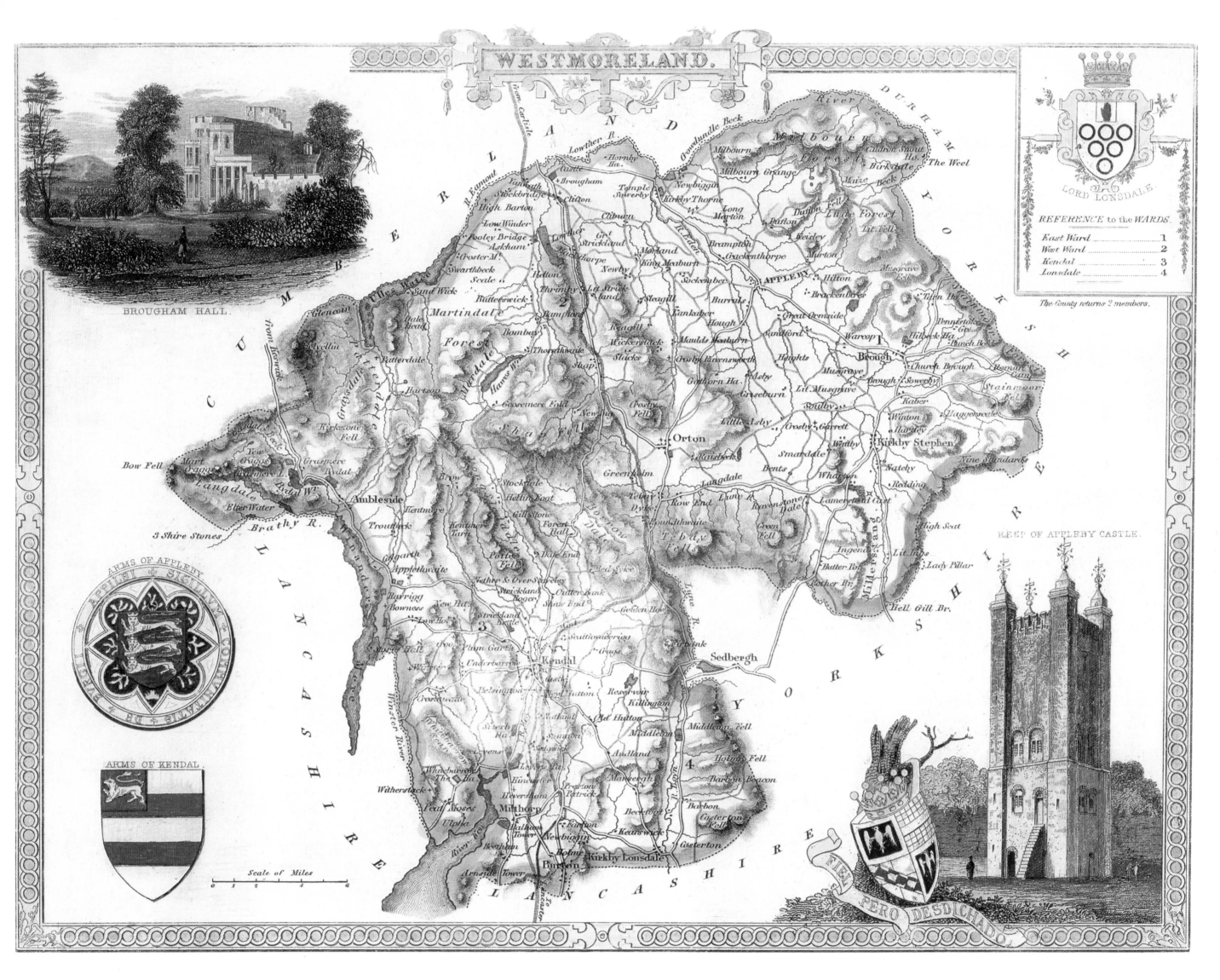

WESTMORELAND.

BROUGHAM HALL.

LORD LONSDALE

REFERENCE to the WARDS.

East Ward 1
West Ward 2
Kendal 3
Lonsdale 4

The County returns 2 members.

ARMS OF APPLEBY

ARMS OF KENDAL

Scale of Miles

KEEP OF APPLEBY CASTLE.

FIEL PERO DESDICHADO

CUMBERLAND

DURHAM

YORKSHIRE

LANCASHIRE

ISLE OF WIGHT

The Isle of Wight is situated in the English Channel, and is separated from the coast of Hampshire by a strait, formerly styled the Solent, and more recently the Sound, or the Western Channel. The island is about seven miles in breadth at the eastern side, and also in other parts, excepting at the western extremity; where it is scarcely more than a mile across. It is divided into the Liberties of East and West Medina or *Medham,* so called from a river which runs across the island, from south to north, separating it into two nearly equal portions, and falling into the sea at Cowes. The surface of the country is agreeably diversified, and the soil is fertile: the downs, extending across the island from Bembridge to the Needles, through the centre, afford good pasturage for sheep; cows for the dairy are kept in the lower grounds. The cliffs on the western coast are the esort of a multitude of sea fowl, as gulls, puffins, cormorants, razor bills, and Cornish choughs, and also of wild pigeons and starlings. Various kinds of timber trees are found throughout the island, though the woods have been greatly thinned for the supply of the Royal Dockyards at Portsmouth. At the western side of the island are those remarkable rocks called the Needles. Fish of various kinds are caught in the surrounding seas, especially crabs, lobsters, shrimps, and prawns, which are large and of an excellent quality; samphire grows in abundance on the cliffs and rocks, and is collected for sale.

The ancient lords of the island, by grant of King Henry I., had their own courts of judicature, and the right of nomination to all offices requisite for the peace of the island, and the return of all the King's writs. The tenants held their lands as of the Castle of Carisbrook, and were bound to assist in its defence at their own charges, for the space of forty days: they were bound also to attend there on the owners coming to the island, and on his quitting it, as well as in various other services. One remnant of feudal times is the Knighten or *Knight's* Court, kept by the captain's steward of the island, in the town-hall of Newport, on Monday, every three weeks. Its jurisdiction extends through the whole island, the corporation of Newport excepted; and it takes cognizance of all actions of debt and trespasses under the value of forty shillings; the actions are adjudged by the court without jury, and the judges are freeholders who hold of his Majesty's Castle of Carisbrook. From the time that the island passed out of the hands of its feudal proprietors, in consequence of a purchase made by King Edward I. from Isabella de Fortibus, Countess of Albemarle, it has been governed by wardens or captains appointed by the crown; these titles have been changed to that of governor. The present governor is the Earl of Malmsbury, who resides at Heron Court, near Ringwood.

In the year 1445, the titular dignity of King of the Isle of Wight was conferred, by Henry VI., on Henry Beauchamp, Duke of Warwick. A representation of the Duke, as King of the Island, with a crown on his head, and a sceptre before, him, was painted in glass, for one of the windows of the church of Warwick. Antony Widvile, Earl Rivers also bore the title of Lord of the Isle of Wight, having received from King Edward IV. a grant of the island and castle, with other rights belonging to the lordship. The original appellation of the island, was Ictis, and it was afterwards called Vectis, by the Romans, both which names are supposed to be derived from the British Guith, signifying separated.

ISLE OF WIGHT

REFERENCE.

West Medina _____ 1
East D° _____ 2

The County returns 1 member:

Portsmouth Harbour

GOSPORT   PORTSEA   PORTS-MOUTH

Haslar Hospital   S. Sea Castle

LYMINGTON

THE SOLENT

SPITHEAD

Beaulieu River   Calshot Castle   Southampton Water   to Southampton 15 Miles

Gurnet Bay   W. Cowes   Norris Castle   Mother Bank
Thorney Bay   Gurnet E.   East Cowes   Osborne House   Kings Quay
Rew Street   Cockleton   Barton F.   Wood Ho.   Binstead   RYDE
Nodes F.   Whippingham   Whippingham Street   Wootton Br.   Quarr Abbey   Ryde Ho.   Appley
Halfway Ho.   Medina River   Wootton   Wootton Creek   Kite Hill   Stone Pits F.   Sea View   Nettlestone Pt.
E. Hampstead   Northwood   Palmers   Fern Hill   Ninham   St. Johns   Old Fort
Norris Cross   White Ho.   Marks Corner   Scots   Medina   Claybrook   Haven Street   Aldermoor   Small Brook   W. Brook   Nettlestone Green   Priory
W. Hampstead   Lambsleas F.   Gate   W.   Mill   Gt.   Black Br.   Whitefield F.   Park F.   Watch House Pt.
Cranmore Farm   Parkhurst   Prior Ho.   Bridlesford   Lynn F.   Gatehouse F.   St. Helens
Newtown   Signal Seat   New Kairles   Staplers Heath   Chillingwood   St. Helens Green   Sea Mark
Shalfleet   Vields F.   Barracks   Forest   Alvington   2   Bembridge Pt.
Wellow   Street Place   Gt. Watchingwell   Carisbrook   NEWPORT Wilt.   Brading Har.   Foreland
Fullholding F.   Swainstone Lit. Park   Vills   Slade Br.   Combley   Ashey F.   Ashey   Bembri Farm   Knowles
Tapnel   Apes Down   Casile   Whitcomb   Durton F.   Ashey Down   Little Stand   White Cliff Bay
Calbourn   Goldens   Plash   Birchfield   Arreton   Knighton   Brading Down   Brading
Lynch   Bowcomb   Marwell   Black-water   Arreton Str.   Grove   Yar Br.   Long Land   Culver Cliff
Idlecomb   Sandway   Gatcomb   Skinner's   Howringford   Newchurch   Adgeston   Martin   Sandown Bay
Roughboro   Pidford   Gt. Birchmore   Merston   Wackland   Lee F.   Winford   Fort Barracks
Cheverton   Gatcomb   Chillerton Street   Reckley   Pangham   Hele F.   Spicers   Black Pan   Cheverton
N. Court   Chillerton Down   Yard   G. Budbridge   Brenson   Lake
Shorwell   Chillerton Farm   Sandford   Wingham   Batchelors   Shanklin
Brixton   Hill   Rossland   Black Down   Godshill   Hide   Shanklin Chine
W. Court   Sandy Way   River Medina   Winson   Dunnose
Lamerston   Dagwich   Appuldur Comb House   Appuldcomb   Shanklin Down   Luccomb Chine
Yaford   Kingston   Billinghurst House   Blake Down   Berry F.   Sheepwash   Whitehall   Chine Head
L. Atherfield   Appleford F.   Strood Gr.   Span F.   Litcomb   Bonchurch
Sutton   Atherfield Green   Black Down   Rew F.   Ventnor
Ship Ledge   Hermitage   Stenbury F.   Nettlecomb   Bontnor Down   St. Lawrence
Barnes Chine   Chale   Weeks F.   Old Park   Woolverton
Brixton Bay   Holbrooks   Bog F.   Boniface   Sea Cottages
Cowleaze Chine   Bare Lea   Whitwell   Sloane Hill   Mirables   U
Atherfield Rocks   Niton   Puckaster Cove
White Chine   Walpen   Barrack   Tenvnor Cove   Sheep Bull Cove
Chale Bay   Watherstone   Beacon   Blacknang Chine   St. Catherines   Light Ho.   Knowle   Rocken End   Buckaster Cove

Scale of Miles.
1 2 3 4 5 6

CARISBROOKE CASTLE

WILTSHIRE

THIS county is bounded on the north by Gloucestershire, on the east by Berkshire and Hampshire, on the south by Dorsetshire, and on the west by Somersetshire; in length it is fifty-four miles from north to south, thirty from east to west, and in circumference it is one hundred and fifty miles. In early times this part of the country was inhabited by the Belgæ, and there are British earthworks at Southley Wood, near Heytesbury, Bokerly Ditch, Elder Valley, Grymsditch, Hamshill Ditches, Wansdyke and Sutton Common; at Avebury, Brome, near Swindon, and Stonehenge, are British remains; and there are Cromlechs at Clatford Bottom, Littleton Drew, and Rockley. The British encampments are at Bratton, Knook, Whitestreet Hill, and Yarnbury. Under the Romans, Wiltshire was included in the province of Britannia Prima, and within its boundaries were some important stations, Cunetio, Folly Farm, near Marlborough, Mutuantonis, Easton Grey, Sorbiodunum, Old Sarum, and Verlucio, near Wanstown; there are Roman encampments at Amesbury, Badbury, Bagdon, Barbury, Battlesbury, Beacon Hill, Bilbury Rings, Blunsden Hill, Broad Chalk, Casterley, Castle Rings, Chesbury, Chidbury, Chiselbury, Church Ditches, Clearbury Ring, Cotley Hill, Haydon, Martinsale, Newton Toney, Oldborough Castle, Old Castle, Roddenbury, Rolston, Round-away-Hill, Scratchbury Hill, Thirston, Warminster, Whichbury, Winkelbury, and Woodyates Inn. The castles of its ancient lords were at Calne, Castlecomb, Devizes, Downton, Farley, Lacock, Ludgershall, Malmesbury, Marlborough, Mere, Sarum, Stourton, Trowbridge, and Wardour. There were abbeys at Bradford, Kingswood, Malmesbury, and Stanleigh; priories at Avebury, Bradenstoke, Bradfield, Brioptune, Bromham, Great Charlton, Chissenbury, Clarendon, Clatford, Corsham, Ivy Church, Longleat, Maiden Bradley, Marlborough, Monkton Deverill, Monkton Farley, Poulton, Ramsbury, Stratton, Tisselbury, and Uphaven; besides the nunneries at Amesbury, Kington, Lacock, Malmesbury and Wilton.

Wiltshire contains one city,—25 market towns,—304 parishes,—41,702 houses,—and 222,157 inhabitants. It returns eighteen Members to Parliament: one for Calne, two for Chippenham, two for Cricklade, two for Devizes, one for Malmesbury, two for Marlborough, two for Salisbury, one for Wertbury, one for Wilton, and four for the county; who, at present, are Paul Methuen, Esq., of Corsham House, near Chippenham; and Walter Long, Esq., of Chalcot House, near Westbury, for the northern division; and John Benett, Esq., of Pyt House, near Salisbury, and the Honourable Sidney Herbert, for the southern division.

This county is divided into north and south Wiltshire, which are separated by the rivers Kennet and Lower Avon, and by the canal which unites them. North Wiltshire is a fertile district with an undulated surface, extending from the base of the Cotswold Hills to the borders of Salisbury Plain; this tract, formerly covered with forests, and now interspersed with woods, affords rich pasture for cattle kept for the dairy, and is famous for its produce of cheese. The greater part of south Wiltshire is included in Salisbury Plain. In this county, which is considerably elevated, several rivers have their rise; near the northern boundary some of the streams rise, which unite in forming the Thames; here also are the sources of the lower Avon, which unite at Marlborough, pass Chippenham and Melksham, and leave the county at Bath. The Kennet rising on Marlborough Downs, flows by Marlborough, Ramsbury, and Chilton, into Berkshire. The upper Avon has its source amongst the hills eastward of Devizes, and passing Uphaven and Amesbury to Salisbury, receives the united stream of the Wily and the Nadder, and afterwards the Bourne, passing Downton into Hampshire. The Wily rises at the foot of Clay Hill, near Warminster, and, passing Heytesbury and Wilton, joins the Nadder; the other rivers of the county of less note are the Brue, the Colne, the Deverill, the Marle, the Stour, and the Were.

The principal eminences of the county are Beacon Hill, near Amesbury, Bidcombe Hill, Box, Cheril Hill, Clay Hill, East Knoyle, Hermitage Hill at Codford, Topwood Hill, Stourhead, and Westbury Down. This county anciently contained the royal forests of Bradon, Blackmore or Melksham, Pewsham or Chippenham, Savernake, Pannshill, and Melshet, all which have either been disafforested or alienated from the crown. Savernake Forest, near Marlborough, about sixteen miles in circuit, is the only forest remaining in a state of woodland. Pannshill, or Clarendon Forest, near Salisbury, formerly the site of a royal palace, is now known as Clarendon Park; and Cranbourne Chase, partly in this county, is stripped of its feudal privileges. Verndtich Chase is in a state of cultivation; and Grovely Wood, near Wilton, is in the grounds of the Earl of Pembroke. A fine variety of free-stone, used for building, is found at Chilmark, Box, and other places. To John Anstie, of Devizes, who died in 1830, the woollen manufacture of this county, and the west of England generally, was indebted for its extension and subsequent prosperity, through the introduction of improved machinery; his ingenuity and knowledge of the varieties of wool first suggested its combination with silk, in the manufacture of fancy cloths, which he successfully introduced and finally perfected to the exclusion of foreign competition. As chairman of the wool committee, he furthered the objects and interests of that body by his enlarged views of the subject. Bow Wood, near Calne, is the seat of the Marquess of Lansdowne, the lord lieutenant of the County.

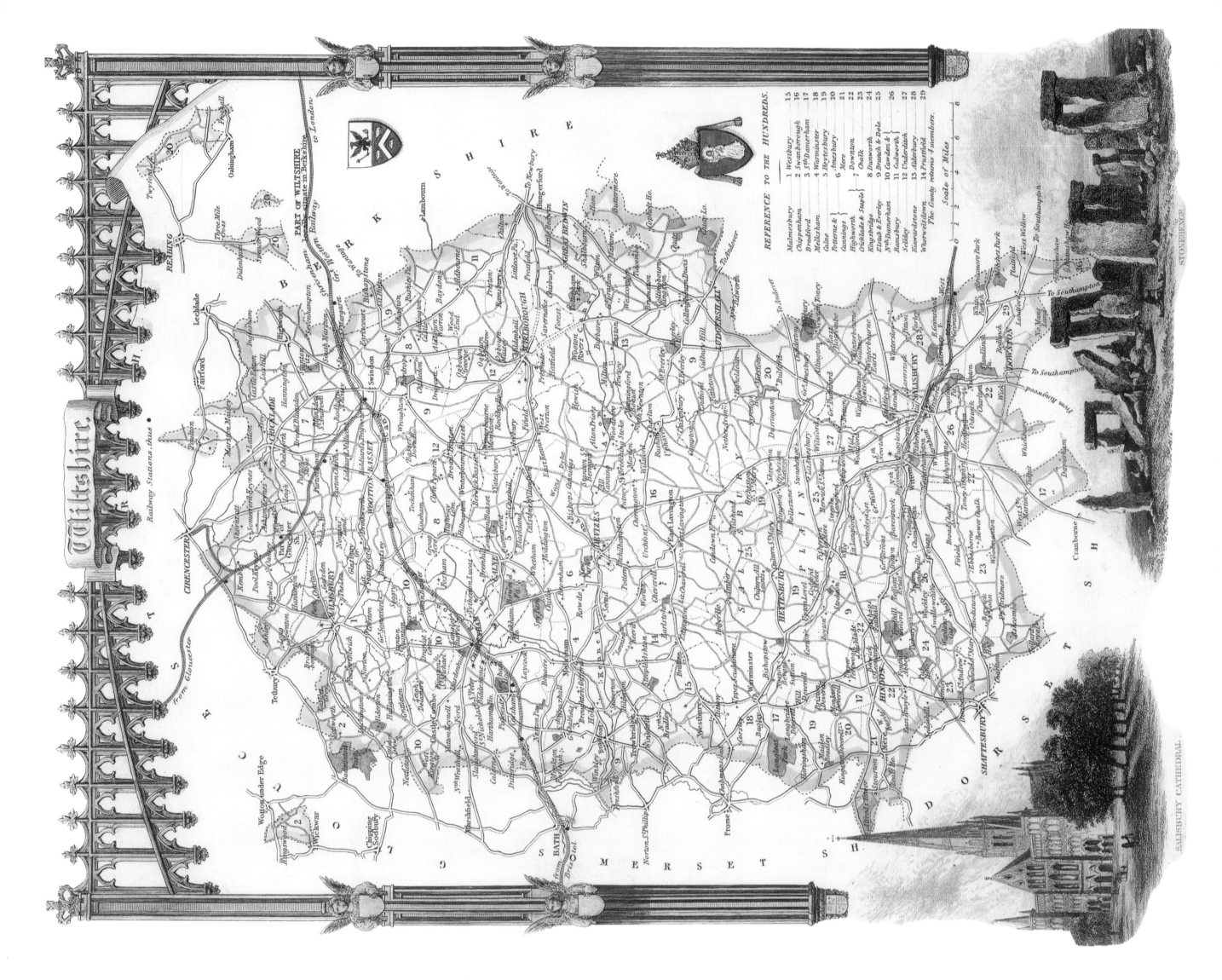

WORCESTERSHIRE

This county, which is towards the centre of the kingdom, is bounded on the north by Staffordshire and Shropshire; on the east by Warwickshire; on the south by Gloucestershire and on the west by Herefordshire and Shropshire. The greatest length is thirty-six miles, being twenty-six in breadth, and one hundred and thirty in circumference. It was included in the Roman province Flavia Cæsariensis, and was inhabited by the Cornavii or Dobuni. During the Saxon Heptarchy, Worcestershire formed a part of the kingdom of Mercia. There are encampments at Bredon, Kemsey, Malvern Hill, Wichbury Hill and Woodbury Hill, and there were formerly abbeys at Bordesley, Evesham, Pershore, and Worcester; also priories at Astley, Blockley, Bredon, Claines, Cokehill, Dodford, Kemsey, Little Malvern, Great Malvern, Wicton and Westwood. The castles of its earlier lords were at Bengworth, Castle-Morton, Elmley, Hagley, Hanley, Hartlebury, Holt, Caldwell, Weoly, and Worcester. The ancient forests were Feckenham, Ombersley, Horewell and Malvern. This county contains one city, Worcester, eleven market towns, one hundred and fifty-two parishes, 34,738 inhabited houses, and 184,424 inhabitants. It is in the province of Canterbury, and in the diocese of Worcester, excepting Tenbury, which is in the diocese of Hereford.

Worcestershire returns nine members to Parliament; two for Worcester, one for Bewdley, two for Droitwich, two for Evesham, and two for the county—the Honourable H.B. Lygon, brother of the Earl Beauchamp, and the Honourable T. Foley. The air is soft, warm and healthy, there being but few lakes and little boggy land; the soil south of Worcester is mostly a rich clay or marl; north of the city it is chiefly gravel or sand. The part of the Malvern Hills, which is distinguished from the Herefordshire range by the name of the Worcestershire Beacon, rises 1300 feet above the level of the plain. This range of hills appears to be one vast rock, principally of limestone towards the west, and quartz towards the east. A variety of springs rise in these hills, the most noted of which are the Malvern Wells, which have acquired a reputation for curing many disorders. The view from the summit of the hill is peculiarly extensive and delightful; and in the month of May, when the orchards in Herefordshire are in full blossom, presents one of the most enchanting landscapes in the kingdom. The Lickey Hills are on the north, the Bredon Hills on the south-east and the Abberley Hills on the north-west. The valleys of this county are particularly rich and fertile, and the productiveness of the Vale of Evesham is not exceeded by any tract in the kingdom. The rivers of Worcestershire are the Arrow, Upper Avon, Leden, Rea, Salwarpe, Severn, Stour and Teme. The Severn, famous for its salmon, rises in Plinlimmon Hill in Montgomeryshire, and enters this county a little above Bewdley. At Mitton it receives from the east the Stour, and pursuing a southern course it is further augmented by the Salwarpe; it then runs with a swift current through the city of Worcester, two miles below which it receives the river Teme; and after washing Stoke and Upton, enters Gloucestershire where it is joined by the Upper Avon, which rises in Northamptonshire, and traversing Warwickshire enters Worcestershire at Cleeve Prior, flows through Evesham, and having united with the Little Stour near the last town, turns to the south at Pershore and falls into the Severn at Tewksbury. The Teme rises in Radnorshire, enters this county above Tenbury, and falls into the Severn two miles below Worcester, after having watered a rich country particularly famous for its many hop grounds. The canals of Worcestershire are the Droitwich, Dudley, Leominster, Staffordshire, Stourport, and the Worcester and Birmingham. The chief manufactures are hardware, iron, china, and glass, carpets and worsted shag. Croome Park, near Pershore, is the seat of the Earl of Coventry, Lord Lieutenant of the County.

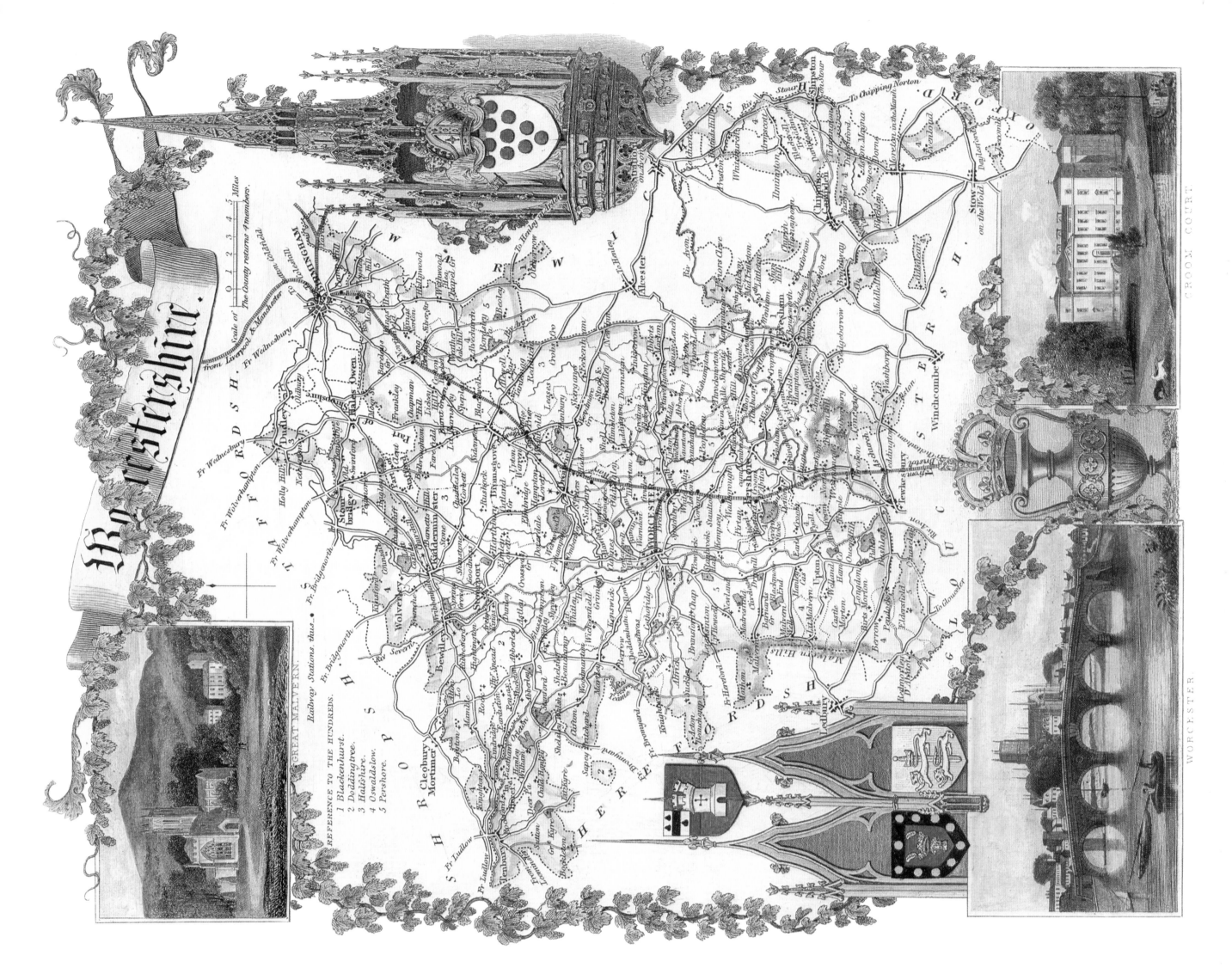

Worcestershire.

Scale of Miles
0 1 2 3 4 5

The County returns 4 members.

REFERENCE TO THE HUNDREDS.
1 Blackenhurst.
2 Doddingtree.
3 Halfshire.
4 Oswaldslow.
5 Pershore.

Railway Stations, thus _

GREAT MALVERN.

GROOM COURT.

WORCESTER.

YORKSHIRE

This county is bounded on the north by Westmorland and Durham, the border line being formed by the river Tees; on the east by the German Ocean; on the South by the river Humber, and the counties of Lincoln, Nottingham, Derby, and a small part of Chester; and on the west by Lancashire. It greatly exceeds in size every other county in the kingdom, its length from east to west being about one hundred miles, its breadth from north to south about eighty miles, and in circumference it is about three hundred and twenty.

Yorkshire was part of the country of the Brigantes, which extended over a wide tract, and under the Romans formed a part of the province named Maxima Cæsariensis. The Roman stations of most note were Eboracum, York; Catarraton, Catteric; Lataræ, Bowes; Olicana, Ilkley; Isurium, Aldborough; Cambodunum, Slack; Calcaria, Tadcaster; Præturium, near Flamborough Head; Legiolum, at Castleford, near Pontefract; and Ad Danum at Doncaster.

This county formed part of the kingdom of Deira, under the Anglo Saxons; was united with Bernicia, in the name of Northumbria, and formed a province under an Earl, who resided at York. The county of York from its extent and variety of surface may be considered as an epitome of the whole kingdom, in its soil, products, and aspect. The three great divisions or Ridings, are named from their relative situation— East, North, and West Riding; the Ainstey of York, situated between the three ridings may be regarded as constituting a fourth division. It is separated from the North Riding by the rivers Nid and Ouse, from the East Riding by the Ouse, and from the West Riding principally by the river Wharfe. The Ainstey was formerly a Forest, and corresponds with the other parts of the vale of York in its scenery.

The natural disposition of the rivers of this county is peculiar and interesting; they generally rise on the mountainous borders, and uniting as their streams flow towards the centre, terminate in the estuary of the Humber. The most important of these rivers are the Ouse, the Swale, the Ure, the Wharfe, the Derwent, the A(i)re, the Calder, the Don, and the Rother, besides the Tees which skirts the northern boundary of the county, and the Ribble a river of Lancashire, which has its source in the western hills of this county. The climate varies in different parts, mists being very frequent in the marshy level districts, while the heights are cold, and the air is frequently disturbed by tempests. Yorkshire has long been noted for the excellence of its breed of horses, especially those of the North and East Ridings; coach, and saddle horses, are generally sold at the fairs of Beverley, Malton, York, and Howden, and distributed to different parts of the kingdom, and even sent to the continent. For size and beauty the Yorkshire horses are superior to those of every other part of the world, and are capable of performing what no others ever could. By a judicious mixture of the several kinds, and the superior skill of management, they are known to excel the Arabians in size and swiftness; to be more durable than the Barb, and more hardy than the Persian steeds. The West Riding is famous for the Craven breed of long-horned cattle and the Tees-water breed, are well known under the name of Holderness cattle. The Penistone breed of sheep is supposed to be indigenous.

Within the county were formerly the Royal forests of Galtries, Hardwick, Arkelgarthdale, Knaresborough, Pickering, Wharfedale, Swynden, Okeden, Harlow, Fullwith, Coverdale, and the Chase of Hatfield, all which have been alienated from the crown and disafforested.

The sea coast from Scarborough nearly to the mouth of the Tees, is bold and rocky, the cliffs rising from sixty to one hundred and fifty-feet, and at Stoupe Brow, southward of Whitby, the height is not less than eight hundred and ninety feet. The surface of the county generally rises rapidly from the shore towards the interior, to about the height of four hundred feet, at which level is a considerable extent of fertile soil; more inland, the hills become loftier, till they reach the eastern moorlands, near the borders of which, some of the heights command extensive prospects, particularly Roseberry Topping. Northward of these mountains is the vale of Cleveland, bounded on the north by the Tees. Part of the vale of York lies between the eastern and western moorlands, the latter are of greater elevation, of a bolder character than the former, and intersected by a multitude of vallies, watered by numerous streams. Eastward of the Ouse the county exhibits considerable diversity of surface, and the vale of York is level and marshy, but the more central part consists of gentle eminences exhibiting much fine scenery.

The western, and north-western parts of the county are rugged and mountainous, and contain some of the loftiest hills of England, particularly Ingleborough, and Whernside. Interspersed with the heights are the beautiful vallies of Wharfedale, Nidderdale, and the vale of the A(i)re. In Craven, are several small lakes, one of which, Malham Water, is situated on a lofty moor. The wolds of Yorkshire, consist of a lofty range of chalk hills, extending from the banks of the Humber, to the vicinity of Malton on the river Derwent, and thence eastward, terminating in Flamborough Head. The surface of the southern coast is flat and marshy, and terminates in Spurn Head, westward of which is Sunk Island, recovered from the sea. The Yorkshire Levels is an uninteresting but fertile tract.

The whole of this county is within the diocese of York, excepting a part of the North Riding, which belongs to that of Chester. Besides the magnificent cathedral at York, Yorkshire contains numerous remains of interesting monastic edifices. The abbeys of Kirkstall, Selby, Roche, Fountains, Byland, Rievaux, and Whitby. The priories of Bolton and Knaresborough. There are also the ancient castles of Conisborough, Cawood, Harewood, Knaresborough, Pontefract, Skipton, Richmond, Skelton and Clifford's tower at York.

THE NORTH RIDING

The Norrh Riding is bounded on the north by the river Tees, which separates it from Durham; on the east by the German Ocean; on the south by the Ainstey of York and the West Riding, and on the west by the county of Westmorland and Lancashire. Its greatest length, from east to west, is eighty-three miles; its greatest breadth, from north to south, is thirty-eight miles, and in circumference it is about one hundred and sixty miles. It contains nineteen market towns, 35,765 houses, and 183,381 inhabitants. This Riding returns eleven members to parliament; two for Malton, one for Northallerton, two for Richmond, two for Scarborough, one for Thirsk, one for Whitby, and two for the Riding, who, at present are the Hon. W. Duncombe and E.S. Cayley, Esq. Hornby castle is the seat of the Duke of Leeds, Lord Lieutenant of the North Riding.

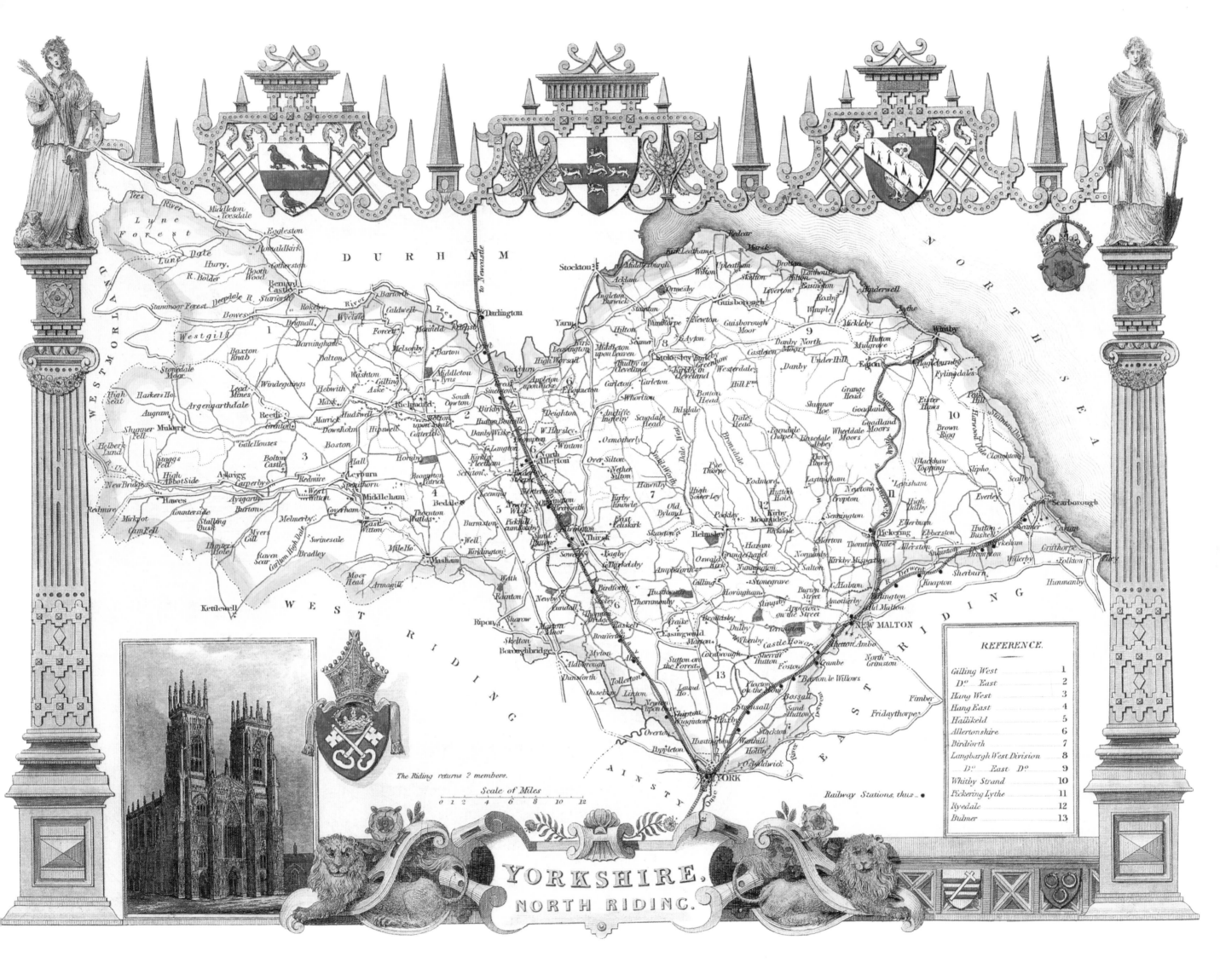

YORKSHIRE,
NORTH RIDING.

The Riding returns 2 members.

Scale of Miles
0 1 2   4   6   8   10   12

Railway Stations, thus •

REFERENCE.

Gilling West	1
D° East	2
Hang West	3
Hang East	4
Halikeld	5
Allertonshire	6
Birdforth	7
Langbargh West Division	8
D° East D°	9
Whitby Strand	10
Pickering Lythe	11
Ryedale	12
Bulmer	13

THE WEST RIDING

The West Riding is bounded on the north by the North Riding; on the east by the East Riding, the Ainsty of York, and Lincolnshire; on the south by Nottinghamshire, Derbyshire, and Cheshire; and on the west by Lancashire and Westmorland. Its greatest length is 95 miles, and its breadth 48; in circumference it is about 250 miles. The West Riding contains thirty-four market towns, 192 parishes, 154,314 houses and 799,357 inhabitants. It sends eighteen members to parliament; two for Bradford, two for Halifax, one for Huddersfield, two for Knaresborough, two for Leeds, two for Pontefract, two for Ripon, two for Sheffield, one for Wakefield, and two for the Riding, who, at present, are Viscount Morpeth and Sir George Strickland, Bart., of Hildenley-hall, near Malton. Harewood-house is the seat of the earl of Harewood, Lord Lieutenant of the West Riding.

HAREWOOD HOUSE.

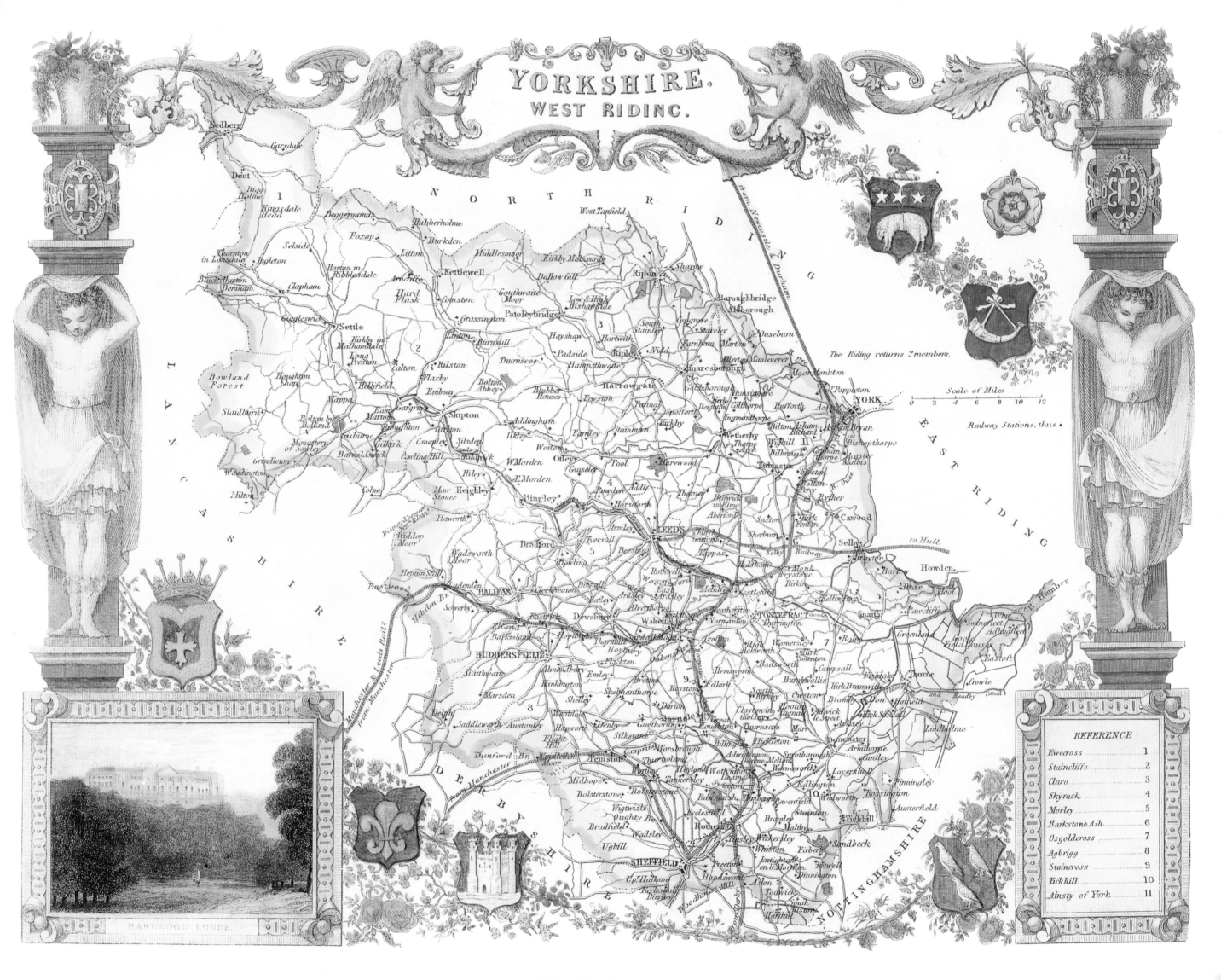

YORKSHIRE,
WEST RIDING.

N O R T H   R I D I N G

L A N C A S H I R E

E A S T   R I D I N G

D E R B Y S H I R E

N O T T I N G H A M S H I R E

The Riding returns 2 members.

Scale of Miles

Railway Stations, thus •

REFERENCE

Ewecross	1
Staincliffe	2
Claro	3
Skyrack	4
Morley	5
Barkstone Ash	6
Osgoldcross	7
Agbrigg	8
Staincross	9
Tickhill	10
Ainsty of York	11

HARDWOOD HOUSE.

THE EAST RIDING

East Riding is bounded on the north by the river Derwent; on the east by the German Ocean; on the south by the river Humber; and on the west by the river Ouse. Its greatest length is fifty-five miles; its breadth thirty-three; and in circumference, it is about one hundred and seventy-five miles. It contains the city of York, six market towns, 184 parishes, 34,390 houses, and 190,449 inhabitants. It returns eight members to parliament; two for the city of York, two for Beverley, two for Hull, and two for the East Riding, who at present are R. Bethel, Esq., and P.P. Thompson, Esq. Castle Howard is the seat of the Earl of Carlisle, Lord Lieutenant of the East Riding.

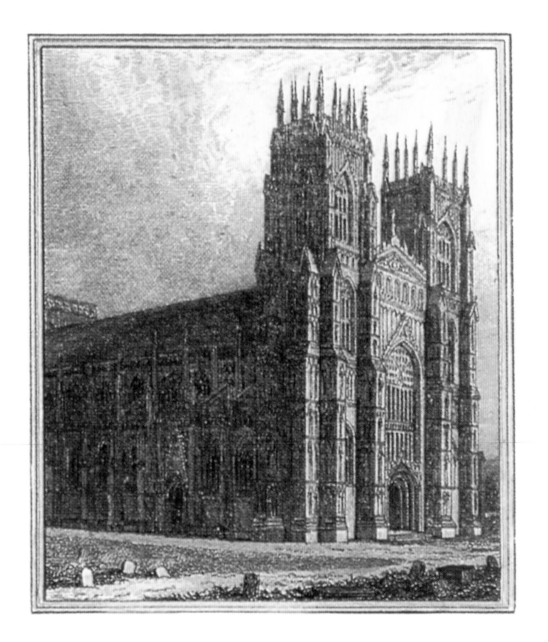

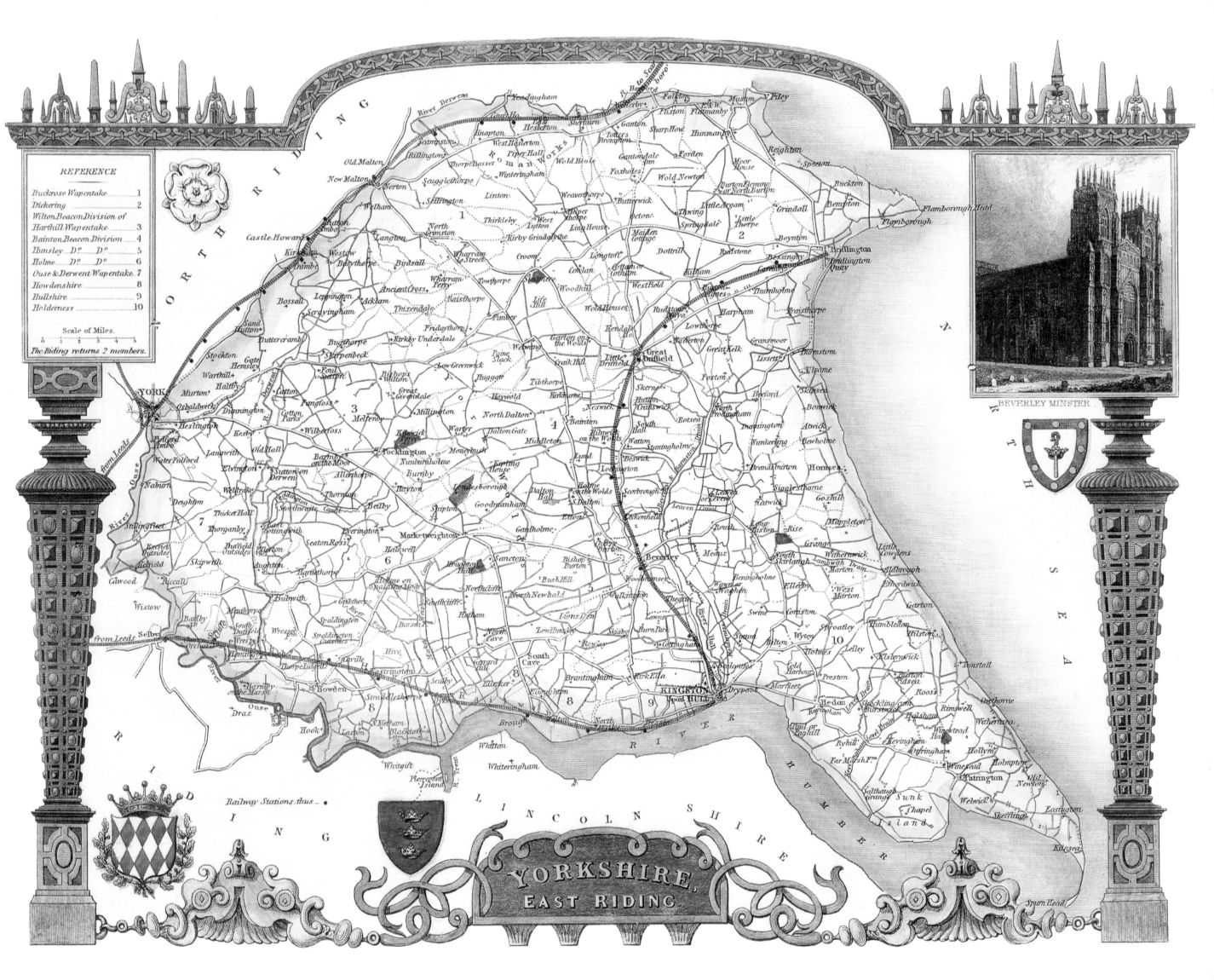

YORKSHIRE, EAST RIDING.

BEVERLEY MINSTER.

FURTHER READING AND SOURCES

FURTHER READING

Barclay, James (Rev.), Revised by Henry W. Dewhurst *A complete and universal English dictionary*, various editions, George Virtue, London 1842, 1844, 1845, 1848, 1852

Barber, Peter & Harper, Tom *Magnificent Maps: Power, Propaganda and Art* The British Library, London 2010

Barber, Peter *London: A History in Maps* The British Library, London 2012

Black, Jeremy *The Grand Tour: The British Abroad in the Eighteenth Century* Sutton Publishing, Stroud 2003

Blanchard, E L *Bradshaw's Illustrated Hand Book to London and its Environs* Bradshaw's Guide Office, London & Manchester 1862

Bradshaw, George *Descriptive Railway Handbook of Britain and Ireland* Bradshaw's Guide Office, London & Manchester 1863

Campbell, Tony *The original monthly numbers of Moules "English Counties"*, Map Collector journal, No. 31, 1985

Curwen, Henry *The History of Booksellers: The Old and the New* Chatto And Windus, London 1873

Crane, Nicholas *The Making of the British Landscape* Weidenfeld & Nicolson/Orion, London 2016

Foster, Joseph *The Dictionary of Heraldry: Feudal Coasts of Arms and Pedigrees*, Studio Editions, London 1992

Hamilton, James *Turner: A Life* Hodder and Stoughton, London 1997

Hewitt, Rachel *Map of a Nation: A Biography of the Ordnance Survey*, Granta Publications, London 2010

Hibbert, Christopher & Weinreb, Ben *The London Encyclopedia*, (Revised Edition), Macmillan, London 1995

Hill, Rosemary *God's Architect: Pugin and the Building of Romantic Britain*, Allen Lane/Penguin, London 2007

Moule, Thomas *Bibliotheca Heraldica Magnæ Britanniæ. An Analytical Catalogue of Books in Genealogy, Heraldry, Nobility, Knighthood, and Ceremonies*, Lackington & Co., London, 1822

Moule, Thomas *Antiquities in Westminster Abbey, ancient oil paintings and sepulchural brasses*, London, 1825

Moule, Thomas *An Essay on the Roman Villas of the Augustan Age, their architectural disposition and enrichments, and on the Remains of Roman Domestic Edifices discovered in Great Britain*, London, 1833

Moule, Thomas *Winckle's Illustrations of the Cathedral Churches of England and Wales, Effingham Wilson*, London, 1836

Moule, Thomas *The English counties delineated; or a topographical description of England. Illustrated by a map of London, and a complete series of county maps*. 2 Vol.s George Virue, London 1837

Moule, Thomas, *Heraldry of Fish: Notices of the principal families bearing fish in their arms*, London 1842

Moule, Thomas & Barron, Roderick (Introduction) *The County Maps of Old England*, Studio Editions, London 1990

Nurminen, Marjo, *The Mapmakers' World*, The Pool of London Press, London, 2015

Parker, Philip *History of Britain in Maps*, HarperCollins, Glasgow 2017

Potter, Jonathan *Collecting Antique Maps*, Jonathan Potter, London 2001

Shaw, Henry FSA, *Details of Elizabethan Architecture* , Introduction by Thomas Moule, William Pickering, London, 1839

Smith, David *Victorian Maps of the British Isles*, B T Batsford, London 1985

Speed, John *Britain's Tudor Maps: County by County* Introduction by Nigel Nicolson and county commentaries by Alasdair Hawkyard, B T Batsford, London 2017

Tomalin, Claire *Charles Dickens: A Life*, Viking/Penguin, London 2011

Tooley, R V *Maps and Mapmakers*, (Sixth Edition) B T Batsford, London 1978

Westall, William *Great Britain Illustrated*, Descriptions by Thomas Moule, Charles Tilt, London, 1830

Westall, William *Illustrations of the Works of Walter Scott, Seven essays by Thomas Moule*, London, 1834

Winchester, Simon *The Map that Changed the World: William Smith and the Birth of Modern Geology* Harper Perennial New York 2002

SOURCES

The staff and resources of the map reading room at London's British Library are incredibly helpful in any study of this nature. Equally all map dealers have an excellent knowledge of their collections.

There are many editions and versions of Moule's county maps available to the collector and cartographic enthusiast or, as has ever been, those requiring something beautiful, historic and worthy of conversation to hang on one's wall. The above-cited *Map Collector* article by Tony Campbell is an excellent, deeply researched and clearly organised introduction to various editions.

Original single editions of the maps that form the collection published in this book of Moule's English counties are widely available at reasonable prices from a variety of sources, and new collections frequently come onto the market. Furthermore, copies of both *The English Counties Delineated* and *Barclay's Universal English Dictionary* regularly come up for sale at antiquarian booksellers and can be researched using Abebooks.com.

The following antique and map dealers would be a great place to commence researching and acquiring a selection of maps by Thomas Moule and, of course, his fellow cartographers:

Barron Maps	www.barronmaps.com
Steve Battrick Antique Prints & Maps	www.antiqueprints.com
Copperplate Antique Maps and Prints	www.copperplate.co.uk
Peter Harrington	www.peterharrington.co.uk
The Map House	www.themaphouse.com
Jonathan Potter Limited	www.jpmaps.co.uk
Storey's	www.storeysltd.co.uk
Welland Antique Maps,	www.wellandantiquemaps.co.uk

Reproduction versions of various Moule's maps will also be available to order via the Pool of London Press website: www.poooflondon.com.